Assessing Speaking in Context

SECOND LANGUAGE ACQUISITION

Series Editors: **Professor David Singleton**, *University of Pannonia, Hungary* and Fellow Emeritus, *Trinity College, Dublin, Ireland* and **Associate Professor Simone E. Pfenninger**, *University of Salzburg, Austria*

This series brings together titles dealing with a variety of aspects of language acquisition and processing in situations where a language or languages other than the native language is involved. Second language is thus interpreted in its broadest possible sense. The volumes included in the series all offer in their different ways, on the one hand, exposition and discussion of empirical findings and, on the other, some degree of theoretical reflection. In this latter connection, no particular theoretical stance is privileged in the series; nor is any relevant perspective – sociolinguistic, psycholinguistic, neurolinguistic, etc. – deemed out of place. The intended readership of the series includes final-year undergraduates working on second language acquisition projects, postgraduate students involved in second language acquisition research, and researchers, teachers and policy makers in general whose interests include a second language acquisition component.

All books in this series are externally peer-reviewed.

Full details of all the books in this series and of all our other publications can be found on http://www.multilingual-matters.com, or by writing to Multilingual Matters, St Nicholas House, 31–34 High Street, Bristol BS1 2AW, UK.

SECOND LANGUAGE ACQUISITION: 149

Assessing Speaking in Context

Expanding the Construct and its Applications

Edited by
M. Rafael Salaberry and Alfred Rue Burch

MULTILINGUAL MATTERS
Bristol • Blue Ridge Summit

DOI https://doi.org/10.21832/SALABE3811
Library of Congress Cataloging in Publication Data
A catalog record for this book is available from the Library of Congress.
Names: Salaberry, M. Rafael, editor. | Burch, Alfred Rue, editor.
Title: Assessing Speaking in Context: Expanding the Construct and its Applications/Edited by M. Rafael Salaberry and Alfred Rue Burch.
Description: Bristol; Blue Ridge Summit: Multilingual Matters, [2021] | Series: Second Language Acquisition: 149 | Includes bibliographical references and index. | Summary: "This book takes a critical perspective of research on assessing speaking in second and foreign languages. Chapters focus on the complexity brought about by actual interactional competence in speaking tasks and discuss how testing and assessment models and practices can incorporate recent research on the dynamic and situated nature of language use"— Provided by publisher.
Identifiers: LCCN 2021013283 (print) | LCCN 2021013284 (ebook) | ISBN 9781788923811 (hardback) | ISBN 9781788923804 (paperback) | ISBN 9781788923828 (pdf) | ISBN 9781788923835 (epub)
Subjects: LCSH: Second language acquisition. | Language and languages—Study and teaching. | Speech—Study and teaching. | Language and languages—Ability testing.
Classification: LCC P118.2 .A85 2021 (print) | LCC P118.2 (ebook) | DDC 401/.93—dc23
LC record available at https://lccn.loc.gov/2021013283
LC ebook record available at https://lccn.loc.gov/2021013284

British Library Cataloguing in Publication Data
A catalogue entry for this book is available from the British Library.

ISBN-13: 978-1-78892-381-1 (hbk)
ISBN-13: 978-1-78892-380-4 (pbk)

Multilingual Matters
UK: St Nicholas House, 31–34 High Street, Bristol BS1 2AW, UK.
USA: NBN, Blue Ridge Summit, PA, USA.

Website: www.multilingual-matters.com
Twitter: Multi_Ling_Mat
Facebook: https://www.facebook.com/multilingualmatters
Blog: www.channelviewpublications.wordpress.com

The policy of Multilingual Matters/Channel View Publications is to use papers that are natural, renewable and recyclable products, made from wood grown in sustainable forests. In the manufacturing process of our books, and to further support our policy, preference is given to printers that have FSC and PEFC Chain of Custody certification. The FSC and/or PEFC logos will appear on those books where full certification has been granted to the printer concerned.

Typeset by Nova Techset Private Limited, Bengaluru and Chennai, India.
Printed and bound in the UK by the CPI Books Group Ltd.
Printed and bound in the US by NBN.

Contents

Contributors

Dagmar Barth-Weingarten is Professor of Present-Day English Language and Linguistics at the University of Potsdam (Germany). Her research takes an interactional-linguistic perspective and centers around grammar and prosody in everyday social interaction. More recently, it also includes the description and assessment of interactional skills of learners of English as a foreign language aiming to help improve teacher training.

Alfred Rue Burch is an Associate Professor at Kobe University, Japan. His research interests include conversation analysis, discursive psychology, second language acquisition and use, and task-based language teaching and testing.

Shi Chen is a PhD candidate in applied linguistics at Northern Arizona University. Her current research interests revolve around language testing and assessment, pragmatic competence, second language speaking and research methods. Shi received her BA in teaching Chinese as a second language from Wuhan Institute of Technology (China) and her MA in TESOL from the University of Southern California.

Rémi A. van Compernolle is an Associate Professor of Second Language Acquisition and French and Francophone Studies at Carnegie Mellon University. His research and teaching centers around extensions of cultural-historical psychology to L2 development, instruction, and assessment. Thematically, his work focuses primarily on sociolinguistics, pragmatics, and interaction in L2 contexts.

David Wei Dai is a Lecturer in the Faculty of Medicine, Nursing and Health Sciences at Monash University (Australia). His research has focused on broadening test constructs in language assessment, drawing on concepts in lingua franca communication, interactional competence and second language pragmatics. David published his Masters thesis in *Language Assessment Quarterly* on assessing English listening in lingua franca contexts. He is currently completing a PhD dissertation on the design and validation of an interactional competence test for second language Chinese speakers.

Shane Dunkle has been teaching ESL for over 20 years in both the United States and Japan. He received his MA in applied linguistics in 2010 from the University of Illinois at Chicago and is currently a language pedagogy specialist in the University of Chicago's English Language Institute. His research interest include pragmatics and intercultural communicative competence.

Britta Freitag-Hild is Professor of English Language Education at the University of Potsdam. Her research areas include English language teacher education, teaching literature and culture, intercultural competence and global education, as well as genre-based language learning and developing speaking skills and language teachers' diagnostic competence.

Wei-Li Hsu received her PhD in second language studies at the University of Hawai'i at Mānoa, specializing in Chinese and English as a second language (L2), L2 assessment and L2 reading. Her research interests include assessing L2 interactional competence, validating tests with a communicative framework, and real-time L2 Chinese reading strategies.

Noriko Iwashita is Associate Professor in Applied Linguistics at the University of Queensland (Australia). She has been involved in several validation projects for speaking assessments funded by ETS, IELTS and the British Council. In 2018, Noriko co-edited the special volume on *Revisiting the Speaking Construct* for *Language Testing* with India Plough (Michigan State University) and Jayanti Banerjee (Trinity College).

Gabriele Kasper is Professor of Second Language Studies at the University of Hawai'i at Mānoa. In her research she adopts conversation analysis to examine the organization of social interaction among multilingual speakers, with an emphasis on interaction in institutional settings.

Katharina Kley is a Lecturer in German in the Center for Languages and Intercultural Communication at Rice University (USA). She holds a PhD in second language acquisition from the University of Iowa. Katharina's research interests include classroom-based assessment, assessing speaking and the teaching and testing of interactional competence.

Silvia Kunitz completed her PhD at the University of Illinois at Urbana-Champaign in 2013. In her research she adopts a conversation-analytic approach to study how students and teachers do learning/teaching/testing as socially situated activities in and through embodied talk-in-interaction. So far, Silvia has focused on task accomplishment in the classroom, multipart oral exams and instructed interactional competence.

Lyn May is a Senior Lecturer in TESOL at Queensland University of Technology (Australia). Her research interests include L2 speaking assessment, interactional competence and learning oriented assessment. Lyn has published in journals including *Language Testing*, *Language Assessment Quarterly* and *Assessment in Education: Principles, Policy and Practice*.

Paul J. Moore is convenor of the Applied Linguistics program at the University of Queensland. His teaching and research interests include sociocognitive perspectives on task-based interaction (FtF and online), intercultural language teaching, and the dynamic roles of the L1 in L2 interaction. Recent publications include co-edited issues in *Language Learning & Technology* and *Australian Review of Applied Linguistics*.

India Plough is Associate Professor in the Residential College in the Arts and Humanities (RCAH) at Michigan State University. She teaches sociolinguistics and is Director of the RCAH Language Proficiency Program. India's research includes second language teaching, learning and assessment. Her current work focuses on the role of interactional competence and nonverbal behavior in defining the second language speaking construct.

Carsten Roever is Associate Professor in Applied Linguistics at the University of Melbourne (Australia). His teaching and research interests include second language pragmatics, conversation analysis, quantitative research methods and second language acquisition. Carsten is the author of *Teaching and Testing Second Language Pragmatics and Interaction: A Practical Guide* (2021, Routledge) and co-author (with Naoko Taguchi) of *Second Language Pragmatics* (2017, Oxford).

M. Rafael Salaberry is Gibbs Jones Professor of Humanities in the Department of Modern and Classical Literatures and Cultures at Rice University. His research and teaching focus on second language acquisition and teaching, morphological, syntactic and discursive development of tense and aspect, bilingualism and bilingual education, and educational applications of technology.

Erica Sandlund is Associate Professor of English Linguistics at Karlstad University (Sweden). Her research centers on social interaction in institutional settings, including language testing, language teaching, rater training, performance appraisal interviews and broadcast interaction. With a conversation analytic approach, Erica's special interests include reported speech, code-switching, assessments, and apologies and their receipt.

Jayoung Song received her PhD in foreign language education from the University of Texas at Austin. Currently, she is an Assistant Professor of Korean in the Department of Asian Studies at Pennsylvania State University. Jayoung's research focuses on Korean applied linguistics, computer-assisted language learning, intercultural communication and second language reading, all of which she incorporates in her teaching.

Pia Sundqvist is Associate Professor of English Education at the University of Oslo (Norway). Her main research interests are in the field of applied English linguistics, with a focus on informal language learning (extramural English and gaming), assessment of L2 oral proficiency and English language teaching. Pia is co-author (with Liss Kerstin Sylvén) of *Extramural English in Teaching and Learning* (Palgrave, 2016).

Meng Yeh, Teaching Professor in the Center for Languages & Intercultural Communication at Rice University (USA), specializes in language pedagogy, assessment, curriculum design and second language acquisition. Her recent pedagogical research focuses on developing and evaluating students' interactional and pragmatic competence, as well as instructional design and the effect of teaching Chinese characters and reading skills.

Soo Jung Youn is an Assistant Professor in the English Education Department at Daegu National University of Education (Korea). Her research interests include language testing and assessment, L2 pragmatics, interactional competence, task-based language teaching and mixed-methods research. Soo Jung's research has recently been published in *TESOL Quarterly, Language Testing, System, Applied Linguistics Review* and the *Journal of English for Academic Purposes.*

Part 1

Conceptual and Theoretical Issues

1 Assessing Speaking in Context: Expanding the Construct and the Applications

M. Rafael Salaberry and Alfred Rue Burch

This edited volume, based upon the Rice University Center for Languages and Intercultural Communication's conference of the same name held in May 2018, draws together research that takes a critical eye towards assessing speaking in second/foreign languages, with special attention given to reconceptualizing or adapting existing approaches and frameworks. The main contribution of this volume is the explicit focus on and analysis of the effect of an expanded sociolinguistic definition of speaking that incorporates recent research findings on interactional dynamics of conversations, interviews, etc.

1 Background

Over the last three decades, the field of second language acquisition (SLA) has witnessed two major turning points that have influenced the way we define a second language: the social turn (e.g. Block, 2003; Duff, 2015; Eskildsen & Majlesi, 2018; Firth & Wagner, 1997, 2007; Lantolf, 2011; Norton, 2000); and the multilingual turn (e.g. Cook, 1992; Douglas Fir Group, 2016; García & Flores, 2014; May, 2011, 2014; Norton, 2014; Ortega, 2014). A common concern of both the social and the multilingual turn has been the expansion of an outdated definition of language (confined until rather recently to the realm of individual cognition) to incorporate, among other new constructs, the notion of interactional competence and the concept of the multilingual learner and speaker.

This critical reconceptualization of language needs to be reflected in the redesign of testing instruments that properly assess this broad definition of second language proficiency (e.g. Chalhoub-Deville, 2003; Lantolf & Poehner, 2011; McNamara & Roever, 2006; Roever & Kasper, 2018; Shohamy, 2011; Valdés & Figueroa, 1994). The potential opportunities to redesign testing instruments aligned with the new conceptualizations of language are limited, however, by the prevailing institutional infrastructure of testing instruments, testing standards and testing policies that were developed around narrow definitions of language. In effect, despite their avowed focus on the interactional dynamics of speaking in context, current assessment models used in institutional settings (e.g. ACTFL in the USA, CEFR in Europe) largely eschew the complexity brought about by actual interactional competence in speaking tasks (e.g. Brown, 2003; Fulcher, 2004; Galaczi, 2008, 2013; Johnson, 2001; Kormos, 1999; Patharakorn, 2018; Plough, 2018; Roever & Kasper, 2018; Weir, 2005; Youn, 2015; Young, 2011).

For instance, paired speaking test formats introduced to the assessment profession in the 1990s (Stansfield & Kenyon, 1992; McNamara, 1996) have been deemed problematic to assess the L2 proficiency of individual students due to the effect of interlocutors' differences in proficiency, familiarity, gender and other factors (e.g. Brown, 2003; Davis, 2009; Ducasse & Brown, 2009; Lazaraton, 1996). Similarly, in contrast with scripted interview questionnaires, unguided informal conversations have been regarded as detrimental to the collection of relevant language samples to perform a fair assessment of proficiency across a large number of students due to the lack of standardization of the procedures used to collect language samples (e.g. Bachman, 2007; Young, 2011). Finally, there have been few attempts at expanding the realm of assessment of language ability to include paralinguistic and nonlinguistic facets of interactional settings of communication (Plough *et al.*, 2018; Roever & Kasper, 2018; Ross, 2018).

Overall, there is a gap between the most recent research studies (e.g. Galaczi, 2008; Roever & Kasper, 2018; Youn, 2015) and the current structure of major institutional testing models of speaking. Considering the significant challenges to assessing speaking in context as described above, it is not surprising that such a gap would exist. To identify the major points of disparity between the type of testing instrument necessary to assess a socially contextualized definition of language and the features of the current models of language assessment embodied in the traditional testing instruments, we review the main features of the theoretical foundation of both assessment frameworks.[1]

2 Previous Theoretical Construct: Communicative Competence

The starting point to describing the concept of language proficiency enshrined in the established models of assessment is the notion of communicative competence. The latter concept, described by Hymes (1972), focused on the type of linguistic knowledge that is not only possible in a language, but that is also actually used in socially contextualized situations (Hymes also discussed the type of knowledge associated with what is feasible and what is appropriate). Notably in Hymes' position is his early reference to a key component of the concept of interactional competence, making explicit reference to the 'evidence for linguistic competence [that] co-varies with interlocutor' (Hymes, 1972: 276). The theoretical framework developed by Canale and Swain (1980) almost a decade later introduced a tripartite division of the concept of communicative competence: grammatical competence, sociolinguistic competence and strategic competence (a separate fourth component of discourse competence was added later by Canale, 1983). The objective of Canale and Swain's article was to identify a series of principles that would be useful to develop a foundation (and guidelines) for second language teaching and testing, including 'more valid and reliable measurement of second language communication skills' (Canale & Swain, 1980: 1). For the purpose of our discussion, Canale and Swain explicitly distinguished between *communicative competence* and *communicative performance*, leading them to advocate for the inclusion of testing procedures in the context of 'realistic communicative situations', during which there would be 'little time to reflect on and monitor language input and output' (Canale & Swain, 1980: 34). Canale and Swain noted that this direct type of assessment (at the time exemplified, as stated by the authors, by the FSI Oral Proficiency Interview and communicative tests) increases the face validity of the test.

To address this newly developing focus on L2 communicative competence, and in particular the spoken components of this competence, the American Council for the Teaching of Foreign Languages-Oral Proficiency Interview (ACTFL-OPI) became an important institutional instrument for that purpose. Even though the ACTFL Proficiency Guidelines claimed to be a theoretical, their professed focus on proficiency seems to be aligned with an implied communicative approach model that had been evolving during the 1970s and 1980s as described above: the ACTFL Proficiency Guidelines 'are descriptions of what individuals can do with language ... in real-world situations in a spontaneous and non-rehearsed context' (Swender *et al.*, 2012: 3). Furthermore, the test is described as a conversation: 'it mirrors a typical spontaneous conversation inasmuch as the interviewer's line of questioning and posing of tasks are determined by the way in which the interviewee responds' (Glisan *et al.*, 2013: 267). Kormos (1999: 165), nevertheless, points out that a conversation is 'an unplanned face-to-face interaction with unpredictable sequence and outcome ... and in which speakers' turns are reactively or mutually contingent' (see also van Lier, 1989). Johnson (2001: 142) explained further that 'the OPI tests speaking ability in the context of an interview, and, to be more precise, in the context of two types of interviews, sociolinguistic and survey research'. Johnson noted that:

> in a survey research interview, questions and answers are regarded as stimuli and responses. All 'extraneous material' is suppressed in order that the finding may be generalized to a larger population. ... The context is not viewed as an important factor influencing participants' interaction. (Johnson, 2001: 59)

Thus, there are two obvious problems with the use of the ACTFL-OPI to measure general language competence: first, an interview is of limited value for extrapolating to other interactional contexts; and second, the lack of attention to bringing up contextual factors further constrains the definition of conversational interaction.[2]

3 Interactional Competence

The view of communicative competence described above differs in significant ways from the concept of interactional competence (IC) described in detail by He and Young (1998): interactional competence is 'co-constructed by all participants in an interactive practice and is specific to that practice' (He & Young, 1998: 7). Apart from linguistic resources identified in previous models of communicative competence, the construct of IC highlights the role played by identity resources such as participation frameworks and interactional resources such as turn-taking, sequence and preference organization, and repair (Young, 2011). Furthermore, the concept of linguistic resources is expanded to include not just verbal, but also embodied means of communication such as gaze, facial expressions and gestures (e.g. Burch & Kasper, 2016). Overall, interactional resources enable speakers both to design their turns for a particular recipient in a particular context to accomplish social actions (e.g. invitations, requests, rejections to invitations, etc.), and also to react appropriately to the actions produced by other participants (Pekarek Doehler & Pochon-Berger, 2015).

3.1 Two problems: Local context and co-construction of meaning

By its very definition, IC is inherently characterized by a dynamic and emergent understanding of the interaction as it unfolds in real time as part of a locally co-constructed communicative act. For the purpose of assessment, however, Bachman (2007) points out that the definition of IC brings up two problems: it is determined by the local context (thus, not generalizable) and it is based on the co-construction of meaning (thus, language ability cannot be attributed to one individual alone).

The first problem identified by Bachman (2007: 63) focuses on the problem of generalizability of findings: '[i]f the construct is strictly local and co-constructed by all the participants in the discursive practice, this would imply that each interaction is unique ... then we have no basis for generalizing about the characteristics of [contexts or participants]'. Furthermore, not only is the assessment of IC complex due to the high level of contextualization of interactional events, it is also clear that the inherently emic nature of IC (i.e. participant-based) is incompatible with the inherently etic viewpoint (i.e. observer-based) of the testing profession (e.g. Young, 2011). The two problems identified by Bachman seem to make the testing of IC incompatible with the type of standardized language tests that have been prevalent for the last 50 years.

3.2 Standardized tests of language proficiency

Liskin-Gasparro (2003: 483) notes that 'our profession has produced models of proficiency at the rate of at least one or two per decade'. Out of all those proposals, however, she points out that the ACTFL Proficiency Guidelines is the model that stands out as the most well-known and most widely used, the one that has 'become an integral part of the professional landscape of foreign language instruction, test development, and policy making in the United States' (Liskin-Gasparro, 2003: 486). The success of the ACTFL-OPI test in the United States and the CEFR test in Europe showcases the benefit of implementing some type of institutionalized, systematic procedure to assess language competence. The success of these models, despite the obvious lacunae in their representation of the process of language development or the nature of language interaction of proficiency, rests primarily on their pragmatic (i.e. practical) approach to the implementations of assessment instruments.

In line with the pragmatic approach to developing a testing instrument such as the ACTFL-OPI, Spolsky (1997: 246) noted that '(m)any if not most of the important decisions we have to make in life are made in a state of insufficient empirical evidence'. It should be noted, however, that Spolsky added a qualification to his position: '(o)nce we accept the need for a gatekeeping function, we are ethically bound to seek the most complete information available'. In this respect, despite the difficulties of assessing IC, the potential benefit of an IC-based syllabus cannot be underestimated. In the United States, for example, about 80% of all college students who study a second language do not continue beyond the first two years of instruction (Goldberg *et al.*, 2015). The lack of focus on interactional abilities, especially for beginning students, may deprive these students of the opportunity to develop a more realistic, contextualized definition of language (e.g. Carter & McCarthy, 2004; O'Keefe *et al.*, 2007), and of the opportunity to practice their language skills accordingly.

Arguably, there have been some modifications of the ACTFL-OPI over the last 30-plus years. It is clear, however, that these changes have not introduced the type of significant changes needed to address some of the critiques advanced by the social turn and the multilingual turn. On the other hand, after reviewing various critiques about the validity of the ACTFL-OPI test, Liskin-Gasparro (2003) conceded that:

> its empirical basis is shaky, and its claim to be conversational does not hold up. It is clear that oral proficiency ratings predict far less about an individual's future performance in a range of communicative situations than promoters of the OPI would like them to. (Liskin-Gasparro, 2003: 488)

The apparent call for action to make improvements to the ACTFL-OPI test, voiced by one of the original designers of the test, is promising. Nevertheless, Ross (2018) points out that some of the latest scholarly writings on IC are too recent to have had any significant impact on the design of the ACTFL-OPI and, more importantly, that the construct of IC may be 'difficult to operationalize in conventional assessment tasks'.

4 Addressing the Challenges of IC: From Theory to Practice

It is hardly surprising that the assessment of a definition of language proficiency *broader* than the one used by ACTFL-OPI (and similar tests like the CEFR) represents a challenge. The assessment of complex constructs (as opposed to 'real-life tasks') implies that there are compromises to be made on the path towards developing testing instruments that can be used by a large number of people. To address the challenges outlined by Bachman (i.e. the effect of the local context and the co-construction of meaning) and develop a viable and practical testing instrument to evaluate IC, we need to appraise both the affordances and the constraints posed by institutionalized assessment practices.

The significant number of theoretical and empirical studies shedding light on the interactional nature of discourse and the multilingual identity of test-takers published over the last two decades has provided a strong foundation for the expansion of institutionalized models of proficiency. There are at least two important developments that point in the direction of significant changes that may pave the way for the assessment of speaking in context. First, over the last two decades there has been a significant effort to design and implement a variety of teaching procedures aimed at providing classroom instruction on contextualized speaking activities with a focus on IC (e.g. Barraja-Rohan, 1997, 2011; Betz & Huth, 2014; Huth, 2006; Huth & Betz, 2019; Huth & Taleghani-Nikazm, 2006). Furthermore, a handful of recent studies have attempted to operationalize the assessment of this broad type of contextualized speaking practice (e.g. Ikeda, 2017; Kley, 2019; Sandlund & Sundqvist, 2019; Youn, 2015).

These studies have become instrumental in addressing the challenge for the adoption of an IC-oriented syllabus (e.g. Bachman, 2007; Chalhoub-Deville, 2003): the difficulty of assigning individual grades to a co-constructed performance (i.e. language ability cannot be attributed to one individual alone) determined by the local context (thus, not generalizable). Not surprisingly, there have been numerous studies measuring the competence of test-takers in interactional settings (e.g. Galaczi, 2013; Ross & Kasper, 2013; Youn, 2015; Young, 2011). We describe the relevance of some of these studies.

4.1 Contextualization of interaction: Focusing on generic practices

While it is true that He and Young (1998) proposed that the skills developed in one local environment 'either do not apply or apply in a different configuration to different practices', a decade later Young (2009) further explained that

> … interactional competence includes the skill to mindfully and efficiently recognize contexts in which resources are employed and to use them when participating in unfamiliar practices to help them make sense of the unknown. (Young, 2009: 214)

For instance, when faced with the need to turn down an invitation (i.e. a dispreferred action), competent speakers must be able to choose among various relevant pragmatically sensitive options that do not inadvertently convey hostility or impatience (e.g. delays, appreciations, accounts, etc.) to reject the invitation. That is, interactional resources can be 'transported' across communication settings (Young, 2011). To promote the learning of this specific type of interactional knowledge, Young points out that we need to engage learners in a 'close analysis of naturally occurring discourse and social interaction [to] reveal the standards that apply in reality in particular settings' (McNamara, 1997: 457).

Even though the localized nature of language interactions may be difficult to assess through standardized assessment procedures, the close analysis of naturally occurring data may provide an option for language testers to sample fundamental features of IC. Huth (2014), for instance, shows that the design of classroom tasks based on natural language samples can be used to assess learners' understanding of the sequential organization of closings in telephone conversations in L2 German (and contrasting their use with L1 English closings). Huth and Betz (2019) note that in Huth's and other successful cases of IC testing, the assessment tasks are focused on the existence of routinized, generic practices (cf. Young, 2009). Even though the specific sequence of actions may be dependent on some factors relevant to the specific interaction, the generic process to make the selection of the appropriate action falls within the range of a reasonable set of options.

The benefit of a focus on generic practices is that it allows test designers to explore options other than direct testing formats. Along those lines, Huth and Betz describe possible uses of indirect written tests to circumvent the logistical problems prompted by the local co-construction of oral testing. For instance, they provide additional examples of the assessment of IC whereby learners may be asked to put sequences of turns in the right order, match the function with the relevant linguistic resource, unscramble sequences of turns, complete conversations with the appropriate linguistic markers, provide an account for their selections, guess next turns, etc. In essence, the development (i.e. learning) of IC, although highly contextualized by the characteristics of each interactional context, is possible through an explicit process of analysis and synthesis that can (only) be implemented with the use of naturalistic samples of language data.

4.2 Emic and etic perspectives: Developing rubrics and ratings

The apparent success of the ACTFL-OPI may provide us with some ideas of how to proceed. The benefit of relying on a construct-driven approach (i.e. the assessment of the well-circumscribed theoretical notion of IC) over a task-driven approach (i.e. the 'real-life speaking test' represented in the OPI interview) has been discussed before (Bachman, 2007; Messick, 1994; Roever & Kasper, 2018; Young, 2011). On the other hand, whether such an optimal approach is possible or feasible is dependent on 'the selection or construction of relevant tasks as well as the rational development of scoring criteria and rubrics' (Messick, 1994: 22).

In this respect, the complexity of the process to rate speech samples in the context of an interview increases exponentially for the ratings of speech samples to assess IC. However, what in principle would be an even less tractable problem has prompted test designers to find practical solutions to rate speech samples without reducing the informational value added by the increased number of factors that define interactional dynamics. Along those lines, Kley (2019) proposes the use of a data-driven approach for the development of rubrics intended for speaking tests. More concretely, she argues for the use of a two-step sequence that entails first the analysis of the 'students' test discourse from an emic (participant-based) perspective before creating etic (instructor-based) rating categories for rubrics'. Complementing the work of Kley on the development of rubrics, Sandlund and Sundqvist (2019) focus their attention on the opposite task: raters' interpretations of rubrics through collaborative grading of a paired speaking test. Rubrics, by necessity, are abbreviated definitions of the IC construct. Therefore, the analysis carried out by Sandlund and Sundqvist reveals that the process of training raters can be as much if not more important than the initial writing of the rubric.

5 Conversation Analysis and Assessment

The previous historical review of the assessment of communicative competence and interactional competence highlights the relevance of research methodologies. In effect, several chapters in this volume employ conversation analysis (CA) to examine assessment procedures and outcomes (Barth-Weingarten & Freitag-Hild; Burch & Kasper; Kley, Kunitz & Yeh; Roever & Dai; van Compernolle), while others make significant reference to CA methodologies (Iwashita, May & Moore; Plough; Sandlund & Sundqvist; Youn & Chen). This is justified given that in the roughly decade and a half since the conceptualization of IC, by far the lion's share of research done in this sphere has been conducted through CA (e.g. Gardner & Wagner, 2004; Nguyen & Kasper, 2009; Pallotti & Wagner, 2011; Hall *et al.*, 2011; Greer *et al.*, 2017; Salaberry & Kunitz, 2019).

At its heart, and drawing upon its roots in ethnomethodology (Garfinkel, 1967; Heritage, 1984, *inter alia*), CA is a qualitative methodology that examines in fine detail the particulars of *talk and other conduct in interaction* (Schegloff, 1992) in both mundane contexts and institutional settings. It relies, first and foremost, upon audio- or video-recordings of situated interactions, most commonly interactions that would occur regardless of research purposes. Through repeated listening or viewing, fine-grained transcriptions, commonly using the conventions developed by Gail Jefferson (2004), are made and recursively refined. These transcriptions often include minute details regarding timing and pauses, intonational features, mis-starts, overlaps, and (more recently) nonverbal conduct such as gestures, gaze direction, facial expressions and orientations to objects or materials in the environment. This degree of detail, although initially opaque or intimidating to those who are unfamiliar, reflects a standard practice in CA research of not dismissing any detail *a priori* as irrelevant until after a thorough analysis has been completed. It also affords the opportunity for the reader to confirm or question the analysis by granting access to the particulars of the data (which can be further enhanced through sharing the recordings as well).

This attention to detail – details that are most importantly observable to the participants themselves – further reflects other aspects of CA's epistemological framework. Here we will highlight three aspects that are particularly relevant to CA work on language assessment: the co-constructed nature of interaction; CA's perspective on cognitive or psychological topics; and CA's *emic* orientation.

Heritage (1984) points out that turns and other contributions to an interaction are both *context-shaped* and *context-renewing*. Each contribution, as an action, is situated within the context that has come before, and in particular builds upon and displays an understanding of the prior turns and actions (see also Goodwin, 2018; Sacks, 1992). At the same time, it provides the context for actions that are to come. As such, all interaction is inescapably *co-constructed* (Hall & Pekarek Doehler, 2011; He & Young, 1998) by the participants, and contributions must be understood through how they relate to the ongoing activity. Indeed, viewing a contribution to an interaction in a discrete, decontextualized manner risks impoverishing the analytic understanding of that contribution.

The focus on the details of interaction also relates to CA's general abstention from individualistic, unobservable psychological or cognitive explanations for the actions conducted in talk. It is not that CA research denies individual cognition (Kasper, 2009, although see the debate that is laid out in te Molder & Potter, 2005). Instead, it espouses a degree of 'cognitive agnosticism' (Hopper, 2005; Markee, 2011), relying upon an analysis of observable actions and participant orientations without recourse to unobservable happenings within the mind. When psychological or cognitive phenomena are relevant, it is because the participants themselves orient to them as such (Edwards & Potter, 2005), often through accounts of their own or others' actions or in reference to the 'psychological thesaurus' (Edwards & Potter, 2005) of ways of describing psychological or emotional phenomena.

The final epistemological stance taken within CA, intrinsically related to the prior two, is the *emic* perspective on interaction, particularly as to how it relates to categorization and coding. CA's reliance on participants' orientations reflects its ethnomethodological (and earlier, phenomenological; see Heritage, 1984) roots. This perspective views the participant as the arbiter of what is relevant in, to, and for the interaction; by displaying their understanding of the context and prior actions, the participant is also engaged in an ongoing analysis that the researcher in turn explicates. As a consequence, CA avoids *a priori* categorization or coding, as these may not be relevant to the participants' own analysis of the interaction (Burch, 2014; Hauser, 2005), and may indeed draw attention away from the participants' co-constructed accomplishments within the activity.

It is this final point that provides the greatest friction between the goals of CA and the goals of language assessment. While assessment procedures and practices can be designed to account for co-construction, and are not required to make assumptions about cognitive phenomena (i.e. criterion-referenced achievement and diagnostic assessments can focus on learner production), rubrics and standards are by their very nature *etic* formulations – descriptions that reflect the values and goals of the teacher, curriculum and/or the test designer. Even rubrics thoroughly informed by CA findings must undergo what could be called a process of *de-emicization* (see Barth-Weingarten & Freitag-Hild, this volume, for further discussion) in order to serve their purpose and to provide the appropriate degrees of validity. This is a very real challenge, and the studies presented here, as well as work by others (Galaczi, 2013; Galaczi & Taylor, 2018; Plough *et al.*, 2018; Roever & Kasper, 2018) take a variety of approaches in dealing with it.

Despite these challenges, research employing CA for the understanding of SLA and language assessment in the wake of Firth and Wagner's (1997) call for more socially grounded approaches to SLA research, and Young and He's (1998) volume on discursive approaches to language assessment, has provided much insight, as represented not only in these pages, but in the work presented in Ross and Kasper (2013), Seedhouse and Nakatsuhara (2018), McNamara (2019) and Salaberry and Kunitz (2019), among many others.

6 The Chapters in this Volume

This volume is divided into three parts. Part 1 is comprised of two chapters that simultaneously outline prospective challenges facing the assessment of interaction (or, as Roever & Kasper, 2018, put it, 'talking' as opposed to 'speaking'), while also reflecting on and building upon the papers presented in Plough, Banarjee and Iwashita's (2018) special issue of *Language Testing.*

One of these challenges, inherent to assessment in general but particularly pressing for the assessment of interactional abilities, is to delineate which domains and features are relevantly assessable. Roever and Dai point out that L2 IC research (Al-Gahtani & Roever, 2015, 2018; Pekarek Doehler & Pochon-Berger, 2011, among others) rarely provides a rationale for why specific actions such as requests or disagreements are targeted for scrutiny or why those actions as opposed to others ought to make their way into a curriculum – an issue that the authors point out is remedied through needs analyses. Potentially ratable markers for IC, such as the generic practices discussed above, should be similarly principled and reasoned, not least for the sake of construct validity and distinguishing from constructs that extant psycholinguistically based assessment instruments such as the TOEFL or ACTFL-OPI can already cover. One such marker is 'social role enactment' within a roleplay. Roever and Dai introduce an innovative approach to operationalizing this marker by making use of membership categorization analysis (Sacks, 1974; Stokoe, 2012), and highlighting how learners of Chinese of differing proficiency levels are able to display their IC through orientations to relevant social categories.

Plough, maintaining the focus on assessing interactional abilities, draws attention to the role that *nonverbal behavior* (NVB) plays in interaction, arguing that assessments that aim to measure interactional abilities ought to account for embodied behavior such as gesture or facial expression. This is not only in recognition of how NVB may impact raters' perceptions of the test-taker's performance, but also that NVB is fundamental and integral in face-to-face communication.[3] However, NVB presents a further challenge for valid assessment due to variations in use between individual participants, interactional contexts and at the linguacultural level. While this challenge is daunting, Plough – referencing McNamara (1996) – notes that we cannot just define NVB 'out of existence' for the sake of simplification and provides an early attempt at how to operationalize NVB in assessment rubrics.

Part 2 collects chapters that examine a variety of procedural and constitutive elements implicated in speaking assessments, drawing upon data from both test-takers (Burch & Kasper) and raters (Youn & Chen; Sandlund & Sundqvist).

Burch and Kasper examine four video-recorded Japanese as a foreign language oral proficiency interviews (OPIs), focusing on how the interviewer and test-takers transition between the interview and roleplay activities. While the interactions that occur in these transitions are not officially recognized as ratable speech samples (Ross, 2017), analysis of these phases highlights how troubles in understanding that have consequences for how the test procedures move forward may arise, thus becoming 'unofficial ratables' (Ross, 2017). The chapter further draws analytic attention to the role that embodied behaviors (gesture, gaze, posture), textual objects (roleplay cards) and environmental configurations (seating positions, placement of documents on a table) play in the procedures for transitioning between activities during an assessment activity.

In order to understand assessment procedures, it is as important to scrutinize those who assess as it is to examine those who are assessed. The following two chapters shift the focus to the raters. Building upon Youn's (2015, 2018) previous work, Youn and Chen studied the processes and strategies raters go through by using think-aloud protocols before and after training on recognizing IC-related phenomena. Prior to training, raters tended to focus on factors such as task completion, accuracy or fluency (*editor's note*: the latter two categories fall within Canale & Swain's 1980 category of grammatical competence, and may reflect the enduring influence of the communicative language teaching model that came in the wake of that ground-breaking work). After training, raters were able to identify relevant IC-implicative factors, although many still faced difficulty in matching these factors to the appropriate thickly described rubric categories, suggesting that even more rigorous training is necessary, and that raters need ample time to 'internalize' their training.

Sandlund and Sundqvist also examine raters in relation to rater training, but through the application of membership categorization analysis (see also Roever & Dai, this volume) to discussions between raters with regard to the severity of their ratings. The authors note that, by and large, leniency was treated by the participants as more problematic in relation to professional identity, while at the same time being attributed to inexperience or excessive generosity. On the other hand, severity was related to both excessive strictness and to professional caution on the part of the rater. These findings provide a new approach to understanding rater variability and open a new avenue for research on how to minimize the negative effect rater variability can have on assessment validity.

Finally, the various chapters in Part 3 describe and assess new or improved options to implement the types of speaking assessment that are constitutive of the features discussed in the previous parts.

Kley, Kunitz and Yeh address a concern that faces language teachers who want to assess IC at the classroom level: the potential incongruity of preconceived IC markers and the test-taker's actual, *in situ* usage. Drawing upon data from a CA-informed pedagogical intervention in a Chinese as a foreign language classroom, the authors focus on *repair* (Schegloff *et al.*, 1977, *inter alia*), the practices by which participants in an interaction restore and maintain mutual understanding after the occurrence of interactional trouble. The authors find that the stated objectives regarding repair practices, as reflected in the assessment rubric, were not all met during an interactive assessment task with L1 speakers and, furthermore, that the rubric was not able to discriminate appropriately between higher and lower level learners, prompting the authors to propose refinements to the objectives, rubrics and assessment procedures. This study highlights the challenges of assessing IC in a way that is pedagogically sound (i.e. following and measuring stated objectives), but also reflects the current understandings of interaction as co-constructed and contextually shaped and shaping (Heritage, 1984).

Van Compernolle expands on previous work on dynamic strategic interaction scenarios (DSIS) as a tool for assessing L2 IC (e.g. repair, turn-taking management). One of the most important benefits of the assessment of IC with the help of DSIS is that we obtain a more granular description of the scaffolded nature of interaction than with standard procedures (e.g. straight interviews) and that, consequently, we can trace the growth of a learner's repertoire (e.g. resources for managing turn-taking and repair) and his or her ability to deploy resources in a context-sensitive way over time. Van Compernolle makes his case for the benefits of DSIS with the analysis of data from US elementary and intermediate university students of French who completed a series of six scenarios. The objective of his study was to focus primarily on the mediation mechanisms occurring in the samples analyzed to track both manifest and emerging capabilities through mediation to assess what a learner can do alone and what becomes possible with support. While examples of IC were present in all the data, the specific focus was on cases where troubles in interaction arose. Van Compernolle's analysis showcases several examples of both the co-constructed nature of IC and the mediation mechanisms at play. In one case, for instance, one student initiated a repair sequence, but the repair itself was managed by both students. Drawing on the displays of understanding of his interlocutor, one of the students modified his speech to repair the problem at hand, and once the interlocutor was able to continue, he closed the sequence. Other examples show the use of L1 English as a resource for dealing with troubles in interaction and the management of turn-taking. In these cases, the data show how participants were able to take up as well as seek out assistance from a more competent person through the use of English, demonstrating how the multiplicity of resources available to learners were used to manage the learning/interactional process.

In his chapter, Dunkle proposes the use of social deduction board games as a formative assessment tool for the production of certain pragmatic skill sets. He argues that the assessment of student utterances produced in such interactive environments are more reliable than the speech acts produced in archetypal contexts used to elicit language assessment data such as roleplays. Dunkle argues that the use of social deduction board games provides a more direct access to assess learners' ability to engage in social interactions negotiating communicative norms and conventions that are central components of IC, namely 'the ability to deploy language in interactive situations for social purposes' (cf. Roever & Kasper, 2018). Dunkle provides an empirical assessment of learners' improvements on three target skills that can be profitably developed through social deduction board games: bluffing, negotiation and turn-taking (specifically giving turns). He collected data from 16 international students (full-time graduate, doctoral or post-doctoral students) who, at the time, were enrolled in a university-level English communication course. Their competence in English was rated as Intermediate Mid to Advanced High (on the ACTFL scale). Over the course of three separate classes, Dunkle collected comparative data on language production during the participants' engagement with both target board games and traditional roleplays. The overall results of his study show that the social deduction board games provided a better context for target pragmatic forms for turn-taking and bluffing than roleplays. Data for the other target skill (i.e. negotiation) were at least equal to those of the roleplay group. One important outcome of the overall qualitative analysis shows that the participation in social deduction board games showed a tendency to produce short, phrase-level utterances that more closely resemble the 'natural' and 'fluent' speech that native speakers use. In contrast, the roleplay groups generated turns that are more properly aligned with monologues rather than dialogues.

In their chapter, Barth-Weingarten and Freitag-Hild focus on the important challenge of administering scarce institutional resources to implement an assessment program that addresses the complexity of the construct of IC. Their proposal is oriented towards helping German high school second language teachers include IC in their testing procedures based on an efficient use of assessment resources (but their suggestions are applicable across languages and school settings). They describe IC in terms of generic organizational contingencies required for interaction in general – turn-taking, action formation, sequence organization, overall structural organization and dealing with trouble. Barth-Weingarten and Freitag-Hild argue, however, that we can selectively but systematically focus on a small number of IC subskills, at the same time as we delimit the comprehensiveness of the analysis. For the purposes of this chapter, they focus specifically on turn-taking as part of learners' IC for which they develop a rubric to assess students' performance in roleplays tailored to their limited resources situation. The objective was to preserve a focus on the main subskills of turn-taking (turn-holding, turn-yielding and turn-taking proper) as well as timing considerations and the appropriate use of all language-specific resources. Their description of the process to use their streamlined rubric focuses on two of their learners that they regard as representative of their study, in order to showcase the range of the analysis needed to gather sufficient evidence that demonstrates IC.

Finally, the last part of the volume reviews the potential of new technologies to support the design and administration of language assessment instruments that incorporate a sociolinguistic definition of a second language.

Song and Hsu focus on the challenges faced by new technological tools used in assessment to integrate the crucial role of contextualization effects in the assessment of speaking abilities, and pragmatics more specifically. They argue that such contextualization cues tend to be lacking in the type of technology-aided and virtual oral interactions in which test-takers respond to audio- or video-recorded prompts, semi-interactive avatar-based virtual environments and other similar contexts. To that effect, Song and Hsu propose that the immersive quality of VR experiences can create socially authentic environments in which test-takers feel that they are in the same place as the interlocutor and, more importantly, that would allow them to analyze important cues and features of the social situation that are critical components of pragmatic competence given the positive effect of co-presence and social presence implemented through VR technologies.

Song and Hsu collected data from 25 L2 Korean students using virtual reality (VR) technology to examine its feasibility for the assessment of L2 interactive oral abilities, focusing primarily on identifying the types of language ability that can be elicited and scored using the VR testing mode, the language functions that are elicited by the VR testing mode and the students' perceptions of the VR testing mode. To address this broad range of questions, they collected data comprising a wide range of options: test scores, CA of their performance, a survey of their perceptions about VR in assessment, and interviews. Their analysis shows that the assessment of speaking abilities with VR technology was successful in eliciting most language functions and ratable speech samples without major technical issues. There were, however, some language functions that the assessment failed to elicit. In particular, the recorded nature of the assessment might have limited the test-takers' use of some of the language functions, especially the negotiation of meaning. On the positive side, the students generally showed positive attitudes towards the VR assessment in terms of ease and enjoyment. The study suggests practical implications for test developers or language practitioners in terms of VR test design, its benefits and limitations.

Along the lines of the important topic raised by Song and Hsu about the potential under-representation of the construct of IC with the use of recent technological advances, Iwashita, May and Moore note two concurrent trends in the assessment of speaking skills with such tools: publishers of large-scale standardized tests are trying to find ways to leverage the affordances offered by new technologies, at the same time as modern communication is increasingly technologically mediated. Notwithstanding the important benefits of new technologies, the concern raised by Iwashita *et al.* is focused on the possible limitations of speech samples collected in the context of standardized, high-stakes, computer-mediated L2 speaking tests to elicit features of IC. Iwashita, May and Moore first describe in detail the two most common computer-mediated approaches to the assessment of IC: pre-recorded questions or tasks that prompt test-takers to produce monologues, and videoconferencing that generates real face-to-face interviews/interactions. They then turn to the analysis of the potential of three goal-oriented set ups (with both old and new technologies) to elicit data viable to assess various aspects of IC: videoconferencing technologies (but focused on paired and group speaking tests); virtual environments (focused on simulation of contextualized group discussions); and automated speech recognition and interactive spoken dialogue systems (for multi-turn interactions). After a detailed analysis of the potential of these new interactive environments, Iwashita, May and Moore conclude that, despite the limitations of current technological environments to incorporate the assessment of IC, continuing technological advances and the ongoing efforts of language testing researchers will pave the way for innovative and rational choices to elicit and assess IC in the future.

Notes

(1) For the sake of space, we focus on the model prevalent in the United States (ACTFL-OPI), although the model used in Europe (CEFR) has a similar theoretical foundation.
(2) Despite several calls for modifications in the early 2000s (e.g. Chalhoub-Deville, 2003; Chalhoub-Deville & Fulcher, 2003; Salaberry, 2000), the ACTFL proficiency model remains mostly unchanged since the time of its original publication in 1982 (the latest revision is from 2012).
(3) This holds true even in cases where some might expect lack of visual access to lessen the importance of NVB, such as in interactions between deafblind participants (Willoughby et al., 2019).

References

Al-Gahtani, S. and Roever, C. (2015) The development of requests by L2 learners of modern standard Arabic: A longitudinal and cross-sectional study. *Foreign Language Annals* 48 (4), 570–583.
Al-Gahtani, S. and Roever, C. (2018) Proficiency and preference organization in second language refusals. *Journal of Pragmatics* 129, 140–153
Bachman, L.F. (2007) What is the construct? The dialectic of abilities and contexts in defining constructs in language assessment. In J. Fox, M. Wesche, D. Bayliss, L. Cheng, C.E. Turner and C. Doe (eds) *Language Testing Reconsidered* (pp. 41–71). Ottawa: University of Ottawa Press.
Barraja-Rohan, A.M. (1997) Teaching conversation and sociocultural norms with conversation analysis. *Australian Review of Applied Linguistics* 14, 71–88.
Barraja-Rohan, A.M. (2011) Using conversation analysis in the second language classroom to teach interactional competence. *Language Teaching Research* 15 (4), 479–507.
Betz, E. and Huth, T. (2014) Beyond grammar: Teaching interaction in the German language Classroom. *Die Unterrichtspraxis/Teaching German* 47, 140–163.
Block, D. (2003) *The Social Turn in Second Language Acquisition*. Washington, DC: Georgetown University Press.
Brown, A. (2003) Interviewer variation and the co-construction of speaking proficiency. *Language Testing* 20 (1), 1–25.
Burch, A.R. (2014) Pursuing information: A conversation analytic perspective on communication strategies. *Language Learning* 64 (3), 651–684.

Burch, A.R. and Kasper, G. (2016) Like Godzilla. In M. Prior and G. Kasper (eds) *Emotion in Multilingual Interaction* (pp. 57–85). Philadelphia, PA: John Benjamins.

Canale, M. (1983) On some dimensions of language proficiency. In J.W. Oller Jr. (ed.) *Issues in Language Testing Research* (pp. 332–342). Rowley, MA: Newbury House.

Canale, M. and Swain, M. (1980) Theoretical bases of communicative approaches to second language teaching and testing. *Applied Linguistics* 1 (1), 1–47.

Carter, R. and McCarthy, M. (2004) Talking, creating: Interactional language, creativity, and context. *Applied Linguistics* 25 (1), 62–88.

Chalhoub-Deville, M. (2003) Second language interaction: Current perspectives and future trends. *Language Testing* 20 (4), 369–383.

Chalhoub-Deville, M. and Fulcher, G. (2003) The oral proficiency interview: A research agenda. *Foreign Language Annals* 36 (4), 498–506.

Cook, V.J. (1992) Evidence for multicompetence. *Language Learning* 42 (4), 557–591.

Davis, L. (2009) The influence of interlocutor proficiency in a paired oral assessment. *Language Testing* 26 (3), 367–396.

Douglas Fir Group (2016) A transdisciplinary framework for SLA in a multilingual world. *The Modern Language Journal* 100 (S1), 19–47.

Ducasse, A.M. and Brown, A. (2009) Assessing paired orals: Raters' orientation to interaction. *Language Testing* 26 (3), 423–443.

Duff, P.A. (2015) Transnationalism, multilingualism, and identity. *Annual Review of Applied Linguistics* 35, 57–80.

Edwards, D. and Potter, J. (2005) Discursive psychology, mental states and descriptions. In H. te Molder and J. Potter (eds) *Conversation and Cognition* (pp. 241–259). Cambridge: Cambridge University Press.

Eskildsen, S.W. and Majlesi, A.R. (2018) Learnables and teachables in second language talk: Advancing a social reconceptualization of central SLA tenets. Introduction to the special issue. *The Modern Language Journal* 102, 3–10.

Firth, A. and Wagner, J. (1997) On discourse, communication, and (some) fundamental concepts in SLA research. *The Modern Language Journal* 81 (3), 285–300.

Firth, A. and Wagner, J. (2007) Second/foreign language learning as a social accomplishment: Elaborations on a reconceptualized SLA. *The Modern Language Journal* 91, 800–819.

Fulcher, G. (2004) Deluded by artifices? The common European framework and harmonization. *Language Assessment Quarterly: An International Journal* 1 (4), 253–266.

Galaczi, E.D. (2008) Peer-peer interaction in a speaking test: The case of the First Certificate in English examination. *Language Assessment Quarterly* 5 (2), 89–119.

Galaczi, E.D. (2013) Interactional competence across proficiency levels: How do learners manage interaction in paired speaking tests? *Applied Linguistics* 35 (5), 553–574.

Galaczi, E. and Taylor, L. (2018) Interactional competence: Conceptualisations, operationalisations, and outstanding questions. *Language Assessment Quarterly* 15 (3), 219–236.

García, O. and Flores, N. (2014) Multilingualism and Common Core State Standards in the United States. In S. May (ed.) *The Multilingual Turn: Implications for SLA, TESOL and Bilingual Education* (pp. 147–166). New York: Routledge.

Gardner, R. and Wagner, J. (eds) (2004) *Second Language Conversations*. London: Continuum.

Garfinkel, H. (1967) *Studies in Ethnomethodology*. Englewood Cliffs, NJ: Prentice-Hall.

Glisan, E.W., Swender, E. and Surface, E.A. (2013) Oral proficiency standards and foreign language teacher candidates: Current findings and future research directions. *Foreign Language Annals* 46 (2), 264–289.

Goldberg, D., Looney, D. and Lusin, N. (2015) Enrollments in languages other than English in United States institutions of higher education, Fall 2013. Retrieved April 19, 2021 from https. apps.mla.org/pdf/2013_enrollment_survey. pdf.

Goodwin, C. (2018) *Co-operative Action*. Cambridge: Cambridge University Press.

Greer, T., Ishida, M. and Tateyama, Y. (eds) (2017) *Interactional Competence in Japanese as an Additional Language*. Honolulu, HI: National Foreign Language Resource Center.

Hall, J.K. and Pekarek Doehler, S. (2011) L2 interactional competence and development. In J.K. Hall, J. Hellermann and S. Pekarek Doehler (eds) *L2 Interactional Competence and Development* (pp. 1–18). Bristol: Multilingual Matters.

Hall, J.K., Hellermann, J. and Pekarek Doehler, S. (eds) (2011) *L2 Interactional Competence and Development*. Bristol: Multilingual Matters.

Hauser, E. (2005) Coding 'corrective recasts': The maintenance of meaning and more fundamental problems. *Applied Linguistics* 26 (3), 293–316.

He, A.W. and Young, R. (1998) Language proficiency interviews: A discourse approach. In R. Young and A.W. He (eds) *Talking and Testing: Discourse Approaches to the Assessment of Oral Proficiency* (pp. 1–24). Amsterdam: John Benjamins.

Heritage, J. (1984) *Garfinkel and Ethnomethodology*. Cambridge: Polity Press.

Hopper, R. (2005) A cognitive agnostic in conversation analysis: When do strategies affect spoken interaction? In H. te Molder and J. Potter (eds) *Conversation and Cognition* (pp. 134–58). Cambridge: Cambridge University Press.

Huth, T. (2006) Negotiating structure and culture: L2 learners' realization of L2 compliment-response sequences in talk-in-interaction. *Journal of Pragmatics* 38, 2025–2050.

Huth, T. (2014) 'When in Berlin ...': Teaching German telephone openings. *Die Unterrichtspraxis/Teaching German* 47 (2), 164–179.

Huth, T. and Betz, E. (2019) Testing interactional competence in second language classrooms: Goals, formats and caveats. In M. Salaberry and S. Kunitz (eds) *Teaching and Testing L2 Interactional Competence: Bridging Theory and Practice* (pp. 322–356). New York: Routledge.

Huth, T. and Taleghani-Nikazm, C. (2006) How can insights from conversation analysis be directly applied to teaching L2 pragmatics? *Language Teaching Research* 10 (1), 53–79.

Hymes, D.H. (1972) On communicative competence. In J.B. Pride and J. Holmes (eds) *Sociolinguistics: Selected Readings* (pp. 269–293). Harmondsworth: Penguin.

Ikeda, N. (2017) Measuring L2 Oral Pragmatic Abilities for Use in Social Contexts: Development and Validation of an Assessment Instrument for L2 Pragmatics Performance in University Settings. Unpublished doctoral dissertation, University of Melbourne, Australia.

Jefferson, G. (2004) Glossary of transcript symbols with an introduction. In G. Lerner (ed.) *Conversation Analysis: Studies from the First Generation* (pp. 13–31). Amsterdam: John Benjamins.

Johnson, M. (2001) *The Art of Non-Conversation: A Reexamination of the Validity of the Oral Proficiency Interview*. New Haven, CT: Yale University Press.

Kasper, G. (2009) Locating cognition in second language interaction and learning: Inside the skull or in public view? *International Review of Applied Linguistics* 47, 11–36.

Kley, K. (2019) What counts as evidence for interactional competence? Developing rating criteria for a German classroom-based paired speaking test. In M. Salaberry and S. Kunitz (eds) *Teaching and Testing L2 Interactional Competence: Bridging Theory and Practice* (291–321). New York: Routledge.

Kormos, J. (1999) Simulating conversations in oral-proficiency assessment: A conversation analysis of role plays and non-scripted interviews in language exams. *Language Testing* 16 (2), 163–188.

Lantolf, J.P. (2011) The sociocultural approach to second language acquisition: Sociocultural theory, second language acquisition, and artificial L2 development. In D. Atkinson (ed.) *Alternative Approaches to Second Language Acquisition* (pp. 24–47). New York: Routledge.

Lantolf, J.P. and Poehner, M.E. (2011) Dynamic assessment in the classroom: Vygotskian praxis for second language development. *Language Teaching Research* 15 (1), 11–33.

Lazaraton, A. (1996) Interlocutor support in oral proficiency interviews: The case of CASE. *Language Testing* 13 (2), 151–172.

Liskin-Gasparro, J.E. (2003) The ACTFL proficiency guidelines and the oral proficiency interview: A brief history and analysis of their survival. *Foreign Language Annals* 36 (4), 483–490.

Markee, N. (2011) Doing, and justifying doing, avoidance. *Journal of Pragmatics* 43, 602–615.

May, S. (2011) The disciplinary constraints of SLA and TESOL: Additive bilingualism and second language acquisition, teaching and learning. *Linguistics and Education* 22 (3), 233–247.

May, S. (ed.) (2014) *The Multilingual Turn: Implications for SLA, TESOL and Bilingual Education.* New York: Routledge.

McNamara, T.F. (1996) *Measuring Second Language Performance.* London: Addison Wesley Longman.

McNamara, T.F. (1997) 'Interaction' in second language performance assessment: Whose performance? *Applied Linguistics* 18 (4), 446–466.

McNamara, T.F. (2019) *Language and Subjectivity.* Cambridge: Cambridge University Press.

McNamara, T. and Roever, C. (2006) *Language Testing: The Social Dimension* (Vol. 1). John Wiley & Sons.

Messick, S. (1994) The interplay of evidence and consequences in the validation of performance assessments. *Educational Researcher* 23 (2), 13–23.

Nguyen, H.T. and Kasper, G. (eds) (2009) *Talk-in-Interaction: Multilingual Perspectives.* Honolulu, HI: National Foreign Language Resource Center.

Norton, B. (2000) *Identity and Language Learning: Social Processes and Educational Practice* (1st edn). New York: Longman.

Norton, B. (2014) Identity, literacy, and the multilingual classroom. In S. May (ed.) *The Multilingual Turn: Implications for SLA, TESOL, and Bilingual Education* (pp. 103–122). New York: Routledge.

O'Keefe, A., McCarthy, M. and Carter, R. (2007) *From Corpus to Classroom: Language Use and Language Teaching.* Cambridge: Cambridge University Press.

Ortega, L. (2014) Ways forward for a bi/multilingual turn in SLA. In S. May (ed.) *The Multilingual Turn: Implications for SLA, TESOL and Bilingual Education* (pp. 32–53). New York: Routledge.

Pallotti, G. and Wagner, J. (eds) (2011) *L2 Learning as Social Practice: Conversation-Analytic Perspectives.* Honolulu, HI: National Foreign Language Resource Center.

Patharakorn, P. (2018) Assessing interactional competence in a multiparty roleplay task: A mixed-methods study. Doctoral dissertation, University of Hawai'i at Manoa.

Pekarek Doehler, S. and Pochon-Berger, E. (2011) Developing 'methods' for interaction: A cross-sectional study of disagreement sequences in French L2. In J.K. Hall, J. Hellermann and S. Pekarek Doehler (eds) *L2 Interactional Competence and Development* (pp. 206–243). Bristol: Multilingual Matters.

Pekarek Doehler, S. and Pochon-Berger, E. (2015) The development of L2 interactional competence: Evidence from turn-taking organization, sequence organization, repair organization and preference organization. In T. Cadierno and S.W. Eskildsen (eds) *Usage-based Perspectives on Second Language Learning* (pp. 233–268). Berlin: Mouton De Gruyter.

Plough, I. (2018) Revisiting the speaking construct: The question of interactional competence. *Language Testing* 35 (3), 325–329.

Plough, I., Banerjee, J. and Iwashita, N. (2018) Interactional competence: Genie out of the bottle. *Language Testing* 35 (3), 427–445.

Roever, C. and Kasper, G. (2018) Speaking in turns and sequences: Interactional competence as a target construct in testing speaking. *Language Testing* 35 (3), 331–355.

Ross, S. (2017) *Interviewing for Language Proficiency: Interaction and Interpretation.* Basingstoke: Palgrave Macmillan.

Ross, S. (2018) Listener response as a facet of interactional competence. *Language Testing* 35 (3), 357–375.

Ross, S.J. and Kasper, G. (eds) (2013) *Assessing Second Language Pragmatics*. Basingstoke: Palgrave Macmillan.

Sacks, H. (1974) On the analysability of stories by children. In R. Turner (ed.) *Ethnomethodology: Selected Readings* (pp. 216–232). Harmondsworth: Penguin.

Sacks, H. (1992) *Lectures on Conversation* (2 vols). Oxford: Blackwell.

Salaberry, M.R. (2000) Revising the revised format of the ACTFL Oral Proficiency Interview. *Language Testing* 17 (3), 289–310.

Salaberry, R. and Kunitz, S. (eds) (2019) *Teaching and Testing L2 Interactional Competence: Bridging Theory and Practice*. New York: Routledge.

Sandlund, E. and Sundqvist, P. (2019) Doing versus assessing interactional competence. In M. Salaberry and S. Kunitz (eds) *Teaching and Testing L2 Interactional Competence: Bridging Theory and Practice* (pp. 357–396). New York: Routledge.

Schegloff, E.A. (1992) On talk and its institutional occasions. In J. Heritage and P. Drew (eds) *Talk at Work: Interaction in Institutional Settings* (pp. 101–134). Cambridge: Cambridge University Press.

Schegloff, E.A., Jefferson, G. and Sacks, H. (1977) The preference for self-correction in the organization of repair in conversation. *Language* 53, 361–382.

Seedhouse, P. and Nakatsuhara, F. (2018) *The Discourse of the IELTS Speaking Test: Interactional Design and Practice*. Cambridge: Cambridge University Press.

Shohamy, E. (2011) Assessing multilingual competencies: Adopting construct valid assessment policies. *The Modern Language Journal* 95 (3), 418–429.

Spolsky, B. (1997) The ethics of gatekeeping tests: What have we learned in a hundred years? *Language Testing* 14 (3), 242–247.

Stansfield, C. and Kenyon, D. (1992) Research on the comparability of the oral proficiency interview and the simulated oral proficiency interview. *System* 20 (3), 347–364.

Stokoe, E. (2012) Moving forward with membership categorization analysis: Methods for systematic analysis. *Discourse Studies* 14 (3), 277–303.

Swender, E., Breiner-Sanders, K., Mujica Laughlin, L., Lowe, P. and Miles, J. (1999) *ACTFL Oral Proficiency Interview Tester Training Manual*. Stamford, CT: American Council on the Teaching of Foreign Languages.

Swender, E., Conrad, D.J. and Vicars, R. (2012) *ACTFL Proficiency Guidelines 2012*. Fairfax, VA: American Council on the Teaching of Foreign Languages.

te Molder, H. and Potter, J. (eds) (2005) *Conversation and Cognition*. Cambridge: Cambridge University Press.

Valdés, G. and Figueroa, R.A. (1994) *Bilingualism and Testing: A Special Case of Bias*. New York: Ablex.

van Lier, L. (1989) Reeling, writhing, drawling, stretching, and fainting in coils: Oral proficiency interviews as conversation. *TESOL Quarterly* 23 (3), 489–508.

Weir, C.J. (2005) Limitations of the Common European Framework for developing comparable examinations and tests. *Language Testing* 22 (3), 281–300.

Willoughby, L., Manns, H., Iwasaki, S. and Bartlett, M. (2019) Are you trying to be funny? Communicating humour in deafblind conversations. *Discourse Studies* 21 (5), 584–602.

Youn, S.J. (2015) Validity argument for assessing L2 pragmatics in interaction using mixed methods. *Language Testing* 32 (2), 199–225.

Youn, S.J. (2018) Rater variability across examinees and rating criteria in paired speaking assessment. *Papers in Language Testing and Assessment* 7, 32–60.

Young, R.F. (2009) Contexts of teaching and testing. *Language Learning* 58, 183–226. https://doi.org/10.1111/j.1467-9922.2009.00493.x

Young, R.F. (2011) Interactional competence in language learning, teaching, and testing. In E. Hinkel (ed.) *Handbook of Research in Second Language Teaching and Learning, Vol. 2* (pp. 233–268). New York: Routledge.

Young, R.F. and He, A.W. (eds) (1998) *Talking and Testing: Discourse Approaches to the Assessment of Oral Proficiency*. Amsterdam: John Benjamins.

2 Reconceptualising Interactional Competence for Language Testing

Carsten Roever and David Wei Dai

There has recently been strong interest in the assessment of interactional competence (IC) as witnessed by a special issue of the journal *Language Testing* (Plough *et al.*, 2018) devoted entirely to IC, a special issue on the employment of conversation analysis in assessing IC of the journal *Papers in Language Testing Assessment* (Youn & Burch, 2020) and the prominent role of IC assessment in the special issue of the journal *Language Assessment Quarterly* on speaking assessment (Lim, 2018). However, to this date no major language test assesses IC, and this chapter is intended to contribute to ending this lamentable state of affairs. We will do so by discussing why the absence of IC assessment is problematic, why simply assessing proficiency does not give information about test-takers' IC, what particular challenges IC test designers face and how the IC construct can be broadened to incorporate social role enactment as a rating criterion via membership categorisation analysis (MCA).

1 Why Test IC?

In the widely used argument-based approach to assessment (Kane, 2006, 2012), the purpose of a test is to generate desirable consequences or, more specifically, to provide information in the form of scores about the strength of an attribute of interest in test-takers, such as language skills, to enable decisions about these test-takers (see Chapelle *et al.*, 2008, 2010, for examples). In the case of language tests, decisions informed by language test scores might include such high-stakes decisions as admission to a foreign university, suitability for practising as a medical professional or permission to settle permanently in the host country. A test is arguably doing its job well if it enables good decisions, e.g. foreign medical graduates really do have the necessary language skills to communicate with patients and fellow professionals.

In the overwhelmingly typical case where test-takers' real-world language use involves interacting with others, it seems clear that their ability to do so should be a core part of the information gathered on their language ability. Language is a tool to make private thoughts public and visible (audible) to others, obtain access to their private thoughts and thereby enable coordinated social actions. Language users' ability to deploy language for accomplishing social actions has been conceptualised as their interactional competence, defined by Hall and Pekarek Doehler (2011: 2) as the 'ability to accomplish meaningful social actions, to respond to co-participants' previous actions and to make recognisable for others what our actions are and how these relate to their own actions'. This includes behaviours by which social roles are enacted in a given context, context-specific ways of organising turn-taking and communicative practices, as well as the use of linguistic and non-linguistic resources to accomplish these goals. While writing and reading are also to some degree forms of interaction, the immediate coordination of social actions between people on a moment-by-moment basis relies most strongly on speaking and listening. Language users' social actions are specifically designed with regard to their recipient (Drew, 2013) and every utterance accomplishes a social action which provides a context for the interlocutor's subsequent actions (Heritage, 1984): this is the core meaning of inter-action.

It seems logical that language tests should mirror this interactive use of language in order to obtain a representative picture of what the user can do in the real world and allow extrapolation from the sample of language use situations in the test to real-world language use. Alas, they do not. Language tests frequently do not include interaction in a second language and, where they do, they do not assess it, instead just using the resulting talk as a language sample to be rated on non-interactive criteria. For example, TOEFL and PTE contain monologic speaking tasks where test-takers react to prompts and input materials without engaging with an interlocutor. Tests like the ACTFL OPI and the IELTS speaking test involve a live interlocutor but their rating scales do not include measure of interactional abilities, and their main purpose is simply the elicitation of samples of spoken language. Various empirical studies have demonstrated the non-equivalence of interview-based speaking tests and natural conversation (e.g. Johnson, 2001; Lazaraton, 1992; van Lier, 1989).

The Cambridge English scales for assessing speaking performance (Cambridge English, n.d.) used for the Cambridge main suite exams go a step further and contain a rubric for interactive communication. However, this rubric is strongly influenced by the test format and focuses on maintaining interaction, responding to the interlocutor and linking contributions to the interlocutor's, thereby likely abbreviating the construct of interaction. Finally, the Common European Framework of Reference for Languages (CEFR; Council of Europe, 2001, 2018) has a number of scales for different interactive activities (casual conversation, interview, negotiation) and 'interaction strategies' (taking the floor, ensuring understanding, repair), but pays little attention to social action implementation and social role enactment. Tests of languages other than English, such as the Test of German as a Foreign Language (TestDaF) or the Chinese Standard Exam (Hanyu Shuiping Kaoshi, HSK) also do not score IC.

This lack of attention to IC means that most language tests privilege speaking over talking, to use Roever and Kasper's (2018) parlance. Roever and Kasper (2018) view talking as interactive language use, including designing utterances for a specific interlocutor and comprehending implied social actions. By contrast, speaking is simply a monologic response to a stimulus not designed to achieve a social action vis-à-vis an interlocutor. While people usually talk to others and rarely just speak to nobody, the latter is exactly what the vast majority of language tests assess.

Given that large-scale, high-stakes language tests do not assess what people use language for, there is a serious risk that their results are flawed and that construct underrepresentation threatens the defensibility of decisions and conclusions based on scores (Messick, 1989). There would be no problem if speaking were the same as talking, i.e. if people who are good at speaking are invariably good at talking, and people who are good at talking are invariably good at speaking. We will start our deliberations by showing that speaking is in fact not the same as talking, and then we will discuss ways of making language tests more representative of what people do with language.

2 Are Talking and Speaking the Same?

Speaking ability following the classic model by Levelt (1989, 1999), which explicitly informs tests such as PTE, requires fast access to vocabulary, automatisation of grammatical knowledge and high-speed phonetic encoding and articulation. This enables fluent, smooth, easily comprehensible speech, captured well in the construct of facility in L2, which Bernstein *et al.* (2010: 356) freely admit 'provides a measure of performance with the language without reference to any specific domain of use'. Similarly, the IELTS band descriptors (IDP IELTS, 2021) for the speaking test rate test-taker performance in four categories: fluency and coherence, lexical resource, grammatical range and accuracy, and pronunciation. There is no mention of interactional abilities, even though IELTS speaking involves a face-to-face interview, and research exists on the interactional construction of this interview (Brown, 2003; Seedhouse & Egbert, 2006; Seedhouse & Nakatsuhara, 2018).

Roever and Kasper (2018) term this the psycholinguistic view of speaking, and it sees speaking ability as consisting of a set of components that can be assessed without reference to their conversational use. Still, it assumes that such an assessment will provide useful information since these abilities are required across a wide variety of contexts. This is probably not entirely unreasonable: if speakers have ready access to vocabulary and can implement a broad range of grammatical functions under real-time conditions, this will help them under any circumstances, be it a conversation in a pub, a job interview or a classroom discussion.

However, this view is akin to assessing driving by having a candidate drive alone on a closed course, and then assuming that they will do equally well in rush hour traffic. This is clearly a daring assumption: while the basic skills needed for successful driving (such as accelerating, braking, steering) are called upon in both situations, driving in rush hour traffic goes beyond basic driving skills. It requires coordinating one's actions with others, predicting what they might do, reacting to their actions and adapting to changing conditions.

While driving on a closed course is like speaking, driving in rush hour traffic is like talking: you need to be able to speak in order to talk (although not in all circumstances, as we will elaborate on below), but talking requires more than speaking. In addition to basic speaking skills, talking also requires understanding of the interlocutor, and adjusting of one's speaking to the interlocutor. Both are crucial, so let us take them in turn.

Understanding of the interlocutor involves real-time decoding of incoming language on a semantic level of word meaning, as well as on a pragmatic level of social action and interpersonal meaning. To be able to respond, interlocutors must understand the content of what is being said, but to be able to respond appropriately they must also understand what action is being done and how the utterance frames the relationship between the interactants. All of this happens before the interlocutor has even finished speaking, as otherwise there would simply not be enough time, given that assembling a response takes about 0.6 seconds but gaps between turns in English-language conversation are only about 0.2 seconds (Levinson & Torreira, 2015).

Knowing what social action is being performed is crucial for designing a response, as social actions tend to only have a limited range of typical response. For example, in responding to the informal greeting, 'How is it going?', a response like 'Not bad, you?' is quite typical because it consists of a second pair part commonly associated with this type of greeting. However, an account of one's health status ('How is it going?' – 'I've had really bad hay fever recently.') is atypical, as it recasts the social action of greeting as an inquiry after well-being. Finally, a response like 'I'm going by train.' indicates a semantic lack of understanding and would most likely be taken as a mis-hearing, which may be repaired or ignored.

In addition to responding to a social action with a type-fitting action, utterances must be recipient-designed. In the CA literature (e.g. Drew, 2013), recipient design refers mostly to taking into account shared knowledge between interlocutors. For example, when a speaker talks about their partner, Mike, to a stranger who can be assumed not to know Mike, they are likely to refer to Mike as 'my partner'. However, when they talk to a close friend who knows Mike well, they are likely to refer to him as 'Mike'; in fact, referring to him as 'my partner' would be decidedly odd.

Talk can be specifically designed for a recipient in other ways as well. A great deal of research in pragmatics, based in speech act theory (Austin, 1962; Searle, 1969) and taking off from Brown and Levinson's (1987) seminal work on the social context of interaction, has focused on social factors that impact how people talk to each other, with most research focusing on politeness in making requests. Brown and Levinson posit three major factors that influence the politeness level of utterances: Power, Social Distance and Degree of Imposition. Power refers to the degree that one interlocutor can exert control over the other one's behaviour; e.g. in a workplace situation, a manager would have power over an employee they supervise. Social Distance is the degree of acquaintanceship or common membership in a social group between interlocutors; e.g. close friends have low social distance whereas strangers have high social distance. Finally, the Degree of Imposition describes the 'cost' to the hearer in terms of money, time, effort or social sanction for complying with the speaker. For example, asking someone for the time is a low imposition request, but asking them to go out of their way to help carry a heavy item is high imposition. It is worth noting that these factors do not deterministically govern how people talk to each other; other factors come into play as well. For example, Curl and Drew (2008), taking a CA approach, showed that the perceived degree of entitlement for making a request in emergency calls strongly affects request formulation.

Finally, work in sociolinguistics has identified a number of other factors that impact talking, most famously encapsulated in Hymes's (1974) SPEAKING model, which takes into account (among others) the physical setting of the interaction, its overall tone, the channel through which it is conducted and the cultural norms through which interlocutors make judgments about meanings.

Given the numerous additional factors that impact talking as opposed to speaking, it is difficult to imagine that simply measuring speaking would give testers a strong basis for making inferences about the ability to talk. However, this is really an empirical question. If strong speaking ability invariably leads to strong talking ability, it is sufficient to test speaking and then simply infer talking. This may seem unlikely, and speaking will probably not account for all the variance in talking, but even if it just accounts for a large amount of variance, that may be sufficient for a test. However, if a dissociation between speaking and talking can be demonstrated, where you can be good at speaking but not talking and vice versa, talking would need to be tested separately to enable defensible inferences from test scores.

2.1 Can you be good at speaking but not talking?

It certainly appears that way, as anecdotal evidence abounds about test-takers who do well in the testing situation but not so well in real-life interaction, e.g. in medical communication (Eggly *et al.*, 1999; Hall *et al.*, 2004). In fact, end-user complaints about apparent mismatches between candidates' scores on the Occupational English Test (OET) taken by medical professionals and those test-takers' real-world performance were a major impetus in the revision of the OET to include a stronger focus on role-appropriate interaction in the rating criteria (Pill, 2016). This divergence is likely due to tests being rated on language-focused criteria, which tend to privilege speaking, and not criteria indigenous to users (see Jacoby, 1998), which tend to privilege talking. Sato (2014) supports this conclusion, showing that different aspects of speaking performance matter to naïve judges assessing a performance on their general impression of the test-taker as a skilled communicator, as compared to trained raters assessing on language-focused criteria. This dissociation between the criteria used in language tests and real-world language requirements also likely accounts for the less-than-overwhelming confidence of students, academics and employers in the predictive value of language tests for real-world performance (see Murray *et al.*, 2014, for IELTS; Malone & Montee, 2014, for TOEFL).

It appears that speaking ability as measured by such a test is not a good predictor of the ability to talk in the real world, which does not bode well for language tests. However, two counter-arguments to this line of reasoning could be adduced to defend general language tests: first, it could be claimed that specific-purpose language tests like the OET not only require a general ability to interact but a role-specific ability to interact. To put it simply, not only do you have to talk well, you have to talk recognisably like a doctor, nurse, dentist, etc. A potential argument is that this ability is not required in general proficiency tests. Second, it could be argued that no test performance ever extrapolates perfectly to real-world performance, and so the apparent gap between speaking in a test and talking in the real world is simply an unavoidable gap between eliciting performance in a controlled test environment and performing 'in the wild'. In our view, both points are akin to desperate rear-guard battles trying to stave off the inevitable loss.

Role-specific interactional abilities are always required in talking. There is no such thing as language use unbounded to a social role. Interlocutors are always speaking as a friend, colleague, supervisor, customer, partner, neighbour, student, with all the social requirements of talking appropriately to that role. These requirements can be subtle: Bella (2014) found that although advanced learners of modern Greek had control of the pragmalinguistic tools for performing refusals in roleplays, they overused some and underused others when compared to native speakers. In other words, just because you have grammar and vocabulary that you can deploy in speaking does not mean you can deploy it in conventional ways when talking from the perspective of a particular social role. This is more obvious in specific-purpose assessment, but no different in other language tests.

While language use in tests is not the same as language use in the real world, strengthening the extrapolation inference should be the main mission of language testers. O'Sullivan (2019) lays out the problem very clearly, and the larger the gap between test performance and real-world performance (i.e. the weaker the extrapolation inference in Kane's, 2006, framework), the less value test scores have for end-users because they do not enable the decisions for which end-users need them. Tests based on a universe of generalisation that is mostly chosen to be practically measurable will not do well on extrapolation. This is precisely the issue with measuring speaking versus measuring talking: in particular, tests that use monologic measures and thereby measure speaking have an advantage in terms of administration, standardisation and scoring, but they do not measure the skills associated with talking, such as designing talk for the recipient, responding, organising talk sequentially, enacting befitting social roles, etc. Similarly, tests that simply use interaction to elicit ratable samples of language to be rated without any reference to interactional abilities sell the talking construct short. Scores from these tests run precisely the risk of being mismatched with end-user impressions of ability, which can eventually bring down the whole language testing enterprise: Why should end-users go through the trouble of obtaining test scores if these scores do not tell them what they want to know? This is a broader question than just speaking versus talking, but because of the pervasiveness and everyday necessity of being able to talk, speaking versus talking is a particularly important aspect of this problem in language testing.

2.2 Can you be good at talking but not speaking?

It may seem counter-intuitive that a language user could be better at talking than speaking since we have so far portrayed talking as 'speaking plus': interactants need basic speaking skills, but to talk they need to be able to configure and deploy them within a particular physical, social and interactional context. However, it is possible to talk with little or even no language proficiency. Levinson (2006) describes an interaction during field research with a deaf signer on Rossel Island, an island in the far south-east of Papua New Guinea. Levinson and his interlocutor shared no language and little background knowledge but successfully managed a storytelling. While this may seem like an extreme case, it is actually fairly mundane: anybody who has travelled to a country without speaking the local language knows that it is possible to communicate to some extent through pointing, miming and gesturing. This is not sufficient for discussing abstract, complex topics, but it demonstrates that talking in the sense of communicating is possible with very little speaking proficiency.

A case closer to the experience of applied linguists is the well-known case study of Wes (Schmidt, 1983). Wes is a native Japanese speaker who migrated to the United States as an adult, and Schmidt collected tape recordings and field notes of Wes's use of English over several years. He found little and stagnating grammatical development, but rapid development and high levels of performance in spoken discourse. Wes had an active social life with many friends and managed everyday interactions in English successfully. While Schmidt described Wes's language ability in order to test Schumann's acculturation theory (1978), the disjunct he found between grammatical ability and interactional/sociolinguistic abilities is a good illustration of a highly interactionally competent language user with low grammatical ability. Schmidt writes: 'If language is seen as a means of initiating, maintaining, and regulating relationships and carrying on the business of living, then perhaps Wes is a good learner. If one views language as a system of elements and rules, with syntax playing a major role, then Wes is clearly a very poor learner' (Schmidt, 1983: 164). Wes was good at talking but not so good at speaking, and it is probably safe to say that he would not have performed well on formal language tests where his lack of grammatical accuracy and limited vocabulary range would have likely been penalised.

To conclude, the above discussion offers theoretical and conceptual evidence that speaking and talking are two overlapping but still distinctive forms of competence. This lends support to assessing talking/IC in its own right in testing settings so as to better gauge test-takers' ability to interact in real life. But what are some of the caveats in talking/IC assessment?

3 How Can Talking Be Tested Better?

The second part of this chapter focuses on four practical concerns in operationalising a 'talking'/IC construct in testing settings. The first three concerns are target domain delineation, IC construct validity and IC marker selection and the last one is social role enactment. Although previous IC developmental and assessment studies have interrogated the first three concerns to varying degrees, we argue that these concerns warrant more thorough deliberation if test designers want to develop a defensible interpretative framework for an IC construct. The last concern, social role enactment, is unexplored in existing IC research and we aim to demonstrate its relevance in an IC construct with the analytical toolkit of MCA.

3.1 Target domain delineation

Galaczi and Taylor (2018: 227) offer a tree-shaped visual representation of IC which is helpful in framing our discussion of IC assessment. Their IC tree grows into branches and leaves, with branches indexing general IC markers such as 'turn management' and 'interactive listening', and leaves indexing finer IC markers such as 'maintaining turns' and 'pausing', under the branch of turn management. Going downwards, the authors specify the roots for the IC tree in three concentric circles: speech acts (or social actions in CA parlance), speech events and speech situations. Although such contextual factors situate, nourish and support the investigation of IC, they are rarely given the consideration they deserve. In terms of the first two circles, although previous L2 IC research has examined a range of social actions such as requests (Al-Gahtani & Roever, 2015), refusals (Al-Gahtani & Roever, 2018), storytelling (Waring, 2013; Watanabe, 2016) and disagreements (Pekarek Doehler & Pochon-Berger, 2011), the rationale for researchers' choices of social actions is rarely provided. Understandably for developmental IC studies, social actions merely serve as vehicles for analysts to observe differential IC, so what social action is used to elicit L2 speakers' performances is a minor concern. However, from a test design perspective, which social action to include in or exclude from the target domain needs to be a carefully considered and empirically justifiable decision. For example, there needs to be a rationale for testing L2 Arabic speakers' ability in launching a request, instead of a disagreement or a complaint.

When we move beyond speech acts and speech events in Galaczi and Taylor's (2018) IC tree, we encounter the largest circle, speech situations where social actions take place. The authors' conceptualisation of speech situations draws from Hymes (1974) where speech situations are decidedly sociocultural. This further complicates the picture for IC assessment. Cross-linguistic CA research has offered evidence that speakers adopt different methods and sequentially structure their talk differently across languages and cultures when they conduct social actions (Golato, 2002; Huth, 2006). Developmental L2 IC studies have also noted that L2 speakers increasingly diversify their methods to adapt to and align with routinised interactional patterns commonly found in the host culture (Cekaite, 2007; Pekarek Doehler & Pochon-Berger, 2015). The cultural specificity of social action implementation requires test designers to go one step further: they need to demonstrate the relevance of their chosen social actions to the particular L2 context. In other words, the question now is not just choosing between requests, disagreements or complaints for an unspecified L2 speaker population, but it is to decide between these social actions for an IC test specifically targeting, for example, L2 Arabic speakers. Why should requests be singled out in an L2 Arabic test? Is it because requests in Arabic are particularly frequent, complex or difficult? Or do L2 Arabic speakers struggle with requests in particular due to some sequential, interactional or sociocultural differences in how requests are formatted in the host community? Fortunately, there is a ready remedy for this problem: needs analysis.

Needs analyses can assist L2 IC test designers in their depiction of the IC target domain and identify social actions that are most pertinent to or challenging for their specific test-taker population. Youn (2015) followed this procedure by grounding the design of her IC test in a needs analysis on the English for academic purposes (EAP) domain. Her needs analysis, later published as Youn (2018), triangulated the perspectives from programme administrators, instructors and students and utilised two data elicitation methods: interviews and questionnaires. Her data revealed a wide range of social actions where EAP students struggle, which then fed into the two interactional tasks she designed. The two tasks in Youn (2015) require test-takers to roleplay with a professor and a classmate and elicit actions such as making a request for a recommendation letter and agreeing on a meeting time. In a similar vein, Dai (2019) conducted a task-based needs analysis of the interactional needs of L2 Chinese speakers for the design of his IC test. Utilising Socratic-Hermeneutic interviews (Dinkins, 2005) and follow-up written communication and triangulating the perspectives from L2 Chinese speakers, Chinese teachers and native speakers who frequently interact with L2 speakers, Dai elicited rich qualitative data on where L2 Chinese speakers encounter problems when interacting in Chinese in China. Dai then designed nine roleplay tasks targeting the top-ranking social actions that L2 Chinese speakers struggle with the most (Dai & Roever, 2019). To conclude, although every social action is worth investigating from a developmental perspective, due to the limited resources in testing settings, test designers need to define their target domain clearly and select social actions that are most germane to their respective L2 groups. A methodic needs analysis serves this purpose and can assist test designers in narrowing down the target domain to items in a test.

3.2 IC construct validity

The second concern links back to our previous discussion on differentiating talking from speaking. If an IC construct claims to cover 'talking' variance not already covered by existing tests that measure 'speaking' or general proficiency, it needs to be able to demonstrate it in a statistical sense. Having this goal in mind and then looking at existing research in L2 IC, the issue of differentiating between IC and speaking, or proficiency in general, quickly becomes a chicken-and-egg question. Longitudinal studies on L2 IC development document L2 speakers' changing methods or interactional patterns but it is difficult to tease apart how much of those changes are attributable to increase in IC or increase in general proficiency (Hellermann, 2007, 2008; Pekarek Doehler & Pochon-Berger, 2016). Cross-sectional studies, on the other hand, start with pre-grouping L2 speakers by proficiency and investigate if speakers from different proficiency levels mobilise different methods in implementing the same social action (Al-Gahtani & Roever, 2018; Pekarek Doehler, 2018; Pekarek Doehler & Pochon-Berger, 2011). Their grouping criteria are either proficiency frameworks based largely on the speaking construct (e.g. CEFR) or researchers' intuition. The few IC assessment studies that exist also adopt a cross-sectional design and although they provide statistical evidence that L2 speakers do differ on researchers' IC measures, we cannot know for sure if proficiency or 'speaking variance' can already account for such IC differences (Galaczi, 2013; Ikeda, 2017; Youn, 2015).

Nevertheless, there is some incipient evidence that IC does measure unique variance not encompassed by speaking, or a psycholinguistic conceptualisation of proficiency. Lee and Hellermann (2014) offer cross-sectional data where a low-proficiency speaker, Larissa, demonstrates the capacity to launch a storytelling sequence despite her lack of linguistic resources. In their data Larissa, who is from Russia, is conversing with another low-proficiency speaker Jamie, who is from Mexico, and before the turn that launches the storytelling sequence in focus, a sequence on Thanksgiving was completed with an agreement token by Larissa. After a 2.5-second gap, Larissa self-selects, and launches her storytelling sequence with 'mm husband #uh::# call my uncle.' (Lee & Hellermann (2014: 772). Lee and Hellermann argue that although Larissa's storytelling announcement turn lacks explicit time reference devices such as 'yesterday', which are common in high-proficiency L2 speakers' talk, she still designs her turn to adumbrate a forthcoming story. Accompanying this turn, Larissa employs body language mimicking a person making a call, suggesting that her husband is calling her uncle to talk about the American tradition of having turkeys at Thanksgiving. It is also worth noting that in this turn Larissa evokes family categories 'husband' and 'uncle' which, combined with other linguistic and paralinguistic resources, pave the way for inferences such as 'husband is living with Larissa in USA', 'husband is calling Larissa's uncle to tell the story of American Thanksgiving' and 'uncle is most likely still living in Russia'. These inferences are crucial to Larissa's storytelling in subsequent turns. Therefore, despite Larissa's linguistic inadequacies, she is still interactionally competent in securing a storytelling sequence through the mobilisation of turn design, body language and category evocation. Regrettably, these markers of interactional resourcefulness are not covered in any existing speaking rubric. In summary, developmental IC studies have offered fruitful insight into how L2 speakers differ in different facets of talking, but we need more evidence to prove that such differences can add variance to our existing speaking tests.

Different from the qualitative evidence in Lee and Hellermann (2014), Ockey et al. (2015) is a rare testing study that explicitly compares IC measures with proficiency measures. The researchers compare 222 Japanese university students' TOEFL iBT performances with their performances on three language tasks (group discussion, picture description and oral presentation). One component score for the three language tasks is IC, which is defined as 'participation and smoothness of interaction (e.g. turn-taking, responding to others, asking questions, introducing new gambits, paraphrasing, and hedging)' (Ockey et al., 2015: 46).

Pearson correlations reveal high correlations between test-takers' TOEFL scores and their component scores on pronunciation, fluency and vocabulary in the three tasks. However, only moderate correlation is achieved between TOEFL scores and their IC component scores. Such a finding offers evidence that TOEFL, a psycholinguistically grounded speaking test, can offer good prediction on real-life performances in terms of pronunciation and fluency but not IC. It also shows that the asynchronous monologic speaking tasks employed by TOEFL can barely cover basic IC variance such as turn-turning or hedging. We speculate that higher-order talking/IC sub-traits such as action formation and social role enactment are even harder to predict from existing speaking constructs and rubrics, but such speculations are only tentative until corroborated by empirical evidence.

When piloting his L2 Chinese IC test, Dai also garnered emergent quantitative evidence supporting the separation between talking competence/IC and speaking competence/proficiency. Dai piloted his nine-item test on 22 test-takers, comprising 11 native speakers (NSs) and 11 non-native speakers (NNSs) of differing proficiency in Chinese. Three L1-Chinese raters provided intuitive IC rating on all 198 performances (9 items*22 test-takers), with 'successful interaction' coded as 3, 'average interaction' coded as 2 and 'unsuccessful interaction' coded as 1 in the IC ability measure.

Rating results were analysed via many-facet Rasch measurement, and fair scores (which correct for rater severity and item difficulty) are presented in Table 2.1. Although NSs dominate the higher end of the scale, many NSs did not outperform NNSs in the middle range of the scale and one NS (ID 13) even scored below all 11 NNSs. Within the middle range, it is also telling to note that test-taker 12 is a beginner-level NNS, overtaking not only five NSs but also eight NNSs of much higher Chinese proficiency. Such findings challenge our conventional wisdom that NSs and highly proficient NNSs are invariably better at interaction than lower-proficiency NNSs, which lends preliminary support to IC being a distinctive construct from the traditional proficiency construct.

3.3 IC marker selection

The third concern is the selection of IC markers, which can offer backing to both scoring and explanation inferences in Kane's framework. Drawing on copious findings from CA, developmental IC studies have offered a wide array of potential IC markers such as progressivity (Balaman & Sert, 2017), alignment (Dings, 2014), post-expansion (Greer, 2016), dispreference structure (Al-Gahtani & Roever, 2012) and recipient design (Al-Gahtani & Roever, 2018). However, the choice of IC markers, just like the choice of social actions, should be a purposeful one from a test operationalisation perspective. The markers selected should be

Table 2.1 NS and NNS test-takers in Dai's (2019) study

ID	Group	Score
5	NS	2.99
4	NS	2.97
8	NS	2.90
7	NS	2.73
18	NS	2.59
2	NS	2.55
3	NNS	2.55
6	NNS	2.47
12	NNS	2.43
14	NNS	2.36
16	NS	2.36
11	NNS	2.28
20	NS	2.28
19	NNS	2.20
9	NNS	2.16
10	NS	2.16
15	NNS	2.08
21	NNS	2.04
1	NNS	1.95
22	NS	1.91
17	NNS	1.60
13	NS	1.34

consistently observable, ratable and scalable in test-taker performances. They should be those aspects of human interaction that make a speaker like Wes (Schmidt, 1983) interactionally competent despite their linguistic deficiencies. In terms of the scoring inference, IC markers and their rubrics are what translate test-taker performances into numbers, and a poor choice of markers can potentially mislead raters, directing their attention to aspects of talk not related to the IC construct. In terms of the explanation inference, IC markers carry the responsibility of construct validation explicated in the previous section as it is these markers that cover the added variance that existing speaking tests might fail to capture. Finally, due to the constraints of assessment, only a limited number of markers can be selected and incorporated into assessment rubrics. Therefore, the privileging of, for example, topic management over turn-taking, needs to have empirical support. Test designers should hence select markers that cover greater IC variance and that make a more tangible impact on the performance of talking.

One approach to purposeful marker selection is to combine etic, researcher-based judgment with emic, data-based evidence. Researchers can develop indigenous criteria through eliciting target group members' assessment on sample test-taker performances (Dai, 2020; Elder & McNamara, 2016; Knoch & Macqueen, 2019; Pill, 2016). Let us take the two added criteria, 'clinician engagement' and 'management of interaction' in OET, as an example. Pill (2016) developed both criteria by first obtaining medical educators' and clinical supervisors' judgments on simulated clinical performances from trainee healthcare professionals. He then conducted a thematic analysis on the data and generated these two new criteria, which were not covered by the previous OET rubric. Although Pill did not employ CA, it is evident that CA can be productively applied to the analysis of the 'management of interaction' criterion to collect micro-level evidence of how interaction is co-constructed. 'Clinical engagement', on the other hand, requires the ability to talk in a manner befitting the role of a doctor, a physiotherapist or a nurse. In other words, medical professionals' language should evoke their respective professional categories in relation to their interlocutors. Sequential CA, with its predominant concern for sequential properties, is clearly limited in collecting such information. This brings us to our last concern in IC assessment: social role enactment and MCA.

3.4 Social role enactment

As discussed earlier, there is no language use unbounded to social roles. In EAP contexts test-takers talk as a student or a classmate, whereas in OET contexts they talk as a doctor, a nurse or a physiotherapist. However, the ability to perform a particular social role is largely ignored by existing language tests, with OET being a rare example. A recent study on domain experts' indigenous criteria of L2 Chinese IC has identified role enactment as one of the five IC rating criteria that are most salient to and considered most crucial by domain experts (Dai, 2020). Here we argue that social role enactment should be foregrounded in our conceptualisation of IC and we should combine the analytic power of both CA and MCA to further our understanding of social role enactment as an IC marker.

Although MCA was developing rather slowly while CA flourished following Sack's seminal work (Sacks, 1992), we are now seeing a renaissance of interest in MCA (Stokoe, 2012), with a recent edited book on advances in MCA (Fitzgerald & Housley, 2015) and a special MCA section in the *Journal of Pragmatics* (Fitzgerald *et al.*, 2017). This shows that CA analysts have acknowledged that, apart from the many sequential concerns of talk, there is also a categorical aspect of talk that is worthy of investigation. How speakers evoke categories such as doctors, nurses and students indexes their members' knowledge of social roles in their host society and culture. L2 developmental studies are yet to grapple with the affordances and challenges of MCA, although Lee and Hellermann (2014) offer some nascent findings in this regard. MCA also has not made inroads into L2 IC assessment, as IC rubrics so far still focus solely on sequential markers such as turn-taking, topic development, adjacency pairs and back-channelling without situating such markers in test-takers' categorical knowledge (Galaczi, 2013; Ikeda, 2017; Youn, 2015). The last section of this chapter aims to make an exploratory attempt at demonstrating how MCA can be productively applied to the analysis of test-taker performances on the rating criterion, social role enactment.

4 MCA and Testing

Dai's (2019) needs analysis-grounded IC test of L2 Chinese explicitly assessed social role enactment as a marker of IC. Each item is delivered to test-takers in video format with three still images and a soundtrack of a scenario script recorded in Chinese. The English translation of the script for one such item is presented below and the three still images of this item are presented in Figures 2.1–2.3.

Video script in English:

You recently went to a different city for work for six months and sub-let the apartment you rented to Wang Hao's son Wang Bin. Wang Hao is your best friend and has helped you greatly over the years. You have also met Wang Bin before when you visited Wang Hao and have a good impression of him. Today the body corporation of your apartment building calls you, telling you that lately there has been a lot of noise and loud music in your apartment late at night. Sometimes the neighbours also see drunken youths coming in and out of your apartment. You want to discuss this with Wang Bin but since you are still away so you decide to talk to him via video chat.

As the prompt makes clear, Wang Bin (the interlocutor) is making too much noise late at night and causing annoyance to the test-taker's neighbours. The prompt does not prescribe what social actions the test-taker

Figure 2.1 The test-taker sub-letting his apartment to his best friend's son (interlocutor)

Figure 2.2 The test-taker receives a call from the building manager about noise in their apartment

Figure 2.3 The test-taker decides to have a video chat with the interlocutor about this incident

needs to implement but most test-takers orient to criticising the interlocutor. Despite unanimity on the social action, different test-takers construct, evoke and utilise different aspects of their categories vis-à-vis the categories of their interlocutor. Here we focus on two performances from intermediate L2 Chinese test-taker Brian (Test-taker ID 19 in Table 2.1) and beginner L2 Chinese test-taker Hans (Test-taker ID 12 in Table 2.1), each playing the role of the aggrieved apartment owner.

Brian: 'I want to be good to you'

Excerpt 2.1 is the start of the role play between Brian and the NS interlocutor.

Excerpt 2.1 Brian's greeting sequence

```
1   B      .tch (0.2) Wang Bin        [ni hǎo:
                   (full name)         hello
           '.tch (0.2) Wang Bin       [hello'


2   I                                 [Ai
                                       PRT
                                      ['Hi'


3   I  →   (.) Ai      Brian          shushu   hao
               PRT    (first name)    uncle    good
           '(.) Hi Uncle Brian,hello'


4         (0.9)


5   B      .tch (0.2) .tch Zui↑jin   zenme    ↓YANG?
                          Lately     how      condition
           '.tch (0.2) .tch how have you ↓been? la↑tely'


6         (0.4)


7   I     AAA:    >°zuijin   haihao°<      jiu     xuexi   >°shenme de°<
          PRT     lately     pretty good   just    study   what     NOM
          'AHH: >°Pretty good lately°< just studying >°and the sort°<'
```

In Line 1, Brian (abbreviated as B in the transcript) launches a greeting sequence, addressing the interlocutor (I in the transcript) by the full name of his role, Wang Bin. The interlocutor overlaps with Brian's talk, produces an acknowledgement token in Line 2 and returns the greeting in Line 3, suggesting that Brian's greeting is formatted in an easily recognisable manner. What is of analytical interest here is that the interlocutor addresses Brian by using his English name, followed by a Chinese kinship term '*shushu*' (uncle). On the interlocutor's prompt we do not specify how the test-taker should be addressed, but here the NS interlocutor draws on his member's knowledge and decides to address Brian with a kinship term *in situ* and *in vivo*. '*Shushu*' in Chinese is not reserved only for blood relatives but is an inference-rich address term that carries specific duties, obligations and expectations. Instead of resisting the interlocutor's attempt at categorising, Brian starts in Line 5 with a question enquiring about the interlocutor's well-being. Brian's implicit sanctioning of the category '*shushu*' shows that the interlocutor's activity is permissible and pre-existent in both parties' shared category knowledge.[1] By establishing intersubjectivity, it also licenses Brian to exploit the inferences bestowed by the '*shushu*' category.

Excerpt 2.2 Brian laying groundwork for criticising

```
1    B    >NI    ZHIDAO  WO   shi<  (1.7) ni       BA,
          You    know    I    be          your     father
          '>YOU KNOW I am< (1.7) your DAD'

2    B    jiu (.)  >wo de     hao     pengyou<
          just     I   ASSOC  good    friend
          just (.) >is my good friend<'

3         (0.4)

4    I    Dui=dui=°dui°
          Yes  yes yes
          'Yes=yes=°yes°'

5         (0.7)

6    B →  Aaa:::  (0.3) Suoyi (.)    wo   xiāng ↓DUI        ni      hao
          PRT              therefore  I   want  towards    you     good
          'Ahh:::  (0.3) Therefore (.) I want to be good ↓TOWARDS you'

7    B    (0.3)Wo ye     ↑XI↑WANG   ni: (0.1)   ni    ye:
          I    also   hope       you           you   also
          '(0.3) I also ↑HOPE you: (0.1) you also'

8         (0.9)

9    B →  dui      WO:   hao.
          towards  I     good
          'are good towards ME'

10        (0.4)

11   I    Ye::    ↓en↑hen     (0.3) ye?
          PRT     PRT  PRT           PRT
          'Yes::   ↓um↑hum (0.3) Yeah?'
```

Excerpt 2.2 takes place a few turns after Excerpt 2.1 where Brian makes use of his '*shushu*' category when he criticises the interlocutor. Brian first makes an explicit attempt at self-categorisation, abandons it, topicalises the test-taker's father, and establishes a standardised relational pair between test-taker's father and himself from Lines 1–2. A standardised relational pair is a pair of categories that carry mutual obligations and responsibilities (Stokoe, 2012), such as patient-doctor, salesperson-customer and friend-friend. By categorising the interlocutor's father as his good friend, Brian also self-categorises as a good friend to the interlocutor's father, as friendship cannot be claimed one-sided. Brian's relational pair and self-categorisation are quickly endorsed by the interlocutor with repeated acceptance tokens in Line 4. When we combine the categorisation work of '*shushu*' in Excerpt 2.1 and the relational pair in Excerpt 2.2, we can see how three categories, father, son and uncle, emerge as duplicatively organised (Francis & Hart, 1997). This makes explicit a commonsensical practice in Chinese society: if a male Chinese speaker is on close terms with another male Chinese speaker of similar age, the son of one of the speakers is bound to call the other speaker '*shushu*' (uncle), despite there being no blood connection between the son and the other speaker. Such knowledge is neither explicated in nor mandated by the scenario script for test-takers or the prompt for NS interlocutors. It is both parties' members' knowledge of their respective social roles that makes them co-construct this duplicative organisation.

Having examined the category-building work from both Brian and the interlocutor, now let us look at how Brian makes his laborious categorisation work for him. Categories are not void concepts. Sacks first noted that categories have activities bound to them, such as in his famous example, the baby (category) cried (activity) and the mommy (category) picked it up (activity) (Sacks, 1974). Subsequent work on MCA has further substantiated the activities (also called predicates) tied to categories, such as entitlements, duties and knowledge (Jayyusi, 1984; Payne, 1976; Watson, 1978). In Excerpt 2.2, after sanctioning his category as '*shushu*' and the interlocutor's category as 'close friend's son', in Line 6 Brian makes explicit the obligations he perceives to have been engendered by their relational categories: 'I (*shushu*) wanted to be good towards you (close friend's son)' and 'I (*shushu*) hope you (close friend's son) are also good towards me (*shushu*)'. Note Brian's choice of verbs here. When he explicates his moral obligation as a '*shushu*', he uses 'want' (*xiang*) in Line 6, a word indexing strong agency. When he describes the obligation of his friend's son, he chooses 'hope' (*xi wang*) in Line 7, a word that hedges the proposition. The word 'also' (*ye*) similarly offers a softening effect as it emphasises reciprocity.

In Line 11, the interlocutor first issues an affiliative token '*ye*' with a downward intonation, licensing Brian's category inferences and acknowledging the mutual obligations that Brian purposely establishes. The subsequent rising and falling intonation of the particles '*en hen*' is particularly intriguing here. '*En hen*' suggests that the interlocutor predicts that there is more to come from Brian as Brian's exposition of mutual obligations is knowledge that already exists in their shared category knowledge. The fact that Brian has painstakingly spelt out such details of their category predicates could only implicate one thing: Brian wants to make use of such predicates. Indeed, although not reproduced here, Brian's 'I wanted to be good towards you' later paves the way into his more attentive enquiries about what the interlocutor does at night, what kind of people he brings home and whether they have been drinking irresponsibly. Brian's 'I hope you will be good to me too' provides grounds for Brian's criticising of the interlocutor's behaviour, as what the interlocutor does obviously is not 'being good' to '*shushu*'. Everything takes on a different hue after the meticulous category groundwork Brian has laid for his criticising action. Although what the interlocutor has done is irresponsible in itself (e.g. disturbing the neighbours), Brian adds ammunition to his criticism by evoking the moral obligations rooted in their categories. Therefore, what the interlocutor has done has thus become not just irresponsible, but also immoral.

'Guai haizi'

Previous excerpts demonstrate that test-takers do not solely focus on launching the intended social action implied in the scenario video. They contextualise actions in a manner that is congruent to their social roles and carefully design their talk so that it is role appropriate. It should also be noted that role enactment is a joint process by both parties, as evidenced by the duplicative organisation 'father-son-uncle' in Brian's example. However, as Brian has skilfully demonstrated, test-takers have the ability to utilise categorisation work to their advantage in an interactionally relevant fashion. The following excerpts feature a beginner-level test-taker Hans, who shows us that even low-proficiency L2 speakers have an awareness of role enactment and can mobilise category knowledge to their benefit, despite limited linguistic resources.

Excerpt 2.3 Hans (abbreviated as H in the transcript) categorising the interlocutor as a 'guai haizi'

```
1   H      Wo=wo=wo=wo   xiang:  ni    shi
             I  I  I  I    think   you   be
             'I=I=I=I thought: you were'

2   H  →   yi   ge   guai   hai (.) zǐ (.) suoyi
             one  C    good   kid            therefore
             'a good ki(.)d(.) therefore'

3   H      (0.3)

4   H      Anm:(.)yexu (0.1) e:  (0.3) YOU shihou (0.3) juede (0.5)
             PRT    perhaps  PRT        be time          think
             'Hmm: (.)perhaps (0.1) Err: (0.3) There ARE times I think'
```

```
5   H    E:    gen      pengyou  he:      (0.1)  yi    liang  bei
         PRT   with     friend   drink           one   two    C
         'En:(.)you might have(0.1)one or two (0.3) drinks with friends'

6   H    (0.3)En (0.6) suoyi (0.2) bu  hui  you  wenti  dè=   buguo
                       therefore   N   AUX  be   problem NOM   but
         '(0.3)Hmm (0.6)therefore (0.2) it wouldn't be any problems=but'
```

Line 1 in Excerpt 2.3 follows Hans's storytelling of him receiving a call from the neighbour saying that lately there has been a lot of noise in his apartment. Hans makes multiple attempts at starting the turn but gets stuck at the subject 'I' (*wo*). When he finally succeeds at the fourth attempt, he smoothly delivers his assessment of the interlocutor in Line 2, calling him a '*guai haizi*' (good/obedient kid). It is worth noting that Hans categorises the interlocutor as a '*haizi*' (kid), despite the fact that his 'friend's son' is old enough to host parties and drink recklessly. Hans calling his friend's son '*haizi*' positions the interlocutor at the lower end of a hierarchical relational pair compared to Hans, as Hans is the 'grown-up' here while the interlocutor is the 'kid' (Stokoe, 2012). Therefore, when a '*haizi*' misbehaves, a grown-up has sufficient moral grounds to criticise him, which is exactly what Hans's turn foreshadows.

Another interesting feature is the adjective '*guai*' that Hans predicates on '*haizi*'. '*Guai*' is a cultural-specific description that does not lend itself well to translation. Semantically it falls between 'being good', 'being nice', 'being obedient', 'do not cause trouble' and 'do not contradict'. '*Guai*' can only be used by a senior member on a junior member in Chinese society and the senior and junior members are related on an intimate personal level. For example, a younger person in Chinese society would not use '*guai*' as a quality expected of a person older than them. An older person would also not randomly call out people younger than them as '*guai*' as there is no entitlement for such an expectation. What licenses Hans's usage of '*guai*' is the same duplicative father-son-uncle organisation explicated before. Similar to Brian's categorisation, '*guai*' also carries a strong moral obligation as there is a preference for a category like '*haizi*' to co-select with its bound predicates like '*guai*' (Hester & Eglin, 1997). '*Guai*' as a predicate is a cultural expectation of the '*haizi*' category, which in this particular instance manifests as 'being nice to *shushu*', 'do not contradict *shushu*' and certainly 'do not drink irresponsibly and cause trouble for *shushu*'. Therefore, Hans's characterisation work is purposeful as now the interlocutor's behaviour is not just unsociable, but also flouts the moral obligations implicated in his category.

In terms of Hans's production of '*guai haizi*', it is smoothly delivered in Line 2, despite a micropause between '*hai*' and '*zi*'. This contrasts greatly with the following Line 3–Line 6 where Hans struggles to describe what the interlocutor was doing. Considering Hans's beginner-learner proficiency level, it is understandable that he finds it challenging to mobilise language in his recount of the interlocutor's irresponsible drinking episodes. However, Hans easily formats a predicate + category combination (*guai haizi*), which suggests that such a categorisation, its bound predicate and inferences are not constructed on the spot. This combination is locally regulated, culturally pre-packaged and contextually embedded in the very social role of Hans vis-à-vis the role of the interlocutor.

Excerpt 2.4 Hans's closing sequence where 'guai' resurfaces

```
1    I    Wo   hui=wo=>wo hui      zhuyi           de< (0.1)
          I    AUX I    I  AUX     pay attention   NOM
          'I will=I=>I will be more careful< (0.1)'

2    I    °Bu  hao  yisi°    (0.3) °Hai                    shushu°
          I'm sorry                (Hans's family name)   uncle
          '°I'm sorry° (0.3) °Uncle Hai°'

3         (1.7)

4    H  → Hao      a: (0.3) Guai:
          good     PRT      obedient
          'Ok: (0.3) Be good:'

5         (0.3)

6    I    °E (0.1) hao     de°
          PRT      good    NOM
          'Oh (0.1) Okey'

7         (0.6)

8    I    Xin   na   wo=°na   wo  yihou   hui   zhuyi            de°=
          Ok    then I    then I   future  AUX   pay attention   NOM
          'Okey, so I=°so I will be more careful in the future'

9    I    =na      xiexie  shushu
          then     thank   uncle
          '=so thank you uncle'

10        (1.1)

11   H    En
          PRT
          'Ok'

12        (0.6)

13   I    Hao     de
          Good    NOM
          'Okey'
```

Lastly, the '*guai haizi*' categorisation is not a one-off isolated incident, as Hans also makes it interactionally relevant in his closing sequence. Excerpt 2.4 is towards the end of the interaction and starts off with the interlocutor promising not to misbehave in the future. After issuing a positive assessment '*hao*' in Line 4, Hans recycles '*guai*' with emphasis and elongation, only this time as an imperative. '*Guai*' here takes on different functions as before: it is an assessment as in 'I underwrite what you just promised as *guai* behaviour'; it is also a veiled admonition as in 'be a *guai* kid and don't misbehave again'. In Line 6 the interlocutor first issues a change-of-state token '*E*', which is similar to 'Oh' in English (Heritage, 1990). This token could be occasioned by surprise at the warning tone in Hans's '*guai*', or incredulity at Hans's highly idiomatic use of '*guai*' and his cultural knowledge of how Chinese people reprimand kids. Regardless of the mental state behind '*E*', the interlocutor quickly proffers an agreement token and, after a 0.6 gap, reformats his promise from Line 1 in Line 8 and thanks Hans for his assessment/admonition in Line 9. The interlocutor's behaviour from Line 6 to Line 9 ratifies the legitimacy of Hans's use of '*guai*' and Hai's implicated moral rights. It would be highly problematic if the interlocutor rebutted by saying, 'Hang on, why should I be *guai* or be a *guai haizi*?' or 'Who do you think you are to talk to me in such a patronising manner?'. This would be synonymous to a mother saying 'Why should I pick up my baby just because they are crying?', in Sack's example. It is the inherent moral order residing in categories that makes the claims from category-bound predicates irrefutable.

We hope that the above analyses have illustrated our point that MCA can be applied to L2 speakers' talk to describe their competence in social role enactment. As we have argued multiple times in this chapter, there is no language use unbounded to social roles. Hence, we maintain that the ability to enact appropriate social roles should be integrated into the IC construct. Drawing on the MCA analysis in this chapter, role enactment can entail the ability to 'assign categories to oneself and the interlocutor as appropriate in the roleplay scenario' and to 'evoke category-congruent predicates/activities to facilitate interaction'. Brian's and Hans's performances indicate that this ability is unaccounted for in existing speaking frameworks. From CA transcription we can observe numerous cases where Brian's and to a much larger extent Hans's language is linguistically inadequate, including excessively long gaps, awkward turn designs, infelicitous lexical choices and non-native prosodic features. However, inadequacies in 'speaking' do not obfuscate their ability to 'talk', to undertake categorisation or to make their categorisation work for them interactionally. This mismatch between 'speaking competence' and 'talking competence' can go a long way towards strengthening the construct validity of IC assessment.

5 Conclusion

This chapter makes a case for moving from the 'psycholinguistic-individualist perspective' to a 'sociolinguistic-interactional perspective' in our assessment of L2 speakers' competence in interaction (Roever & Kasper, 2018: 332). We argue that existing speaking tests fail to assess test-takers' ability to interact, to launch social actions and to enact social roles. Such speaking tests cannot generate reliable inferences for stakeholders to make accurate prediction of test-takers' IC in real-world settings. To combat this deficiency, we survey existing attempts at IC assessment and highlight four concerns that are particularly pertinent to IC test designers. We also draw special attention to one much-overlooked sub-trait of IC – social role enactment – and propose that MCA can serve as a potential analytic candidate to unpack this trait and the categorical features of interaction. Future research can draw on the analyses and suggestions from this chapter to further our understanding and depiction of IC in assessment contexts.

Note

(1)   There are also cases in the dataset where test-takers explicitly self-categorise as 'shushu' or 'ayi', which is the equivalent female category to shushu. Due to space limitations, these data are not presented but they reinforce the argument that the category knowledge of 'shushu/ayi' is shared between test-takers and NS interlocutors.

References

Al-Gahtani, S. and Roever, C. (2012) Proficiency and sequential organization of L2 requests. *Applied Linguistics* 33 (1), 42–65.

Al-Gahtani, S. and Roever, C. (2015) The development of requests by L2 learners of modern standard Arabic: A longitudinal and cross-sectional study. *Foreign Language Annals* 48 (4), 570–583.

Al-Gahtani, S. and Roever, C. (2018) Proficiency and preference organization in second language refusals. *Journal of Pragmatics* 129, 140–153

Austin, J.L. (1962) *How to Do Things with Words*. Oxford: Clarendon Press.

Balaman, U. and Sert, O. (2017) Development of L2 interactional resources for online collaborative task accomplishment. *Computer Assisted Language Learning* 30 (7), 601–630.

Bella, S. (2014) Developing the ability to refuse: A cross-sectional study of Greek FL refusals. *Journal of Pragmatics* 61, 35–62.

Bernstein, J., Van Moere, A. and Cheng, J. (2010) Validating automated speaking tests. *Language Testing* 27 (3), 355–377.

Brown, A. (2003) Interviewer variation and the co-construction of speaking proficiency. *Language Testing* 20 (1), 1–25.

Brown, P. and Levinson, S. (1987) *Politeness: Some Universals in Language*. Cambridge: Cambridge University Press.

Cekaite, A. (2007) A child's development of interactional competence in a Swedish L2 classroom. *The Modern Language Journal* 91 (1), 45–62.

Chapelle, C.A., Enright, M.K. and Jamieson, J.M. (eds) (2008) *Building a Validity Argument for the Test of English as a Foreign Language*. London: Routledge.

Chapelle, C.A., Enright, M.K. and Jamieson, J.M. (2010) Does an argument-based approach to validity make a difference? *Educational Measurement: Issues and Practice* 29 (1), 3–13.

Council of Europe (2001) *Common European Framework of Reference for Languages: Learning, Teaching, Assessment*. Cambridge: Cambridge University Press.

Council of Europe (2018) *Common European Framework of Reference for Languages: Learning, Teaching, Assessment. Companion Volume with New Descriptors*. Strasbourg: Council of Europe.

Curl, T.S. and Drew, P. (2008) Contingency and action: A comparison of two forms of requesting. *Research on Language and Social Interaction* 41 (2), 129–153.

Dai, D.W. (2019) A task-based needs analysis of interactional competence in Chinese as a second language. Manuscript in preparation.

Dai, D.W. (2020) Conversation-analytically validating domain experts' indigenous interactional competence rating criteria in test-taker exemplar responses. Manuscript submitted for publication.

Dai, D.W. and Roever, C. (2019) A task-based needs analysis of interactional competence in L2 Chinese. Paper presented at the 2019 American Association for Applied Linguistics conference, Atlanta, GA.

Dings, A. (2014) Interactional competence and the development of alignment activity. *The Modern Language Journal* 98 (3), 742–756.

Dinkins, C.S. (2005) Shared inquiry: Socratic-hermeneutic interpre-viewing. In P.M. Ironside (ed.) *Beyond Method: Philosophical Conversations in Healthcare Research and Scholarship* (pp. 111–147). Madison, WI: University of Wisconsin Press.

Drew, P. (2013) Turn design. In J. Sidnell and T. Stivers (eds) *The Handbook of Conversation Analysis* (pp. 131–149). Hoboken, NJ: Wiley-Blackwell.

Eggly, S., Musial, J. and Smulowitz, J. (1999) The relationship between English language proficiency and success as a medical resident. *English for Specific Purposes* 18, 201–208.

Elder, C. and McNamara, T. (2016) The hunt for 'indigenous criteria' in assessing communication in the physiotherapy workplace. *Language Testing* 33 (2), 153–174.

Fitzgerald, R. and Housley, W. (eds) (2015) *Advances in Membership Categorisation Analysis*. London: Sage.

Fitzgerald, R., Housley, W. and Rintel, S. (ed.) (2017) Membership categorisation analysis. Technologies of social action (Special issue). *Journal of Pragmatics* 118.

Francis, D. and Hart, C. (1997) Narrative intelligibility and membership categorization in a television commercial. In S. Hester and P. Eglin (eds) *Culture in Action: Studies in Membership Categorization Analysis* (pp. 123–152). Washington D.C.: International Institute for Ethnomethodology and Conversation Analysis and University Press of America.

Galaczi, E.D. (2013) Interactional competence across proficiency levels: How do learners manage interaction in paired speaking tests? *Applied Linguistics* 35 (5), 553–574.

Galaczi, E. and Taylor, L. (2018) Interactional competence: Conceptualisations, operationalisations, and outstanding questions. *Language Assessment Quarterly* 15 (3), 219–236.

Golato, A. (2002) German compliment responses. *Journal of Pragmatics* 34, 547–571.

Greer, T. (2016) Learner initiative in action: Post-expansion sequences in a novice ESL survey interview task. *Linguistics and Education* 35, 78–87.

Hall, J.K. and Pekarek Dohler, S. (2011) L2 interactional competence and development. In J.K. Hall, J. Hellermann and S. Pekarek Doehler (eds) *L2 Interactional Competence and Development* (pp. 1–15). Bristol: Multilingual Matters.

Hall, P., Keely, E., Dojeiji, E., Byszewski, A. and Marks, M. (2004) Communication skills, cultural challenges and individual support: Challenges of international medical graduates in a Canadian healthcare environment. *Medical Teacher* 26 (2), 120–125.

Hellermann, J. (2007) The development of practices for action in classroom dyadic interaction: Focus on task openings. *The Modern Language Journal* 91 (1), 83–96.

Hellermann, J. (2008) *Social Actions for Classroom Language Learning*. Clevedon: Multilingual Matters.

Heritage, J. (1984) *Garfinkel and Ethnomethodology*. Cambridge: Polity Press.

Heritage, J. (1990) Intention, meaning and strategy: Observations on constraints on interaction analysis. *Research on Language and Social Interaction* 24 (1–4), 311–332.

Hester, S. and Eglin, P. (eds) (1997) *Culture in Action: Studies in Membership Categorization Analysis*. Washington, DC: University Press of America.

Huth, T. (2006) Negotiating structure and culture: L2 learners' realization of L2 compliment-response sequences in talk-in-interaction. *Journal of Pragmatics* 38 (12), 2025–2050.

Hymes, D. (1974) *Foundations in Sociolinguistics: An Ethnographic Approach.* Philadelphia, PA: University of Pennsylvania Press.

IDP IELTS (2021) *Understanding the IELTS Speaking Band Descriptors.* https://ielts.idp. com/prepare/article-understanding-the-ielts-speaking-band-descriptors

Ikeda, N. (2017) Measuring L2 oral pragmatic abilities for use in social contexts: Development and validation of an assessment instrument for L2 pragmatics performance in university settings. Unpublished PhD dissertation, University of Melbourne.

Jacoby, S.W. (1998) Science as performance: Socializing scientific discourse through conference talk rehearsals. Unpublished doctoral dissertation, University of California.

Jayyusi, L. (1984) *Categorisation and the Moral Order.* London: Routledge & Kegan Paul.

Johnson, M. (2001) *The Art of Nonconversation.* New Haven, CT: Yale University Press.

Kane, M.T. (2006) Validation. In R.L. Brennan (ed.) *Educational Measurement* (4th edn) (pp. 17–64). Westport, CT: Greenwood.

Kane, M.T. (2012) Validating score interpretations and uses. *Language Testing* 29 (1), 3–17.

Knoch, U. and Macqueen, S. (2019) *Assessing English for Professional Purposes.* London: Routledge.

Lazaraton, A. (1992) The structural organization of a language interview: A conversation analytic perspective. *System* 20 (3), 373–386.

Lee, Y.A. and Hellermann, J. (2014) Tracing developmental changes through conversation analysis: Cross-sectional and longitudinal analysis. *TESOL Quarterly* 48 (4), 763–788.

Levelt, W.J.M. (1989) *Speaking: From Intention to Articulation.* Cambridge, MA: MIT Press.

Levelt, W.J.M. (1999) Producing spoken language: A blueprint of the speaker. In C. Brown and P. Hagoort (eds) *The Neurocognition of Language* (pp. 83–122). Oxford: Oxford University Press.

Levinson, S.C. (2006) On the human 'interaction engine'. In N.J. Enfield and S.C. Levinson (eds) *Roots of Human Sociality* (pp. 39–69). Oxford: Berg.

Levinson, S.C. and Torreira, F. (2015) Timing in turn-taking and its implications for processing models of language. *Frontiers in Psychology* 6, 731.

Lim, G.S. (2018) Conceptualizing and operationalizing second language speaking assessment: Updating the construct for a new century. *Language Assessment Quarterly* 15 (3), 215–218.

Malone, M.E. and Montee, M. (2014) Stakeholders' beliefs about the TOEFL iBT® test as a measure of academic language ability. *ETS Research Report Series* 2, 1–51.

Messick, S. (1989) Validity. In R.L. Linn (ed.) *Educational Measurement* (3rd edn) (pp. 13–103). New York: Macmillan.

Murray, J.C., Cross, J.L. and Cruickshank, K. (2014) Stakeholder perceptions of IELTS as a gateway to the professional workplace: The case of employers of overseas trained teachers. *IELTS Research Reports Online* 78.

Ockey, G.J., Koyama, D., Setoguchi, E. and Sun, A. (2015) The extent to which TOEFL iBT speaking scores are associated with performance on oral language tasks and oral ability components for Japanese university students. *Language Testing* 32 (1), 39–62.

O'Sullivan, B. (2019) The future of language testing. In C. Roever and G. Wigglesworth (eds) *Social Perspectives on Language Testing* (pp. 197–216). Frankfurt: Peter Lang.

Payne, G.C.F. (1976) Making a lesson happen: An ethnomethodological analysis. In M. Hammersley and P. Woods (eds) *The Process of Schooling.* London and Henley: Routledge & Kegan Paul/Open University Press.

Pekarek Doehler, S. (2018) Elaborations on L2 interactional competence: The development of L2 grammar-for-interaction. *Classroom Discourse* 9 (1), 3–24.

Pekarek Doehler, S. and Pochon-Berger, E. (2011) Developing 'methods' for interaction: A cross-sectional study of disagreement sequences in French L2. In J.K. Hall, J. Hellermann and S. Pekarek Doehler (eds) *L2 Interactional Competence and Development* (pp. 206–243). Bristol: Multilingual Matters.

Pekarek Doehler, S. and Pochon-Berger, E. (2015) The development of L2 interactional competence: Evidence from turn-taking organization, sequence organization, repair organization and preference organization. In T. Cadierno and S.W. Eskildsen (eds) *Usage-based Perspectives on Second Language Learning* (pp. 233–268). Berlin: Mouton de Gruyter.

Pekarek Doehler, S. and Pochon-Berger, E. (2016) L2 interactional competence as increased ability for context-sensitive conduct: A longitudinal study of story-openings. *Applied Linguistics* 39 (4), 555–578.

Pill, J. (2016) Drawing on indigenous criteria for more authentic assessment in a specific-purpose language test: Health professionals interacting with patients. *Language Testing* 33 (2), 175–193.

Plough, I., Banerjee, J. and Iwashita, N. (eds) (2018) Special issue on Interactional Competence. *Language Testing* 35 (3).

Roever, C. and Kasper, G. (2018) Speaking in turns and sequences: Interactional competence as a target construct in testing speaking. *Language Testing* 35 (3), 331–355.

Sacks, H. (1974) On the analysability of stories by children. In R. Turner (ed.) *Ethnomethodology: Selected Readings* (pp. 216–232). Harmondsworth: Penguin.

Sacks, H. (1992) *Lectures on Conversation* (2 vols). Oxford: Blackwell.

Sato, M. (2014) Exploring the construct of interactional oral fluency: Second language acquisition and language testing approaches. *System* 45, 79–91.

Schmidt, R. (1983) Interaction, acculturation and the acquisition of communicative competence. In N. Wolfson and E. Judd (eds) *Sociolinguistics and Second Language Acquisition* (pp. 137–174). New York: Newbury House.

Schumann, J.H. (1978) *The Pidginization Process: A Model for Second Language Acquisition* (pp. 367–379). Rowley, MA: Newbury House.

Searle, J. (1969) *Speech Acts*. Cambridge: Cambridge University Press.

Seedhouse, P. and Egbert, M. (2006) The interactional organisation of the IELTS speaking test. International English Language Testing System (IELTS). *Research Reports* 2006 (6), 1.

Seedhouse, P. and Nakatsuhara, F. (2018) *The Discourse of the IELTS Speaking Test: Interactional Design and Practice*. Cambridge: Cambridge University Press.

Stokoe, E. (2012) Moving forward with membership categorization analysis: Methods for systematic analysis. *Discourse Studies* 14 (3), 277–303.

van Lier, L. (1989) Reeling, writhing, drawling, stretching, and fainting in coils: Oral proficiency interviews as conversation. *TESOL Quarterly* 23 (3), 489–508.

Waring, H.Z. (2013) 'How was your weekend?': Developing the interactional competence in managing routine inquiries. *Language Awareness* 22 (1), 1–16.

Watanabe, A. (2016) Engaging in an interactional routine in EFL classroom: The development of L2 interactional competence over time. *Novitas-ROYAL (Research on Youth and Language)* 10 (1), 48–70.

Watson, D.R. (1978) Categorisation, authorisation and blame-negotiation in conversation. *Sociology* 12 (1), 105–113.

Youn, S.J. (2015) Validity argument for assessing L2 pragmatics in interaction using mixed methods. *Language Testing* 32 (2), 199–225.

Youn, S.J. (2018) Task-based needs analysis of L2 pragmatics in an EAP context. *Journal of English for Academic Purposes* 36, 86–98.

Youn, S.J. and Burch, A.R. (eds) (2020) Where conversation analysis meets language assessment. *Papers in Language Testing and Assessment* 9 (1).

3 A Case for Nonverbal Behavior: Implications for Construct, Performance and Assessment

India Plough

1 Introduction

A recent bibliometric analysis of visible nonverbal behavior produced a list of the 1000 most cited articles, published in 297 different journals. These articles represented a range of disciplines, including medicine, biology, anthropology, computer science, engineering and communication, to name a few. Interestingly, more than 50% of the articles were published in 33 journals in neuroscience, psychology, psychiatry or the behavioral sciences. As the authors note, 'such a wide variety of disciplines shows how visible nonverbal behavior is a highly multi- and interdisciplinary research field and how scientific knowledge about nonverbal communication goes far beyond social psychology' (Plusquellec & Denault, 2018: 367–368).

Based within a socio-interactional approach to second language learning, teaching and assessment, the goal of this chapter is to provide evidence for the incorporation of nonverbal behavior (NVB) into the second language speaking construct. This argument rests on two sequential assumptions. First, interaction is a *sine qua non* of speaking proficiency and, second, nonverbal behavior is a *sine qua non* of interaction. The first assumption is approaching axiom status 'the primordial purpose of speaking is social interaction' (Eskildsen & Markee, 2018: 73). An ever-growing body of literature (e.g. Ellis, 2019; Eskildsen & Majlesi, 2018; Eskildsen & Markee, 2018; Plough *et al.*, 2018; Salaberry & Kunitz, 2019) from multiple research approaches (e.g. usage-based, sociocultural, conversation analytic) to second language acquisition, learning, pedagogy and assessment maintains that language cannot be abstracted from contextualized use. Regardless of one's epistemic stance on interaction, its definition or its relationship to cognition, there is overwhelming consensus that interaction is an essential ability of L2 speaking proficiency. Within L2 speaking assessment, we are now seeing interaction increasingly taken into consideration in test design (task types), format (paired) *or* rating scales (interactive language use) of local as well as large-scale standardized tests such as ACTFL OPI, Michigan Language Assessment Examination for the Certificate of Proficiency in English Speaking test and Cambridge Main Suite Exams. Simultaneously, robust research into interactional competence (IC) has informed our understanding of this construct. For example, Roever and Dai (this volume) provide theoretical arguments that 'speaking and talking are overlapping but still distinctive forms of competence' and that IC is necessarily about talking (an interactive endeavor) and not about speaking (a monologic endeavor). As such, no large-scale, high-stakes test attends to IC in test design, format *and* rating. Indeed, NVB constitutes a meaningful and essential 'IC marker'.

This assertion rests on the second assumption: NVB is fundamental to communication. Even though scholarly debate continues in first and second language gesture research regarding the ontological status of NVB, including its origins and development, its relationship to thought, emotion and language as well as its context-specific manifestations (e.g. culture, interlocutors), a substantial body of research now supports this position (e.g. Hall & Knapp, 2013; Hall *et al.*, 2019; Matsumoto *et al.*, 2016). In this chapter I discuss relevant literature in order to address the key task: *How* might we incorporate NVB in second language speaking assessment?

I begin with a discussion of the frameworks of Ekman and Friesen (1969, 1971; Ekman, 2004), Kendon (1972) and McNeill (1992), the three seminal, and relatively similar, frameworks emanating from anthropology and (social) psychology that have formed the foundation for much of the gesture research in first and second languages. These frameworks have been thoroughly explained and summarized elsewhere (e.g. see Kendon, 2004, for a comprehensive history). Therefore, as background, Gullberg's (2006a) concise overview of some of the commonalities in the three categorization frameworks is provided. I explicate specific divergences in theoretical assumptions regarding interaction and intention between the aforementioned frameworks and a socio-interactional perspective of L2 learning and assessment. I suggest that the L2 assessment research in which NVB has surfaced as influencing raters as well as candidates can make meaningful contributions to the broader field. In a summary of L2 gestures studies, I note those findings that are particularly relevant for L2 assessment. I propose that ethnomethodological conversation analysis holds the most promise in order to take full account of NVB in L2 face-to-face speaking tests. The chapter concludes with a description of an operational scoring process, which provides an example of one way in which NVB can be incorporated into L2 speaking assessment, thus aligning theory and practice.

The chapter is situated within a non-Cartesian perspective that views language cognition as 'essentially embodied, environmentally embedded, autopoietically enacted, and socially encultured ... languages [are] emergent, social, integrated phenomena' (Ellis, 2019: 46). Additionally, this chapter applies exclusively to face-to-face interaction. Furthermore, gestures are considered to be a subset of NVB, which is a broader category of actions that includes, in addition to those movements encompassed within gesture studies: paralinguistic features (e.g. prosody, voice quality, non-lexical vocalizations); posture; all body movement; glances, gaze, eye contact; and facial expressions.[1] Finally, speaker intention is not predetermined (by the researcher or examiner) and as such is not a necessary condition in order to include a particular form of NVB as the object of study.

2 Gesture Frameworks

The majority of gesture studies find their origins in the work of Efron (1941), Ekman (2004), Ekman and Friesen (1969, 1971), Kendon (1972) or McNeill (1992). Gulberg (2006a: 105) notes that all frameworks include a category of fixed, conventionalized forms that are culture specific (e.g. Ekman's 'emblems' and Kendon's 'quotables'); all 'identify representational and rhythmic gestures ... that have no standard of well-formedness but are created spontaneously ... during speech' (e.g. McNeil's spontaneous gesture), and all gestures have structural characteristics based on the articulators (hand, arm, etc.), spatial location of movement and manner of movement. Determination of the internal structure of gestures (e.g. gestural units, phases) is methodologically critical in matching gesture and speech, which in turn is used to hypothesize the relationships between the two. Other directed 'interactional functions include turn regulation, feedback eliciting, agreement marking, attention directing (pointing), etc. Self-directed functions include ... organizing thought for expression', emphasizing, supplementing or complementing one's message.

Ekman and Friesen used interpretations of attitude and emotional state from body movements and facial expressions, comparisons of facial expressions across cultures and detection of deception to create a systematic means by which to investigate NVB, which includes: the *Origin* of a person's NVB; the context of its *Usage*; and the rules (*Coding*) that explain the information that is conveyed. Five categories of NVB are described in terms of Origin, Usage and Coding.

Of interest to the present discussion, they proposed three general divisions for the Origin of nonverbal behavior: behaviors that are 'built into the nervous system' (Ekman & Friesen, 1969: 59) and are a response to some external stimulus; those that are common to all humans and are acquired; and those that are learned either implicitly or explicitly through social interaction and may vary by culture, class, family or individual. Building on the work of Tomkins and McCarter (1964) and employing his categorization framework, Ekman (1971) proposed a neurocultural theory of emotion. According to this theory, certain emotions are hard-wired and there is a one-to-one correlation between a person's emotion and the manifested facial expression (i.e. 'neuro'). Additionally, in non-social contexts, this correlation is universal. However, in social situations, humans consciously control these expressions through the use of learned 'display rules', which vary across cultures (i.e. 'cultural'). In this way, an emotional display can be decreased, increased or neutralized according to cultural norms.

In a critical review of Ekman's neurocultural theory, Crivelli and Fridlund (2019) note the rigid separation established between biology and culture and their roles. The theory maintains that 'because of our common phylogeny, humans [share] certain "facial expressions of emotion" that [express] those specific emotions; and culture [acts] to supervene on and modify the innate, prototypic expressions' (Crivelli & Fridlund, 2019: 169). Crivelli and Fridlund suggest that the seemingly unquestioning acceptance of basic emotions theories results in part from the fact that the majority of researchers in this area are Westerners with little or no direct experience of or familiarity with 'diverse non-industrialized societies and their con-ceptions and rituals, except as seen through a Western ... lens (Crivelli et al., 2016). Among these Western preconceptions is one that "emotions" ... are linked inextricably to facial expressions, even though the evidence suggests otherwise (Durán et al., 2017)' (Crivelli & Fridlund, 2019: 186).[2]

2.1 Interaction

Ekman and Friesen (1972) do acknowledge interaction. For example, Usage is divided into informative, communicative and/or interactive non-verbal behavior. These subcategories incorporate shared meanings, intended meaning, and nonverbal behavior that modifies another person's behavior, whether or not it was intended. However, they also suggest that the individual must be the starting point of any systematic investigation:

> While the study of interpersonal interactions can reveal information about each of the individual interactants ... People have experiences as individuals when alone, changes in feelings and mood. Nonverbal behav-ior may then be the only source of information about their experience, since people rarely speak when alone ... If we are to understand the influ-ence of social rules about nonverbal behavior in interpersonal interac-tions ... we must also examine the individual when he [sic] is alone. (Ekman & Friesen, 1972: 353–354)

In sum, the nature–nurture divide and the focus solely on the individual position Ekman's theory in opposition to a socio-interactional approach to L2 assessment, but with an awareness of these contradictory theoretical underpinnings, research from multiple perspectives can be mutually beneficial.

As noted above, the models created by Kendon and McNeill share structural and functional similarities. Kendon (2004: 15–16) defines the object of study as those actions that are perceived to be controlled by an individual and are performed specifically to express meaning and serve a communicative intent. 'Participants in interaction recognize [these] actions and ... are held responsible ... whether an action is deemed to be intended or not is something that is dependent entirely upon how that action appears to others'. Kendon elaborates on the essential role of context: 'What forms of gesture are created and used depends upon the circumstances of use, the person's specific communicative purposes and what other modes of expression are also available' (Kendon, 2004: 84).

Following from this, gestures can serve pragmatic functions as well as interactive functions. Pragmatic functions are 'any of the ways in which gestures may relate to features of an utterance's meaning that are not a part of its referential meaning or propositional content' (Kendon, 2004: 158). They are further divided into: modal functions, which indicate intended interpretation such as the speaker's stance or attitude; performative functions, which show the speaker's interactional move or speech act; and parsing functions, which mark different components (e.g. conceptual components) of speech. In terms of interactional/interactive functions of gestures, Kendon provides examples of the integration of gestures and speech to convey referential meaning, to mark topic-comment and to serve pragmatic functions, as well as to manage interactions.

The focus for McNeill (1992) is spontaneous gestures, which by definition co-occur with speech ('gesticulation' in Kendon's representation). McNeill (2006: 1) maintains that 'gesture and language are best thought of as [two inseparable] components of a single system'. In contrast to Kendon, who makes no distinction between gesture and sign, McNeill has established a categorical distinction between the two. McNeill (2006) has pointed out, however, that the 'categories' are 'not truly categorical' and should be considered dimensions (i.e. iconicity, metaphoricity, temporal highlighting, deixis and social interactivity), as a single gesture may include multiple dimensions. Furthermore, 'gestures are like thoughts themselves. They belong, not to the outside world, but to the inside one of memory, thought, and mental images' (Müller, 2018: 12). An utterance emerges from a 'growth point'; the imagistic is represented by a gesture and the linguistic by speech.

Spontaneous gestures serve many functions and can serve multiple functions simultaneously. Functions include adding or emphasizing information, reducing a speaker's cognitive load and helping speakers organize information or retrieve lexical items. Finally, spontaneous gestures may be used as indicators of active listening as well as for turn-taking management (Ishino & Stam, 2011). McNeill (1992) has proposed a 'pragmatic synchrony rule', a logical extension of his attention to gestures that only accompany speech. According to this rule, speech and gesture, when produced together, perform the same pragmatic function. In theory, then, all pragmatic functions that can be performed through speech can also be performed through gesture.

One sees that interaction, in terms of pragmatic functions, is incorporated into the models proposed by Kendon and McNeill. However, what is absent is an account of the dynamic, integrated processes of interaction where, for example, participant goals are negotiated, transformed and realized through an amalgamation of cognitive and affective resources, prior experiences and expectations within a socially situated context.

2.2 Intention

These models are founded on a cognitive-philosophical approach in which intention is considered an a priori mental state of speakers. In contrast, in sociocultural-interactional pragmatics, intention is typically conceptualized as a post facto participant resource that emerges through interaction (Haugh, 2008; see also Kasper, 2006, 2009, for discussions of discursive approaches to cognition).

A view of communication that assumes a relatively static view of intentionality (and of interaction more generally) and that relies on listener inference of meaning poses unique challenges for L2 (speaking) assessment. The importance of pragmatic knowledge to proficiency has been noted for more than 40 years, and an active research agenda continues to develop assessments of sociopragmatic as well as pragmalinguistic knowledge of learner as speaker and learner as listener (e.g. Kasper & Ross, 2007, 2013; Kasper & Youn, 2018; McNamara & Roever, 2006; Roever, 2011, 2013; Ross & O'Connell, 2013; Youn, 2015). While L2 assessment research has begun to highlight rater interpretations of candidate NVB as a reflection of interactional ability, this does not entail the rater (correctly) determining the speaker's communicative intentions and then evaluating the listener's interpretation. In fact, as pointed out by Salaberry and Kunitz (2019: 4) within the context of research on IC, the issue for these models within the socio-interactional approach adopted here is the 'entry point to data analysis, which for some researchers should be entirely emic (i.e. participant-relevant; Hauser, 2019; Markee, 2019), while for others it can be etic (i.e. researcher-relevant; Pekarek Doehler, 2018, 2019)'. I return to a discussion of emic- and etic-based research in Section 6 on Moving Forward.

3 Gestures in L2 Studies

Nonetheless, research in second language acquisition and gestures, which draws primarily on Kendian and McNeillian frameworks, continues to increase and expand our understanding of face-to-face interaction as multimodal, involving both verbal and nonverbal communication

(Stam, 2008). This research encompasses investigations of: the frequency of gesture use in various contexts (e.g. proficiency levels, age groups); the compensatory functions of gestures; the role of gesture in L2 development; and cross-linguistic comparisons of gesture use among learners of different L1s and L2s (Gullberg & McCafferty, 2008).

Findings from studies conducted in L2 classrooms and in quasi-experimental contexts indicate that learners tend to produce more gestures in their L2 than in their L1 (Gullberg, 2006b, 2013) and some studies indicate that these may serve a compensatory function for linguistic difficulties (Gullberg, 2011). Studies examining level of proficiency and gesture production are increasing, in part because of what they might reveal about the relationships between gesture and language. A number of studies, which included L1 speakers of Chinese, Dutch, French or Swedish and L2 speakers of French, English or Swedish, indicated an inverse relationship between proficiency and use of co-referent gestures (Gullberg, 2006b, 2008; Yoshioka & Kellerman, 2006). Additionally, use of beat gestures became more target-like, serving meta-pragmatic purposes rather than simply marking prosodic features (McCafferty, 2006) as proficiency increased. Finally, studies (e.g. Özyürek, 2002; So *et al.*, 2013; Stam, 2008) have investigated the production of gestures among learners of typologically diverse languages in which temporality, space, motion, manner or path are marked differently lexically and syntactically. Overall, findings indicate a close correlation between linguistic information, corresponding gestures and proficiency levels, generating various hypotheses (e.g. interface hypothesis, Kita *et al.*, 2007), and leading Stam (2008: 253) to state that 'looking at learners' gestures and speech can give us a clearer picture of their proficiency in their L2 than looking at speech alone'.

Cross-linguistic and developmental studies continue to provide valuable information on the relationship between gesture and speech. Graziano and Gullberg (2018) investigated the compensatory function of gestures and speech dysfluencies through a cross-linguistic comparison between adult L1 speakers of Dutch and L1 speakers of Italian, a developmental comparison between children and adult L1 speakers of Italian and, finally, a developmental comparison between adult L1 speakers of Dutch and L2 speakers of French. Findings indicated that in all groups gesture use was more frequent during fluent speech, that gestures were held during dysfluent speech, but the small number of gestures that did proceed served pragmatic and referential functions, and that adult L2 speakers are more likely to gesture during dysfluency, and to use referential gestures. The researchers only found 'a cross-linguistic difference in the production of pragmatic gestures during fluent stretches, with Italian adults producing more such gestures than Dutch adults and Italian children' (Graziano & Gullberg, 2018: 11–12).

Graziano and Gullberg point out that there are contradictory findings among various studies examining the connections between gesture use and (dis)fluent speech. They suggest that this may be due in large part to methodological inconsistencies between studies. For example, in the aforementioned study, Graziano and Gullberg followed Kendon's coding and definitions of gesture functions. In other studies, researchers have included head and body movement, or focused on gestures of a single function (e.g. referential). Additionally, the precise definition of what was considered dysfluent speech as well as which part of the gesture was considered when linking (dis)fluent speech and gestures has varied. As a result, these irregularities make comparison across studies difficult, preventing valid generalizations.

However, findings from these studies should not be dismissed straight away. With attention to any caveats, this research must be taken into account in the L2 assessment research community if we are to advance our understanding of the nature of the multimodal nature of communication. As noted by Ellis (2019: 39), 'Looking at languages through any one single lens does not do the phenomena justice. Taking the social turn does not entail restricting our research focus to the social. Nor does it obviate more traditional approaches to second language acquisition. Instead it calls for greater transdisciplinarity, diversity, and collaborative work'. I suggest that the L2 gesture research on cross-linguistic and developmental comparisons holds the most potential for its applicability to L2 assessment *when* it is combined with emic-based research that includes the full range of NVB in a testing context and goes beyond the analysis of co-expressive gestures alone to include all embodied actions. I return to this discussion below.

4 Nonverbal Behavior[3] in L2 Testing

NVB has emerged in L2 testing research investigating the development of rating scales and learner-oriented assessment tools, the effects of proficiency level and personality traits of one's conversational partner on performance, the comparison of different modes of test delivery and, finally, the construct of IC. The contexts of these tests have included classrooms as well as local and large-scale testing situations. Formats have ranged from one-on-one (examiner: candidate) and paired (two examiners: two candidates) to group oral exams. That NVB has surfaced in various contexts and test formats indicates that it would be premature to dismiss it as idiosyncratic to a particular individual or to a specific context.

In the development of an empirically based rating scale for an end-of-semester paired format test for English speakers learning Spanish, Ducasse and Brown (2009) conducted content analyses of rater commentary of video-recorded tests. The authors found evidence that raters perceived the use of NVB as contributing to the 'success' of an interaction. Similarly, May (2009, 2011) examined a paired format classroom speaking task for Chinese speakers learning English. Employing stimulated recall of video-recorded tasks and analyzing rater notes, she discovered that raters considered nonverbal behavior (e.g. eye contact, gestures and facial expressions) to play a role in effective interaction.

With a goal of creating learner-oriented assessment tools of IC, Nakatsuhara *et al.* (2016b) conducted an in-depth thematic analysis of the stimulated verbal recall of six trained examiners of the *Cambridge English: B2 First*, a paired format test. Examiners, who were also teachers, viewed 12 video-recorded tests and scored candidates. *Communicative Interactive* scores of high, mid and low were confirmed. Among the eight macro themes identified from the verbal recall, two are particularly relevant as they highlight examiners' attention to the [in]appropriate use of NVB by candidates. Macro Theme 6, Interactive Listening, and Macro Theme 7, Body Language, included NVB indicative of IC such as nodding, smiling, making eye contact with one's speaking partner, forward leaning posture and the use of deictic gestures. Notably, examiners commented negatively on the absence of certain NVB such as lack of facial expression and the lack of eye contact. This investigation resulted in a resource for teachers that included recommendations in addition to a checklist and descriptions of skills that can be used to offer feedback for learners in terms of IC. The researchers call for additional studies that focus specifically on the relationship between features of interactional competence and proficiency level.

Turning to the possible effects of one's conversational partner(s) in group tests, Nakatsuhara (2011) focused on the individual characteristic of introversion/extroversion and on proficiency level. She administered a performance-based test to 269 Japanese secondary school students who worked in groups of three and four students. Using both qualitative and quantitative analyses of the video-recorded tests, Nakatsuhara noted that gesturing was employed in several of the groups of four. Functions included making suggestions for turn-taking order, proposing that a specific individual take the turn, encouraging more reserved students to participate and indicating a pass in one's own turn. Nakatsuhara reports that in this study 'group members' characteristics played a significant role in contributing to the creation of a context where some test-takers display their communication skills to fit their conversants' (Nakatsuhara, 2011: 503–504). While specifically examining the effects of extroversion and proficiency on the use of NVB was not the aim of this study, it is interesting to note that it did emerge as a salient feature in the analysis.

Research into the construct of IC in L2 speaking assessments has yielded primarily anecdotal evidence of a possible role of NVB. For example, Galaczi (2014) examined the video-recorded tests of 41 pairs of candidates taking Cambridge English tests for those features of IC that mark different proficiency levels. Galaczi notes 'that non-verbal features such as gaze and body language are part of the IC construct. They were not captured in the transcripts in a systematic way, however, and will not be reported here' (Galaczi, 2014: 559). This expectation that NVB, theoretically, is a part of IC has been supported in a number of studies (Kim, 2018; Roever & Kasper, 2018; Ross, 2018) that highlighted the increased importance of proficient verbal communication when visual input was not available.

5 A Focus on NVB in L2 Assessment

Jenkins and Parra (2003) were the first researchers to focus specifically on NVB in their investigation of a local test of English proficiency for prospective international teaching assistants. Situating their study within seminal research in the area of NVB (e.g. Birdwhistell, 1970; Goffman, 1974, 1981; Kendon, 1990; McNeill, 1992; Mehrabian, 1972; Scheflen, 1972), the authors examined the influence of paralinguistic features and NVB on examiners' ratings of four Spanish-speaking and four Chinese-speaking international students. Their microanalyses of the transcripts of video-taped posttest interviews as well as examiners' notes during the tests indicated that NVB contributed to examiners' perceptions of a candidate's IC. The researchers were able to identify specific signals (e.g. smiling, frowning) that were rated positively and specific signals (e.g. no eye contact) that were rated negatively. As a result of this work, examiner training now includes NVB and the scoring rubric has been revised to 'include listening comprehension and communicative competence ... defined as including verbal, nonverbal, and paralinguistic interaction' (Jenkins & Parra, 2003: 102–103).

It is interesting to note that examiners also noticed the absence of NVB, commentary that is echoed by teacher-examiners in the study by Nakatsuhara *et al.* (2016b) discussed previously. From their investigation of this specific context, Jenkins and Parra concluded that linguistically weaker students, who were seen to exhibit NVB associated with IC and were also considered 'borderline' proficiency, passed the test. However, linguistically weaker students who did not employ NVB did not pass the test. Those students who were considered very low proficiency did not pass the test, regardless of the NVB employed. Similarly, linguistically strong students passed the test regardless of their NVB. The finding that some students whose linguistic proficiency was lower but who employed NVB were able to pass the test was interpreted as NVB serving a compensatory role, which has been supported in more recent studies (Banerjee & Plough, 2016; Gan & Davison, 2011; Gullberg, 2006b, 2013).

Gan and Davison (2011) investigated the use of gestures in an ESL classroom-based group oral exam. Using conversation analysis, the authors analyzed two training and calibration videos used by the Hong Kong Examinations and Assessment Authority. Each video included four students taking the exam: one video consisted of 'lower-scoring students' and the other of 'higher-scoring students'. The authors' examination of the videos indicated that the gestures and other NVB (e.g. eye contact, posture, facial expression) of the higher-scoring group were 'well synchronized ... and integrated during the interaction'. Additionally, the quantity and range of NVB was greater in this group. In contrast, the lower-scoring group employed minimal gestures and NVB, and when they did, it seemed to be detached from their discourse and the interaction. In fact, some teachers interpreted the NVB of the lower-proficiency group to be indicative of 'language difficulties, disfluency, tension, and lack of confidence'. Cautioning against causality, the authors conclude that 'the data seem to support the claim that there is a fundamental relationship between teacher scoring patterns and gesture in face-to-face peer group L2 interaction in these group oral assessment situations' (Gan & Davison, 2011: 116).

In an ongoing investigation of the relationship between candidate proficiency and the use of NVB, Banerjee and Plough (2016) analyze video-recordings of the speaking component of the Michigan Language Assessment Examination for the Certificate of Proficiency in English, a paired format test. Preliminary findings from an examination of ten candidates indicate differences in the kind and amount of NVB between higher rated and lower rated speakers. Higher rated speakers tend to exhibit more NVB associated with active engagement (e.g. nodding, eye contact, smiling, forward leaning posture). In contrast, lower rated speakers exhibit decreased engagement through such NVB as lack of eye contact, lowered head and slumped, stationary posture. Additionally, while higher rated speakers used illustrators (e.g. using one's finger to outline the shape of an object being described) to complement and emphasize speech, lower rated speakers used illustrators (e.g. deictic gestures) as substitutes for speech. Observations of the NVB of lower rated speakers supports earlier work (e.g. Gan & Davison, 2011; Jenkins & Parra, 2003) indicating that NVB may be used as a compensatory strategy.

Using grounded ethnography and situated within Goffman's (1981) concept of footing, Plough and Bogart (2008) investigated the perceptions of an examiner's NVB in a one-on-one roleplay task that was part of an oral performance test for prospective international teaching assistants (TA). The task requires the international student to assume the role of the TA and an examiner[4] assumes the role of an undergraduate student coming to office hours. In posttest feedback sessions, video-recordings of the roleplay were viewed separately with the examiner who assumed the role of the undergraduate student (examiner/undergraduate), a second examiner/researcher who participates in all other tasks of the test, one researcher and four Chinese-speaking candidates. In addition to remarking on their own performance and noting that the task content and context were 'real' to them, candidates commented that the examiner's/ undergraduate's behavior also contributed to the realism. Findings indicated that the examiner's/undergraduate's NVB such as lowering his head, slouched posture, lack of eye contact and false starts was salient to the candidates, who interpreted this as the examiner/undergraduate appearing 'somewhat confused and sincere about wanting help' (Plough & Bogart, 2008: 209). The examiner also remarked on his posture and physical positioning, stating that it is just 'how I often am' (Plough & Bogart, 2008: 211). The examiner/researcher and the researcher also noted the NVB and interpreted this in terms of power and dominance, suggesting that this NVB allowed for a shift in the power dynamics, particularly in light of its salience to the candidates.

Nakatsuhara *et al.* (2016a, 2017) investigated delivery of the IELTS Speaking Test via video-conferencing and via the standard face-to-face delivery. The researchers compared 'test takers' scores and linguistic output … examiners' test management and rating behaviors' (Nakatsuhara *et al.*, 2016a: 10), and both the test-takers' and the examiners' perceptions of the two delivery conditions. Among their findings, Nakatsuhara *et al.* noted that more test-takers elaborated on their opinions during video-conferencing and suggested that this was due to test-takers misreading the NVB of examiners to indicate that they needed to speak more. Additionally, many test-takers commented that the ability to see the examiner's NVB during the face-to-face test made it easier for them to understand the examiner. Interestingly, examiners noted that they were much more aware of their speech articulation, speaking more slowly and enunciating clearly, during the video-conferencing. Additionally, the examiners were conscious of the effect of their gestures and body language but seemed unsure how to use 'natural' gestures in the video-conferencing mode.

6 Moving Forward

The emic-based approach employed in the studies by Plough and Bogart (2008) and by Nakatsuhara *et al.* (2016b, 2017) allowed the researchers to gain an understanding of examiner and candidate behavior from the perspectives of all participants in the exchange. Notably, NVB surfaced in the commentary of all involved. As noted by Plough and Bogart (2008: 213–214), '[a]lthough studies have found that an examiner's perception of candidate *performance* [emphasis added] is influenced by the nonverbal behavior of candidates … [these two studies make explicit the influence that the NVB of examiners have on] the testing event and ultimately the possible effect on candidate performance'.

While an etic-based methodology may yield similar results, the emic-based approach of ethnomethodological conversation analysis (EMCA) holds the most promise for L2 face-to-face speaking assessment research and test validation. From the extensive theoretical and empirical literature on EMCA in second language studies (e.g. Eskilden & Majlesi, 2018; Eskildsen & Markee, 2018; Kasper & Wagner, 2018), I extract one general tenet of EMCA as it pertains to L2 speaking assessment. Kasper and

Wagner (2018: 82) note that '... EMCA does not support factor models ... of the relationship of (inter)action, participants, and context more generally, but explores the ways social actions are built by the participants, contingent on and indexical for the specifics in any situation'. This poses unique challenges for L2 assessment research. After all, in an attempt to improve test authenticity, validity and generalizability, we have a long tradition of conceptualizing and then isolating those factors that will most accurately and fully represent the construct. One of the implicit arguments in this chapter is that the speaking construct in face-to-face interactions is underrepresented if NVB is excluded. At the same time, it has been suggested that NVB is not a static variable that can be categorized; rather it is part of dynamic interactional processes.

Second language speaking assessment research investigating NVB directly is minimal; nonetheless, there is a growing body of work noting the influence of NVB. This behavior has included hand, arm and head movements, posture, physical positioning, eye gaze and paralinguistic cues. Gesture in the absence of these other nonverbal behaviors has not been identified as the only feature emerging in these studies. Adhering to a research methodology that does not encompass the NVB present in the L2 assessment data would ignore key evidence. Additionally, isolating gestures must be justified; one would need to show fundamental differences (beyond structural) between gestures and other NVB to explain why they have been extracted from 'the dynamic interplay of the totality of behavior' (Knapp, 2006: 10).

7 Application: Challenges for L2 Assessment

Incorporating NVB into the speaking construct introduces important challenges for L2 assessment that directly impact test validity. However, we are obligated to create rubrics that, to the extent possible, account for the full range of performance (on which candidates are evaluated). Perhaps a unique characteristic of NVB that makes it particularly elusive is its fluidity and contextual variation – individual variation in the interpretations of the same NVB as well as individual variation in the production of NVB. It is part of the fabric of a linguaculture (Risager, 2013) and of an individual. That NVB, on the whole, cannot be taught and that any attempts to do so would result in behavior similar to inauthentic, memorized speech, can be partially attributable to this.

Plough *et al.* (2018) outlined a preliminary research agenda addressing the *what* of NVB. This included: the relationships between NVB forms and functions; the relationships between NVB, tasks and individual characteristics; the criteria for evaluating NVB, including rater training; and the relationship between NVB and proficiency. To this I would add the relationships between NVB and various linguacultures. Additionally, with respect to forms and functions, this does not imply creation of a strict one-to-one correlation or categorizations. Rather, context of use, participants' commentary on and interpretations of NVB serve as the starting point in an analysis of NVB. As noted previously, researchers in L2 gesture studies are beginning to gather data from comparative cross-linguistic and developmental studies, which serve as meaningful supplements to an emic-based analysis. I next offer a preliminary working model for determining the criteria by which to evaluate NVB (i.e. the *how*).

7.1 Context

I briefly describe a local high-stakes speaking test of a language other than English administered to undergraduate students enrolled in the Residential College in the Arts and Humanities (RCAH), which is located within Michigan State University. The RCAH has a world language graduation requirement, which students can fulfill through study abroad, coursework or passing the RCAH's performance-based test.[5] The purpose is to assess the ability of students to engage in and contribute to the development of purposeful discourse on personal, professional or academic topics. The test measures students' use of linguistic and interactional resources to engage in planned and unplanned interactions. The test employs a paired format (two students and two examiners) and includes three tasks: a warm-up; a prepared presentation; and a negotiated consensus task. Following the International Test Commission (ITC) Guidelines for Test Adaptation (Hambleton *et al.*, 2005), the test has been developed in Arabic, Chinese, French, German, Haitian Creole, Hebrew, Italian, Korean, Spanish and Vietnamese; it has been administered in Chinese, French, Hebrew and Spanish.

The test was initially trialed with native speakers of English, which the researcher administered along with an undergraduate research assistant. Test administration training sessions were conducted with native speakers of French, German and Spanish, who then administered test trials in those languages. Feedback sessions with all participants immediately followed test trials. During post-trial discussions, examiners remarked on the NVB of volunteer test-takers. Feedback sessions with all participants (i.e. examiners and student test-takers) after operational tests remain an important feature of the testing procedure. In this way, immediate commentary from participants is gathered, which is then used for test and rubric revisions.

7.2 Scale development and implementation

The scoring rubric was created using an intuitive (experiential) method (Fulcher, 2003) and consulting validated, operational scales and proficiency descriptors (e.g. ACTFL, CEFR). The rubric consists of ten (yes-no) binary items, seven Likert items, and four holistic descriptors that encompass grammar and vocabulary, pronunciation and intelligibility, listening comprehension and interactional abilities. The latter category includes an open-ended question on the appropriateness and effectiveness of NVB, descriptors that initially emerged in the remarks of all participants during test trials. Review of the rubric and calibration exercises are part of examiner training. However, while NVB is explicitly discussed with the examiners, it is not included in calibration. Scoring is done in real time.

At this point, the operationalization of the item on NVB can be characterized as a compilation of descriptors. It is important to note that it is one item within one category and thus is not heavily weighted. Valuable commentary on the NVB of American undergraduates from the perspectives of the undergraduates and from examiners representing a wide range of linguacultures is slowly being collected. For example, (female) students repositioning themselves during the negotiated consensus task has been salient for multiple examiners. If students shift to directly face each other, examiners comment that this indicates to them that the students are truly engaged in the task. However, not making this shift is not judged negatively. Examiners have not indicated that these observations affected their evaluations of student performance.

Another example, which applies specifically to student performance, comes from the students' perception of examiner NVB during the introduction of the negotiated consensus task. Students are provided with a written description (in the world language) of the task and are told that they can ask about any vocabulary that they do not know. During the Chinese test, both students had questions and both examiners moved from their seats and knelt by the students to explain (in the world language) unknown vocabulary. After the test, students commented that this movement lowered the formality of the test and helped reduce their nervousness, which one could speculate altered (improved) their performance.

Currently, a continuum is under construction that includes a range of (im)permissible behaviors, beginning with the extremes. That is, NVB that is clearly unacceptable or incomprehensible is on one end of the continuum and NVB that is both acceptable and that meaningfully contributes to the interaction is on the other end. Andrén (2014) may inform this endeavor. In an attempt to move away from a dichotomous conceptualization of gesture versus non-gesture, he has proposed a continuum of communicative explicitness and one of representational complexity. Additionally, Jenkins and Parra (2003: 91) continue to revise examiner training materials and the scoring rubric which, as noted, now includes NVB, through a review of research examining a 'language threshold level beneath which compensatory strategies or pragmatic skills do not make up for linguistic problems' within testing and classroom contexts.

As noted previously, findings from emic-based studies combined with those of Gullberg and colleagues into cross-linguistic and developmental comparisons can eventually result in descriptions of meaningful relationships and interactions between context, L1s, L2s, proficiency levels and NVB. Additionally, large-scale, standardized tests that employ face-to-face speaking tests can contribute to this body of knowledge by attending to NVB in test validation procedures, similar to the series of IELTS studies conducted by Nakatsuhara and colleagues. Minimally, NVB should be included in all rater training as NVB consists of those 'elements that we are at once consciously unaware and yet unconsciously, profoundly aware' (Burgoon *et al.*, 2010: 374).

We have a long row to hoe. However, as McNamara (1996: 83) noted more than 20 years ago when creating a model of speaking proficiency, 'too often, efforts are made to dispose of the difficulties by simply defining them out of existence'. My intent in this chapter has been to provide evidence from existing theoretical and empirical research that NVB is essential to interaction, which is fundamental to speaking proficiency. We should not define it away.

Notes

(1) Gullberg (2006a) defines gestures as a set of actions that are usually limited to movements of the arms and hands. This definition excludes functional (e.g. drinking) and symptomatic (e.g. scratching) actions as well as posture and proxemics, which 'are not communicatively irrelevant but ... are not typically part of the message that the speaker intends to convey' (Gullberg, 2006a: 104).

(2) There are also methodological issues with a lack of consensus on definitions of emotions; additionally, the criteria that are established to confirm universality of facial expressions of emotion have varied and appeared somewhat arbitrary.

(3) There is debate over the expression of nonverbal as it creates a false dichotomy, assuming that verbal and nonverbal are separate, distinct channels of communication. By using it here, no such dichotomy is claimed. Rather, it is used for lack of a more concise, transparent term for the topic under discussion.

(4) Examiners in this role have recently completed their undergraduate degrees, thus lending credibility to their role as an undergraduate student.

(5) Additional details about the test, including its development, can be found in Plough (2014).

References

Andrén, M. (2014) On the lower limit of gesture. In M. Seyfeddinipur and M. Gullberg (eds) *From Gesture in Conversation to Visible Action as Utterance: Essays in Honor of Adam Kendon* (pp. 153–174). Philadelphia, PA: John Benjamins.

Banerjee, J. and Plough, I. (2016) Behavior in speaking tests: A preliminary model of interaction. Work-in-progress presented at the Annual Language Testing Research Colloquium (LTRC), Palermo, Italy, June.

Birdwhistell, R.L. (1970) *Kinesics and Context: Essays on Body Motion Communication.* Philadelphia, PA: University of Pennsylvania Press.

Burgoon, J.K., Guerrero, L.K. and Floyd, K. (2010) *Nonverbal Communication.* New York: Routledge.

Crivelli, C. and Fridlund, A.J. (2019) Inside-out: From basic emotions theory to the behavioral ecology view. *Journal of Nonverbal Behavior* 43, 161–194. doi:10.1007/s10919-019-00294-2

Crivelli, C., Jarillo, S. and Fridlund, A.J. (2016) A multidisciplinary approach to research in small-scale societies: Emotions and facial expressions in the field. *Frontiers in Psychology* 7 (1073), 1–12.

Ducasse, A. and Brown, A. (2009) Assessing paired orals: Raters' orientation to interaction. *Language Testing* 26 (3), 423–443.

Durán, J.I., Reisenzein, R. and Fernández-Dols, J.M. (2017) Coherence between emotions and facial expressions. In J.M. Fernández-Dols and J.A. Russell (eds) *The Science of Facial Expression* (pp. 107–129). New York: Oxford University Press.

Efron, D. (1941) *Gesture, Race, and Culture*. The Hague: Mouton.

Ekman, P. (1971) Universal and cultural differences in facial expressions of emotion. In J. R. Cole (ed.) *Nebraska Symposium on Motivation:* 19 (pp. 207–283). Lincoln, NE: Nebraska University Press.

Ekman, P. (2004) Emotional and conversational nonverbal signals. In J.M. Larrazabal and L.A. Perez Miranda (eds) *Language, Knowledge, and Representation* (pp. 39–50). Dordrecht: Kluwer Academic.

Ekman, P. and Friesen, W.V. (1969) The repertoire of nonverbal behavior: Categories, origin, usage, and coding. *Semiotica* 1, 49–98.

Ekman, P. and Friesen, W.V. (1971) Constants across cultures in the face and emotion. *Journal of Personality and Social Psychology* 17 (2), 124–129.

Ekman, P. and Friesen, W. (1972) Hand movements. *Journal of Communication* 22, 353–374.

Ellis, N.C. (2019) Essentials of a theory of language cognition. *The Modern Language Journal* 103 (Suppl.), 39–60. doi:10.1111/modl.12532

Eskildsen, S.W. and Majlesi, A.R. (eds) (2018) Learnables and teachables in second language talk: Advancing a social reconceptualization of central SLA tenets. *Special Issue, The Modern Language Journal* 102, 3–10.

Eskildsen, S.W. and Markee, N. (2018) L2 talk as social accomplishment. In R.A. Alonso (ed.) *Speaking in a Second Language*. Philadelphia, PA: John Benjamins.

Fulcher, G. (2003) *Testing Second Language Speaking*. London: Pearson Education.

Galaczi, E. (2014) Interactional competence across proficiency levels: How do learners manage interaction in paired speaking tests? *Applied Linguistics* 35 (5), 553–574.

Gan, Z. and Davison, C. (2011) Gestural behavior in group oral assessment: A case study of higher- and lower-scoring students. *International Journal of Applied Linguistics* 21 (1), 95–120.

Goffman, E. (1974) *Frame Analysis*. New York: Harper & Row.

Goffman, E. (1981) *Forms of Talk*. Philadelphia, PA: University of Pennsylvania Press.

Graziano, M. and Gullberg, M. (2018) When speech stops, gesture stops: Evidence from developmental and crosslinguistic comparisons. *Frontiers in Psychology* 879, 1–17.

Gullberg, M. (2006a) Some reasons for studying gesture and second language acquisition (homage à Adam Kendon). *International Review of Applied Linguistics* 44, 103–124.

Gullberg, M. (2006b) Handling discourse: Gestures, reference tracking, and communication strategies in early L2. *Language Learning* 56 (1), 155–196.

Gullberg, M. (2008) A helping hand? Gestures, L2 learners, and grammar. In S.G. McCafferty and G. Stam (eds) *Gesture: Second Language Acquisition and Classroom Research* (pp. 185–210). New York: Routledge.

Gullberg, M. (2011) Multilingual multimodality: Communicative difficulties and their solutions in second language use. In J. Streeck, C. Goodwin and C. LeBaron (eds) *Embodied Interaction: Language and Body in the Material World* (pp. 137–151). Cambridge: Cambridge University Press.

Gullberg, M. (2013) Gesture analysis in second language acquisition. In C. Chapelle (ed.) *The Encyclopedia of Applied Linguistics*. Oxford: Wiley-Blackwell. doi:10.1002/9781405198431.wbeal0455

Gullberg, M. and McCafferty, S.G. (2008) Introduction to gesture and SLA: Toward an integrated approach. *Studies in Second Language Acquisition* 30, 133–146.

Hall, J.A. and Knapp, M.I. (eds) (2013) *Nonverbal Communication*. Berlin: DeGruyter Mouton.

Hall, J.A., Horgan, T.G. and Murphy, N.A. (2019) Nonverbal communication. *Annual Review of Psychology* 70, 271–294.

Hambleton, R.K., Merenda, P.F. and Spielberger, C.D. (eds) (2005) *Adapting Educational and Psychological Tests for Cross-cultural Assessment*. Mahwah, NJ: Lawrence Erlbaum.

Haugh, M. (2008) Intention in pragmatics. *Intercultural Journal of Pragmatics* 5 (2), 99–110.

Hauser, E. (2019) The construction of interactional incompetence in L2 interaction. In R. Salaberry and S. Kunitz (eds) *Teaching and Testing L2 Interactional Competence: Bridging Theory and Practice* (pp. 77–121). New York: Routledge.

Ishino, M. and Stam, G. (2011) Introduction. In G. Stam and M. Ishino (eds) *Integrating Gestures: The Interdisciplinary Nature of Gesture* (pp. 3–15). Philadelphia, PA: John Benjamins.

Jenkins, S. and Parra, I. (2003) Multiple layers of meaning in an oral proficiency test: The complementary roles of nonverbal, paralinguistic, and verbal behaviors in assessment decisions. *The Modern Language Journal* 87 (1), 90–107.

Kasper, G. (2006) Speech acts in interaction: Towards discursive pragmatics. In K. Barvodi-Harlig, C. Felix-Brasdefer and A. Omar (eds) *Pragmatics and Language Learning* (pp. 281–314). Honolulu, HI: National Foreign Language Resource Center.

Kasper, G. (2009) Locating cognition in second language interaction and learning: Inside the skull or in public view? *International Review of Applied Linguistics* 47, 11–36.

Kasper, G. and Ross, S.J. (2007) Multiple questions in oral proficiency interviews. *Journal of Pragmatics* 39, 2045–2070.

Kasper, G. and Ross, S.J. (2013) Assessing second language pragmatics: An overview and introductions. In S.J. Ross and G. Kasper (eds) *Assessing Second Language Pragmatics* (pp. 1–40). Basingstoke: Palgrave Macmillan.

Kasper, G. and Wagner, J. (2018) Epistemological reorientations and L2 interactional settings: A postscript to the special issue. *Special Issue, The Modern Language Journal* 102, 82–90.

Kasper, G. and Youn, S.J. (2018) Transforming instruction to activity: Roleplay in language assessment. *Applied Linguistics Review* 9 (4), 585–616. doi:10.1515/applirev-2017–0020

Kendon, A. (1972) Some relationships between body motion and speech: An analysis of an example. In A.W. Siegman and B. Pope (eds) *Studies in Dyadic Communication* (pp. 177–210). New York: Pergamon. doi:10.1016/B978-0-08-015867-9.50013-7

Kendon, A. (1990) *Conducting Interaction: Patterns of Behavior in Focused Encounters*. New York: Cambridge University Press.

Kendon, A. (2004) *Gesture: Visible Action as Utterance*. Cambridge: Cambridge University Press.

Kim, H. (2018) What constitutes professional communication in aviation: Is language proficiency enough for testing purposes? *Special Issue, Language Testing* 35 (3), 403–426.

Kita, S., Özyürek, A., Allen, S., Brown, A., Furman, R. and Ishizuka, T. (2007) Relations between syntactic encoding and co-speech gestures: Implications for a model of speech and gesture production. *Language and Cognitive Processes* 22 (8), 1212–1236. doi:10.1080/01690960701461426

Knapp, M.L. (2006) An historical overview of nonverbal research. In V. Manusov and M.L. Patterson (eds) *The Sage Handbook of Nonverbal Communication* (pp. 3–19). Thousand Oaks, CA: Sage.

Markee, N. (2019) Some theoretical reflections on the construct of interactional competence. In R. Salaberry and S. Kunitz (eds) *Teaching and Testing L2 Interactional Competence: Bridging Theory and Practice* (pp. 60–75). New York: Routledge.

Matsumoto, D., Hwang, H.C. and Frank, M.G. (eds) (2016) *APA Handbook of Nonverbal Communication*. Washington, DC: American Psychological Association.

May, L. (2009) Co-constructed interaction in a paired speaking test: The rater's perspective. *Language Testing* 26 (3), 397–421.

May, L. (2011) Interactional competence in a paired speaking test: Features salient to raters. *Language Assessment Quarterly* 8 (2), 127–145.

McCafferty, S.G. (2006) Gesture and the materialization of second language prosody. *International Review of Applied Linguistics* 44 (2), 195–207.

McNamara, T. (1996) *Measuring Second Language Performance*. London: Addison Wesley Longman.

McNamara, T.F. and Roever, C. (2006) *Language Testing: The Social Dimension*. Malden, MA: Blackwell.

McNeill, D. (1992) *Hand and Mind: What the Hands Reveal about Thought*. Chicago, IL: University of Chicago Press.

McNeill, D. (2006) Gesture: A psycholinguistic approach. In K. Brown (ed.) *The Encyclopedia of Language and Linguistics* (pp. 1–15). Amsterdam: Elsevier.

Mehrabian, A. (1972) *Nonverbal Communication*. Chicago, IL: Aldine-Atherton.

Müller, C. (2018) Gesture and sign: Cataclysmic break or dynamic relations? *Frontiers in Psychology* 9 (1651), 1–20. doi:10.3389/fpsyg.2018.01651

Nakatsuhara, F. (2011) Effects of test-taker characteristics and the number of participants in group oral tests. *Language Testing* 28 (4), 483–508.

Nakatsuhara, F., Inoue, C., Berry, V. and Galaczi, E. (2016a) Exploring performance across two delivery modes: Face-to-face and video-conferencing delivery a preliminary comparison of test taker and examiner behavior. IELTS Partnership Research Paper No. 1. British Council, Cambridge English Language Assessment and IDP:IELTS Australia. See https://www.ielts.org/teaching-and-research/research-reports.

Nakatsuhara, F., May, L., Lam, D. and Galaczi, E. (2016b) Learning oriented feedback and interactional competence. *Cambridge Assessment English Research Notes* 70.

Nakatsuhara, F., Inoue, C., Berry, V. and Galaczi, E. (2017) Exploring the use of video-conferencing technology in the assessment of spoken language: A mixed-methods study. *Language Assessment Quarterly* 14 (1), 1–18.

Özyürek, A. (2002) Speech-gesture synchrony in typologically different languages and second language acquisition. In B. Skarabela, S. Fish and A.H.J. Do (eds) *Proceedings of the 26th Annual Boston University Conference on Language Development* (pp. 500–509). Somerville, MA: Cascadilla Press.

Pekarek Doehler, S. (2018) Elaborations in L2 interactional competence: The development of L2 grammar-for-interaction. *Classroom Discourse* 9 (1), 3–21.

Pekarek Doehler, S. (2019) On the nature and development of L2 interactional competence: State of the art and implications for praxis. In R. Salaberry and S. Kunitz (eds) *Teaching and Testing L2 Interactional Competence Bridging Theory and Practice* (pp. 25–59). New York: Routledge.

Plough, I. (2014) Development of an exit-level proficiency exam in multiple languages. *Special Issue, Papers in Language Testing and Assessment* 1, 27–52.

Plough, I.C. and Bogart, P.S.H. (2008) Candidate perceptions of examiner behavior in oral performance testing. *Language Assessment Quarterly* 5 (3), 1–23.

Plough, I., Banerjee, J. and Iwashita, N. (2018) Interactional competence: Genie out of the bottle. *Special Issue, Language Testing* 35 (3), 427–445.

Plusquellec, P. and Denault, V. (2018) The 1000 most cited papers on visible nonverbal behavior: A bibliometric analysis. *Journal of Nonverbal Behavior* 42, 347–377. doi:10.1007/s10919-018-0280-9

Risager, K. (2013) Linguaculture. In C.A. Chapelle (ed.) *Encyclopedia of Applied Linguistics* (pp. 3418–3421). London: Blackwell.

Roever, C. (2011) Tests of second language pragmatics: Past and future. *Language Testing* 28, 463–481.

Roever, C. (2013) Testing implicature under operational conditions. In S.J. Ross and G. Kasper (eds) *Assessing Second Language Pragmatics* (43–64). Basingstoke: Palgrave Macmillan.

Roever, C. and Kasper, G. (2018) Speaking in turns and sequences: Interactional competence as a target construct in testing speaking. *Special Issue, Language Testing* 35 (3), 331–355.

Ross, S.J. (2018) Listener response as a facet of interactional competence. *Special Issue, Language Testing* 35 (3), 351–375.

Ross, S.J. and O'Connell, S. (2013) The situation with complication as a site for strategic competence. In S.J. Ross and G. Kasper (eds) *Assessing Second Language Pragmatics* (pp. 311–326). Basingstoke: Palgrave Macmillan.

Salaberry, R. and Kunitz, S. (2019) *Teaching and Testing L2 Interactional Competence: Bridging Theory and Practice.* New York: Routledge.

Scheflen, A. (1972) *Body Language and Social Order: Communication as Behavioral Control.* Englewood Cliffs, NJ: Prentice Hall.

So, W.C., Kita, S. and Goldin-Meadow, S. (2013) When do speakers use gestures to specify who does what to whom? The role of language proficiency and type of gestures in narratives. *Journal of Psycholinguistic Research* 42, 581–594.

Stam, G. (2008) What gestures reveal about second language acquisition. In S.G. McCafferty and S. Stam (eds) *Gesture Second Language Acquisition and Classroom Research.* New York: Routledge.

Tomkins, S.S. and McCarter, R. (1964) What and where are the primary affects? Some evidence for a theory. *Perceptual and Motor Skills* 18, 119–158.

Yoshioka, K. and Kellerman, E. (2006) Gestural introduction of ground reference in L2 narrative discourse. *IRAL International Review of Applied Linguistics in Language Teaching* 44 (2), 173–195.

Youn, S.J. (2015) Validity argument for assessing L2 pragmatics in interaction using mixed methods. *Language Testing* 32, 199–225.

Part 2

Collecting and Rating Speaking Data

4 Task Instruction in OPI Roleplays

Alfred Rue Burch and Gabriele Kasper

1 Introduction

The notion of task is fundamental in language assessment. Tasks are treated as elicitation devices that model language use activities in the real world. The challenge for language testers is to design test tasks that embody relevant dimensions of 'target language use tasks' (Bachman & Palmer, 1996) and therefore enable valid inferences from test scores to test construct – a challenge that is magnified in tests of second language speaking (Fulcher, 2003). In the highly complex, multidimensional target domains of oral language use, 'speaking' means to talk in some form of social interaction. Speaking tests thus have to meet two essential design requirements: (1) to enjoin test-takers' participation in, and active contribution to, *social interaction* by taking turns at talk; and (2) to construct participation opportunities as *test tasks* that elicit ratable speech samples for inferences to performance in the target domain. In addition, a design consideration for proficiency tests is that they offer a *standardized* measure of second language speaking, a particularly pressing concern in large-scale and high-stakes test contexts.

The oldest test format that strives to meet all three criteria is an interview-structured activity between an examiner and an examinee, such as the International English Language Testing System (IELTS) Speaking Test, the Interagency Language Roundtable (ILR) Language Proficiency Interview (LPI), the Test of English for International Communication (TOEIC) and the American Council for the Teaching of Foreign Languages (ACTFL) Oral Proficiency Interview (OPI). Collectively, these tests are commonly referred to as OPI.[1] Ross (2017: 13) describes the format as 'one of the most developed task-based language assessments methods in use'.

Unlike interviews conducted for the purpose of eliciting the interviewee's beliefs and opinions on some topic, the interview format in the OPI serves as a platform for task delivery (Ross, 2017: Ch. 2). The repurposing of the interview format is made possible through the generic adjacency pair structure and how participant roles are fixed in regard to who initiates and responds. That is, the first pair part is bound to the category of interviewer or examiner and the second pair part is bound to the category of inter-viewee or examinee. The critical difference between interviews for topical information and the OPI is in the categories of *action* that the adjacency pair organization supports. While the paired actions in the standard inter-view are questions and answers, the actions in the OPI are various task instructions and the projected task uptake. These do include questions and answers, but the questions are only one possible format of task formula-tion. The first pair parts also implement instructions and directives for a range of actions, among them reporting facts, describing objects, events and spaces as well as future plans and hypothetical scenarios, telling per-sonal stories and news stories, and formulating and supporting assess-ments and opinions.

Still, the interview format imposes structural limitations on the range of afforded actions and therefore may underrepresent the test construct (Kasper & Ross, 2013), a threat to construct validity (Messick, 1989). A common solution is to integrate a roleplay component in the OPI, and all of the OPI versions listed above include a roleplay component. Roleplays are designed to transform the participation framework of the interview (Okada, 2010) and enable a wider range of speaking opportunities from first and second position, such as requesting, suggesting, inviting, advis-ing, persuading or complaining in mundane scenarios of varying complex-ity. In the OPI context, roleplays figure as another task-based activity.

2 Task Instructions

As an organization for generating ratable examinee performance of multiple tasks, the OPI confronts examiners with several problems of task management. One is to transition between tasks so that the examinee recognizes that the current task is nearing completion and can be ready for the next task. Task boundaries also have to be recognizable for second or third raters who do not participate in the OPI (Ross, 2017). Lastly, the examiner has to design the task instruction in such a way that the exam-inee understands it and undertakes the task as instructed. Previous research on task instruction within the interview-structured portion of the OPI has shown that examiners vary considerably in setting up a new task, with demonstrated effects on examinee performance (Brown, 2003; Ross, 2007). Relatedly, examinees frequently display problems in under-standing the instructions, or the examiner treats the task uptake as inad-equate (Kasper, 2013; Kasper & Ross, 2007; Ross, 1996, 2017). Based on extensive evidence from ILR OPIs, Ross (2017) proposes that effective task instructions, or 'task frames', are composed of multiple actions (topi-calization, ratification, confirmation, delimitation) tailored towards the type and complexity of the task. For instance, narrations of past and pres-ent events, descriptions and fact reporting require the complete task fram-ing sequence, while delimitations of the task are built into the topicalization component for eliciting narrations of future events, supporting opinions and hypothetical scenarios (Ross, 2017: 143).

Ross demonstrates that examinees' problems in understanding the task instruction and producing task-relevant uptake can frequently be traced to incomplete or ambiguous task framing and require (sometimes extensive) repair. In the economy of the OPI, such repair sequences can have undesirable consequences. As the repair inevitably stalls the progression of the test, it cuts into the time available for working through the set of tasks. The repair is also a liability for the examinee because interviewer and raters may attribute the trouble to the examinee's language ability. As Ross (2017: 144) notes, 'Whenever there is confusion about the task, raters are likely to assume that the reason is a lack of proficiency on the part of the candidate'. There are thus compelling arguments for designing task instructions that preempt the need for repair, and for examiners to consistently use a standard instructional procedure adapted to the local assessment context and interactional contingencies. At the same time, examinees' participation in the task instructions requires further scrutiny to better understand the conditions for successful and problematic uptake.

3 Roleplays as the Next Task in the OPI

Interaction research on roleplays in language assessment has typically examined how the talk unfolds once the participants have shifted into the roleplay frame (Grabowski, 2013; Kasper & Youn, 2018; Kormos, 1999; Okada & Greer, 2013; Ross & O'Connell, 2013; Walters, 2013; Youn, 2015, 2020). In contrast, little analytic attention has been paid to the transition from the interview-structured portion of the OPI to the roleplay. This may be because proficiency is operationalized as task performance, with the implication being that transitional talk between tasks counts as construct irrelevant and hence unassessable. However, as in the case of all task transitions, the examinee's participation in the roleplay instructions may still figure as an unofficial assessable and contribute to the awarded score (Ross, 2017). From the perspective of test fairness (Kunnan, 2004), it is therefore important to shed light on how roleplay instructions are delivered and how the participants accomplish the transition to the roleplay.

The few studies on these topics to date note that roleplay instructions routinely include a written description of the scenario and the simulated identities that the participants will assume, printed on a laminated card (Okada, 2010; Ross, 2017). In ILR OPI protocol, the examiner reads out the selected prompt card, written in the target language, to the examinee. The examinee is then given a version of the card in their first language or the target language, depending on proficiency level, for silent reading (Ross, 2017). So, in this protocol, the prompt cards demonstrably figure as constitutive textual resources in the delivery of the roleplay instruction. However, the audio-recorded data examined in published research on roleplay in language testing do not give access to how the participants manage the cards as objects that not only have a textual but also a material quality. As conversation analytic (CA) research on instruction (Lindwell *et al.*, 2015) and activity transitions (Mikkola & Lehtinen, 2014; Robinson & Stivers, 2001) across a range of social activities shows, the accomplishment of these activities is not limited to talk but critically involves material resources and embodied action. This study will therefore examine roleplay instructions using video-recorded OPIs as data and multimodal CA (Mondada, 2014) for analysis. These methodological extensions will allow us to show how the roleplay instructions are organized as a sequentially unfolding, cooperative social activity through formulations and multimodal practices. Against this backdrop, we will particularly inspect moments in the instruction that pose understanding problems for the examinees and the repair practices that address these troubles. Overall, the analysis aims to reveal how the roleplay instructions unfold as informal assessables in the interstitial spaces between the tasks as formal assessables.

4 Data and Method

The data come from a corpus of 57 ACTFL OPIs for Japanese as a target language. The examinees are senior undergraduate students at a US university majoring in Japanese. The examiner is an ACTFL-certified OPI tester and L1 speaker of Japanese. The dyadic face-to-face interviews were audio- and video-recorded with the participants' consent. From the total corpus, a stratified random sample of 15 OPIs was drawn, resulting in sets of three OPIs for each of the five levels from Intermediate-Low to Advanced-Mid on the ACTFL proficiency scale (Tominaga, 2013, 2017).

For this study, we selected four excerpts from OPIs with examinees rated at the Intermediate level to represent roleplay instruction sequences that evolve from minor delays in the progression of the instruction to severe trouble in examinee uptake. Data are transcribed using standard CA conventions to represent the talk (adapted from Jefferson, 2004), with conventions from Burch (2014) to represent embodied conduct and conventions modified from Goodwin (1984) for the representation of gaze direction. The original Japanese talk is Romanized according to a modified Hepburn system and glossed using the conventions in Greer *et al.* (2017: xviii). The method of data analysis is multimodal CA (Mondada, 2014).

5 Analysis

In the entire OPI corpus, the participants maintain a consistent spatial arrangement (Figure 4.1). The prompt cards, color-coded for proficiency

Figure 4.1 Spatial arrangement of OPI

level, are placed in the front right corner of the examiner's side of the table, with the printed side up in the examiner's direction. As the cards are in full view for both participants, the examinee may anticipate that the cards will be utilized in the OPI at some stage. At the same time, the placement of the cards gives the examiner privileged visual access to the role-play prompts and in this way embodies her superior epistemic and deontic status in the OPI. The spatial configuration also affords the opportunity for both the examiner and examinee to visually monitor each other's ongoing embodied activities.

5.1 Phase structure of roleplay instructions

Throughout the corpus, the roleplay instruction evolves through distinct sequentially ordered phases (Heritage & Clayman, 2010). Each of these sequences is initiated by the examiner and thus displays her category-bound responsibility to manage the progression of the OPI. The instruction begins with an *announcement* of the roleplay as the next activity ('Now we are going to do something different. We are going to do a role-play in which we will act out a situation', (ACTFL - Swender, Conrad & Vicars, 2012). In the Japanese OPIs, the examiner announces the roleplay with a version of the formulation *jaa chotto koko de roorupuree o shite moraitai n desu ne* 'so now I would like you to do a roleplay for me, okay?'. The announcement advises the examinee of the upcoming activity category and a shift in participation framework. Next, the examiner makes the selected card with the roleplay prompt written in English visually accessible to the examinee and *directs* them *to read the card aloud in English* (*kore o eego de koe ni dashite yonde kudasai* 'please read this out loud in English'). The written prompt instructs the examinee in the specific scenario and the role they will be taking on. When the examinee has complied with the reading directive, the examiner routinely *checks* the examinee's *readiness* to proceed with the specified roleplay (*ii desu ka?* 'Okay?'). This sequence does not advance the instruction but offers the examinee an opportunity for clarification before the roleplay gets under way (compare the 'confirmation' component in Ross's task framing sequence). Lastly the examiner *identifies her role* in the scenario and *prompts* the examinee *to begin* the roleplay (*chotto hanashite kudasai* 'please talk to me'). In the instruction sequence, this final directive is *the* directive that projects the start of the roleplay as its second pair part. It prefigures the shift in participation framework to the enacted identities in the scenario and announces to the non-present raters that the ratable talk is to begin. In the overall sequential organization of the instruction, the announcement, directive to read the role prompt and examiner's role information not only precede the directive to start the roleplay temporally but successively provide the examinee with the information needed to conduct the roleplay. The examinee's alignment with the examiner's initiating actions clear the way for the examiner to move the instruction forward. The preliminary phases can therefore be understood as a sequence of pre-sequences (Schegloff, 2007) that preface the directive to start the roleplay.

The phase structure of the roleplay instruction is remarkably stable in the Japanese OPI corpus and largely matches the instruction sequences documented by Okada (2010) and Ross (2017). The most salient difference is the requirement that the examinee read the roleplay prompt aloud in English. As we will show below, this feature of the instruction protocol becomes a fragile moment in all four cases in this study. In the following sections we will examine how the phase structure of the instruction is locally achieved and adapted in cooperation by examiner and examinees, and the various ways in which the prompt cards figure as essential objects (Weilenmann & Lymer, 2014) in the transition to the roleplay. We call the examinees (EEs) Nicole (N), George (G), Alyssa (A) and Jacob (J).

5.2 Announcing the roleplay

During the closing of the interview phase, the examiner (ER) has selected a (candidate) prompt card from the displayed set and shown embodied orientation to the cards while making the selection. Once the instruction sequence begins, the cards become the primary focus of attention.

Excerpt 4.1 Roleplay announcement – Nicole

```
     ng:    ER---------------↑↑↑↑↑↑↑↑↑↑↑↑↑ER
     erg:   REC---------------------CARD---
                                     *FG. N8
8    ER:    .hh jaa  chotto ano: .hh *koko de
            then little  H            here  P
```

N8

```
     ng:    ER--------------CARD---
     erg:   CARD-------------------
     er:    +leans toward cards
     er:    +LHIF up---------------|
                            *FG. N9
9    ER:    +hitotsu +rooru*puree o
            one        role-play  O
```

N9

```
     ng:    CARD-----------------------
     erg:   CARD-----------------------
10   ER:    shitemoraitai  n desu [ne:¿
            want-you-to-do N CP      IP
            So, uhm, now I'd like you to do a role-play, ok?

     n:                          +nod
11   N:                          [+hai.
                                  yes
     Okay.
```

The announcement is designed with a near identical version of the standard formulation shown in Section 5.1 above. The pre-beginning (Schegloff, 1996) and turn-initial markers portend a departure of the upcoming activity from the direction of the prior talk (Heritage, 2013). Concurrent with the onset of the announcement proper (*koko de*), ER shifts her gaze to the prompt cards (FG N8) and subsequently leans towards the cards. By the time ER has produced the first component of the activity category *roorupuree*, Nicole has shifted her gaze to the prompt cards too so that the cards are now the attentional focus for both participants (Goodwin, 2018). Nicole registers the announcement with the affirmative marker *hai* 'okay', in this environment a signal of understanding and readiness to go along with the announced activity (Beach, 1993). Also note that Nicole produces the affirmation in transitional overlap, which indicates unproblematic understanding although the announcement comes rather suddenly. This suggests that Nicole recognizes that the cards are related to the announced activity and that the already established status of the cards as a joint attentional object makes that inference possible.[2]

Nicole's unproblematic alignment to the roleplay announcement is representative of the cases in the collection. Although the examiner's embodied orientation to the prompt cards prior to the announcement varies in detail, it is always present and guides the examinees' attention and expectations. All examinees produce a *hai* token without delay and thereby signal to the examiner their readiness to move forward in the instruction.

5.3 Directive to read the prompt card

The joint embodied orientation to the prompt cards and the examiner's verbal announcement prepare the examinees for the roleplay as the upcoming activity. The next phase of the instruction advises the examinees of the specific roleplay that the examiner has selected for them. In contrast to the examinees' uniform and unproblematic response to the roleplay announcement, the directive to read the prompt card aloud in English generates more diverse and problematic uptake, ranging from minimal (Excerpts 4.2 and 4.3) and non-minimal repairs (Excerpt 4.4) to major delays in the progression of the instruction (Excerpt 4.5).

In Excerpts 4.2 and 4.3 it is the examiner who locates the trouble source initially.

Excerpt 4.2 Directive to read the prompt card – Nicole

```
     ng:   CARD---------------ER-CARD
     erg:  CARD----------------------
     er:              +BH>card +BH move card
                      *FG. N12
12   ER:   de   ano: *+jaa (.) +kore o
            then H         then    this O
```

N12

```
     ng:   CARD-------------------
     n:                    +leans toward card
     erg:  CARD-------------------
     er:   +BH flip card to face N
     er:            +BH place card in front of N
     er:                  +RHIF>card
13   ER:   +chotto +(.) +ni- niho-
            little       Ja- Japa
```

```
     ng:   CARD-----------
     erg:  CARD-----------
           *FG. N14
14   ER:   *eego    de¿ (.)
            English P
            So, please read this in Ja- Japa- English,
```

N14

```
     erg:  CARD----------------
     ng:   CARD----------------
     n:          +nods
           *FG. N15
15   N:    *[+hai.
             yes
            Uh huh.
```

N15

```
     er:          +RH moves in a semicircle
16   ER:   [+koe    ni dashite
             voice P  put
```

```
     ng:   CARD-------ER----------CARD
     erg:  CARD-------------------N
     er:                  +BH fold together
                          *FG. N17
17   ER:   (.) chotto yonde *+kudasai.
            little read        please
            Please read it aloud.
```

N17

```
        erg:  N----------
        ng:   CARD-------
        n:    +BH move toward card
18      N:    +eego     de?
              English P
              In English?

        ng:   CARD-----
        n:    +BH lift card slightly
        erg:  CARD-----
19      ER:   +hai [hai.
              yes   yes
              Yes, yes.

20      N:         [(hai/uhm).
                    yes
              (Okay/Uhm).
```

Concurrently with formulating the directive, ER repositions the selected prompt card on the table so that the text becomes readable for Nicole. The transfer of the card begins as ER marks the start of the directive with the conjunction *jaa* 'so' (Line 12) and proceeds through successive actions (Lines 12–13), closely followed by Nicole's gaze. Although the verbal directive has not yet reached its substantive elements, Nicole shows her understanding of ER's multimodal action by bending her torso towards the card in a display of readiness to engage with the object (Line 13). Simultaneously with Nicole's bodily realignment, ER points her index finger on the card as she produces the first component of the directive. Together, the pointing gesture and the formulation of the language medium make the language of the text on the card salient for Nicole.

As she formulates the directive, ER starts with an incipient production of *nihongo* 'Japanese', which is immediately self-repaired to the more contextually appropriate *eego* 'English' (Lines 13–14). The repair is issued with a slightly rising intonation that invites and gets Nicole's acknowledgment (Line 15). Proceeding with the directive, ER says *koe ni dashite* 'aloud' while moving her right hand in a semicircle in front of her mouth (Line 16, FG N15). In this way the direction is delivered as a multimodal package of mutually enhancing iconic gesture and formulation. However, as shown in frame-grabs N14 and N15, ER and Nicole maintain their gaze on the card as the object of joint attention, and therefore Nicole may not register the gesture. While moving her hands to the card in preparation to read, Nicole seeks confirmation of her hearing by repeating *eego de?* 'In English?' (Line 18), which ER confirms (Line 19). In this case, the repair initiation might be related to ER's prior self-repair regarding the language in which to read. However, as the next excerpts will show, the language medium component of the directive generates understanding problems when no such prior trouble occurred. Following a third-turn response (Line 20), Nicole starts to read the prompt card (Excerpt 4.6), thus demonstrating (as opposed to only claiming) understanding of the directive.

Excerpt 4.2 also shows how the participants co-configure the stages in the directive sequence with different bodily orientations. While the directive is ongoing, ER and EE turn their torsos toward each other and their gaze at the prompt card in an 'ecological huddle' (Goffman, 1964: 64) that visibly establishes the card as a shared object of scrutiny (FGs N14 and N15). In contrast, when the directive turn reaches completion (Line 17), ER and Nicole reestablish mutual gaze and in this way signal readiness for the activity to progress after the solitary task. Furthermore, ER retracts her torso from the shared space and clasps her hands closely in front of her chest (FG N17), a bodily arrangement that conveys the projected turnover of primary responsibility for action to Nicole.

In the remaining cases, the directive turn and concurrent transfer of the prompt card progress without delay. Troubles surface *after* both actions have been completed. Excerpt 4.3 illustrates a minimal delay.

Excerpt 4.3 Directive to read the prompt card – Alyssa

```
     er:   +RH picks up card        +places card
     er:                            +RHIF>card
     a:                  +moves forward
     a:                            +BH>table
                                      *FG. A26
26   ER:   +ano: ja  +kore +o (.) *+eego de (.)
            H    then  this O       English P
```

A26

```
     ag:   ER-------------------------CARD
     erg:  A-------------------         A--
     er:     +LH moves forward in a semicircle
             *FG. A27
27   ER:   *+koe   ni dashite (.) yonde kudasai.
            voice P  put          read  please
           Please read this aloud in English.
```

A27

```
     erg:  A-----
     ag:   CARD--
     a:      torso slightly bends forward
             *FG. A28
28         *(0.6)
```

```
     ag:   CARD-------
     erg:  A----------
29   ER:   eego    de¿
           English P
           In English.
```

A28

```
     erg:  A---
     ag:   CARD
     a:    slight nod
30         (.)
```

```
     erg:        +down
31   A:    after +finishing a good meal …
```

Upon completion of the directive, Alyssa inspects the text on the card in silence (Line 28). Her action could be seen as a preparation to comply with the directive, but ER's repetition of *eego de¿* 'In English' (Line 29) orients to the absence of a verbal response as signaling trouble and proactively locates the language medium component of the directive as the candidate problem. Alyssa claims understanding with a slight nod (Line 30) before she begins to read the card as instructed.

In Excerpts 4.2 and 4.3, the only trouble source in the directive is the language medium component. Excerpts 4.4 and 4.5 reveal both components of the directive – reading in English and reading aloud – as trouble-prone.

Excerpt 4.4 Directive to read the prompt card – George

```
        gg:   CARD-------------------------
        g:                +leans forward slightly
        erg:  CARD-------------------------
        er:   +flips card to face G
        er:                +places card in front of G
        er:                +RHIF>card
                           *FG. G14
14      ER:   +kore o (.) *+eego   de (.)
               this O       English P
```

G14

```
        gg:   CARD-------------------------
        g:    +LH>card
        erg:  CARD-------G-----------
        er:   +RHIF traces a sentence on card
        er:            +LHIF>throat
                       *FG. G15
15      ER:   +koe   ni *+dashite¿ (.)
               voice P    put
```

G15

```
        gg:   CARD---------------
        erg:  G-----------------
        er:   +withdraws BH
16      ER:   +yonde kuremasen ka?
               read  give-NG   Q
              Would you please read this (.) aloud (.) in English?
```

```
        erg:  G--------
        gg:   CARD-----
        g:    +leans toward card
17            +(0.7)
```

```
        erg:  G--
        gg:   CARD
              *FG. G18
18      G:    *e?
              huh
              Huh?
```

G18

```
        erg:  CARD
        gg:   IR--
19            (.)
```

```
        erg:     CARD-------G-----
        er:   +RH moves forward
        gg:      ER--------CARD--
              *FG. G20
20      ER:   *+koe   ni dashite,
               voice P  put
              Aloud.
```

G20

```
        erg:  G----
        gg:   CARD-
21            (1.3)
```

```
        erg:   G----------------
        gg:    CARD-----ER------
                         *FG. G22
22      G:     read in *English?

        gg:    ER--------CARD
        erg:   _____G---
        er:    +nodding
23      ER:    +>hai hai. En-<
                 yes  yes
               Yes, in En-( Eng)

        erg:   G---
        gg:    CARD
24      G:     °a°
                oh
               Oh.

        gg:    CARD-----------
        erg:   G--------------
25      ER:    °hai. eego    de.°
                 yes  English P
               Yes, in English (Jpn).

        erg:      +down
26      G:     af+ter finishing a good meal …
```

G22

Here, ER's directive to read the card aloud in English (Lines 13–16) generates a non-minimal repair sequence (Kendrick, 2015) that exposes the vulnerability of both components. In response to the transfer of the prompt card, George has established the text on the card as an object of scrutiny by gazing at it (Line 14, FG G17) and resting his left hand on its bottom edge while ER is tracing a line in the text with her right index finger (Line 15, FG G18). George's visible multisensorial engagement with the card appears to become interactionally consequential. Following a gap of silence during which George continues to gaze at the card, he initiates repair with an open-class practice (Drew, 1997; Kendrick, 2015) *e?* 'huh?' that leaves the trouble source unspecified (Line 18). Perhaps in orientation to George's scrutiny of the text on the card, ER locates the problem in the stipulation to read *aloud* by repeating *koe ni dashite* while producing a version of the iconic gesture (FG G20, Line 20) that she routinely employs as a concurrent embodied elaboration. ER's attribution of the trouble might suggest that she takes George's intense inspection of the card to indicate that he registers the language in which the text is written. However, another gap of silence ensues (Line 21), suggesting that the modality of reading was not the trouble source. In a subsequent round of repair, George upgrades the repair initiation with a candidate understanding *read in English?* (Line 22) that specifies the problem (see Svennevig, 2008, on 'weaker' and 'stronger' other-repair initiators). ER responds affirmatively (Line 23) and confirms that George is to read the text in English. After a minimal post-completion sequence, mutual understanding has been achieved as George begins to read the text aloud.

Although the non-minimal repair sequence above addresses both components of the directive, the problematic understandings are resolved swiftly and thus do not run afoul of the time constraints of the OPI (Ross, 2017). In contrast, Excerpt 4.5 presents a case in which the directive generates multiple repair sequences that substantially delay the progression of the instruction.

Excerpt 4.5a Directive to read the prompt card – Jacob

J21

```
     jg:   CARDS-------------------
     j:               +BH move toward card
     j:                         +RH2Fs>card
     erg:  CARDS-------------------
     er:   +LH places card on table
     er:               +RHIF>card
                     *FG. J21
21   ER:   +kore o *+(.) +eego   +de
            this O          English  P
```

```
     jg:   CARDS-------------------
     j:             +BH pull card slightly
     erg:  CARDS-------------------
     er:   +withdraws BH, reseats herself
22   ER:   +(.) +koe   ni dashite:
                 voice P  put
```

```
     jg:   CARDS-------------
     erg:  CARDS-----------J-
     er:   +folds arms
23   ER:   +yonde kuremasen ka.
            read   give-NG   Q
            would you please read this aloud in English?
```

```
     erg:  J----
     jg:   CARD-
     j:    RH lifts card slightly
24         (0.9)
```

```
     jg:   CARD------------
     j:    BH holding card
     erg:  J---------------
     er:   LH moves in a circular motion
25   ER:   koe   ni dashite.
            voice P  put
            Aloud.
```

```
     erg:  J----
     jg:   CARD-
26         (1.5)
```

J27

```
     jg:   CARD------------ER-
     erg:  J-----------------
     er:             +LH out toward J, smiling
                   *FG. J27
27   ER:   ano (.) *+hanashite.
            H           speak
            Please speak.
```

```
     erg:  J--CARD
     jg:   ER-CARD
28         (0.5)
```

```
     erg:  CARD-J-
     er:   +RHIF points at card
     jg:   CARD-
     j:    +withdraws LH, RH still holding card
29   J:    +a!
            oh
            Oh.
```

```
     jg:   CARD---------------
     erg:  J------------------
     er:             +nods slightly, smiling
30   ER:   (de)   yo+nde. hai.
            (and) read    yes
            (And) please read it. Uh huh.
```

During the directive and after its completion, Jacob successively intensifies his embodied scrutiny of the prompt card (FG J21; Line 22). ER takes his silent lifting of the card (Line 24) as signaling trouble. This time she identifies the problem as relating to the direction to read aloud and repeats *koe ni dashite* (Line 25) together with the 'speaking' gesture (FG J25). However, with no response forthcoming (Line 26), she reformulates the directive as *hanashite* 'please speak' (Line 27) while making an inviting hand gesture, which temporarily draws Jacob's gaze to her (FG J27). After a gap of silence in which he resumes gazing at the card, Jacob claims with *a!* that he has gained a new understanding of the course of action (Heritage, 1984). In response, ER repeats the final element of the directive (*yonde* 'read', Line 30) while nodding and smiling, and the added affirmation with *hai* 'uhu huh' treats the trouble as resolved. This, however, is not the case, as shown below.

Excerpt 4.5b Directive to read the prompt card – Jacob

```
      erg:   J--------CARD----
      jg:    CARD---------IR-
      j:        +BH>card
31    J:     a! +ima   kara uh:
             oh  now   from  H
             Oh from now...


      jg:    IR-----------------------------
      erg:   CARD---------------------------
      er:    +nods slightly
      er:              +LH moves toward card
32    ER:    +eego    [+de
             English   P
             In English


      j:              +RH quickly moves up and down
      er:                      +LHIF points at card
33    J:     [+kangaenai+de: (a- soo)
             think-NG        oh  so
             without thinking, (I see).


      jg:    IR--------CARD----------------
      erg:   CARD-------------------J-------
      er:                    +withdraws LH
34    ER:    hai hai tada (.) +kore o yonde.
             yes yes just      this O read
             Yes, please just read this.


      erg:   J---------
      er:    +BH together at chest
      jg:    CARD------
      j:     +withdraws LH, RH still holding card
      j:     +slightly leans more toward card
35    J:     +aa aa aa.
             Oh oh oh
             Oh, oh, oh


      jg:    CARD--
      erg:   J-----
36    ER:    °hai.°
              yes
             Uh huh.


      erg:   J-------------------------------------
      jg:    CARD---------IR---------------------
37    J:     ano: (1.0) a go- (.) cho- cho- cho-
             H          H        li-  li-  li-
```

```
        erg:    J-----------------------------------
        jg:     IR----------------------------------
38      J:      [chotto wakarimasen.
                 little understand-NG
                I don't understand.


        er:     +RH moves forward in a semicircle
39      ER:     [+$ko- (.) k(h)oe  ni dashite¿$
                               voice  P  put
                Aloud?


        erg:    J---
        jg:     IR--
40      J:      a¿
                huh
                Huh?


        jg:     IR------CARD------------------------
        erg:    J--------------------------CARD----
        er:     +RH>chest       +RH out       +RHIF>card
41      ER:     +$koe    ni  (.) +dashit(hh)e$ +.hh (.)
                 voice  P        put
                Aloud


        jg:     CARD----------------
        er:     CARD----------------
        er:                    +RHIF traces sentence on card
42      ER:     kore o  (.) +sonomama
                 this O       as-it-is
                as it says.


        erg:    J---------------
        jg:     CARD—IR----------
        j:      +slight jump
43      J:      +aa! [eego    de?
                 oh   English P
                Oh! In English?


44      ER:          [ (yuu)
                       say
                (Say)


        jg:     ER-------------
        erg:    J--------------
        er:     +nods, smiling
        er:            +RH strokes down, palm facing down
45      ER:     +soo +eego    de.
                 so   English P
                Yes in English,


        erg:    J------
        jg:     CARD---
        j:      +BH>card
46      J:      +aa(i)=
                 oh
                Oh


        jg:     CARD----------
        erg:    J-------------
        er:     +BH together at chest
        er:     +nod
47      ER:     =+yonde kudasai.
                 read  please
                please read it.
```

Instead of the projected compliance, Jacob continues to wrestle with grasping the directive. The repair trajectory evolves through successive other-initiations of repair ('multiples', Schegloff, 2000) that include displays (Lines 31, 33) and claims of changed understanding (Line 35) before

Jacob reluctantly admits non-understanding (Lines 37–38). In the contingent unfolding of the participants' struggle to achieve understanding, this moment becomes a turning point. Concurrently with Jacob's claim of non-understanding, ER repeats *koe ni dashite¿* 'aloud' together with the iconic 'speaking' gesture (Line 39). Perhaps due to the overlap, Jacob responds with an open-class repair initiator *a¿* 'huh?' (Line 40) that appears to prompt ER to repeat a version of the previous multimodal ensemble (Line 41). This time she expands the repair with another TCU in which she recycles the beginning of the standard directive *kore o* 'this' and adds a specifying *sonomama* 'as is' (Line 42), concurrently tracing the text lines on the card with her finger while Jacob is watching. Through the repackaging of the repair, ER treats the whole task directive (rather than the two separate components) as repairable. In response, Jacob produces a multimodal claim of changed understanding (a slight jump while producing an emphatic *aa!* 'oh!'), followed by a candidate understanding *eego de?* 'In English?' (Line 43) that ER confirms with a *so* 'yes' marked repetition (Line 45). After a post-completion in which ER repeats the final element of the directive *yonde kudasai* 'please read' (Line 47), Jacob proceeds to read the text as instructed and so finally delivers the outstanding second pair part to the directive.

With as many as five other-initiations of repair that address the same trouble source turn (Schegloff, 2000), Jacob's persistent understanding difficulties in Excerpt 4.5 significantly delay the progression of the instruction and thus work against the time constraints of the OPI. While the excerpt is an outlier in this regard, it has important commonalities with the instruction delivery throughout the collection. For one, the demanded public departure from Japanese as the normative language of the OPI is a recurrent trouble source.[3] For another, in the concurrent delivery of the directive and transfer of the prompt card, the participants temporarily reorganize their participation framework from talk-centered to an object-focused 'contextual configuration' (Goodwin, 2018: 170) in which talk, gaze, gesture and the prompt card as a material and textual object are mutually elaborative. In each of Excerpts 4.2 to 4.5, the frame-grabs show how ER and EE reconfigure their bodily orientation as an 'ecological huddle' (Goffman, 1964), an embodied arrangement that allows them to establish the prompt card as an object of joint attention and together generate the ecological conditions for EE to comply with the directive.

5.4 Readiness check, role identification and initiation of roleplay

After the participants have achieved mutual understanding of the directive to read the prompt card, EE proceeds to read the prompt. Excerpt 4.6 shows how the ordered activities from reading the prompt to starting the roleplay advance unproblematically. In Excerpt 4.7, several of EE's responses are delayed as he appears to be working out the prompt. However actual problems do not surface, and EE successfully shifts into the roleplay as directed. Excerpt 4.8 presents a contrast case. Here EE claims not to understand what the prompt directs her to do. As a remedy she receives a new prompt that proves accessible for her.

Excerpt 4.6 *Prompt reading through roleplay initiation – Nicole*

```
     erg:  N----_____
     ng:   CARD---------------------
                 *FG. N21
21   N:    you  *recently purchased …
           ((lines 22-26 omitted))
```

N21

```
     erg:  N-RIGHT-N-----
     ng:   CARD----------
27         a full  refund.

28         (.)

     ng:   CARD---------
     erg:  N------------
29   ER:   ii    desu ka?
           good CP   Q
           Is it okay?
```

```
     erg:  N---------------____
     ng:   CARD---------------
                   *FG. N30
30   N:    *hai. daijoobu  desu.
           yes     all-right CP
           Yes. It's fine.
```

N30

```
     ng:   CARD--------------------
     erg:                  N------
     er:        +BH>chest
                  *FG. N31
31   ER:   jaa *+atashi: wa omise no
           then  I         TP store LK
```

N31

```
     ng:   ER------------CARD
     erg:  N--------------__
     er:                +RH wave toward self
32   ER:   hito   na   no[+de,
           person CP   because
           So, I'm the shop keeper, so
```

```
     n:                    +nod
                         *FG. N33
33   N:                  *[+hai.
                           yes
           Uh huh.
```

N33

```
     ng:   CARD--------------------
     erg:  ___N--------------------
34   ER:   chotto hanashite kudasai.
           little  talk       please
           Please talk to me.
```

```
     ng:   CARD-----
     erg:  N-------
     er:   +BH>table
     er:   +nods
           *FG. N35
35   ER:   *+°hai.°
              yes
           Yeah.
```

N35

```
     erg:  N-----
     ng:   CARD--
36         (1.5)
```

```
     erg:   N------------        N--
     ng:    CARD---------ER------
     n:     +BH move to lap
     n:               +torso swings slightly forward
                         *FG. N37
37   N:     +˚(ja) *+haitte˚ (.)
              then    enter
             So, I enter (the store),
```

N37

```
     erg:          N----------
     ng:    ER---------
                  *FG. N38
38   N:     a, *suimasen.
            oh  excuse-me
            Oh, excuse me.
```

N38

```
     ng:    ER—CARD--------
     erg:          N--------------
39   ER:    hai irasshaimase.=
            Yes welcome
            Yes. Welcome.
```

```
     erg:   N----------
     ng:    ER---CARD--
40   N      =hai. ano::
            yes   uhm
            Yes. Uhm...
```

As Nicole begins to read the prompt, ER shifts her gaze downwards (FG N21) while maintaining her embodied withdrawal to the periphery of the shared space (Excerpt 4.2, FG N17). With these practices, ER can be seen to treat Nicole's reading aloud as a solitary activity. In contrast, when the reading approaches conclusion (Line 27), ER turns her gaze to Nicole[4] as a practice of resuming the joint activity. In response to ER's routine readiness check with *ii desu ka?* 'okay?' (Line 29), Nicole confirms promptly with two practices (*hai. daijoobu desu.* 'okay. I'm good.') that convey a sense of confidence about moving forward. As a next step in the instruction, ER informs Nicole of the role that she will take in the roleplay (Lines 31–32), elaborated by self-directed gestures (FGs N31 and N32), and directs Nicole to take the initiating turn (Line 34), both of which get aligning minimal responses from Nicole (Lines 33 and 35). After a 1.5-second gap during which Nicole appears to further scrutinize the prompt (Line 36), she initiates the roleplay by describing her character's entry to the imagined space (Line 37) before changing footing to perform the role of the customer (Line 38).

The following cases show that each of the steps towards the start of the roleplay is vulnerable to interactional trouble that can delay the progress of the activity. In Excerpt 4.7 the passage evolves with substantial delay but without manifest trouble.

Excerpt 4.7 Readiness check through roleplay initiation – George

```
     gg:    CARD---------
     g:     LHIF remains on card
     erg:   G-----------
              *FG. G33
33   ER:    *ii   des   ka?
            good  CP    Q
            Is it okay?
```

G33

```
       erg:  CARD---------
       gg:   CARD---------
       g:      leans over card
       g:      LH traces sentences on card
             *FG. G34
34           *(6.4)
```

G34

```
       erg:  CARD---
       gg:   CARD---ER
35     G:    °Okay°
```

```
       gg:      ER--------------------
       erg:     G----_____
       er:                    +RH>chest
                           *FG. G36
36     ER:   +hai! [(.) jaa **atashi
              yes        then   I
```

```
37     G:         [(°alright°)
```

G36

```
       gg:      ER--------------------
       erg:     _____G---------------
       er:                    +RH wave toward self
38     ER:   wei(.)toresu des +ne?
              waitress    CP   IP
              Okay, so, I am the waitress.
```

```
       erg:     _____G--------
       gg:      ER--------------------CARD---
       g:        +nods
             *FG. G39
39     G:    *[+(°hai.°)
                  yes
              Uh huh.
```

G39

```
       er:      +flips RH inwards twice
40     ER:   [+jaa   atashi ni hanashikakete
              then me      P  talk-to
```

```
       gg:   CARD---
       erg:  G------
41     ER:   kudasai.
              please
              So, please talk to me.
```

```
       erg:  CARD---
       gg:   G---___
       g:      leans toward card
42           (0.5)
```

```
       erg:     _____G's LH-G--
       er:                    nod
       gg:   CARD-----------------
       g:                +LH>card
                        *FG. G43
43     G:    a- (.) ano: *+(1.8)
                      H
```

G43

```
       erg:  G--------------------
       gg:   CARD-----------------
       g:      LH on card-----------
44     G:    a- (.) ano: sumimasen.
                      H      excuse-me
              Uh um excuse me.
```

```
       erg:  G---
       er:      +nods
       gg:   ER—
       g:      LH on card
             *FG. G45
45     ER:   *+hai.
                  yes
              Yes.
```

G45

```
        erg:   G-----CARD-----
        gg:    CARD----------
        g:     LH on card
46      G:     eeto:, (.) uh::
               uhm
               Uhm, uh::
```

While reading the prompt aloud, George has been tracing the text lines with his left index finger. His hand and gaze remain on the card (FG G33) when ER issues the readiness check (Line 33). Instead of the projected verbal response, George leans over the card (FG G34) and traces the text lines again during an extended silence of 6.4 seconds (Line 34) before he delivers the not-yet-provided confirmation (Line 35). In the local sequential environment, George's ostensible re-reading suggests that he may be verifying his understanding of the text in order to respond to the readiness check. Positionally and functionally, his silent reading bears similarity to a pre-second insert expansion[5] (Schegloff, 2007: 106), in that the reading serves to 'establish the resources necessary to implement the second pair part which is pending', and puts the ongoing action on hold. ER's refraining from pursuing a response during George's silent reading offers emic support for this analysis. It is after first saying *okay* that George shifts his gaze to ER and in this way addresses ER as recipient of his confirmation retrospectively. A final difference from the readiness check sequence with Nicole (Excerpt 4.6) is that ER post-completes the sequence with a sequence-closing *hai!* (Line 36) before moving on to announce the role that she will be taking (Lines 36–38), which may be recognizing the readiness claim as the result of the visible and considerable effort George put towards understanding the task.

Following the role informing sequence (Lines 36–39), George complies with ER's directive to take the first turn in the roleplay (Lines 40–41) after a brief delay in which he again examines the prompt (Line 42). Even after he begins to speak as a character in the roleplay (Line 43), George only briefly shifts his gaze to ER when she responds to his summons (Line 45), and his left hand remains on the card. In this way, George treats the prompt card as a resource that he literally keeps at hand to support his roleplay performance (FG G45).

In contrast to Excerpts 4.6 and 4.7, Excerpt 4.8 shows a case in which the prompt reading fails to generate the projected uptake. In the readiness check sequence, the participants display a visible mismatch of stance that portends the failure of the selected roleplay. The analysis will show how the participants get to the point where the selected roleplay is abandoned and how they jointly manage to launch an alternative roleplay.

Excerpt 4.8.1 Alyssa

```
        ag:    CARD----------
        erg:   _____A-------
        er:    +smiling
38      ER:    +ii    des  ka?
               good  CP   Q
               Is it okay?
```

```
      erg:  A---
      ag:   CARD
39          (.)

      erg:  A------
      ag:   CARD---
            *FG. A40
40    A:    *˚hai.˚
            yes
            Yes.
```

A40

```
      erg:  A----------
      ag:   CARD------
      a:              +slightly tilts torso back
                      +puzzled facial expression
41          (0.7) +(.)

      ag:   CARD---------
      a:    +smiling
      erg:  A-----------
            *FG. A42
42    A:    *+hhehheh hheh
```

A42

While ER gazes at Alyssa with a smile that reinforces the expectancy of confirmation (Line 38), Alyssa gazes at the card with a facial expression that treats the text she just read aloud as perplexing. Although her *hai* 'okay' (Line 40) implements a preferred type-conforming response (Raymond, 2003), the low volume together with her embodied stance adumbrate a dispreferred action. Her display of confusion (Drew, 2005) at the roleplay instruction is upgraded with a slight backwards tilt of her torso (Line 41), and with smiling and laughing (Line 42, FG A42) while keeping her gaze trained at the card as the source of her trouble. Glenn and Holt (2013: 15) note that laughter regularly appears in interactional contexts that are 'delicate, tricky, dispreferred, or in some other way problematic', and the absence of reciprocating laughter by ER suggests that she treats Alyssa's displayed stance as such.

Excerpt 4.8.2 Alyssa

```
      erg:  A------------------CARD
      ag:   CARD-----------------
43    A:    ˚(xx) wa doo sureba hheh˚
                  TP how do-if
            What should I do hheh

      ag:   CARD-ER
      erg:  CARD---
      er:   +leans forward
44    ER:   +˚hheh˚

      ag:   CARD----------
      a:              +tilts head slightly
      erg:  CARD-------A---
                      *FG. A45
45          (.) +(.) *(0.7)
```

A45

```
     erg:   A---OTHER CARDS-------A---------
     ag:    CARD--↑↑↑↑CARD------------------
            *FG. A46
46   A:     n: *(1.7) watashi doo sureb(hh)a
            H         I       how  do-if

     erg:   A----------OTHER CARDS---------
     ag:    CARD--------------------------
47   A:     ii [no (kana)
            good N   IP
            (I wonder) what I should do.
```

A46

The ensemble of embodied and vocal actions in Lines 40–41 prefigures Alyssa's (grammatically incomplete) formulation of her predicament with *doo sureba* 'what should I do' (Line 43) which cancels her earlier confirmation. The turn formulates an unspecified difficulty with implementing the roleplay instruction[6] and is repeated, after a substantial 1.7-second intra-turn pause, in a grammatically more complete version (Lines 46–47) when the first saying does not generate a substantive response from ER. During the ongoing trouble formulation, Alyssa continues her vocal and bodily displays of stance towards her own action (the turn-final, Line 43, and interpolated laugh particles, Line 46, marking dispreference) and towards the text on the card as the problem source (the head tilt while gazing at the card, Line 45, FG A45).

Meanwhile, ER begins to enact a solution to Alyssa's trouble. On the one hand, her only vocal response to Alyssa's first trouble formulation is a laugh particle reused from Alyssa's preceding turn (*hheh*, Line 44), which registers Alyssa's problem display but does not offer assistance. On the other hand, ER's gaze and bodily actions show that she is working towards a remedy. Starting with a gaze shift from Alyssa to the active prompt card in response to Alyssa's ongoing problem formulation (Line 43), ER next leans forward in preparation for turning her head towards the set of prompt cards on her right as a site of attention and visually selects one of the cards (card2 in Excerpt 4.8.2) by gaze (Lines 44–47, FG A46). By the time Alyssa repeats her problem formulation (Lines 46–47), she and ER have established diverging orientations to the prompt cards in front of them, with Alyssa continuing to gaze at the active card while ER visually engages an inactive card. Insofar as they orient to the cards as media for the roleplay instructions, the participants are looking for exits from the impasse in different places – Alyssa in the currently active roleplay prompt, ER in an alternative.

Excerpt 4.8.3 Alyssa

```
     er:          +RH moves toward cards
48   ER:          [+chotto muri      des ka?
                   little impossible CP  Q
            Can't you do it?

     erg:   A---------
     er:    +RH>new card
     ag:    CARD------
            *FG. A49
49   A:     *+hheh hheh
```

A49

```
     ag:    CARD--------------
     erg:   A----------------
     er:    +picks up new card
50   ER:    +iya    des ka.
            dislike CP  Q
            You don't like it.


     erg:   A-----CARD------A-------
     er:    +holding new card
     ag:      ER----_____
     a:                       +LH>hair
               *FG. A51
51   ER:    +jaa *hoka no ni +shite mo
            then    other N  P   do    also


     ag:           _____
     erg:   A-------------
     er:                  +moves card slightly forward
52   ER:    ii    des +kedo.
            good CP   but
            We can do something else if you like.


     erg:   A---------
     ag:            ER--
            *FG. A53
53          *(0.6) (.)


     erg:    A-------------CARD-------
     er:     +BH extend to present card
     ag:     ER------CARD------------
            *FG. A54
54   A:     *+h(h)ai. hheh [sumimasen.
             yes              sorry
            Okay. Sorry.
```

A51

A53

A54

With ER's vocal response to Alyssa's problem formulation, a second round of roleplay initiation becomes their shared interactional concern. ER's *chotto muri desu ka?* 'you can't do it?' (Line 48) offers up her understanding of Alyssa's problem formulation for confirmation, which Alyssa's laughter response can be heard to provide (Line 49). ER's next turn registers Alyssa's response with an epistemically upgraded attribution *iya desu ka*. 'you don't like it.' (Line 50), which prefaces ER's proposal for a solution to the current stalemate with *jaa hoka no ni shite mo ii desu kedo*. 'Then we can do something else if you like.' (Lines 51–52). The proposal sequence is completed as Alyssa accedes to the proposal (*h(h)ai. hheh sumimasen*. 'Okay. Sorry.', Line 54), orienting to the announced course of action as an undesirable solution with vocal and embodied stance displays (the laughter tokens and grooming action, FGs A53 and A54) and assuming fault for it. By proposing and acceding to an alternative roleplay prompt, ER and Alyssa collaboratively treat the original roleplay instruction as failed.

Concurrently with the talk, ER advances the selection of card2 and transforms it into an actionable resource for Alyssa. From the start of the confirmation sequence, ER moves forward from locating card2 by gaze to selecting it manually[7] and making the text visually accessible for Alyssa to read.[8] What is particularly noteworthy in this pivotal phase of the (re)launching of the roleplay activity is that ER's manual selection and transfer of card2 anticipate the outcomes of the confirmation and proposal sequences. In other words, before the participants reach agreement that the original roleplay has officially failed, ER's visible orientation to accelerating the start of an alternative roleplay foregrounds her deontic authority in the institutional setting and her responsibility for managing the OPI within the available time frame.

Excerpt 4.8.4 Alyssa

```
55     ER:                        [jaa  chotto
                                   then  little

       ag:   CARD------------------
       erg:  CARD------------------
       er:   BH place card in front of A
                      *FG. A56
56     ER:   kocchi wa *doo des ka.
             this    TP  how CP  Q
             So, how about this one?

       ag:   CARD--
       erg:  CARD--
       er:   +BH withdraw from card
             *FG. A57
57     ER:   *+hai.=
               yes
             Okay.

       erg:  CARD----
       ag:   CARD----
58     A:    =hai. .hh
               yes
             Okay.

59     A:    ((reads text on card aloud))
```

A56

A57

In the final step of establishing the card in transfer as the operative roleplay prompt, ER places card2 on top of the card in front of Alyssa (FG A56) while formulating the alternative simultaneously (*jaa chotto kocchi wa doo desu ka* 'so how about this one', Lines 55–56). With the transfer completed, the original card is hidden from sight and functionally erased as an actionable resource, while the re-placing card2 has become the participants' shared object of scrutiny. As card2 is now located in Alyssa's space of action, ER withdraws her hands (FG A57) while issuing *hai* 'go ahead' (Line 57), and with the ensemble of embodied and vocal actions directs Alyssa to perform the next action due. Alyssa's reciprocating *hai*, followed by an inbreath (Line 58), shows that she understands ER's multimodal action as a directive for her to read the text on card2 aloud, which she begins in her next turn (Line 59).

In Excerpt 4.8.5 the new roleplay is collaboratively initiated.

Excerpt 4.8.5 Alyssa

```
       (lines 59-66 Alyssa reads text on card aloud, omitted)

       erg:  A------------------------
       er:            +smile
       ag:   CARD--------------------
       a:    smiling
67     A:    °aa: +chotto muzukashiku
             oh    little difficult
```

```
        erg:  A---------
        ag:   CARD------
68      A:    nacchatta.˚
              became
              Oh, it got hard.

        erg:   A---------_____
        ag:    CARD--------------
        a:        +sit back
              *FG. A69
69      A:    *[+hhuhhuh huh
```

A69

```
        er:                 +lean forward
70      ER:   [hhuh hhuh +hhuh hhuh

        erg:  _____A----
        ag:   CARD--------
71      A:    ˚okay˚

        erg:  A---
        ag:   CARD
72            (.)

        ag:   ER-----
        erg:  A------
73      IR    (˚hai.˚)
              yes
              (Go ahead.)

        ag:   ER-
        erg:  A--
74            (.)

        erg:  A--------------___
        ag:    ER---------------
              *FG. A75
75      A:    *moshi$moshi¿$ hhuh=
                hello
              Hello.
```

A75

```
        ag:   ER---------------card2-
        erg:  _____LEFT SIDE DOWN--
        er:          +RH>ear ("phone" gesture)
                *FG. (A76)
76      ER:   =a (.) *+hai moshimoshi.
              oh        yes hello
              Oh, yes  hello.
```

A76

```
        ag:   card2--------------
        erg:  LEFT SIDE DOWN------
77      ER:   tanaka byooin   des.
              Tanaka hospital CP
              This is Tanaka Hospital.
```

Instead of ER's readiness check as the next action after the prompt reading, Alyssa takes the first turn with an assessment that conveys a markedly different stance towards the second prompt than towards the first. The assessment *aa: chotto muzukashiku nacchatta.* 'oh, it got hard.' (Lines 67–68) is said with a smile, followed by the participants' joint laughter while they are smiling at each other (Lines 69–70, FG A69). Notably, it is Alyssa who signals the end of the humorous assessment sequence and initiates the transition to the roleplay (Line 71), which gets ER's ratification (Line 72). In her next turn Alyssa begins the roleplay

(Line 75) by speaking in character, as does ER in response (Lines 76–77). The shift of the participation framework has been jointly accomplished, and the roleplay proceeds.

Excerpt 4.8.5 shows a striking switch in discourse identities between the participants. In contrast to the phase prior to the reading of card2, Alyssa initiates all three sequences while ER provides aligning responses. By taking charge of getting the roleplay off the ground, Alyssa can be seen to orient to her moral obligation to rectify the delay in the progression of the OPI that her problems in understanding the first prompt generated and to reestablish herself as a competent and responsible examinee.

The analysis of Excerpt 4.8 reveals the methodic practices by which the participants arrive at performing the second roleplay. These methods constitute the second launch as one that not only succeeds the first tempo-rally but is specifically configured *as* a second. The organization of the second launch observably builds on the first. It does so by transforming the standard phase structure of the roleplay instruction (Section 5.1 and Excerpts 4.1–4.7) to fit the local interactional contingencies. The game changing moment, quite literally, is the disconfirmation of the readiness check (Excerpt 4.8.2) and subsequent abandonment of the first roleplay (Excerpt 4.8.3). Here, the multimodal proposal sequence (Lines 51–54) works in a sequentially equivalent way to the roleplay announcement (Excerpt 4.1), in that both project a roleplay as the next activity. In Excerpt 4.8.3, the proposal to conduct an alternative roleplay also implies that the abandoned activity is a specific roleplay, not the entire activity category.

As Excerpts 4.8.4 and 4.8.5 show, the activity phases following the announcement up to the start of the roleplay in the standard phase struc-ture are substantially condensed the second time around. Once card2 has been established as the operative prompt and the written instruction on it is within Alyssa's focal vision (Line 56), ER's multimodal go-ahead (Line 57) suffices for Alyssa to mobilize her institutional knowledge of the roleplay initiation protocol and proceed according to the instruction she received the first time (Excerpt 4.3). Likewise, following Alyssa's reading of the prompt on card2, ER dispenses with the sequence of actions that routinely segues into the start of the roleplay, i.e. checking EE's readiness, informing EE of the role ER will take and directing EE to take the first turn in the roleplay (Section 5.1 and Excerpts 4.6 and 4.7). Instead, as our analysis of Excerpt 4.8.5 points out, Alyssa manages the run-up to and start of the roleplay with a sequence of initiating actions. Her first turn in the activity frame of the roleplay, directed at ER as the addressed recipient by gaze (Line 75, Fig. A75), also demonstrates Alyssa's understanding of the instruction on card2 and of the roles assigned to herself and to ER. ER's in-character response affirms Alyssa's under-standing (Lines 76–77, FG A76) and in this way treats the second roleplay as successfully launched.

6 Discussion

As noted earlier in this chapter, the instruction that transitions the OPI interaction from the interview-structured portion to the roleplay is normatively organized as an examiner-led sequence of activity phases (Section 5.1). In each of the cases we examined, the examiner's initiating actions, their order and their formulation are remarkably similar. ER's conduct is thus strongly oriented to standardization as a design feature of the OPI and by implication to the reliability of the OPI as a test instrument (Ross, 2017; Seedhouse & Nakatsuhara, 2018). Previous research on roleplay instruction in OPIs has offered initial evidence that the roleplay prompt figures as a constitutive textual object, and its delivery appears to be standardized as well (Okada, 2010; Ross, 2017). At the same time, different OPI settings (face-to-face versus telephone, Ross, 2017) and protocols shape the modalities of prompt delivery. According to the protocol that guides the roleplay instruction in the Japanese OPI corpus, the examinee has to read the prompt card that the examiner has selected for them. This stipulation requires that the examiner transfer the selected card from its original locality in the examiner's action space (see initial spatial setup, Figure 4.1) to that of the examinee. As shown in the analysis, the transfer is closely coordinated with the verbal directive to read the card. It starts at pre-beginning of ER's directive turn and is completed before (Excerpt 4.2) or at the start of the substantive directive (Excerpts 4.3, 4.4, 4.5). While the audio-recorded data in the earlier studies postulated the card transfer on the basis of inferential evidence, the video-recordings document observably how the transfer progresses through successive manual actions and how it is coordinated with the verbal directive. Parallel to her verbal instruction delivery, the examiner appears to strive for a measure of standardization in her methods of accomplishing the transfer of the prompt card as well.

What is more, the examiner's orientation to standardization extends to her embodied actions beyond the indispensable transfer of the prompt card. As the examinee observably gives the text on the prompt card their full attention, the examiner consistently reconfigures her upper body to a posture of withdrawal to the periphery of the shared interactional space and so treats the prompt reading as the examinee's solitary activity. Furthermore, the examiner routinely mobilizes embodied resources to manage moments in the directive where intersubjectivity is at risk. ER's embodied actions as she formulates the directive seem to prospectively orient to these vulnerabilities, as she points to the card while saying *eego de* 'in English' (Excerpts 4.2, 4.3, 4.5), indexing both the text to be read and that the text is to be read in English as written, while also inviting the examinee to maintain their gaze upon the object as a constitutive resource for EE's projected action. Similarly, as ER issues the directive to read the text aloud, she concurrently produces a speaking gesture in the form of moving one hand forward from her mouth, often in a semi-circular fashion (Excerpts 4.2, 4.3, 4.4). It is of note that in the one case where she does not conduct this gesture (Excerpt 4.5), all of her subsequent reformulations include a variant of the gesture, suggesting that ER treats the multimodal version as an upgraded form of repair. Taken together, ER's routine use of similar talk-gesture ensembles when she issues the directive to read the prompt text aloud in English shows that she anticipates examinees' understanding problems and thus reveals her institutional experience as a professional OPI tester.

At a group level, ER's prospective orientations bear out in the examinees' uptake. At the same time, there is variation across the cases as to which of the two elements of the directive becomes a source of trouble, how severe the problem is and what methods of repair are used to resolve it. In Excerpts 4.2 and 4.3, the trouble source is the language medium. Nicole locates the problem with a candidate understanding that gets immediate confirmation, notably with no gap before or after the confirmation request. As noted, the repair initiation may well be primed by ER's earlier self-repair (Excerpt 4.2). In Alyssa's case (Excerpt 4.3), after a short 0.6-second pause in which Alyssa inspects the prompt text, ER preemptively locates the language medium as the trouble by repeating *eego de* 'in English', upon which Alyssa complies with the directive. There is no interactional evidence, however, that the language medium formulation was in fact problematic for Alyssa. In contrast, in Excerpts 4.4 and 4.5 both directive components prove challenging for EEs' understanding and prompt multiple repairs of the directive. In Excerpt 4.4, George launches the first of two repair sequences with an open other-initiation of repair that requires ER to guess where in her directive turn to locate the problem. Her repetition of the directive to read the card aloud with the routine formulation-gesture package does not reestablish understanding. Instead George issues a candidate understanding of the language medium, which gets ER's confirmation and clears the way for George to read the prompt. Finally, in Excerpt 4.5 both directive components require multiple reformulations by ER and other-initiations of repair with varying degrees of specificity by Jacob to restore intersubjectivity. In this case EE's persistent understanding difficulties significantly delay the progression of the instruction.

The other notable point of vulnerability in the transition to the role-play is the sequence following EEs' reading of the prompt card, routinely initiated by ER's readiness check with *ii desu ka?* 'okay?'. While the action is always understood, it generates a range of responses. Nicole unequivocally confirms her readiness (Excerpt 4.6). George re-reads the prompt silently, showing his continued effort to achieve understanding before giving the go ahead (Excerpt 4.7). Alyssa represents a marked contrast case (Excerpt 4.8). Her embodied and formulated display of confusion about the prompt text (Excerpts 4.8.1 and 4.8.2) sets a sequence of remedial action in motion during which ER and EE jointly abandon the active prompt and launch an alternative roleplay. The second launch visibly builds on the first in that it methodically reconfigures the standard phase structure of the roleplay instruction (Section 5.1 and Excerpts 4.1–4.7) to fit the local contingencies (Excerpts 4.8.3–4.8.5). In particular, when the alternative prompt card has been positioned as an actionable object for Alyssa, two conspicuous transformations occur (Excerpt 4.8.5): (1) the subsequent activity phases are significantly compressed; and (2) following the prompt reading, the discourse identities of ER and EE are reversed in that it is Alyssa who advances the start of the roleplay through successive sequence-initiating actions. Alyssa's taking the lead in moving the interaction forward at this point aligns with studies showing that in IRF-structured classroom interaction, students do take the initiative with actions from first position and in this way shape the course of the activity (Waring, 2011). Departures from the normative distribution of discourse identities in the OPI will be an important topic for future research, as such moments enable inferences about the examinee's proficiency.

While all of the examined cases show that the transition to the roleplay is accomplished as, and through, the participants' cooperative action in the sense of Goodwin (2007, 2018), the stark contrast between Alyssa's response to the first roleplay prompt and to the second also brings to the fore Alyssa's orientation to her *moral* responsibility as examinee in the OPI. The participants' *cooperative* and *instrumental* orientation to the activity runs through the presented data and is well documented in previous work on OPI interaction (Ross, 2017). Excerpt 4.8 also shows up how the task demands engender contextually changing *affective stances* beyond the merely *instrumental* (Goodwin, 2007).

7 Implications

The analysis has several implications for the protocol and practices of roleplay instruction in the OPI. The activity phases that evolved unproblematically (allowing for minor delays and self-repair that do not significantly compromise progressivity) reveal the examinees' familiarity with roleplay as an activity category and their expectation that a roleplay may be a task in the OPI. Such standard components include the roleplay announcement, the readiness check, the examiner informing the examinee of the role they will occupy as a character in the roleplay, and the examiner's directive that the examinee take the first turn in the roleplay. These components work effectively to organize the transition and the data bear no indication for changing them in the instructional protocol. In order to consider how the problem spots in the transition may be addressed, it is useful to borrow Potter and Hepburn's (2012) distinction of 'contingent and necessary challenges' in the organization of another institutional activity (the research interview). Here the contingent challenge is the stipulation in the directive that examinees read the role-play prompt aloud in English. In recent versions of the ACTFL protocol, the stipulation was modified so that the examiner now delivers the prompt verbally in the target language (with or without reading from the prompt card) and the examinee reads a written version (in the target language or their first language) silently.[9] To our knowledge, these changes were not made in response to published research, although our analysis lends them empirical support *ex post facto*.

The 'necessary', unavoidable potential problem spot is the examinee's response to the readiness check. The action format of the check (a positive polarity question) prefers a confirmation, but the very presence of the check in the standard protocol provides for the possibility that it may reveal problems in the examinee's understanding of the prompt which will have to be addressed for the instruction to move forward. As the confirming responses show (Excerpts 4.6 and 4.7), the checking sequence effectively clears the way for the immediate preliminaries to starting the roleplay. The substantive disconfirmation in Excerpt 4.8 rather highlights the critical role of the checking sequence since it not only exposes the examinee's difficulty in grasping the prompt but ultimately leads to a viable alternative.

Excerpt 4.8.3 specifically raises an important question about the sort of remedial action that the examiner takes to address the examinee's problems in understanding the active prompt. When does the examiner treat these problems as repairable and when do they abandon the prompt and select an alternative, as in the case of Alyssa? Either option is costly in light of the parties' joint interactional effort and time constraints. What are the interactional contingencies under which the examiner opts for either solution, and what outcomes do the different trajectories yield? Future research is needed.

Finally, the analysis has direct implications for the quality of data needed to study interaction in oral language assessment in co-present environments. In the large literature of interaction in language proficiency interviews and other forms of interactive oral language tests (Ross, 2017; Young & He, 1998), video-recorded data are virtually absent. As this study documents, video-recordings are indispensable to observe how the participants manage the interaction through their entire repertoire of semiotic resources, including gaze, gesture and body movement as well as verbal and other vocal resources. The need for video-recorded data gets even more urgent when objects have a constitutive part in the organization and progression of the activity. The video-recorded data allowed us to observe how the prompt cards figure as essential objects in the Japanese OPIs and how their textual and material quality becomes consequential for the embodied participation framework (Goodwin, 2007) at different moments in the activity transition. We submit that the implications for data quality are generalizable to research of all oral language tests that incorporate the use of objects for assessment tasks.

Notes

(1) Others, including He and Young (1998) and Ross (2017), have suggested the appellation Language Proficiency Interview (LPI) in order to avoid confusion with ACTFL's specific OPI procedures. As the data examined in this study are taken from an ACTFL OPI, we will continue to use this term throughout.

(2) It is also possible that Nicole is cognizant of the cards' purpose as the recruitment flier announced that a roleplay is part of the OPI.

(3) Subsequent versions of ACTFL OPI protocol changed the stipulation that examinees read the English prompt *aloud* to *silent* reading.

(4) ER's gaze shift shows her familiarity with the text, which enables her to anticipate the conclusion of the reading.

(5) Standard pre-second insert expansions are adjacency pairs embedded within a base adjacency pair, as in this example (adapted from Merritt, 1976: 333):

```
1 Customer: May I have a bottle of Mich?
2 Server: Are you twenty-one?
3 Customer: No.
4 Server: No.
```

Customer's answer (Line 3) provides the information that Server needs to respond to the purchase request (Line 4).

(6) The design of Alyssa's turn shows that she understands the text she read generically, that is, as an instruction to do something, but not any specifics of the instructed action. In that sense her problem formulation bears similarity with an open-class repair initiation.

(7) Lowering the fingers of her right hand on card2 (Line 48), grasping it (Line 49, FG A49), picking it up (Line 50).

(8) Turning card2 so that the text faces Alyssa (Line 53, FG A53), proffering card2 (Line 54, FG A54).

(9) It may be helpful to recall the institutional rationale for both requirements. The instruction for the selected roleplay must be conveyed verbally to the examiner for the benefit of raters who are not present during the OPI. The examinee must read a written version to ensure that they understand the instruction.

References

ACTFL OPI *Tester Training Manual, 2012: 36.* See https://www.actfl.org/resources/actfl-proficiency-guidelines-2012

Bachman, L. and Palmer, A. (1996) *Language Testing in Practice.* Oxford: Oxford University Press.

Beach, W. (1993) Transitional regularities for 'casual' 'Okay' usages. *Journal of Pragmatics* 19, 325–352.

Brown, A. (2003) Interviewer variation and the co-construction of speaking proficiency. *Language Testing* 20, 1–25.

Burch, A. (2014) Pursuing information: A conversation analytic perspective on communication strategies. *Language Learning* 64 (3), 651–684.

Drew, P. (1997) 'Open' class repair initiators in response to sequential sources of troubles in conversation. *Journal of Pragmatics* 28, 69–101.

Drew, P. (2005) Is confusion a state of mind? In H. te Molder and J. Potter (eds) *Conversation and Cognition* (pp. 161–183). Cambridge: Cambridge University Press.

Fulcher, G. (2003) *Testing Second Language Speaking.* Harlow: Pearson-Longman.

Glenn, P. and Holt, E. (2013) Introduction. In P. Glenn and E. Holt (eds) *Studies of Laughter in Interaction* (pp. 1–22). London: Bloomsbury.

Goffman, E. (1964) The neglected situation. *American Anthropologist* 66 (6), 133–136.

Goodwin, C. (1984) Notes on story structure and the organization of participation. In J.M. Atkinson and J. Heritage (eds) *Structures of Social Action: Studies in Conversation Analysis* (pp. 225–246). Cambridge: Cambridge University Press.

Goodwin, C. (2007) Participation, stance and affect in the organization of activities. *Discourse & Society* 18, 53–73.

Goodwin, C. (2018) *Co-operative Action*. New York: Cambridge University Press.

Grabowski, K. (2013) Investigating the construct validity of a role-play test designed to measure grammatical and pragmatic knowledge at multiple proficiency levels. In S. Ross and G. Kasper (eds) *Assessing Second Language Pragmatics* (pp. 149–171). Basingstoke: Palgrave Macmillan.

Greer, T., Ishida, M. and Tateyama, Y. (eds) (2017) *Interactional Competence in Japanese as an Additional Language*. Honolulu, HI: University of Hawai'i, National Foreign Language Resource Center.

He, A. and Young, R. (1998) Language proficiency interviews: A discourse approach. In R. Young and A. He (eds) *Talking and Testing: Discourse Approaches to the Assessment of Oral Proficiency* (pp. 1–24). Amsterdam: John Benjamins.

Heritage, J. (1984) A change-of-state token and aspects of its sequential placement. In J.M. Atkinson and J. Heritage (eds) *Structures of Social Action: Studies in Conversation Analysis* (pp. 299–345). Cambridge: Cambridge University Press.

Heritage, J. (2013) Turn-initial position and some of its occupants. *Journal of Pragmatics* 57, 331–337.

Heritage, J. and Clayman, S. (2010) *Talk in Action: Interactions, Identities and Institutions*. Malden, MA: Wiley-Blackwell.

Jefferson, G. (2004) Glossary of transcript symbols with an introduction. In G. Lerner (ed.) *Conversation Analysis: Studies from the First Generation* (pp. 13–31). Amsterdam: John Benjamins.

Kasper, G. (2013) Managing task uptake in oral proficiency interviews. In S. Ross and G. Kasper (eds) *Assessing Second Language Pragmatics* (pp. 258–287). Basingstoke: Palgrave Macmillan.

Kasper, G. and Ross, S. (2007) Multiple questions in oral proficiency interviews. *Journal of Pragmatics* 39, 2045–2070.

Kasper, G. and Ross, S.J. (2013) Assessing second language pragmatics: An overview and introductions. In S. Ross and G. Kasper (eds) *Assessing Second Language Pragmatics* (pp. 1–40). Basingstoke: Palgrave Macmillan.

Kasper, G. and Youn, S.J. (2018) Transforming instruction to activity: Roleplay in language assessment. *Applied Linguistics Review* 9 (4), 589–616.

Kendrick, K.H. (2015) Other-initiated repair in English. *Open Linguistics* 1, 164–190.

Kormos, J. (1999) Simulating conversations in oral-proficiency assessment: A conversation analysis of role plays and non-scripted interviews in language exams. *Language Testing* 16, 163–188.

Kunnan, A. (2004) Regarding language assessment. *Language Assessment Quarterly* 1 (1), 1–4.

Lindwell, O., Lymer, G. and Greiffenhagen, C. (2015) The sequential analysis of instruction. In N. Markee (ed.) *The Handbook of Classroom Discourse and Interaction* (pp. 375–411). Malden, MA: Wiley-Blackwell.

Merritt, M. (1976) On questions following questions in service encounters. *Language in Society* 5, 315–357.

Messick, S. (1989) Validity. In R.L. Linn (ed.) *Educational Measurement* (3rd edn) (pp. 13–103). New York: American Council on Education and Macmillan.

Mikkola, P. and Lehtinen, E. (2014) Initiating activity shifts through use of appraisal forms as material objects during performance appraisal interviews. In M. Nevile, P.

Haddington, T. Heinemann and M. Rauniomaa (eds) *Interacting With Objects: Language, Materiality, and Social Activity* (pp. 57–78). Amsterdam: John Benjamins.

Mondada, L. (2014) The local constitution of multimodal resources for social interaction. *Journal of Pragmatics* 65, 137–156.

Okada, Y. (2010) Role-play in oral proficiency interviews: Interactive footing and interactional competencies. *Journal of Pragmatics* 42 (6), 1647–1668.

Okada, Y. and Greer, T. (2013) Pursuing a relevant response in oral proficiency interview role plays. In S. Ross and G. Kasper (eds) *Assessing Second Language Pragmatics* (pp. 288–310). Basingstoke: Palgrave Macmillan.

Potter, J. and Hepburn, A. (2012) Eight challenges for interview researchers. In J.F. Gubrium, J.A. Holstein, A.B. Marvasti and K.D. McKinney (eds) The SAGE Handbook of Interview Research (2nd edn) (pp. 555–570). Los Angeles, CA: Sage.

Raymond, G. (2003) Grammar and social organization: Yes/no interrogatives and the structure of responding. *American Sociological Review* 68, 939–967.

Robinson, J. and Stivers, T. (2001) Achieving activity transitions in primary-care encounters. *Human Communication Research* 27 (2), 253–298.

Ross, S. (1996) Formulae and inter-interviewer variation in oral proficiency interview discourse. *Prospect* 11, 3–16.

Ross, S. (2007) A comparative task-in-interaction analysis of OPI backsliding. *Journal of Pragmatics* 39, 2017–2044.

Ross, S. (2017) *Interviewing for Language Proficiency: Interaction and Interpretation.* Basingstoke: Palgrave Macmillan.

Ross, S. and O'Connell, S. (2013) The situation with complication as a site for strategic competence. In S. Ross and G. Kasper (eds) *Assessing Second Language Pragmatics* (pp. 311–326). Basingstoke: Palgrave Macmillan.

Schegloff, E.A. (1996) Turn organization: One intersection of grammar and interaction. In E. Ochs, E.A. Schegloff and S.A. Thompson (eds) *Interaction and Grammar* (pp. 52–133). Cambridge: Cambridge University Press.

Schegloff, E.A. (2000) When 'others' initiate repair. *Applied Linguistics* 21, 205–243.

Schegloff, E. (2007) *Sequence Organization in Interaction: A Primer in Conversation Analysis, Vol. 1.* Cambridge: Cambridge University Press.

Seedhouse, P. and Nakatsuhara, F. (2018) *The Discourse of the IELTS Speaking Test.* Cambridge: Cambridge University Press.

Svennevig, J. (2008) Trying the easiest solution first in other-initiation of repair. *Journal of Pragmatics* 40, 333–348.

Tominaga, W. (2013) The development of extended turns and storytelling in the Japanese oral proficiency interview. In S. Ross and G. Kasper (eds) *Assessing Second Language Pragmatics* (pp. 220–257). Basingstoke: Palgrave Macmillan.

Tominaga, W. (2017) Assessing interactional competence: Storytelling in the Japanese oral proficiency interview. In T. Greer, M. Ishida and Y. Tateyama (eds) *Interactional Competence in Japanese as an Additional Language* (pp. 211–249). Honolulu, HI: University of Hawai'i, National Foreign Language Resource Center.

Walters, F.S. (2013) Interfaces between a discourse completion test and a conversation analysis-informed test of L2 pragmatic competence. In S. Ross and G. Kasper (eds) *Assessing Second Language Pragmatics* (pp. 172–195). Basingstoke: Palgrave Macmillan.

Waring, H.Z. (2011) Learner initiatives and learning opportunities in the language classroom. *Classroom Discourse* 2, 201–218.

Weilenmann, A. and Lymer, G. (2014) Incidental and essential objects in interaction: Paper documents in journalistic work. In M. Nevile, P. Haddington, T. Heinemann and M. Rauniomaa (eds) *Interacting with Objects: Language, Materiality, and Social Activity* (pp. 319–337). Amsterdam: John Benjamins.

Youn, S.J. (2015) Validity argument for assessing L2 pragmatics in interaction using mixed methods. *Language Testing* 32 (2), 199–225.

Youn, S.J. (2020) Managing proposal sequences in role-play assessment: Validity evidence of interactional competence across levels. *Language Testing* 37 (1), 76–106.

Young, R. and He, A.W. (eds) (1998) *Talking and Testing: Discourse Approaches to the Assessment of Oral Proficiency.* Amsterdam: John Benjamins.

5 Investigating Raters' Scoring Processes and Strategies in Paired Speaking Assessment

Soo Jung Youn and Shi Chen

1 Introduction

Recent years have seen an increasing amount of research on assessing interactional competence, including the construct coverage in relation to the theoretical construct (e.g. Burch & Kley, 2020; Galaczi & Taylor, 2018; Roever & Kasper, 2018), the distinct characteristics of interactional competence across levels (e.g. Galaczi, 2014; Youn, 2020), and the effects of pre-task planning time on paired speaking performance (Nitta & Nakatsuhara, 2014), just to name a few. What is under-represented in the assessment research on interactional competence is *how* raters comprehend training and award a score. Given that raters can award the same scores for different reasons on learners' language performances, additional research on the *processes* involved when raters make scoring decisions is crucial. Thus, we investigate the scoring processes and strategies carried out by 12 raters in charge of scoring roleplay-based paired speaking performances using interaction-sensitive analytical rating criteria. To that effect, raters' think-aloud data were analyzed to identify emerging patterns that illustrate scoring strategies and the unique challenges involved in paired speaking assessment.

2 Literature Review

2.1 Paired speaking assessment

Paired speaking assessment has gained popularity due to its advantages of measuring interactional competence compared to monologic speaking tests (Plough *et al.*, 2018; Taylor & Wigglesworth, 2009). Thus, paired speaking tests allow the elicitation of tangible evidence to make inferences about learners' interactional competence. The paired speaking tests' capacities to elicit a broad speaking construct were confirmed by analyzing interactional features that are salient to raters. For example, Ducasse and Brown (2009) reported three elements that raters pay attention to: non-verbal cues, interactional listening and interactional management. In addition to the construct coverage, students might feel more comfortable with participating in a paired speaking test with a fellow student compared to interacting with an interviewer. Furthermore, a paired speaking test can simulate authentic contexts since students interact with each other in ways that are similar to real-life communicative situations.

Despite these benefits, some challenges should be noted. Pairing students for a speaking test requires deliberate consideration because a level difference between two students can influence the characteristics of paired speaking performances. More complicated issues derive from scoring paired speaking performances. Paired speaking assessment requires developing rating criteria and rater training to ensure the reliability and validity of the rating procedure. The rating is particularly important in consideration of qualitatively distinct patterns of paired speaking performances, such as dominant/passive (Storch, 2001) and symmetric/asymmetric performances (Galaczi, 2008). As Douglas and Selinker (1992) rightly noted, speakers' qualitatively different performances can still receive similar ratings from raters and vice versa. How do raters make scoring decisions on qualitatively different performances and how do they understand rating criteria? With these concerns in mind, in this chapter we set out to examine raters' scoring processes.

2.2 Rater cognition and sources of rater variability

In performance assessment, it is inevitably necessary to rely on raters' decisions to elicit scores and make an inference about an individual learner's language ability. Converging findings confirm that even experienced and trained raters can differ widely in their rating decisions and raters can award the same scores for different reasons (e.g. Douglas, 1994; Elder *et al.*, 2007; Knoch, 2011; McNamara, 1996). Sources of rater variability have included raters' L1 backgrounds (e.g. Zhang & Elder, 2014) and the characteristics of learners (e.g. Winke *et al.*, 2012). In order to strengthen scoring validity, a considerable body of research on rater cognition and rater variability has been available for both monologic speaking (e.g. Cai, 2015; Davis, 2016; Hsieh, 2011; Wei & Llosa, 2015; Zhang & Elder, 2014) and interactive speaking assessment (e.g. Galaczi, 2008; May, 2009; Sandlund & Greer, 2020). Research into rater cognition allows the examination of how and why raters vary in their scoring decisions and processes.

In the context of paired speaking assessments, previous research examined the interactional features that are salient to raters and how raters manage scoring asymmetric paired performances that involve either passive or dominant interaction roles (Galaczi, 2008; May, 2009, 2011).

For example, some findings included raters' positive reactions to a collaborative pattern of paired speaking interaction (Galaczi, 2008). May (2009) analyzed raters' comments on an asymmetric paired speaking performance and reported raters' orientation to perceive the features that emerged from paired speaking tests as a mutual achievement. May further reported that raters emphasized the ability to respond in an effective manner and the authenticity of the interaction. Raters' comments illustrate that the distinct dimensions of interactional competence are represented in paired speaking assessment.

These findings on rater cognition in interactive speaking assessments confirm that raters are able to identify the diverse dimensions of interactional competence. At the same time, this does not necessarily guarantee that raters can apply their understandings of interactional competence to match rating criteria descriptors to interactive speaking performances when awarding a score. Noticeable rater biases towards rating criteria in performance assessment have already been established (e.g. Eckes, 2005), illustrating that the ways in which raters interact with rating criteria constitute a noticeable amount of systematic variance. For instance, using multi-faceted Rasch measurement analysis, Youn (2018) found that the raters displayed noticeable bias patterns towards lower-level paired speaking performances, compared to pairs consisting of higher levels. A remaining question is how raters interact with rating criteria with thick descriptions and skillfully make a scoring decision on paired speaking performances. An in-depth account of what raters do and how they make a scoring decision is warranted. Valid rating criteria should reflect varying dimensions of targeted language performances. To this end, rating criteria with thick descriptions (Fulcher, 1996) and empirically derived rating scales (Turner & Upshur, 2002) were suggested to better reflect the quality of test-takers' written or spoken performances. When rating criteria include detailed descriptions and concrete examples to reflect test-takers' performances, the ways in which raters interact with rating criteria need to be further explicated. A remaining question is how raters interact with rating criteria with thick descriptions and skillfully make a scoring decision on paired speaking performances.

3 The Present Study

The purpose of this study is to examine the scoring processes and strategies that raters utilized while awarding a score when using interaction-sensitive rating criteria on roleplay-based paired speaking performances. The following research questions guided the study.

(1) In what ways do raters interact with rating criteria in scoring various types of paired speaking performance?
(2) What scoring strategies do raters utilize when assessing various types of paired speaking performance?

4 Methods

4.1 Instruments

Roleplays. In the roleplays, two test-takers played classmates working on a group project and negotiated an agreeable meeting time and mode (e.g. meeting face-to-face or online) when a third group member is absent. Roleplay cards were used to ensure some degree of standardization among test-takers (see Appendix 5.1). At the same time, the different information provided in the roleplay card for each test-taker enabled the simulation of interaction.

Rating criteria. The rating criteria included five categories (*Content delivery, Language use, Sensitivity to situation, Engaging with interaction, Turn organization*) on a 3-point scale (see Appendix 5.2). Based on the qualitative analysis of test-takers' performances, concrete examples for each category were included.

4.2 Participants

Test-takers. In the original study, 102 test-takers completed the roleplays and were paired according to their proficiency levels which resulted in six pairing types: high-high, high-mid, high-low, mid-mid, mid-low and low-low (Youn, 2015). For this study, seven pairs who received somewhat unstable ratings from raters were intentionally selected from the original database based on multi-faceted Rasch measurement findings (Youn, 2018). Of the seven pairs, three of them (six test-takers) were included in the current study due to the interview time constraint with each rater. The first two pairs were at similar proficiency levels (low-intermediate) but differed in terms of the degree of engaging in the interaction. The first pair was interactionally more fluent compared to the second one. The third pair consisted of high- and intermediate-level learners, which is characterized as asymmetric interaction due to the male speaker's dominant conversational style. The transcriptions of three paired speaking performances are provided in Appendix 5.3.

4.3 Raters

Twelve raters, consisting of three males and nine females, were newly recruited for the currently study. They were not part of the original study (Youn, 2015). All of them had at least three years of teaching and in-house rating experience in various educational contexts. At the time of data collection, they were pursuing a PhD degree in applied linguistics or educational psychology. Three raters were native English speakers. Nine raters were non-native English speakers with varying L1s (Chinese, Farsi, Korean, Portuguese, Russian, Spanish, Thai). Since the literature indicates that there is no meaningful difference between non-native and native

English speakers in terms of rating quality (e.g. Kim, 2009), their L1s were not deemed as important for the purpose of this study.

4.4 Procedure

The audio-recorded 90-minute interview with each rater consisted of three phases.

Initial impression. Before training, the raters were first asked to provide their impressionistic scores on a 3-point scale and explain their scores. In this way, potential factors that tend to influence raters' initial judgment could be identified. Ways in which raters' decisions changed during the training and think-aloud sessions were examined.

Rater training. The researcher conducted a training session with an individual rater focusing on raters' understanding of the rating criteria, which took approximately 30 minutes. The raters were provided with a turn-by-turn transcription of roleplay performances to connect test-takers' performances and rating criteria descriptions.

Think-aloud. After rater training, each rater was asked to verbalize their decision-making processes while awarding scores on paired speaking performances. The researcher was very careful with the selection of questions during the think-aloud sessions to maintain a neutral position.

4.5 Analysis

The audio-recorded think-aloud data (a total of about 720 minutes) were transcribed for content and thematic analyses. The transcription did not capture micropauses. However, all data were captured for the analysis. After identifying emerging themes, the researchers revisited the transcriptions and checked the rest of the data to confirm the findings. Representative excerpts for each theme are presented in Section 5: Results.

5 Results

This section presents the findings under four emerging themes that characterize the raters' scoring processes and strategies with regard to their use of the rating criteria. The themes are not necessarily exclusive to each other. The first theme illustrates the noticeable difference between what the raters oriented to before and after training. The next two themes focus on why raters varied in awarding scores on some paired performances. The last theme presents individual scoring styles and reported strategies.

5.1 Discrepancies between initial judgment and post-training sessions

This section outlines what the raters oriented to before and after training when awarding a score. After training, the raters demonstrated that they understood the rating criteria more thoroughly and commented on each rating category instead of relying on general impressions on fluency, grammatical accuracy and task completion.

Before training. During the initial impression session, a number of raters tended to focus on test-takers' fluency and task completion as a basis for awarding a score (Raters 4, 9 and 11). For example, Rater 4 commented on Pair A (ID65&66, lower-level) saying that *'I think maybe I should give them more credit because they did accomplish the goal. They seem to know, I guess it's paired speaking test. So they did know the goal of them before they started.'* This comment reveals that Rater 4 was attentive to whether the test-takers achieved the communicative goal or not.

Some raters oriented to interactional phenomena related to awkward pauses. For example, Rater 5 noted about Pair A (ID65&66, lower-level) that *'So ... I'm thinking like a conversation is quite awkward in a way like because of the lot of pauses ...'*. Rater 5 specifically commented on the pauses and awkward flow of the conversation. However, Rater 5 did not interpret the meaning of or distinguish between the types of the pauses, such as between- and within-turn pauses. Within-turn pauses refer to pauses present in an individual speaker's turn that are related to the difficulty of delivery. Between-turn pauses occur between consecutive turns produced by different speakers. It was evident that the raters' comments during the initial impression session did not closely reflect the characteristics of L2 pragmatic interaction.

After training. The analysis of the think-aloud data during the post-training sessions revealed that the raters' comments were more concrete and elaborated, illustrating raters' in-depth understanding of detailed characteristics of L2 pragmatic interaction (e.g. smooth topic initiation, back-channeling, negotiation) and familiarity with the rating criteria (see more examples of post-training think-aloud data in the next sections). For example, the raters paid closer attention to turn organizations during scoring (e.g. Raters 4, 5, 8, 9, 11). Rater 5 noted that, *'I'm giving them 2 oh, no, sorry, 1 both of them to organization, because of long pauses and I mean, no not that the other cut off but really long pauses between turns.'* Rater 5 noticed the between-turn pauses, which was not observed before training. Additionally, the raters focused more on pragmatic-related grammatical features after training rather than general comments on grammatical accuracy. For example, Rater 9 said that *'and for the language use, she definitely did not have pragmatically appropriate varied expressions.'*

Towards the end of the training session, the raters were asked to reflect on their experiences. Some raters explicitly noted the change in the features that they attended to before and after training, as reflected in the comments from Raters 3 and 9 below.

> *There was a difference [after training] and I think one thing that stood out to me was like pronunciation and, like, intonation was something that, when I listened to that first sample, I was like, oh this question is*

asked really weirdly. And although there were other good things in that interaction, like that sort of stood out to me as, like, an issue, whereas now if I were to do that one again I would probably be like- I would probably pay more attention to turns. So, like, do they actually interact? Like, is like- does one understand the other? Is there like an appropriate flow of information from one to the other? Um, so I guess yeah, less- less focus on nitpicking language pronunciation things and more focus now on, like, the turns and the engagement. (Rater 3)

uhm I think my experience was interesting. Uhm I was I definitely was getting more and more familiar with the rubric as I was listening to the dialogues, by the third dialogue I think I was more confident and more familiar with each category. (Rater 9)

As we can see from these comments, after training the raters paid attention to broader qualities of speaking performance and became more familiar with using the rating criteria. This finding highlights the important role of rater training.

5.2 Different pragmatic norms among raters

The raters' understanding of the construct improved noticeably over the training. However, the raters varied in terms of the pragmatic norms expected for the communicative situations, which resulted in different scores on two rating categories (*Sensitivity to situation, Language use*). In the role-play situation, the test-takers were asked to negotiate an agreeable meeting time as classmates working on a group project. Thus, they exchanged their schedules to reach an agreeable time. Faced with this situation, different raters expressed different pragmatic norms, which influenced the scores given to one of the test-takers considerably (ID85, Pair C), who dominated the conversation, as evidenced by numerous lengthy turns and frequent cut-offs (see Appendix 5.3 for a transcript). The following comments reveal the contrasting opinions among Raters 11, 3 and 9 on the test-taker (ID85).

Jesse wasn't just cooperative, but I don't know if that is going to affect their role-play tasks, but yeah so Jesse is definitely a dominating speaker here .... I think the turn taking is a little bit worse in this case, because he just didn't give her an opportunity to talk, uhm, just dumped his whole schedule, and he wasn't very willing to find the time to meet nor talk to Tom. (Rater 11)

And then I think- I think turn I might also do more of a 2, because it does seem- sometimes it abruptly cuts off. Um. Well, I don't know, it's hard. Um. And then also this inconsistent evidence of awareness and sensitivity to situations would make me kind of consider a 2 for him for that just because, you know, again he's giving a ton of, like his own 'I'm busy I'm busy. I have to this I have to do that,' instead of, you know, like trying to figure out the situation. So I'd say 2 for that. But then his language was good. So I think language use was probably a 3. (Rater 3)

> *For sensitivity to situations, I think he was very uhm sensitive as well because when the female speaker said that she couldn't do a certain day he was sensitive to that and was trying to make it work. Yeah so he was very sensitive to the situation.* (Rater 9)

Rater 11 explicitly noted that Jesse (a generic pseudonym given to one of the test-taker roles, in this case referring to ID85) was not cooperative and provided concrete reasons, such as the lack of willingness to find an agreeable meeting time. Rater 3 offered similar opinions. On the other hand, as seen from the comment, Rater 9 thought that ID85 was 'very sensitive' and accordingly awarded the highest score. It should be noted that raters' varied evaluations of ID85 also influenced their scoring decisions for the student he was paired up with. Raters 11 and 3 displayed sympathy and ended up giving more credit to the peer test-taker (ID86, intermediate-level) who accommodated ID85's rather dominant interactional style.

In addition, the raters' varied pragmatic norms influenced expected linguistic expressions and accordingly scores on the *Language use* category. In the rating criteria, concrete examples of linguistic expressions were included (e.g. modal verbs, past progressive tense, conditionals), which were identified based on the qualitative analysis of test-takers' performances at varying levels (Youn, 2020). The following comments illustrate varied views towards the expected linguistic expressions in the roleplay situation.

> *I do that all the time, I think when you get super close to them, I don't really care about, oh would you mind asking Tom, oh could we meet there, no, we're going to meet at the library, okay? 1pm, uhm, you can make it? all right sounds good, ask Tom about it.* (Rater 10)

> *... I know they're just examples, but biclausal, conditional, past progressive, like, um. You know how often are you going to have a conversation that uses that many things. Like when I, I don't know, when I talk to my friends like, 'hey do you want to meet Saturday? Okay, cool.' You know? It's like really short, so, um.* (Rater 3)

As seen in these comments, Rater 10 noted rather direct expressions that she typically uses when talking with a classmate. Instead of *'would you mind'* and a question format with a modal verb (e.g. could we meet there?), she preferred a statement format with rising intonation (*you can make it?*) and more direct expressions (*ask Tom about it*). Rater 3 also noted a similar opinion by commenting that she preferred expressions that tended to be short for the conversations among friends.

On the other hand, other raters expected polite expressions even among classmates. Rater 5, as seen below, explicitly noted the absence of complex grammatical expressions in Pair B's performance (ID57&58, lower-level).

He didn't I don't think that he said anything like using the pragmatically showing … He just asked like 'how about you? I will be free today … how about you' without asking like I'm wondering if we could meet and stuff like that, (Rater 5)

Nonetheless, it is noteworthy that Rater 10, who preferred more direct linguistic expressions among classmates, was severe about *Language use* in general for all three pairs' performances. This also illustrates that raters' reported opinions do not necessarily reflect a score awarded to a test-taker.

More elaborated comments on linguistic expressions were noted by Rater 12. Rater 12 was more explicit about expected grammatical resources specific to spoken interaction. She pointed out an expression used by a lower-level test-taker (ID66, Pair A) that went beyond the examples included in the rating criteria. As seen in the conversation below, one of the low-level test-takers (ID66, Pair A) initiated a turn by asking *'are we gonna talk about our presentation'* in Line 3 (see a full transcript in Appendix 5.3).

Pair A (ID65&66) J: Jessie (ID65); P: Phoenix (ID66)

```
1   P: Jessie↑
2   J: hi
3   P: are we gonna talk about our presentation
4   J: okay
5   P: so: (0.3) I have ti:me (0.5) to Wednesday↑ (0.3)
6      af[ter: (0.3) one (0.5) after one pm
7   J:    [Wednesday?
```

In this instance, Rater 12 pointed out that this is *'really rude'* when used to initiate a conversation to propose a meeting time.

when she said 'Jesse'. And then they did exchange a greeting, so okay, but then she said 'are we going to talk about our presentation'. Uhm that's really rude. She could've said, 'hey our presentation is on Friday, can we talk about it?', but like 'are we going to talk about presentation'. Although her tone was very apologetic, so that's a little conflicting. (Rater 12)

Essentially, Rater 12 displayed sensitivity to varied expressions to be used especially in spoken interaction. This comment from Rater 12 is particularly noteworthy given that she emphasizes the role of appropriate grammatical resources in spoken interaction (Pekarek Doehler, 2018). Rater 12 awarded a score of 1 to ID66's performance, while other raters (five out of 12 raters) awarded her a 2 on *Language use*.

5.3 Scoring interactional features

The previous excerpts illustrate examples of how raters awarded scores on the *Language use* and *Sensitivity to situations* categories. This section focuses on whether raters displayed variability with regard to the two rating categories that closely reflect interactional features (i.e. *Engaging with inter-action, Turn organization*). The two categories are somewhat distinct in that *Engaging with interaction* concerns how each turn is relevant to the previous turn and how learners are engaged in the interaction by using acknowledgment tokens. If learners provide turns that are not reflective of a previous turn (e.g. providing less relevant responses to a question) without enough acknowledgment tokens, lower scores on *Engaging with interaction* are awarded. On the other hand, *Turn organization* concerns how each turn is provided in a timely manner. If a turn is delayed or a turn is provided too soon without meaningful pauses, lower scores on *Turn organization* are awarded. Regarding these two related but distinct categories, the raters varied in terms of their abilities to use them. A few raters, such as Rater 1, persistently struggled and expressed the difficulty of separating the two categories, as seen below. Rater 1 commented on ID57's (Pair B) performance where she made an abrupt transition towards the end of the conversation in Lines 31–35, as seen in the excerpt below.

Pair B (ID57&58) J: Jessie (ID57); P: Phoenix (ID58)

```
30 P: How about uh one (.) pm is okay
31 J: okay (0.5) a:h (0.3) bu:t (1.6) I have to: (2.4) I have
32    another class now↑ (0.5) so: I leave (0.3) soon (0.3)
33    so (2.3) ask to Tom (0.5) his opinion (0.5) and make
34    a final (1.1) schedule↑ (1.1) and let me know (0.4)
35    about the schedule
36       (0.8)
37 P: okay (.) I'll (1.2) told him
```

I felt like she had kind of a hard time especially with transitions. She seemed to have only one transition and it wasn't always appropriate when she used it. It was, 'but.' And she kinda just threw it out there sometimes. So like- she's like, 'but I have class now so I'm leaving.' ... And that was. That was choppy. Um yeah I also. I really struggled with the turn organization as well. So for the female student in this situation- in this task I gave a 1.5 because I felt like she had noticeably long pauses when she was thinking about what she was going to say, but she was quick to give a back channel in the affirmative to respond to what her partner had said. (Rater 1)

Rater 1 gave a very specific example to evaluate ID57's performance. In fact, Rater 1 identified distinct interactional features very well, such as making an abrupt transition, noticeable long pauses and back-channeling. However, she expressed the difficulty with a full grasp of the *Turn organization* category. Rater 1 did not differentiate the rating categories and match between the rating descriptors and the performance.

On the other hand, numerous raters correctly understood and distinguished between *Engaging with interaction* and *Turn organization*, as illustrated in the excerpts below. For reference, the lines that Rater 9 referred to are provided here (e.g. Line 10).

Pair B (ID57&58) J: Jessie (ID57); P: Phoenix (ID58)

```
5   P:  (0.4)  a:h meet:  (0.3)  before the Friday so=
6   J:  =yeah
7       (0.7)
8   P:  when  (0.4)  do you have uh  (1.0)  free time
9       (0.9)
10  J:  uh huh
11      (1.9)
12  J:  I:  (0.3)  I mean  (1.5)  I will be free in Saturday
13      (1.6)
14  P:  Saturday
```

> *But there is a question and answer, but there's no engaging with the conversation … she says 'yes, yeah, uh huh', 'Saturday', she just never answers again. Never answered again. 'Yeah', that was her answer. At the end, she says 'you know, we have to talk about Tom, so I have to go', that's it. Right? So there's no engagement I think at all with the conversation ......*
> *yes so she had very like noticeably long pauses. So I was giving 1 to turn organization. And then for engagement uhm I would give her 2 … because she did have some evidence that she was engaged to as she was giving him some clues that she was listening to him.* (Rater 9)

Rater 9 awarded 2 for *Engaging with interaction* and 1 for *Turn organization* for ID57 (Pair B). Rater 9 supported her decision by offering concrete examples (e.g. acknowledgment tokens, the lack of evidence of engaging with the conversation, noticeable long pauses) in relation to the descriptors in the rating criteria. The reason to deduct a point on *Engaging with interaction* for ID57 was that she did not provide a relevant response. Furthermore, the reason to award a lower score on *Turn organization* was the noticeably long pauses between turns which were due to ID57's delayed response (e.g. Line 12). The examples that Rater 9 mentioned closely reflected the rating criteria descriptors, illustrating Rater 9's active engagement with the rating criteria.

5.5 Raters' scoring processes and reported strategies

The think-aloud data illustrated the raters' distinct rating processes and strategies which confirm the highly complex nature of scoring paired speaking performances. First of all, the raters differed in terms of the degree to which they interacted with the rating criteria descriptions and how often they re-listened to the audio files. Some raters (Raters 4, 7 and 8) re-listened to the audio files multiple times to award scores, whereas other raters (e.g. Rater 12) primarily relied on the transcripts. Two excerpts below illustrate two raters (Raters 12 and 9) whose scoring styles were considerably different. Rater 12 spent the longest time on making a scoring decision by revisiting the transcripts and rating criteria multiple times rather than re-listening to the audio files. Rater 9 made a relatively prompt scoring decision. As noted below, Rater 12 reported closely relying on the rating criteria descriptors to ensure accurate ratings. In contrast, Rater 9 reported having relied primarily on the global qualities of performances conforming to what listeners do in real-life interaction.

> *I think my strategy was that I would wait until I finish rating for these four and then do the language use part last, because I wanted to for the accuracy uhm aspect of it, I just wanted to look at the transcript to be 100% sure. I am looking for modal verbs and some indication that they are using pragmatically appropriate language. So I didn't want to trust my memory for that.* (Rater 12)

> *yes I think so [making a prompt decision]. I think I usually uhm when it comes to speaking I usually don't listen to uhm samples more than 3 times, because I'm not trying to uhm grade their knowledge of grammar or their knowledge of vocabulary. I'm looking more at the global things like politeness, or engagement, or turn taking uhm …. speech is usually such a fast skill and uhm like I kind of try to imagine the real-life conversation and then realize that in real-life we don't have this whole time to rate a speech sample so yeah I think I usually don't spend much time because of that.* (Rater 9)

The complexities involved in the scoring processes were further demonstrated in the following comments. Rater 1, who tended to avoid awarding the score of 1, noted the psychological burden associated with low scores.

> *I have a hard time giving lower scores … so I felt there are things that I give much lower than this one, … I don't know where the bottom is so I'm hesitant to call the bottom something. Maybe- I know it's not supposed to be relative, but I- …, just because the delivery is choppy and fragmented and minimal, doesn't mean that that's the bottom, the worst. And it- I guess I shouldn't think of the bottom as the worst, but I do. Cause if I got a one on this test I would feel like I got the worst score.* (Rater 1)

The highly analytical process involved in rating is further confirmed by Rater 11's comment on her tendency to get more analytical and severe as she kept listening to test-takers' performances to award a score. After rater training, Rater 11 rescored the performance and noted the following.

> *they were much worse than I thought. (laugh) as I was saying, like the first impression, we always want to be softer, as we read, and well having you know thinking and listening with the criteria on your mind, then you're really classifying everything according to the criteria. So the score lowers, absolutely.* (Rater 11)

Rater 11 first awarded a higher score during the initial judgment, but gave harsher scores when she re-listened to the performances after training. Rater 11 reported her tendency to become more severe as she closely matched the performances with the rating criteria descriptors.

In terms of reported strategies, the raters noted that they tried to be very conscientious about their scoring decisions and to monitor their own biases towards non-native English speakers' accents. Rater 8 noted that:

> I try to control my biases like for example, as a like non-native speaker of English ... I would pay a lot of attention to accent or you know fluency ... That would make me distracted from the other main points that content points and I might have had that biases but now that I am aware of it. (Rater 8)

Rater 11 further mentioned the benefit of using analytical rating criteria as seen below.

> I think it's easier if you think about different aspects. And have the scores for each thing. Otherwise, it's not really fair, Right? .... It [being analytical] makes it easier, it's not as unfair, because sometimes like the language use is perfect, and the person is just not confident enough, so he hesitates a lot or there are so many pauses, and you know you would give a lower score because of that, but then the language use itself is really good, right? So it's hard to say one score for everything. (Rater 11)

Finally, specific strategies involved in separating two test-takers' paired speaking performances were reported. The raters reported starting awarding a score on rating categories that she or he was most familiar with and then moving on to categories that needed further attention. All raters agreed to award a separate score for each test-taker although two test-takers completed the task, as Rater 1 noted below.

> I tried to listen to everything at the same time. And of course that didn't work. So, I think my strategy was to try to focus on one speaker at a time ..., I feel like it's a task for two people, so if they achieve it together they should get the same grade, which is probably not fair. If I were a student would be mad. Um, so yeah, as I went on I tried to focus first on the first speaker and then next on the second speaker. But, I wrote down notes in the comments section just to remind me what I was thinking or what I heard and then I didn't give the score until I had all my notes because I wanted to go back and remember. (Rater 1)

Rater 1 mentioned the unfairness of awarding the same score to two test-takers and reported the strategy of focusing on an individual speaker per listening while taking notes. These comments illustrate that rating decisions involve highly multi-faceted processes accompanied by individual-specific scoring styles and strategies to ensure quality scoring.

6 Discussion

The findings from this study revealed that the scoring processes followed by raters are highly complex in nature, influenced by raters' varying pragmatic norms and individual styles that affected their decisions. First of all, the noticeable difference between what raters attended to before and after training highlights the important role of rater training. Before training, it was evident that the raters tended to rely on factors such as fluency, grammatical accuracy and task completion. These are relevant, but under-represent other dimensions of interactive speaking performance, such as turn-taking features and engagement with interaction. Even though the raters had previous teaching and rating experience, it is noteworthy that the raters rarely mentioned the characteristics of pragmatic and interactional competence before training. After training, the majority of the raters reported that they became familiar with the rating criteria. As evidenced in their think-aloud data, they actively interacted with the rating criteria. Also, the trained raters focused more on different types of pauses, turn organization and pragmatically appropriate grammatical features, conforming to the rating criteria descriptions. This finding also confirms that raters' previous rating experiences do not necessarily affect scoring quality and consistency (Davis, 2016). It also reveals that it takes time for experienced teachers to achieve a certain degree of confidence and expertise to score interactive speaking performances.

The think-aloud data indicate that the raters closely interacted with the specific features included in the rating criteria. The raters' heavy reliance on the rating criteria also supports a noticeable amount of rater biases across rating criteria detected in previous quantitative research (e.g. Eckes, 2012; Youn, 2018). The ways in which the raters interacted with the rating criteria and made a scoring decision were influenced by several factors. First of all, the raters expressed differential pragmatic norms to rationalize their scoring decisions in relation to the rating categories, particularly *Language use* and *Sensitivity to situation*. For example, the raters oriented to the different linguistic expressions, ranging from direct expressions to more elaborated expressions (e.g. bi-clausal expressions). In particular, the raters' varied pragmatic norms also need to be discussed in light of raters' reactions to asymmetric paired speaking interaction (Galaczi, 2008). As May (2009) reported in her study, the raters considered a low level of equality between speakers and dominant interactional roles as negative factors. In this study, however, not all raters considered the asymmetric nature of performance as a reason to lower a score. For the asymmetric interaction apparent in Pair C, many raters commented on ID85's (Pair C) dominant interactional style. Nevertheless, not all raters lowered their scores for ID85 who dominated the interaction. Some raters (e.g. Raters 2, 9) awarded a 3 on all five categories assigned to ID85's performance. One possible reason for this outcome is that ID85 still had a good control over vocabulary and grammar, which might have been salient features for Raters 2 and 9. This finding also provides supporting evidence of a rater type hypothesis (Eckes, 2008, 2012). In this study, some raters gave more weight to pragmatic appropriateness, whereas other raters overweighted form-related criteria (e.g. grammar, vocabulary), which resemble the speaking rater classification reported in Cai (2015). Given that rater variability is inevitable, identifying rater types can be useful to systematically describe differences among raters.

In addition, although all raters oriented to a range of interactional phenomena, such as between-turn pauses and the degree of engagement, after training, not all raters were able to match these features with the rating criteria descriptors. The rating criteria used in this study included relatively thick descriptions for each category. Two related but distinct categories of interactional competence (*Engaging with interaction* and *Turn organization*) were included. Quantitative findings support that these two categories were distinct in terms of difficulty (Youn, 2015). Nonetheless, as seen in the study, the raters displayed different abilities to match the performance characteristics with each rating category. It should be noted that all raters' think-aloud comments still included relevant interactional phenomena, although this factor does not necessarily guarantee their abilities to use the rating criteria accordingly. These findings further emphasize the importance of rigorous rater training and checking raters' abilities to use the rating criteria.

The findings further confirm the highly multifaceted nature of rating processes. In order to manage the complex scoring processes, the raters utilized varying scoring strategies, such as relying on global qualities, revisiting rating criteria, re-listening to audio files and monitoring their own biases. Interesting cognitive processes, such as becoming more severe as raters re-listen to audio files and a psychological burden underlying awarding a lower score, were revealed. With regard to raters' scoring strategies, the issue of separability of individuals' contribution to the interaction needs to be discussed. There is no doubt that two speakers contribute to mutual accomplishment (May, 2009). At the same time, each speaker contributes to the interaction in a different manner. With regard to this issue, all 12 raters in this study reported that awarding a separate score to an individual test-taker was justifiable. Although both speakers complete the task together, the different degree to which both speakers contribute to the resulting interaction can be still examined. For example, as seen in the data in this study, some raters (e.g. Rater 9) commented that one of the test-takers did not provide a relevant response in a timely manner. Another example is found where a speaker was credited for an additional action of steering the conversation in order to stop a peer test-taker from dominating the interaction (e.g. Pair C). Since each test-taker's contribution to the interaction can be still identifiable and isolated, awarding an individual score for each speaker can be feasible and fair for assessment purposes. At the same time, this approach requires raters' close attention to detailed features specific to an individual speaker, which is time consuming. To this end, additional research on examining features that efficiently contribute to distinguishing among varying performance levels is required.

Limitations of the current study should be noted. First of all, the audio-recorded data used in this study underrepresent the construct of L2 pragmatic interaction, such as paralinguistic resources. While the qualitative investigation provides accounts for underlying rater variability and rating processes, the findings still lack some degree of generalizability. Lastly, the reactivity of think-aloud data (Bowles, 2010) should be taken seriously as well. Due to the fact that the raters were asked to verbalize their thoughts, their reported data may alter their rating behaviors (i.e. reactivity) and the reported data may not represent their real-life scoring behaviors. In response to these limitations, future research can entail the investigation of a rater type (Eckes, 2008, 2012) in paired speaking assessment using multiple research methods.

Despite the limitations, the present findings point to possible implications for rater training and rating criteria development for paired speaking assessment. First, the importance of rigorous training should not be taken lightly. Given the diverse dimensions underlying interactional competence, raters will need enough time to internalize the construct and rating criteria descriptions. Each rater in this study spent at least 1.5 hours on training and verbalizing scoring three paired performances. Although the optimal duration of rater training is an empirical question, at least one hour can be recommended for rater training for paired speaking assessment. In doing so, particular emphasis on helping raters internalize rating criteria and dealing with borderline cases (e.g. asymmetric paired performances) needs to be paid. To this end, additional training on scoring interactional phenomena is crucial. As seen in this study, without training, raters do not necessarily pay attention to interactional phenomena, and even when they do, they are not necessarily able to match between rating criteria descriptors and test-takers' performances to make a consistent scoring decision. Thus, explicit training on how to make relevant decisions according to raters' scoring styles should be provided. In addition, it is evident that the raters rely heavily upon rating criteria. In order to make rating criteria descriptions more concrete and accessible to raters, user-friendly language in rating criteria would be important as well. For example, instead of using technical terms (e.g. adjacency pair), commonly used phrases (e.g. responding to a question, continuity in the conversation) would be appropriate. Equally importantly, critical features that are representative of distinct performance levels need to be included in the criteria.

7 Conclusion

This study investigated the scoring strategies and processes followed by 12 raters in the context of roleplay-based paired speaking assessment. The think-aloud data illustrate that the raters experience highly complex scoring processes that involve individual scoring styles and strategies. Before training, the raters tended to focus on grammatical accuracy, fluency and overall task completion. However, the trained raters gained an in-depth understanding of various dimensions of L2 pragmatic interaction. The findings highlight the indispensable role played by rigorous training in performance assessment and the importance of broadening the construct of L2 speaking into various features of spoken interaction (Roever & Kasper, 2018). Although this study is exploratory in nature, the findings help us understand how and why raters make scoring decisions in paired speaking assessment. Raters inevitably vary in their decision-making processes, influenced by their own pragmatic norms and scoring styles. Thus, aiming for perfect agreement among raters in paired speaking assessment is not feasible. Instead, assisting raters in making valid and reliable scoring decisions using rigorous rater training and quality rating criteria represents a more realistic goal.

Appendix 5.1: Roleplay Tasks and Roleplay Cards

Situation: After class, you are going to talk with your classmate who is doing a class project (article presentation) regarding **when and how your group members will meet** to discuss the project. The third member (Tom) is absent today. Your presentation is next Friday.

Task: You will receive role-play cards that describe what you are going to tell your classmate. Please have a conversations with your classmate naturally.

Roleplay card for Task 1 (Meeting time)

Jessie

Phoenix
1. Approach Jessie and start a conversation about an upcoming class project (article presentation). **Suggest** discussing an appropriate meeting time. Propose an available time slot based on your schedule.

Jessie
1. **Look at your schedule.** Respond to Phoenix' question.

Phoenix

Jessie

Phoenix
2. Respond to Jessie's time availability **based on your own schedule.**

Jessie
2. You need to leave soon since you have another class soon. So, whether you found a good time or not, **suggest** asking the third member (Tom)'s opinion to make a final decision.

Phoenix

Jessie
3. Respond to what Phoenix says

Phoenix
3. Respond to what Jessie says

Jessie's schedule

Monday	Tuesday	Wednesday	Thursday	Friday	Saturday	Sunday
9am–1pm: Classes	Part-time work (10am–5pm)	9am–1pm: Classes	Part-time work (10am–5pm)	9am–1pm: Classes		Part-time work (2–9pm)

Phoenix's schedule

Monday	Tuesday	Wednesday	Thursday	Friday	Saturday	Sunday
10am–3pm: Classes	No class	10am–1pm: Classes	10am–3pm: Classes	Meeting with an advisor at 2pm	BBQ party with friends at 5pm	

Roleplay card for Task 2 (Discussion mode)

Jessie	Phoenix
1. Move the discussion to a discussion mode. **Suggest** discussing how you will meet all together to discuss a project. Propose an option between **face-to-face discussion** and **online discussion (e.g., chatting)** that you personally prefer.	
Jessie	**Phoenix** 1. Respond to what Jessie proposes. **Choose one option that you prefer** and express your own opinion.
Jessie 2. Respond to Phoenix' opinion.	**Phoenix** 2. Respond to Jessie's opinion. **Suggest** that you want to ask the third group member (Tom) who is absent today to make a final decision about how you will meet.
Jessie 3. Wrap up the conversation	**Phoenix** 3. Wrap up the conversation

Appendix 5.2: Rating Criteria

Score	Content delivery	Language use	Sensitivity to situation	Engaging with interaction	Turn organization
3	• Clear, concise, fluent • Smooth topic initiations (i.e. smooth turn initiation) **Rating Phoenix**: *asking time for a meeting* and Phoenix's responses to Jessie's questions **Rating Jessie**: *asking how to meet* and Jessie's responses to Phoenix's questions *Note*: Who initiates 'Asking Tom for a final decision' is not a crucial rating point, but focus more on the delivery of follow-up contents.	• Pragmatically appropriate linguistic expressions (**bi-clausal, conditional, past progressive tense**: I was thinking, I don't think I can; **modal verbs**: would, could, might) • Good control of grammar and vocabulary that doesn't obscure meaning **Focus: asking questions, expressing different opinions and suggestions** *Note*: No need to heavily rely on elaborated complex structures, but diverse grammatical structures for pragmatic meaning need to be observed for '3'.	• Consistent evidence of awareness and sensitivity to situations exists in an appropriate sequence **Examples**: what is needed for a team project (e.g. time negotiation, back-up time slots for Tom), accounts for disagreement, explanations (at least brief) for the time and meeting mode preference, paying attention to classmates' opinions *Note*: Although not all examples need to be observed, a substantial amount of evidence needs to be observed for '3'.	• A next turn shows understandings of a previous turn throughout the interaction (i.e. shared understanding) • Evidence of engaging with the conversation exists (e.g. clarification questions, backchannel, acknowledgment tokens) *Note*: Nonverbal cues also serve as acknowledgment, so no need to heavily rely on the amount of discourse markers.	• Complete adjacency pairs (e.g. question and answer) • Interactionally fluid **without awkward pauses or abrupt overlap** (especially for disagreement *Note*: Interactionally meaningful pauses include those before refusal and disagreement. *Note*: Even with the elaborated language use ('3' in Language use), this may not necessarily be done properly with a pause (especially disagreement). Then, '3' in Turn organization may not necessarily be awarded.
2	• Generally smooth, but **occasionally unclear** (which can confuse a classmate), or **unnecessarily wordy** • **Abrupt** topic initiation (in terms of contents) • **Unclear transitional cues** (e.g. unclear intonation and stress)	• Able to use modal verbs in **mono-clausal** (e.g. could, can, might), but doesn't use various grammatical structures for pragmatic meaning • Linguistic expressions are occasionally inaccurate and a bit limited and sometimes obscure meaning	• Inconsistent evidence of awareness and sensitivity to situations (e.g. provide accounts for opinions, but do not necessarily handle the disagreement situation properly)	• Some evidence of engaging with the conversation, but not consistent (e.g. literally reading the roleplay card) • A next turn does not sometimes show an understanding of a previous turn	• Some turns are **delayed** and a next turn is **absent** in adjacency pairs (e.g. absence of answers) • Sometimes **abruptly cut off** previous turns
1	• Delivery is choppy, fragmented and minimal (due to a lack of language competence)	• Expressions sound **abrupt** or **not polite enough** (e.g. I'm busy, I can't) • Linguistic expressions are inaccurate and quite limited and obscure meaning	• Little evidence of situational sensitivity (e.g. absence of providing accounts for *disagreement in particular*, handle disagreement awkwardly)	• Noticeable absence of discourse markers • Evidence of not achieving a shared understanding	• Noticeably abrupt overlap or no pauses for disagreement and refusal • **Noticeably long pauses** or **noticeable cut-off** between turns

Appendix 5.3: Transcripts

Pair A

ID65&66RP1-1 J: Jessie (ID65); P: Phoenix (ID66)

```
 1  P: Jessie↑
 2  J: hi
 3  P: are we gonna talk about our presentation
 4  J: okay
 5  P: so: (0.3) I have ti:me (0.5) to Wednesday↑ (0.3)
 6     af[ter: (0.3) one (0.5) after one pm
 7  J:   [Wednesday?
 8     (0.4)
 9  J: [after one pm?
10  P: [so do you have time?
11     (0.5)
12  J: oh Wednesday? I have a (.) nine am to one pm classes
13  P: a:h
14  J: so after class (.) okay
15  P: is okay? [yeah so
16  J:          [okay okay
17     (0.3)
18  P: can you↑ (.) ask (0.4) a:h °Tom°?
19     (0.6)
20  J: Tom?
21     (0.3)
22  P: yeah
23  J: ah okay I know Tom's phone number
24  P: ah yeah [hh
25  J:         [hhh
26     (0.4)
27  P: so we need after
28     (0.3)
29  J: after Wed- after
30  P: cl- [class Wednesday
31  J:     [class Wednesday
32  P: yeah
33     (0.7)
34  J: okay
35  P: okay see you °then eh? yeah°
36  J: okay
```

Pair B

ID57&58RP1-1 J: Jessie (ID57); P: Phoenix (ID58)

```
 1  P: ah next Friday↑ we have a (1.5) presentation
 2  J: yes=
 3  P: =so but (.) Tom is (0.4) today absent so [we should
 4  J:                                          [yeah
 5  P: (0.4) a:h meet: (0.3) before the Friday so=
 6  J: =yeah
 7     (0.7)
 8  P: when (0.4) do you have uh (1.0) free time
 9     (0.9)
10  J: uh huh
11     (1.9)
12  J: I: (0.3) I mean (1.5) I will be free in Saturday
13     (1.6)
14  P: Saturday
15  J: yeah how about you?
16     (0.5)
17  P: a:h
18  J: ((coughing))
19     (1.2)
20  P: I have a plan but a:h my plan is started (.) five pm
21     [so before the fi- five pm is okay
22  J: [yeah
23     (0.5)
24  J: uh huh
25     (1.9)
26  J: so: (1.3) we: (1.9) meet in Saturday: (0.3) before the
27     five pm?
28  P: yeah so=
29  J: =yeah
30  P: How about uh one (.) pm is okay
31  J: okay (0.5) a:h (0.3) bu:t (1.6) I have to: (2.4) I have
32     another class now↑ (0.5) so: I leave (0.3) soon (0.3)
33     so (2.3) ask to Tom (0.5) his opinion (0.5) and make
34     a final (1.1) schedule↑ (1.1) and let me know (0.4)
35     about the schedule
36     (0.8)
37  P: okay (.) I'll (1.2) told him
38  J: yeah
```

Pair C

ID85&86RP1-1 J: Jessie (ID85); P: Phoenix (ID86)

```
 1  P: next Fr- next Friday we have <presentation>↑ .hh so
 2     ahm (0.4) a- uhm a- I think we have ahm (0.6) ahm we
 3     have ah .hh free available time to .hh work together
 4     about that↑
 5     (0.5)
 6  J: .hh yeah I know we still have time but I'm very busy
 7     this week a:nd (.) can see that ah tomorrow Thursday
```

```
 8       I have a part time job from ten to five↑ .hh a:nd Friday
 9       I still have class from nine to one .hh (0.3) I'm
10       only available to wo:rk (.) ah maybe Friday afternoon↑
11       (.) >I still have to have< lunch and so[m- something
12 P:                                              [uh huh
13 J:    like that so I will be available I think two: up- (.)
14       two pm on- on Friday↑ .hh ah Saturday I'm very free .hh
15       bu:t my mom- my mom actually already asked me to: (0.8)
16       a:h bring her (.) to buy something .hh I will be available
17       (.) a:h maybe in the afternoon↑ in between one to three↑
18       .hh uh- and Sunday Sunday I still have a work to do and
19       I don't want to do something I still need to finish up
20       my homework .hh [a:h
21 P:                    [uhm
22       (1.0)
23 J:    yeah so [have presen-
24 P:            [how about Tuesday?
25       (0.6)
26 P:    Tuesday
27       (0.9)
28 P:    [at a
29 J:    [Thursday↑ what time is Thursday? Thursday I have a
30       part time work from ten to five
31 P:    ten to five?
32 J:    yeah
33 P:    and after eh after you work we can eh we have a
34       meeting by that
35 J:    o:h I'm not sure for that because five [pm .hh
36 P:                                           [((coughing))
37 J:    five pm >I'm not sure about Tom< as well because
38       I know that Tom is not here today and Tom also have
39       a part time job .hh [and I don't know maybe↑ (.)
40 P:                        [uh huh
41 J:    maybe: we have to ask Tom about that .hh=
42 P:    we can- (.) we can call: call him?
43       (0.7)
44 J:    yeah maybe you can call- (.) call him can you just
45       try to call him and the:n .hh ah because I- a:h in
46       a while I still have a (0.3) a class↑ .hh can you try
47       to call him and then let th- let Tom know that I will
48       be available Friday or Saturday Saturday I have a
49       time in between one to two [.hh and Friday afternoon
50 P:                               [and I have appointment
51       ah [Friday after-?
52 J:       [yeah
53 P:    .hh ah Frida- F- Friday afternoon↑ I have appointment
54       with the an advisor↑
55       (0.7)
56 P:    so I cannot so I think I have an idea↑ a:hm (0.3) when
57       I and you .hh ahm meet each other↑ and after that we
58       send an email to him
59       (1.4)
60 J:    yeah so we- we don't have time right now so (.)
61       probably- how about [Saturday
62 P:                        [TUESday
63       (1.3)
64 P:    how about Tuesday? I talk about Tues- Tuesday
65 J:    next Tuesday? [next Tuesday I also have a part time job
66 P:                  [yeah
```

```
67 J:   .hh [from five
68 P:        [AFTER YOUR WORK
69      (0.5)
70 P:   after [work
71 J:         [after my work
72 P:   [yeah
73 J:   [okay let's try after my work but you have to ask Tom
74      about it first .hh I will be available maybe li- little
75      bit late↑ (.) but I s- I will try to do that
76      (0.5)
77 J:   okay
78 P:   uh huh
79      (0.7)
80 P:   okay
81 J:   okay and then eh- just try to contact Tom and then le-
82      (0.4) let him know that (.) [we: agreed that we will
83 P:                               [yeah
84 J:   meet on Tuesday (0.3) then (0.3) I will (.) I will
85      call you later [see you (.) [then
86 P:                   [yeah        [uh huh
```

References

Bowles, M.A. (2010) *The Think-Aloud Controversy in Second Language Research*. New York: Routledge.

Burch, A.R. and Kley, K. (2020) Assessing interactional competence: The role of intersubjectivity in a paired-speaking assessment task. *Papers in Language Testing and Assessment* 9, 25–63.

Cai, H. (2015) Weight-based classification of raters and rater cognition in an EFL speaking test. *Language Assessment Quarterly* 12, 262–282.

Davis, L. (2016) The influence of training and experience on rater performance in scoring spoken language. *Language Testing* 33, 117–135.

Douglas, D. (1994) Quantity and quality in speaking test performance. *Language Testing* 11, 125–144.

Douglas, D. and Selinker, L. (1992) Analysing oral proficiency test performance in general and specific purpose contexts. *System* 20, 317–328.

Ducasse, A.M. and Brown, A. (2009) Assessing paired orals: Raters' orientation to interaction. *Language Testing* 26, 423–443.

Eckes, T. (2005) Examining rater effects in TestDaF writing and speaking performance assessments: A many-facet Rasch analysis. *Language Assessment Quarterly* 2, 197–221.

Eckes, T. (2008) Rater types in writing performance assessments: A classification approach to rater variability. *Language Testing* 25, 155–185.

Eckes, T. (2012) Operational rater types in writing assessment: Linking rater cognition to rater behavior. *Language Assessment Quarterly* 9, 270–292.

Elder, C., Barkhuizen, G., Knoch, U. and von Randow, J. (2007) Evaluating rater responses to an online training program for L2 writing assessment. *Language Testing* 24, 37–64.

Fulcher, G. (1996) Does thick description lead to smart tests? A data-based approach to rating scale construction. *Language Testing* 13, 208–238.

Galaczi, E. (2008) Peer-peer interaction in a speaking test: The case of the First Certificate in English examination. *Language Assessment Quarterly* 2, 89–119.

Galaczi, E. (2014) Interactional competence across proficiency levels: How do learners manage interaction in paired speaking tests? *Applied Linguistics* 35, 553–574.

Galaczi, E. and Taylor, L. (2018) Interactional competence: Conceptualisations, operationalisations, and outstanding questions. *Language Assessment Quarterly* 3, 219–236.

Hsieh, C.-N. (2011) *Rater Effects in ITA Testing: ESL Teachers' Versus American Undergraduates' Judgments of Accentedness, Comprehensibility, and Oral Proficiency.* Unpublished Ph.D. dissertation. Michigan State University.

Kim, Y.-H. (2009) An investigation into native and non-native teachers' judgments of oral English performance: A mixed methods approach. *Language Testing* 26, 187–217.

Knoch, U. (2011) Investigating the effectiveness of individual feedback to rating behavior – a longitudinal study. *Language Testing* 28, 179–200.

May, L. (2009) Co-constructed interaction in a paired speaking test: The raters' perspective. *Language Testing* 26, 397–421.

May, L. (2011) Interactional competence in a paired speaking test: Features salient to raters. *Language Assessment Quarterly* 8, 127–145.

McNamara, T. (1996) *Measuring Second Language Performance.* New York: Addison Wesley Longman.

Nitta, R. and Nakatsuhara, F. (2014) A multifaceted approach to investigating pre-task planning effects on paired oral test performance. *Language Testing* 31, 147–175.

Pekarek Doehler, S. (2018) Elaborations on L2 interactional competence: The development of L2 grammar-for-interaction. *Classroom Discourse* 9, 3–24.

Plough, I., Banerjee, J. and Iwashita, N. (2018) Interactional competence: Genie out of the bottle. *Language Testing* 35, 427–445.

Roever, C. and Kasper, G. (2018) Speaking in turns and sequences: Interactional competence as a target construct in testing speaking. *Language Testing* 35, 331–355.

Sandlund, E. and Greer, T. (2020) How do raters understand rubrics for assessing L2 interactional engagement? A comparative study of CA- and non-CA-formulated performance descriptors. *Papers in Language Testing and Assessment* 9, 128–163.

Storch, N. (2001) An investigation into the nature of pair work in an ESL classroom and its effect on grammatical development. Unpublished PhD dissertation, University of Melbourne.

Taylor, L. and Wigglesworth, G. (2009) Are two heads better than one? Pair work in L2 assessment contexts. *Language Testing* 26, 325–339.

Turner, C.E. and Upshur, J.A. (2002) Rating scales derived from student samples: Effects of the scale maker and the student sample on scale content and student scores. *TESOL Quarterly* 36, 49–70.

Wei, J. and Llosa, L. (2015) Investigating differences between American and Indian raters in assessing TOEFL iBT speaking tasks. *Language Assessment Quarterly* 12, 283–304.

Winke, P., Gass, S. and Myford, C. (2012) Raters' L2 background as a potential source of bias in rating oral performance. *Language Testing* 30, 231–252.

Youn, S.J. (2015) Validity argument for assessing L2 pragmatics in interaction using mixed methods. *Language Testing* 32, 199–225.

Youn, S.J. (2018) Rater variability across examinees and rating criteria in paired speaking assessment. *Papers in Language Testing and Assessment* 7, 32–60.

Youn, S.J. (2020) Managing proposal sequences in role-play assessment: Validity evidence of interactional competence across levels. *Language Testing* 37, 76–106.

Zhang, Y. and Elder, C. (2014) Investigating native and non-native English-speaking teacher raters' judgments of oral proficiency in the College English Test-Spoken English Test (CET-SET). *Assessment in Education: Principles, Policy & Practice* 21, 306–325.

6 Rating and Reflecting: Displaying Rater Identities in Collegial L2 English Oral Assessment

Erica Sandlund and Pia Sundqvist

1 Introduction

Assessing complex language abilities such as speaking in interaction presents challenges for the development of constructs, scoring rubrics and the practice of assessment. There is a longstanding conviction that training of raters is crucial for the reduction of variance in test scores due to rater factors (e.g. Wilkinson, 1968). Variation in rater severity across rater groups may be the result of many factors, for example, construct interpretations, rater backgrounds and individual biases (Eckes, 2009; Elder *et al.*, 2005). McNamara (1996) discusses four dimensions that may play a role in rater variability: rater consistency, rater leniency or severity, rater's use of the rating scale and rater bias or interaction. Holistic rating scales for speaking and interaction present particular challenges for reaching consensus on performances at different levels, as 'a single score may not do justice to speaking' (Fulcher, 2003: 90) and raters are only required to account for an impression of an overall quality rather than for the presence of a certain number of specified features. Consequently, even when the same score is assigned by different raters, there is no way of ascertaining that raters have based that assessment on the same grounds (Jönsson & Thornberg, 2014), or that raters have understood and used a particular rating scale in the same way. As Fulcher (2003) puts it, there is 'little point in building construct models to support the empirical development of rating scales if raters then pay no attention to it' (Fulcher, 2003: 143), and rater training interventions are generally designed to 'socialize raters into a common understanding of the scale descriptors' (Fulcher, 2003: 145). Such socialization of raters, we argue, could also include opportunities to reflect upon individual rater biases in relation to specific learner performances.

Assessment researchers, as well as policymakers and other stakeholders in education, sometimes promote collaborative assessment (i.e. practices of social moderation or consensus moderation, e.g. Linn, 1993; Sadler, 2013) as a remedy for challenges with assessment equity, especially in the context of large-scale standardized testing, as has been the case with the national tests of core subjects in Sweden (Erickson, 2009; Swedish National Agency for Education, 2009; Swedish Schools Inspectorate, 2013). Moderation is defined 'as a practice of engagement in which teaching team members develop a shared understanding of assessment requirements, standards and the evidence that demonstrates differing qualities of performance' (Grainger *et al.*, 2016: 551), which makes moderation an organized practice for the verification of assessment judgments against standards (Bloxham *et al.*, 2016).

Whether moderation is applied for the sake of achieving validity and reliability in high-stakes grading or as a professional development practice (cf. Jönsson & Thornberg, 2014, on different goals of collaborative assessment, CASS), a closer look at moderation and training as *interactional events* is warranted, as raters' varying perceptions of assessment criteria are reflected in learner scores (cf. Ducasse & Brown, 2009: 425). Raters from different walks of life, carrying different experiences from their own local contexts, may 'attend more or less closely to different sets of criteria, depending on their professional background (...) and a host of other factors' (Eckes, 2009: 43). How raters perceive their own rater characteristics may therefore provide us with insight into one dimension of the professional practice of doing second/foreign language (L2) speaking assessment: the role of rater identities in assigning and accounting for scores in rater training or moderation activities. Like any other collaborative work practice, assessment discussions require participants to reveal their individual views on grading and have their professional judgments challenged by others. As such, the very act of sharing one's professional judgment also means displaying publicly one's professional competence and/or identity. In this chapter, we approach rater variation specifically from the perspective of the raters' displayed perceptions of their rater 'profiles' in collegial assessment activities, that is, when teachers-as-raters jointly and collaboratively assess learner performances, or discuss individually made assessments (cf. Jönsson & Thornberg, 2014). We adopt a qualitative, interactional approach to raters' discussions on L2 speaking in situated assessment talk, and with a conversation analytic (CA) approach we examine how teachers-as-raters, participating in training interventions for the assessment of L2 oral proficiency and interaction, orient to and position themselves as members of particular rater categories.

In line with an interest in rater training which includes *reflections* on professional practice (cf. Mann & Walsh, 2013), we focus specifically on the interactional management of 'rater identities', displayed as raters' orientations to degrees of *severity* and *leniency* when delivering and accounting for assessments of learner productions. Thus, we examine raters' reflection-in-action, as different rater identity positionings are claimed, mitigated, negotiated and linked to the current assessment tasks. The study is grounded mainly in two research areas: rater perspectives in the assessment of L2 speaking; and, methodologically, professional identity work in talk and interaction (e.g. Antaki & Widdicombe, 1998; Benwell & Stokoe, 2006; Richards, 2006; Stokoe, 2012).

2 Assessing L2 Speaking: The Rater Perspective

Assessment of language skills means 'the act of collecting information and making judgments about a language learner's knowledge of a language and ability to use it' (Chapelle & Brindley, 2002: 268); however, assessing L2 proficiency has sometimes been described as capturing 'a moving target' (Leclercq & Edmonds, 2014: 5), and thus a challenge for assessment. High-stakes, standardized testing procedures are part of systems of accountability in education (e.g. Lundahl, 2016), and educational authorities, schools and individual teachers are responsible for aligning teaching and assessment with set standards. As such, for the assessment of speaking and interacting in an L2 to function as intended, raters, as well as teachers-as-raters, must develop their *assessment literacy* (Popham, 2009, 2011) in making professional judgments about a learner's L2 proficiency and interactional skills in line with standards. Ideally, assessments should not deviate from those of other raters. In this section, we review work on efforts to develop raters' assessment skills with a particular focus on the assessment of L2 speaking. For the sake of clarity, we use the term *rater* consistently to refer to professionals assessing such tests, whether teachers or trained expert raters.

2.1 Rater dialogues, moderation and rater training

Popham (2009, 2011) identifies a need to develop more extensive teacher education modules and in-service training programs in order to build up teachers' assessment literacy. The refinement of assessment skills can be viewed as a shared knowledge base for professional learning communities and also as benchmarking for the sake of assessment validity and reliability. Many studies of training efforts report positive outcomes in terms of higher post-training inter-rater reliability and agreement (see Davis, 2016), with novice raters, often 'excessively severe or lenient' (Davis, 2016: 118), seemingly most affected by training. Other studies have shown that rater variation in terms of severity was not reduced to acceptable levels after training (Lumley & McNamara, 1995). Weigle (1998) explored differences in rater severity and consistency and found support for the idea that rater training is more successful in assisting raters to give more predictable scores (intra-rater reliability) than in assisting them to assign identical scores (inter-rater reliability). Elder *et al.* (2005) report positive outcomes of rater training where raters received *individual feedback* on their rating performance, while Knoch (2011) saw no effect of feedback on rater performance over time. However, for the sake of stimulating reflection and awareness, individual feedback can work to prompt self-reflective talk (Sundqvist *et al.*, 2020).

Variants of what Sadler (2013; see also Linn, 1993) refers to as *consensus moderation* or *social moderation* is another route towards increasing raters' shared understanding of constructs and criteria for assessment. While studies of the effects of moderation on equity and rater agreement are scarce, there appears to be consensus regarding the positive effects of moderation activities as a form of professional development. In a review of literature on collaborative assessment, Jönsson and Thornberg (2014) emphasize the pedagogical potential inherent in having teachers work together on assessing authentic learner performances. Furthermore, moderation activities focusing on building learning communities (Wiliam, 2007) for teachers or raters contribute to developing their 'assessment literacy as well as knowledge of standards' (Bloxham *et al.*, 2016: 649), especially when discussions on specific learner performances contain disagreements, which provides opportunities for professional learning and negotiation (cf. also Adie *et al.*, 2012). Central to effective moderation is that the social climate allows for 'the representation and exploration of dissensus', which means that the potential embedded in disagreements and challenges is nurtured as an opportunity for learning (Moss & Schultz, 2001: 65) – even though such disagreements may constitute a threat to members' professional identities (cf. Schnurr & Chan, 2011).

Worth noting is that most studies of moderation work have been based on teachers' self-reported experiences of the effects of moderation (Adie *et al.*, 2012) and not on examinations of the interaction in collaborative assessment activities, which is the focus of the present chapter. Among the few studies conducted, Jølle (2014) examined transcripts of audio-recorded paired rater dialogues on the assessment of L1 writing. Data were analyzed using two main categories: the *referents* that raters drew upon in judging student texts; and the *responses* to collegial contributions (i.e. 'the way the responses distribute between rejections, yes-buts, follow-up questions and acceptance is seen as an indicator of the quality of the assessment dialogue', Jølle, 2014: 42). Jølle (2014: 37) concludes that the quality of the rater dialogues did not change substantially over time, which left the author with 'the impression that raters often reached consensus without much discussion'. In his study of the usefulness of training in CA in assessing L2 pragmatic competence, Walters (2007) employed so-called *hermeneutic dialogues* post-assessment between two raters. One of the aims of the post-assessment conversations was to resolve rating differences dialogically, since 'even identical or similar scores between raters do not necessarily imply similar judgments' (Walters, 2007: 169). However, the study focused primarily on the aspects of pragmatic competence that the raters initially disagreed on rather than on the post-assessment dialogues themselves. May (2011b) was interested in features of paired speaking tests that were salient to raters in relation to interactional competence (IC), and had four raters view a video of a paired speaking test while making notes and recording a stimulated verbal report. Subsequently, raters sat in pairs to discuss their ratings, and their discussions were video-taped. The discussions were then coded with a focus on the features of IC that raters attended to, and reported in the form of sample statements illustrating the different categories. Again, while May's (2011b) study certainly evidences the relevance of examining rater discussions, its main aim was not to examine the rater dialogues as institutional interactions between professionals.

Sandlund and Sundqvist (2019) examined moderation meetings for assessing L2 oral proficiency and interaction, adopting video-recordings of rater discussions and a CA approach. The study aimed to uncover how teachers-as-raters conceptualized IC by examining sequences in which raters reported on specific turns or sequences in the paired test they assessed together. The study concludes that enactments and reports of specific learner contributions served to identify evidence of IC-relevant conduct, to support collaborative views-in-progress and to offer counter-examples to negative assessments in immediately prior talk. The authors conclude that examining rater talk as interaction through a CA lens holds promise for understanding how raters apply scoring rubrics and for developing assessment instructions to raters.

In sum, rater discussions in moderation or training efforts constitute a form of *reflective practice*, where raters do assessment but also reflect upon their own rater performance – something that can then be studied empirically (cf. Eckes, 2009: 44). *Reflection*, then, has been defined as an activity 'in which individuals engage to explore their experiences in order to lead to new understandings and appreciations' (Boud *et al.*, 1985: 19). Mann and Walsh (2013) have emphasized the need for a shift from written reflective practice to reflection as a dialogic, collaborative and data-led process, as such a take on reflective practice 'is more likely to elucidate the "real world" of professional practice and help work towards better outcomes in professional development' (Mann & Walsh, 2013: 293). In adopting such an approach to the design of rater training and moderation, new insights into the role of rater characteristics and reflection thereupon may be accessed through a focus on participants' situated orientations and actions. It is in this vein that this study targets rater positionings in L2 speaking assessment.

3 Data and Analytic Considerations

3.1 Participants and test data

Participants were teachers of English in Sweden, recruited for participation in two different research and professional development projects run by university researchers. The first was a rater training program for

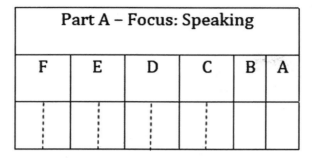

Figure 6.1 Assessment form tick box

assessing the National English Speaking Test (NEST) for Year 6 of compulsory school (NEST 6), and the second was a training workshop for collaborative assessment of the NEST for Year 9 of compulsory school (NEST 9). The NEST is developed by test constructors at the University of Gothenburg on behalf of the Swedish National Agency for Education. As a proficiency test with a traditional design, it includes a productive warm-up task (e.g. picture description or talking about one's family), followed by a peer-peer conversation guided by topic cards. Generally, the test administrator is the students' own English teacher, who thus serves the dual role of administrator and rater (see, for example, Sandlund & Sundqvist, 2019; Sundqvist *et al.*, 2018). Topic cards are used for the test conversations, and they carry statements or questions to prompt the learner conversation (e.g. 'There is nothing wrong with junk food'). On average, a test takes around 10 (NEST 6) or 15 (NEST 9) minutes. NEST performance is assessed on a 10-graded scale, from Grade F to Grade A. Since each of the grades F through C is assessed as either 'low' or 'high', the scale is 10-graded (rather than 6-graded), as illustrated in Figure 6.1, which represents the assessment tick box for teachers to mark their test grade.

As such, teachers considering, for example, a C grade for the test, should select one of the two boxes below C to indicate a strong or weak C grade. The test developers also provide information and samples of old national tests and assessment materials for both NEST 6 and NEST 9 on their website (see NAFS Project, 2021a, 2021b; Swedish National Agency for Education, 2014, 2015). Below, we account for the projects in which the data for the present study was collected.

3.1.1 The NEST 6 project

The data collection tied to NEST 6 was collected as part of a research and development project on assessment in two compulsory school subjects in Sweden: Swedish and English. The main objective was to devise and evaluate a training program that could contribute to equity in assessment in English and Swedish, respectively. Here, we target the training track for the assessment of L2 English speaking only.

Participants in the English track were 11 primary school teachers taking part in the training program (all women; mean age: 43; mean years working as teachers: 9.2). They taught English in Grades 4–6 (aged 10–12) at different schools. A background questionnaire revealed that their academic English education varied from nothing to as much as two semesters of English at university level. On average, participants had assessed NEST 6 almost five times, and they had also assigned term grades in English almost five times.

The rater training program was designed to contribute to equity in assessment by developing participating teachers' *awareness* of their own profiles ('identities') as raters of either English oral proficiency and interaction (the English track) or of Swedish writing proficiency (the Swedish track) – that is, complex productive language abilities. All participants had responded to an open call to participate in the combined research and professional development program. Some parts of the training program were jointly conducted with all teachers, but other parts were subject specific.

The training program had three integrated components (for a detailed description of its contents, see Sundqvist *et al.*, 2020). The first component was detailed feedback on each participant's individual assessment. The second was theoretical input focusing on language assessment, while the third consisted of repeated moderation sessions in small groups. Altogether, the program offered three full-day meetings on campus. The first day is referred to as the 'pretest day' (June), the second as 'rater training day' (when participants were video-recorded during the actual intervention, August) and the third as the 'posttest day' (September). On these three days, we collected assessment and questionnaire data from the participating teachers and they were also offered various lectures. The lectures were considered particularly relevant to their development as raters of L2 English speaking, and central concepts in the field of assessment (such as *benchmarks, construct relevant/irrelevant criteria, formative* versus *summative assessment, high-stakes* versus *low-stakes testing, reliability, standards, test construct* and *validity*) were introduced and discussed.

At the pretest day, 10 student performances in five paired NESTs were assessed by the 11 teachers. Each student was scored independently by each rater on the 10-graded scale, yielding 220 assessments of student performances in total. Following the pretest day, each participant was sent an email containing individual feedback. The purpose of this feedback was to raise each teacher's awareness of her own rater profile. Thus, the feedback included information on each participant's assessments, information about assessments in the rater group as a whole, and *benchmarks* (established reference scores for the ten performances – in this case, scores supplied by the Swedish National Agency for Education). Assessment data revealed that the English group assessed fairly close to the benchmarks at the pretest, and this was made explicit in the emails. To be specific, the mean difference for the group from the benchmarks was 0.40; that is, our

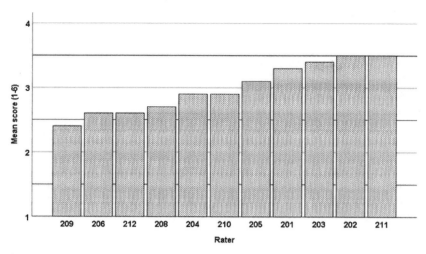

Figure 6.2 Severity continuum: raters' mean scores based on the assessment of 10 student performances on the pretest day, from the strictest rater to the most lenient

11 English raters differed in their assessments on four occasions during the pretest in that they were more strict than the benchmarks (for details, see Sundqvist *et al.*, 2020). In order to further prompt rater profile awareness, the feedback included explanations about how each rater had adopted the grading scale compared to the group (see Figure 6.2). There was also an individual table in the email summarizing each rater's own assessments on the 10 student performances. Finally, as preparation for the rater training day, raters were encouraged to reflect on their own profiles as they surfaced in pretest performances, for example, whether they were lenient or strict (or neither) compared to the benchmarks and to the rater group.

At the rater training day, assessment topics were further discussed and explained in lectures by the authors. Particular attention was given to the assessment criteria for the NEST 6 and the test construct *oral production and interaction*, and to being professional as a teacher in terms of aligning with standards. In order to facilitate the raters' discussions, we introduced three bird metaphors, selected to symbolize aspects of rater severity. The first metaphor was *the rater as a hawk* (that is, a severe rater, traditionally rating lower than the benchmark). The second was *the rater as a dove* (that is, a lenient rater, traditionally rating higher than the benchmark), and the third was *the rater as a blackbird* (that is, a 'benchmark' rater, traditionally rating close to or on the benchmark). The metaphors were explained to participants using examples, and the potential consequences for individual learners and their development were discussed.

For the moderation sessions on the rater training day, the participants were in groups of three or four and these were audio- or video-recorded (see Section 2, Table 6.1). In total, they assessed eight student performances

Table 6.1 Overview of data of 10 rater recordings used in the present study

Recording	Data type	Minutes	Raters (n)	Tests (n)	Students (n)
NEST6_2_A	Video	36	4	1	2
NEST6_2_B	Video	31	4	2	4
NEST6_2_C	Video	26	4	1	2
NEST6_3_A	Audio	21	4	1	2
NEST6_3_B	Audio	20	4	2	4
NEST6_3_C	Audio	7	4	1	2
NEST9_1	Video	52	4	1	2
NEST9_2	Video	51	3	1	2
NEST9_3	Video	42	3	1	2
NEST9_4	Video	55	3	1	2
TOTAL		**341**	**37**	**12**	**24**

in four test recordings. They had been given clear oral and written instructions about listening to one recording at a time, starting each test recording with individual listening and independent assessment (for details, see Sundqvist *et al.*, 2020). As soon as all members of a group had completed their assessments, group moderation sessions began with the opening of an envelope that contained the official assessment comments and benchmark grades for the learner performances from the National Agency for Education. The teachers had been instructed to then 'out' their own rater profile in the group based on how they had understood their individual feedback. The moderation sessions continued with comparisons of the assessments made with regard to the benchmarks. The various components of the moderation sessions together served the purpose of raising rater awareness. After the posttest, effects of the rater training model were investigated using a many-facet Rasch measurement (MFRM) model (Linacre, 2017; Rasch, 1980), and an intraclass correlation coefficient (ICC) two-way random effects model (McGraw & Wong, 1996), which is reported on in Sundqvist *et al.* (2020).

3.1.2 The NEST 9 project

The data collection tied to NEST 9 was done in 2015 as part of a research project on collaborative assessment (CASS). This dataset is comprised of four video-recordings of L2 English teachers involved in CASS of one paired NEST 9 (see Table 6.1). The teachers had signed up for a professional development day for English teachers organized by a research center at a university, which offered a selection of workshops – one of which was organized by the authors. The workshop was announced as an opportunity to engage in CASS of L2 English oral proficiency and participants consented to filling out a brief background questionnaire and to video-recording of the CASS discussions for the purpose of research. In total, 13 teachers (12 women; one man) participated. Questionnaire data revealed that all participants had a teacher degree in English. In terms of experience, on average they had worked for 13 years. All knew the NEST 9 well, except for the least experienced participant who was yet to assess her first NEST 'for real'.

The workshop was divided into three parts. In the first part, the authors gave a lecture on research on L2 oral proficiency testing and assessment. In the second part, a selected, authentic paired NEST 9 test recording (with test-takers Fred and Henrik, pseudonyms) was played to the whole group. Raters were instructed to take notes and make initial independent assessments of the two learner performances (cf. May, 2011a). The third part was the actual moderation meetings. Participants were divided into four groups and assigned separate rooms. In each room, the participants had access to the assessment materials for NEST 9 (tasks and assessment instructions), and a web link to the test recording for re-listening on their smartphones/tablets.Their task as raters was to discuss the performances by Fred and Henrik and reach consensus on grades for each test-taker. Afterwards, each of the four groups handed in a joint rater protocol with arguments supporting their grading. The meetings lasted between 42 and 55 minutes (see Table 6.1) and the researchers were not present. As opposed to the procedure in the NEST 6 project, in which the use of benchmarks aimed to achieve calibration against standards, the NEST 9 project centered on description of moderation activities and participants' displayed understandings of the rubrics. As such, participants were only instructed to discuss their judgments and agree on a grade, but were not presented with benchmarks afterwards.

3.2 Recorded data

Based on data collected in the two projects, we have used 10 rater recordings (audio and video) in the present study, amounting to a total of 341 recorded minutes and involving 37 different raters (see Table 6.1). All recordings were transcribed in their entirety using Jeffersonian conventions (Jefferson, 2004). Translations into English are provided in bold face, and interlinear glosses are provided in cases where the translation significantly changed the syntax or word order of the original turn, or when an idiomatic expression without a suitable English equivalent was used. For this study, the datasets were trawled for sequences in which participants displayed orientations to severity/leniency. These sequences were subsequently transcribed in more detail, and Swedish translations were added.

As Table 6.1 shows, the NEST 9 recordings are longer than the NEST 6 recordings, and while the NEST 9 meetings centered on one paired test for assessment, the two NEST 6 groups discussed several different paired tests across three meetings in the same day.

3.3 Methods of analysis

For the analysis of orientations to rater identities as severe or lenient, CA (Sacks *et al.*, 1974; Sidnell & Stivers, 2013), combined with some observational tools (or 'keys') from membership categorization analysis (MCA; Stokoe, 2012: 280–281), were used. With the descriptor *rater identity*, we broadly refer to displayed orientations to aspects of rater severity and leniency that participants draw upon in the rater discussions, and where such identity orientations constitute participants' 'displays of, or ascription to, membership of some feature-rich category' (Antaki & Widdicombe, 1998: 2). According to Silverman (1998: 77), Harvey Sacks' take on addressing categories in interaction was to 'try to understand when and how members' descriptions are properly produced'. By producing membership categories (or invoking categories more implicitly through descriptions and reference forms), an interactant can 'strengthen the social action that he or she is performing' (Liu, 2015: 1). Categories, performed through various categorical practices in interaction, can be examined from a sequential, participants' perspective (Stokoe, 2012). The present chapter, while principally adopting a CA approach, also analytically examines participants' descriptions as part of sequentially organized action from the lens of membership categories. The two datasets differ in the sense that NEST 6 participants had been explicitly instructed to talk about their individual rater feedback from the pretest day, whereas for NEST 9 participants issues related to rater severity were volunteered in connection with their assessment talk. As such, we believe the two datasets complement each other in uncovering how rater categories are drawn upon in assessment talk.

4 Analysis

Two main sequential environments in which participants oriented to their severity/leniency identities, namely *rater identities in relation to absent 'others'* (Section 4.1) and *rater identities in assessment negotiations* (Section 4.2) were identified in the two datasets. For the sake of illustration, three sequences are analyzed in detail.

4.1 Positioning rater identities in relation to absent 'others'

In our first analytic presentation, we will examine sequences in which the teachers display orientation to rater severity, and mobilize membership in a particular category of raters-as-professionals by reference to relativeness to non-present others. We begin with an extended excerpt from the first session of the rater training day, as raters here explicitly describe themselves along the severity continuum by using the bird metaphors, and account for the self-identification with explanations for their rater performance at the pretest. In this sequence, accounts following membership descriptions contribute to managing the delicacy of having to reveal a professionally problematic category. Subsequently, we examine a sequence from a group discussion from the NEST 6 training program in which orientations to severity also occur in connection with talk about non-present others, but where group members position themselves as affiliating with each other and against non-present others. Because of the length of the sequence, the presentation has been divided up into two segments, and analytic comments are presented in conjunction with each. In what follows, Lines 3–46 are presented first.

As per the instructions for the group work, the raters were told to reveal something to their group members about the pretest feedback they had received by email prior to the rater training day, and talk about their reactions to their rater profiles, before proceeding with discussing the new assessments of tests they had just made individually prior to the rater group meeting. As we enter the group's talk, Rater 201 orients to the instructions, and asks the group where they should begin (Line 1, not shown) before suggesting (in a question format, Line 3) that they begin by 'outing' their rater profiles to each other.

Excerpt 6.1a 'One of the doves'; NEST6_2, Lines 3–46

```
3    201    ska vi: outa oss först.
            should we: out ourselves first.

4    208    kHHHHHhhhh

5           (0.8)

6    208    j[ia↓.
            Y[eah↓

7    201    [hur det gick me:
            [how it went with

8    208    [ me'ren, ]
            [with the,]

9    201    [inte-  ] inte nu me dagens utan me
            [not-   ] not now with today's but with
            [ Not-  ] not the ones today but with

10          förra gångens (.) förtest( et )
            last time's (.) the pretest

11   201    [ah HUR Ä: vi som be[dömare
            [ah how are we as ra[ters
            ah how we are as raters
```

```
12   204    [°Ja just de°         [ja just de
            [°oh yeah right       [oh yeah right=

13   208    =ja:=
            =yes:=

14   201    =ja?
            =yes:=

15         (0.8)

16   202    ja: är ju då: en utav domdäre:h (.) duvor↑na
            I: am PRT then one of those         doves
            So I'm one of the doves then

17   201    m:?

           (1.4)

18   202    .pt e:h lite mer givmild och jag tr↑o:r
            .pt e:h a little more generous and I ↑think

19         att de be↑ror på att när vi har gjort
            that it depends on that when we have done

           + gaze up, circling finger movements
20         +sambedömningar¿ (0.4) så ha ja förstått att
            +co-assessments¿ (0.4) I have learned that

                      +202 both palms pressing down twice
                       + 201 nods twice
21         att många +(.)dömer+ (.) eller bedömer såe:h .pt
            that many +(.) judge (.) or assess so e:h .pt

22   201    hårt.=
            Harshly.=

23   202    =hårt¿
            =harshly¿

24   202    så då har jag varit den som liksom har
            so then have I been the one who kind of has
            then I have been the one to kind of

                      +hands raised
25         ställt frågan +men*e::h* (0.5) kan vi inte
            asked the question but          can we not
            ask bute::h (0.5) can't we see

26         se:r vi inte de hä:r (.) as[så
            see we not this I mean
            can't we see this (.) I    [mean

                                +nods
27   201                        [a:? +
```

```
28  202  för å lätta upp de
         PREP lighten up it
         to lighten things up

29  201  m:?

30  202  å det fortsätter ja me när jag bedömer
         and that continue I with when I assess
         an' I continue with that when I assess

31       själv också¿
         self too
         on my own too¿

32  201  ja?
         Yes?

33  202  å de:- de visar sej precis i de här också .hh
         an' it it shows-RFL precisely in these too
         and it- it is evident in these too.hh

34  201  ja?
         Yes?

35  202  ja har (0.2) bedömt tjejen <li:te>
         I have       assessed girl-the little
         I have (0.2) assessed the girl a little

36       för högt
         too high

37  201  m:

38  202  .h ock- men killen har jag på rätt nivå
         .h and- but guy-the have I on right level.
         .h an- but the guy I have at the right level.

39  201  ↑ja.
         ↑Yes.

40  202  m: (0.3) men så att ja: måste
         m: (0.3) but so that I have to

41       tänka mig för att
         phrasal verb  to
         be careful to

42       inte va riktigt så generös.=
         not be quite so generous.=

43  201  =m:=

44  202  =som ja (1.1) har varit
         =as I (1.1) have been

45  201  m:.

46  202  m:.
```

Rater 201 continues in Lines 7–10 by specifying that this is in reference to the pretest performances rather than to the assessment work they have just conducted, and uses the description 'how we are as raters' (Line 11) to further describe the proposed activity. Rater 204 displays recognition of the suggested activity, and so does Rater 208, with a minimal agreement response. Rater 202, then, volunteers a self-categorization in Line 16. In her turn, Rater 202 categorizes herself as 'one of the doves' – using the bird metaphor used to symbolize rater leniency. By doing so, she explicitly mobilizes the rater severity continuum, with the severe hawks at one end and the lenient doves at the other, and reveals that in her pretest assessments her performance had clearly placed her on the lenient side in comparison with the others. Note, however, that while the researchers had offered the categories, the individual feedback did not contain classifications of the participants as such, but only showed scores of individual ratings compared to benchmarks, and the severity distribution within the rater group (see Figure 6.2). As such, participants may opt to recruit these categories based on their own interpretations of their individual scores, which are unknown to the group. Rater 202 thus volunteers this categorization of herself.

Co-participants (except for the minimal 'm:?' from 201 in Line 17) do not comment on or assess this revelation, but appear to await further elaboration from Rater 202. In Line 18, she elaborates on her revelation, specifying a category-bound predicate (Stokoe, 2012: 281) of a dove rater as 'a little more generous'. She immediately embarks on an account where she reflects upon possible reasons behind her leniency, which indicates that self-categorization is an accountable action. This account (Lines 19–31) centers on her rating experiences outside of the training, where other teachers she has co-assessed with have judged the learners 'harshly' (Line 202, description first provided by Rater 201 in response to Rater 202's possible word search in Line 21), and where she positions herself as someone who has attempted to counter 'harsh' assessments by highlighting positive aspects of learner performances. The account offers an explanation for being lenient that casts Rater 202's approach in a more positive light – in contrast to 'many' of her colleagues, she is the one to highlight strengths by asking her colleagues to 'see this' in order to 'lighten things up'. From just this revelation of a rater profile, we can see that being placed on the far end of the lenient side of the continuum is treated as problematic and accountable. By sharing past experiences, where severe raters are described as rating 'harshly' (rather than described as being 'to the point'), Rater 202 depicts a scenario where her leniency accomplishes an important balance, and thus casts her own 'dove status' as a result of her also paying attention to the strengths in learners' performances. By invoking her leniency as a result of her experience of striving for a more holistic approach, she also invokes severity as paired with actions of excessive strictness in judging learners. She sums up the connection between her pretest performance and her past experience in Lines 30–31, where she states that she tends to continue with the same approach when she grades tests on her own. As co-participants only display receipt of her account, Rater 202 continues in Lines 33 and onwards by specifically referring to the feedback sheet in front of her, stating that her approach to rating is also visible in a particular test from the pretest where she had assessed 'the girl a little too high' (Lines 35–36) but the boy 'at the right level' (Line 38, below). However, the slow production and elongated vowel on <li:te> (a little, Line 35) emphasizes the qualifying adverbial 'a little', which works to downplay the severity of her rater error in relation to the benchmark. Thus, in the evidence she supplies for her own analysis of her rater profile, her turn indicates that it is designed for a specific hearing: that even though she was marginally over-lenient for one learner, she was on the benchmark for the other. Thus, her turn serves to pre-empt recipient understandings of her as *always* being overly lenient or 'wrong' in her professional assessment work. In Lines 40–44, Rater 202 formulates what she needs to think about in her future assessment work as a result of the feedback: she has to be 'careful to not be quite so generous' as she has been in the past, to which Rater 201 provides an acknowledging 'm:'. As such, the self-categorization, followed by an analytic account, ends with a reflective and forward-oriented formulation of desirable future conduct.

Moving forward to the second part of this sequence, presented in Excerpt 6.1b below, Rater 208 follows the self-revelation path set by Rater 202, using the categorization device *hawk* (Line 48) to reveal that she was, in fact, on the other end of the continuum at the pretest:

Excerpt 6.1b 'I am a hawk'; NEST6_2, Lines 48–74

```
                +gaze up to 202
48    208    å +ja är en hök.
             and I am a hawk.
```

```
49    202    m:

50    201    m::,

                +gaze down to documents
51    208    +>ja.< .pt .hhh
             +>yeah<. .pt .hhh|
```

```
52           (1.4)

53    208    ocke:h (0.8) a: när ja skulle försöka
             ande:h (0.8) a: when I was trying to

54           fundera på varför ja va: en hök för ja
             think about why I was a hawk cuz I
```

```
55              (0.3) upplever mig inte va en hök (.)
                (0.3) don't see myself as a hawk (.)

56              annars¿
                otherwise¿

57              vid bedömning men men hä:r var jag ju de
                in assessment but but he:re I was

58              helt klart. |
                no doubt.

59              (0.8)

60      208     e::h

61              (1.7)

62      208     och jag tro:r att ja va: (.) att
                and I think that I was (.) that

                                                +gaze up
63              det ä: lite grann det här jag är +ju själv
                it's a little this that I'm +ju on my own

64              på min skola (.) ja är alldeles själv när ja
                at my school (.) I'm all on my own when I

65              bedömer+ och att de finns en sån
                assess + and that there is such an

                + 201 nods
66              <o+säkerhet>
                <in+security>

67              å när ja då är osäker (.) så sätter ja mej på
                an' if I'm unsure (.) I'll place myself on

68              nån slags (1.2)
                a kind of (1.2)

69              .hha de e lite riskfritt att
                .hha it's sort of risk-free to

70              va ↑hök då
                be a ↑hawk then

71      201     [ja:   just   d e t]
                [Ye:ah that's right]

72      208     [ än å  va:- än å  va
                [than to be:- than to be a

73      208     du:[↑va på nåt sätt
                a ↑do[ve in some ways

74      201        [m:
```

As Rater 208 begins speaking, she shifts her gaze to Rater 202, as if responding specifically to her as the previous speaker. At Line 51, after having produced the description, she shifts her gaze down to the documents on the table and produces a 'yeah.' with falling intonation. In combination with her facial expression, this is a confirming response to the two acknowledgment tokens produced by Raters 201 and 202, but also indicates that there is something problematic about having performed as a hawk. The confirming 'yeah' in combination with the gaze shift, lip smack and inbreath seems also to appeal to a shared sentiment about performing at the extremes of the severity–leniency continuum. As with the prior dove categorization, co-participants await further elaboration, and Rater 208 reports on her own reflection process at the time of receiving the feedback: she was trying to think about why she was a hawk here, because her results did apparently not match her own perception. Her surprise at the feedback is expressed as, 'I don't see myself as a hawk otherwise in assessment', but also acknowledges that her results tell a different story (Lines 55–58).

Having pre-announced an upcoming reflection about severity on the pretest, she prefaces her candidate explanation with 'I think' (Line 62) which, just as Rater 202 did previously, relates her performance to past experiences at her local school, where she happens to be the only English teacher (Lines 63–64). She continues her account by formulating what these conditions generate: that there is such an 'insecurity' as a result of having to make all decisions on her own. She then returns to the severity/ leniency metaphors, and proposes that it is 'sort of risk-free' to exercise severity rather than leniency (Lines 69–70, 73). This yields an affiliative response from Rater 201 before Rater 208 explicitly offers the contrast to a dove (Line 73). In Rater 201's description, then, it is safer, professionally speaking, to exercise severity than risk facing accusations of contribution to grade inflation by awarding high scores.

In this sequence, identification at either end of the continuum is treated as being a problematic rater category, warranting accounts of prior experiences and contexts outside of the current interaction. At the same time, the benchmarks are oriented to as normative, with the implication that displaying category membership in a group that is close to benchmarks is non-accountable. As such, a scale of categories is occasioned – both institutionally and interactionally – where acknowledged membership at either end of the continuum is morally accountable in relation to treatment of benchmark grades as the norm. Scales often operate 'together with notions of normality and markedness' (Bilmes, 2019: 82). Similarly, the understanding of how particular descriptions fit into a given scale requires cultural knowledge as well as 'attention to what scales are relevant and how a particular scale is constructed within the local interaction' (Hauser & Prior, 2019: 76). Raters in our data orient to shared information (figures and images in the feedback documents) as well as to culturally shared norms about professionalism. Their orientations to the benchmarks as normative are evident, for example, in descriptions of rater performance in *relative* terms ('too high', Line

35; 'on the right level', Line 38) and the self-reported conclusions about future conduct, and in the very production of the categorical description (gaze shifts, gaps, intonation) that projects a problem associated with such membership. Also, the categories of hawk and dove, while provided by the workshop organizers, are also locally occasioned in the sequential context of each speaker's analysis of the feedback received, where participants themselves link the contents of the feedback to a rater category metaphor. The two consecutive self-categorizations in the first and second parts of Excerpt 6.1 place the two raters on each end of the scale. While both participants deal with their 'problematic' rater identities in similar ways using accounts, the second account (i.e. the hawk) also *modifies* the scale so that a view of severity as slightly more preferable than leniency (while still problematic in relation to the norm) emerges. In both self-categorizations, individual performance is accounted for in terms of the conduct of others (or lack of others), and these external circumstances are assigned part of the blame for a particular rater's performance.

In the NEST 9 dataset, we also observed orientations to severity, which surfaced in talk about the assessment criteria or in relation to colleagues at their schools, as exemplified in Excerpt 6.2. Here, the discussion has centered on the benchmark tests provided by the test constructors (here referred to as *Skolverket*, i.e. The Swedish National Agency for Education), and in Lines 1–3 Ann announces that she 'often' does not agree with the benchmark grades set as reference points. She presents her claim rather neutrally, thus not revealing whether there is any systematicity in the difference between her views and those of the test constructors, but continues to reveal that this perceived discrepancy is because she feels the benchmark grades are too lenient. Her turn is left incomplete in Line 6, but her 'I think they pass way too-' clearly displays an orientation to the test constructors' set grades as too lenient:

Excerpt 6.2 'went down a notch'; NEST 9_2, Lines 3–18, 19–31

```
1    ANN   men där e:: jag tycker de e ofta de e::m
           but there e:: I think it is often it e::m
           but I often find that

2          (1.1)

           +shaking head repeatedly
3          +skolverket å ja tycker inte samma sak
           +skolverket and I don't think the same

4          ofta asså
           often really

5    KAR   .hhhnä:.hh
           .hhhno: .hh

6    ANN   °ja tycker dom godkä[nner alldeles-,  °]
           °I think they pass way too-,  °
```

```
7   KAR                        [ja och sen bara m-]
                               [yes and also just b-

8        mellan kolleger ↑mä
         between colleagues also

9   LIS  m::?

10  ANN  ja:?
         ye:s?


11  KAR  e:h den ja jobbar närmast med nu: vi är
         e:h the one I work closest with now we are

12       väldit överrens:
         very much in agreement

13       (.)

14  KAR  °men sen:: en annan kollega°
         °but then   another colleague°

15       >hon har gått i pension nu< ↑hon (.) .hhh
         >she has retired now< ↑she (.) .hhh

16       (.)

17  KAR  hade nog lite >vi tog< över lite:
         probably had a little >we took< over some

18       klasser efter henne å d-
         classes from her and d-

19       (.)

20       °var nåra° s(hh)om(hh) åkte ne:r
         °were a few° who went down

21       ett hack.
         a notch

22  ANN  m::

23  KAR  [ja↓]
         [yes↓]

24  LIS  [du:] ä på högstadiet¿
         [you] are at secondary school

25  KAR  +ja::
         +yes
         +nods twice, gaze at LIS

26  KAR  .hh ocke:h (.) ↑a:?
         .hh andu:h (.) well?
```

```
27          (.)


28    KAR   ä: det hon eller vi som har (.) .hh [rätt
            is it her or us who is (.) right


29    ANN                                        [JA DE Ä
                                                 [YES IT IS
30          JU ↑svårt
            PRT
            JU really difficult
```

Ann thus positions herself as a more severe rater, and also provides an (albeit incomplete) assessment of the benchmarks as 'too' lenient, and making it possible to pass 'way' more students than she would. Consequently, leniency in relation to the lowest passing grade (E) is depicted in a negative light, and a higher level of severity, then, is recruited for displaying professionalism. While Ann's turn challenges the epistemic primacy of the norms set by the educational authority, she nevertheless treats it as a norm, albeit a problematic one. In overlap, Kari offers an agreeing 'yes', but instead of exploring the issue of the benchmark grades, she brings forth a parallel context in which differences in severity can arise – between colleagues at one's local school (Line 8). She exemplifies this issue further with an account of how she and her current colleague are 'very much in agreement' (Line 12) but that when a former colleague retired, they took over some of her classes, at which point they had 'a few who went down a notch' (Line 20). As with Ann's example of the benchmark grades, Kari's account is based on a narrative about a third party who, apparently, graded more leniently, resulting in some students' grades being lowered one step when new teachers came in. Kari delivers her account factually, but later acknowledges some uncertainty as to whether the former colleague, or Kari and her current colleague, were 'right' (Line 28). While Ann's contributions positions her own severity as somewhat superior to the benchmark grades from the test constructors, Kari's account, while revealing that she is obviously more severe than a former colleague, mainly functions to assert the presence of discrepancies in assessment between different raters. Ann then provides an agreeing assessment, that it is 'really difficult' (presumably to know which assessment is 'right').

Across both datasets, issues of rater severity is frequently brought up in the context of acknowledging rater differences and preferences. We now turn to the second context in which orientations to rater profiles frequently surface, namely in sequences where assessment decisions are to be made, and disagreement about a particular grade has been revealed.

4.2 Rater identity displays in making collaborative assessment decisions

Unsurprisingly, raters frequently orient to their own perceived position along the severity–leniency continuum when a discrepancy between individually assigned assessments have become evident. In Excerpt 6.3 from the NEST 9 dataset, group members Katherine, Victoria and Alison are discussing a grade for one of the two boys, having revealed their individual grades earlier in the rater meeting and now returning to them in order to agree on a joint grade. In Line 1, Victoria delivers the scope of her preferred grade – a C or a D (Line 3) – and as there is no response apart from the minimal acknowledgment from Katherine, she asserts, using the extreme case formulation *never* (Edwards, 2000), that this is as high as she could go (Line 6). In her rather adamant claim, combined with the formulation 'I think', she is invoking a degree of severity as a property of her assessment decision with regard to the learner as it makes clear that a grade above C would be out of the question for her:

Excerpt 6.3 'maybe it's me who's too strict'; NEST 9_3, Lines 1–37

```
1    VIC   men jag skulle- (0.2)  om ja: s: (0.3)
           but I should-          if I s-

2          ↑HAN skulle ja no va lite mer att jag tänker
           ↑HIM I would probably be more that I think

3          ce: elle de:
           cee:: or dee::

4    KAT   °m:¿°

5          (0.3)

6    VIC   <aldrig högre> än- än dä:
           <never higher> than- than that

7    KAT   ne:↑j ehmen ja sa dä ja är benägen å
           no:↑y uh but I said that I'm inclined to

8          sätta ce: pl[us
           put a ce:: pl[us

9    VIC              [ja:¿
                      [ye:s¿

10   KAT   istället för be:
           instead of be::

11         (1.0)

12   KAT   [ (ja tycker)  ]
           [ ( I think ) | ]
```

13   VIC   [men ↑DU tycker] ↑↑BE:.
            [but ↑YOU think] ↑↑BE:.

14   (0.7)

15   ALI   jamen grejen är att ja::g n- nhhh (0.3) ja
            wellbut the thing is that I:: n- nhhh (0.3) I

16   har <aldrig rättat> nått sånt här .h för↑ut
            have <never graded> anything like this .h be↑fore

17   å ja tänker (0.6) j- n(hh)(0.8)ja (.) liksom
            an' I'm thinking (0.6) I- n(hh)(0.8)I (.) kinda

            +palm held flat in the air, lowering movement
18   +sch- >sänker min: >mina krav (0.7) eftersom
            + sch- >lower my: >my standards (0.7) since

19   det inte äre:hm (0.4) tvåspråk[iga
            it isn't hm   (0.4) bilingu[al

20   VIC   [a:¿ a:¿=
                                         [ye:s¿ ye:s¿

21   KAT   =m:.

22   ALI   så ja tänker ja måste sänka det ganska
            so I'm thinking I have to lower it quite

23   mycke'[rå
            a lot [then

24   KAT   [m::.

25   ALI   men hh [kanske ja sänker det för mycke
            but hh [maybe I'm lowering it too much

26   KAT   [m:.

27   (2.3)

28   KAT   m:

29   (2.1)

30   KAT   mene:h,=
            Bute:h,=

31   VIC   =kanske är ja som är för sträng
            =maybe it's me who's too strict

32   [också?]
            [too?]

33   KAT   [men är du]
            [but are you]

```
34   VIC   så kan de ju va.
           so can it ju be.
           that could be the case.

35   KAT   °annars betraktas ja: som st(hh)rä(hh)ng hh°
           °usually I:'m viewed as st(hh)ri(hh)ct hh°

36         brukar ja ju göra=
           normally I am=

37   VIC   =ja[  HA::   ]
           =a:[HA::     ]
```

In response, Katherine produces an initial 'no' token, which functions as an initial agreement with Victoria's claim (Pomerantz, 1984), but then announces her own grading preference in the shape of a dispreferred disagreeing action ('uh but', Line 7). The formulation 'inclined to put a ce:: plus instead of be::' positions Katherine's preferred grade at a higher level than Victoria's D or C. Here, a grading discrepancy has become publicly available, where Victoria's grade indicates greater severity. Katherine's 'I think' (Line 12) is overlapped by Victoria, who turns to the third rater, Alison. Victoria formulates Alison's stance on the grade for confirmation, emphasizing 'YOU' and the grade 'BE:' with a 'surprised' intonation (Line 13, cf. Wilkinson & Kitzinger, 2006). By displaying surprise although the B grade had been previously revealed and thus is no actual news to Victoria, she also displays some doubt or disbelief at Alison's professional opinion, which is more lenient than Victoria's and even Katherine's. Alison's account in response shows that Victoria's turn projected that she is accountable for explaining her grade, and her account centers on her *inexperience* with rating the NEST: she teaches English as a mother tongue and is therefore used to bilingual learners rather than foreign language learners, and her suggested B grade was the result of her lowering her standards to fit with non-bilinguals (Lines 15–19, 22, 25). Consequently, she is projecting a connection between her lack of experience with a perceived leniency in the graded test. However, while mobilizing a temporary identity as lenient, she is also invoking a higher standard in her everyday professional practice. In Line 25, Alison opens up for deviant views by acknowledging that she is perhaps 'lowering it too much'.

In response, Katherine initiates a disagreeing turn (Line 30), but stops as Victoria produces a self-reflective categorization: 'maybe it's me who's too strict too', which in a way mirrors Alison's indication that she may have been too lenient. In acknowledging that she may just as well be the reason for the discrepancy, she mobilizes the severity–leniency characteristics in affiliating with Alison's displayed uncertainty. Up to this point, then, Victoria has positioned her (more severe) grading view in relation to Katherine and Alison rather strongly, but after Alison's account, she mitigates her earlier claims and treats misplaced severity as equally problematic. In self-identifying as a severe rater who may be too severe in this particular case, public self-reflection is initiated. Interestingly, this occasions another self-categorization from Katherine in Line 35: 'usually I:'m viewed as st(hh)ri(hh)ct hh'. With the emphasis on 'I'm' and the use of 'usually', which recruits non-present others as perception evidence, her turn challenges Victoria's self-categorization as severe by claiming a severe identity for herself. Her production of 'strict' contains laugh particles, and is followed by another reference to her rater profile outside the current context: 'normally I am' (Line 36). Victoria treats this as surprising news in Line 37, and the discussion continues with additional arguments about the particular student they are jointly grading (not included).

The sequence reveals that when diverging perceptions of the learner's performance have been made publicly available, a space for explaining the divergence opens up. This is done through public self-reflection on reasons underlying each rater's view, which is partially accomplished through self-categorization and reflection on the accuracy of these approaches. As Logren *et al.* (2017) have noted, self-reflection in interaction can be identified in 'utterances in which speakers report their own behaviour and experiences and *mark them as a target of reflection*' (Logren *et al.*, 2017: 426, italics in the original), which in this case relates to their grading. While Alison is cast as lenient and accounts for her inexperience as an explanation, Victoria reflects on her possible excessive severity, and Katherine, consequently, claims membership in the severity group of raters by drawing on her experiences in other contexts. Katherine's positioning thus rejects Victoria's indication that it is her general severity that underlies the current discrepancy, since Katherine herself has been viewed as severe in all other contexts. Alison's account, which is accepted, and the 'competition' for membership in the 'severe rater' group also indicate a view of leniency as more problematic than severity, as Katherine displays unwillingness to be identified as lenient, even though she initially proposed a higher grade than Victoria.

5 Discussion

In our analytic section, we have examined three selected sequences in which teachers-as-raters orient to rater severity or leniency in two distinct sequential contexts. Across these three and others in our datasets, participants display an orientation to leniency as a slightly more problematic professional rater identity than severity. Whether using rater metaphors provided, or orienting to severity/leniency in the context of diverging views on particular learner performances, rater leniency is accounted for in relation to inexperience or attributed more positive predicates such as 'generous' in accounts of the excessive severity of others. Severity is linked to excessive strictness, but also to rater insecurity, where severity is accounted for as a safer option, which in turn implies that leniency faces the risk of accusations of unprofessionalism. A scale with a continuum from severe to lenient is not only occasioned from the institution of assessment (in this case, through individual feedback on pretest rating performance, which in itself placed each rater along this continuum), but is also occasioned and made relevant in the situated rater interactions. In their talk, only category membership far away from the benchmark grades is treated as accountable. However, this is also evident when participants question the accuracy of the benchmarks. By critiquing the benchmarks as overly lenient, participants show orientation to them as the norm, but also tilt the moral implications of the scale in favor of the severity category. Consequently, even though both extreme positions are treated as problematic, the scale occasioned in the raters' treatment of the benchmark as the norm allows for professionalism to be displayed through critique of lenient benchmark grades. In all, rater self-categorizations strengthen preferred identity positionings as professionals and/or invite further justifications for rater performance on the extremes of the continuum.

In the NEST 6 project from which data for the present study were drawn, participants returned a month after rater training for a posttest. The posttest analysis revealed that the group scored even closer to the benchmarks than at the pretest, and made greater use of the full range of grades available after participating in training, revealing that changes in assessment practice from pretest to posttest did take place (Sundqvist *et al.*, 2020). For the NEST 9 project, which mainly centered on collaborative assessment rather than rater training, no scoring data were collected at a later occasion. While the present study has focused specifically on interactional trajectories during two types of L2 assessment training events, it is possible that the category memberships formulated by our participants, and the subsequent treatment of them, constitute a core aspect of the development of rater awareness, which in turn contributed to the posttest change. It remains for further research to examine more carefully how such identity positionings and participants' stance towards them may gradually change and even (temporarily) stabilize through participation in rater training activities over time and, in turn, how self-categorizations may form pivotal moments in calibrating assessment practices.

6 Conclusion

Rater variability is naturally a problem in high-stakes language assessment and, as McNamara (1996) notes, rater bias and variations in severity are two of the factors underlying problematic variability. However, these issues have mainly been explored in quantitative studies of rater performance rather than as socially and interactionally constructed and negotiated identities in accomplishing professional activities. Likewise, research on rater training has principally centered on either self-reported experiences or measurable effects and less on the reflective practices involved, such as how raters formulate, negotiate and mobilize their own rater identities in assessment talk. This chapter has targeted how rater identity positionings in situated talk between professionals, frequently adopted through self-categorizations and accounts, enforce, justify or mitigate past assessment performances. Through a CA lens, we have demonstrated some ways in which raters' reflection-in-action can be accessed in descriptions and accounts, partly accomplished through categorization practices (Evans & Fitzgerald, 2016; Hauser, 2011; Sacks, 1992), which can be examined sequentially (Stokoe, 2012). The two sequential contexts examined in moderation interactions between teachers-as-raters – in relation to non-present others and in disagreements about grades – revealed how identity positionings contribute to the establishment of lay/expert roles, and to the shared construction of severity as 'more professional' than leniency. As such, rater positionings taken in interaction have moral implications. This observation is central, as a more positive view on severity may reveal an assessment bias that could hinder equity in high-stakes assessment. We argue that sequential analysis of rater identities in interaction can offer a window into teachers' stepwise modification of rater cognition, and thus holds promise for further studies on assessment (cf. Jönsson & Thornberg, 2014).

References

Adie, L.E., Klenowski, V. and Wyatt-Smith, C. (2012) Towards an understanding of teacher judgment in the context of social moderation. *Educational Review* 64 (2), 223–240. doi:10.1080/00131911.2011.598919

Antaki, C. and Widdicombe, S. (1998) Identity as an achievement and as a tool. In C. Antaki and S. Widdicombe (eds) *Identities in Talk* (pp. 1–14). London: Sage.

Benwell, B. and Stokoe, E. (2006) *Discourse and Identity*. Edinburgh: Edinburgh University Press.

Bilmes, J. (2019) Regrading as a conversational practice. *Journal of Pragmatics* 150, 80–91. See http://www.sciencedirect.com/science/article/pii/S0378216617308007. doi:10.1016/j.pragma.2018.08.020

Bloxham, S., Hughes, C. and Adie, L. (2016) What's the point of moderation? A discussion of the purposes achieved through contemporary moderation practices. *Assessment & Evaluation in Higher Education* 41 (4), 638–653. doi:10.1080/026029 38.2015.1039932

Boud, D., Keogh, R. and Walker, D. (1985) Promoting reflection in learning: A model. In D. Boud, R. Keogh and D. Walker (eds) *Reflection: Turning Experience into Learning* (pp. 18–40). London: Routledge Falmer.

Chapelle, C.A. and Brindley, G. (2002) Assessment. In N. Schmitt (ed.) *An Introduction to Applied Linguistics* (pp. 267–288). New York: Oxford University Press.

Davis, L. (2016) The influence of training and experience on rater performance in scoring spoken language. *Language Testing* 33 (1), 117–135. doi:10.1177/0265532215582282

Ducasse, A.M. and Brown, A. (2009) Assessing paired orals: Raters' orientation to interaction. *Language Testing* 26 (3), 423–443.

Eckes, T. (2009) On common ground? How raters perceive scoring criteria in oral proficiency testing. In A. Brown and K. Hill (eds) *Tasks and Criteria in Performance Assessment* (pp. 43–73). Frankfurt am Main: Peter Lang.

Edwards, D. (2000) Extreme case formulations: Softeners, investment, and doing nonliteral. *Research on Language and Social Interaction* 33 (4), 347–373.

Elder, C., Knoch, U., Barkhuizen, G. and von Randow, J. (2005) Individual feedback to enhance rater training: Does it work? *Language Assessment Quarterly* 2 (3), 175–196.

Erickson, G. (2009) Nationella prov i engelska – en studie av bedömarsamstämmighet. See https://www.gu.se/nationella-prov-frammande-sprak/rapporter-och-skrifter# Studie-av-bed%C3%B6marsamst%C3%A4mmigheti-engelska-%C3%A5k-9

Evans, B. and Fitzgerald, R. (2016) 'It's training man'! Membership categorization and the institutional moral order of basketball training. *Australian Journal of Linguistics* 36 (2), 205–233. doi:10.1080/07268602.2015.1121531

Fulcher, G. (2003) *Testing Second Language Speaking.* Harlow: Pearson Education.

Grainger, P., Adie, L. and Weir, K. (2016) Quality assurance of assessment and moderation discourses involving sessional staff. *Assessment & Evaluation in Higher Education* 41 (4), 548–559.

Hauser, E. (2011) Generalization: A practice of situated categorization in talk. *Human Studies* 34 (2), 183–198. doi:10.1007/s10746-011-9184-y

Hauser, E. and Prior, M.T. (2019) Editorial. Introduction to topicalizing regrading in interaction. *Journal of Pragmatics* 150, 75–79. See http://www.sciencedirect.com/science/article/pii/S0378216619304928. doi:10.1016/j.pragma.2019.07.001

Jefferson, G. (2004) Glossary of transcript symbols with an introduction. In G.H. Lerner (ed.) *Conversation Analysis: Studies from the First Generation* (pp. 13–31). Amsterdam: John Benjamins.

Jølle, L.J. (2014) Pair assessment of pupil writing: A dialogic approach for studying the development of rater competence. *Assessing Writing* 20, 37–52. See http://www.sciencedirect.com/science/article/pii/S1075293514000038. doi:10.1016/j.asw.2014.01.002

Jönsson, A. and Thornberg, P. (2014) Samsyn eller samstämmighet? En diskussion om sambedömning som redskap för likvärdig bedömning i skolan. *Pedagogisk forskning i Sverige* 19 (4–5), 386–402.

Knoch, U. (2011) Investigating the effectiveness of individualized feedback to rating behavior – a longitudinal study. *Language Testing* 28 (2), 179–200. See http://ltj.sagepub.com/cgi/content/abstract/28/2/179. doi:10.1177/0265532210384252

Leclercq, P. and Edmonds, A. (2014) How to assess L2 proficiency? An overview of proficiency assessment research. In P. Leclercq, A. Edmonds and H. Hilton (eds) *Measuring L2 Proficiency: Perspectives from SLA* (pp. 3–23). Bristol: Multilingual Matters.

Linacre, J.M. (2017) Facets® (Version 3.80.0) [computer software]. Beaverton, OR: Winsteps.com.

Linn, R.L. (1993) Linking results of distinct assessments. *Applied Measurement in Education* 6 (1), 83–102.

Liu, R.Y. (2015) Invoking membership categories through marked person reference forms in parent-child interaction. *Working Papers in TESOL & Applied Linguistics* 15 (1), 1–13.

Logren, A., Ruusuvuori, J. and Laitinen, J. (2017) Self-reflective talk in group counselling. *Discourse Studies* 19 (4), 422–440. doi:10.1177/1461445617706771

Lumley, T. and McNamara, T. (1995) Rater characteristics and rater bias: Implications for training. *Language Testing* 12 (1), 54–71. doi:10.1177/026553229501200104

Lundahl, C. (2016) Nationella prov – ett redskap med tvetydiga syften [National tests – a tool with ambiguous aims]. In C. Lundahl and M. Folke-Fichtelius (eds) *Bedömning i och av skolan – praktik, principer, politik* (pp. 243–261). Lund: Studentlitteratur.

Mann, S. and Walsh, S. (2013) RP or 'RIP': A critical perspective on reflective practice. *Applied Linguistics Review* 4 (2), 291–315. doi:10.1515/applirev-2013-0013

May, L. (2011a) *Interaction in a Paired Speaking Test.* Frankfurt am Main: Peter Lang.

May, L. (2011b) Interactional competence in a paired speaking test: Features salient to raters. *Language Assessment Quarterly* 8 (2), 127–145. doi:10.1080/154303.2011.565845

McGraw, K.O. and Wong, S.P. (1996) Forming inferences about some intraclass correlation coefficients. *Psychological Methods* 1 (1), 30–46.

McNamara, T. (1996) *Measuring Second Language Performance.* New York: Longman.

Moss, P.A. and Schultz, A. (2001) Educational standards, assessment, and the search for consensus. *American Educational Research Journal* 38 (1), 37–70.

NAFS Project (2021a) Ämnesprov i engelska för årskurs 6 [English National Test Year 6]. See https://www.gu.se/nationella-prov-frammande-sprak/prov-och-bedomningss tod-i-engelska/engelska-arskurs-1-6/nationellt-prov-i-engelska-for-arskurs-6

NAFS Project (2021b) Ämnesprov i engelska för årskurs 9 [English National Test Year 9]. See https://www.gu.se/nationella-prov-frammande-sprak/prov-och-bedomningss tod-i-engelska/engelska-arskurs-7-9/nationellt-prov-i-engelska-for-arskurs-9

Pomerantz, A. (1984) Agreeing and disagreeing with assessments: Some features of preferred/dispreferred turn shapes. In J.M. Atkinson and J. Heritage (eds) *Structures of Social Action* (pp. 57–101). Cambridge: Cambridge University Press.

Popham, W.J. (2009) Assessment literacy for teachers: Faddish or fundamental? *Theory into Practice* 48, 4–11.

Popham, W.J. (2011) Assessment literacy overlooked: A teacher educator's confession. *The Teacher Educator* 46 (4), 265–273. doi:10.1080/08878730.2011.605048

Rasch, G. (1980) *Probabilistic Models for Some Intelligence and Attainment Tests.* Chicago, IL: University of Chicago Press.

Richards, K. (2006) *Language and Professional Identity: Aspects of Collaborative Interaction.* Basingstoke: Palgrave Macmillan.

Sacks, H. (1992) *Lectures on Conversation, Vols I and II* (ed. G. Jefferson; Introduction by E.A. Schegloff). Oxford: Blackwell.

Sacks, H., Schegloff, E.A. and Jefferson, G. (1974) A simplest systematics for the organization of turn-taking in conversation. *Language* 50 (4), 696–735.

Sadler, D.R. (2013) Assuring academic achievement standards: From moderation to calibration. *Assessment in Education: Principles, Policy & Practice* 20 (1), 5–19. doi:10. 1080/0969594X.2012.714742

Sandlund, E. and Sundqvist, P. (2019) Doing versus assessing interactional competence. In M.R. Salaberry and S. Kunitz (eds) *Teaching and Testing L2 Interactional Competence: Bridging Theory and Practice* (pp. 357–396). Abingdon and New York: Routledge.

Schnurr, S. and Chan, A. (2011) When laughter is not enough: Responding to teasing and self-denigrating humour at work. *Journal of Pragmatics* 43 (1), 20–35. doi:10.1016/j. pragma.2010.09.001

Sidnell, J. and Stivers, T. (eds) (2013) *The Handbook of Conversation Analysis.* Chichester: Wiley-Blackwell.

Silverman, D. (1998) *Harvey Sacks: Social Science and Conversation Analysis.* Cambridge: Polity Press.

Stokoe, E. (2012) Moving forward with membership categorization analysis: Methods for systematic analysis. *Discourse Studies* 14 (3), 277–303. doi:10.1177/1461445612441534

Sundqvist, P., Wikström, P., Sandlund, E. and Nyroos, L. (2018) The teacher as examiner of L2 oral tests: A challenge to standardization. *Language Testing* 35 (2), 217–238. doi:10.1177/0265532217690782

Sundqvist, P., Sandlund, E., Skar, G.B. and Tengberg, M. (2020) Effects of rater training on the assessment of L2 English oral proficiency. *Nordic Journal of Modern Language Methodology* 8 (1), 3–29. doi:10.46364/njmlm.v8i1.605

Swedish National Agency for Education (2009) *Bedömaröverensstämmelse vid bedömning av nationella prov [Rater Agreement in the Assessment of National Tests]*. Dnr/Reg no 2008:286. Stockholm: Swedish National Agency for Education.

Swedish National Agency for Education (2014) *English. Ämnesprov, läsår 2013/2014. Lärarinformation inklusive bedömningsanvisningar till Delprov A. Årskurs 9 [English. National Test 2013/2014. Teacher Information Including Assessment Instructions for Part A. Year 9]*. Stockholm: Swedish National Agency for Education.

Swedish National Agency for Education (2015) *English. Ämnesprov, läsår 2014/2015. Lärarinformation inklusive bedömningsanvisningar till Delprov A. Årskurs 6 [English. National Test, 2014/2015. Teacher Information Including Assessment Instructions for Part A. Year 6]*. Stockholm: Swedish National Agency for Education.

Swedish Schools Inspectorate (2013) *Olikheterna är för stora. Omrättning av nationella prov i grundskolan och gymnasieskolan, 2013 [The Differences Are Too Great. Re-assessing National Tests in Compulsory and Upper Secondary School, 2013]*. Stockholm: Swedish Schools Inspectorate.

Walters, F.S. (2007) A conversation-analytic hermeneutic rating protocol to assess L2 oral pragmatic competence. *Language Testing* 24 (2), 155–183. doi:10.1177/0265532207076362

Weigle, S.C. (1998) Using FACETS to model rater training effects. *Language Testing* 15 (2), 263–287. doi:10.1177/026553229801500205

Wiliam, D. (2007) Content then process: Teacher learning communities in the service of formative assessment. In D. Reeves (ed.) *Ahead of the Curve: The Power of Assessment to Transform Teaching and Learning* (pp. 182–204). Bloomington, IN: Solution Tree.

Wilkinson, A. (1968) The testing of oracy. In A. Davies (ed.) *Language Testing Symposium* (pp. 117–132). Oxford: Oxford University Press.

Wilkinson, S. and Kitzinger, C. (2006) Surprise as an interactional achievement: Reaction tokens in conversation. *Social Psychology Quarterly* 69 (2), 150–182. doi:10.1177/019027250606900203

Part 3

Designing Speaking Assessment Tests

7 Jiazhou? Is It California? Operationalizing Repair in Classroom-based Assessment

Katharina Kley, Silvia Kunitz and Meng Yeh

1 Introduction

Since the late 1990s, a number of language testers (e.g. Chalhoub-Deville, 2003; McNamara, 1997) have criticized interaction in second language (L2) performance assessments as too cognitive in nature. By orienting to conceptualizations of interactional competence (IC) (He & Young, 1998; Kramsch, 1986; Young, 2008, 2011), these scholars acknowledge that interaction in L2 speaking tests is co-constructed in social context and goes beyond individual ability (see also Huth, 2020). In line with others (e.g. Roever & Kasper, 2018), we argue that expanding the speaking construct by a sociolinguistic-interactional component or IC would be beneficial because the range of inferences drawn from an oral assessment can thus be extended.

In a recent paper, Galaczi and Taylor (2018) provide a visual representation of IC as it is currently understood by language teachers and testers. Their definition of IC includes, among other interactional skills, repair practices with the following microfeatures: self- and other-repair, recasts and joint utterance creations. This conceptualization of repair, however, is rather broad and insufficiently fine tuned, as it needs further specificity for purposes of teaching, learning and testing. As a matter of fact, there exists a large body of conversation analytic (CA) research on repair in conversations between English first language speakers (L1S) (e.g. Schegloff, 1992, 1997, 2000; Schegloff et al., 1977) and discourse settings that involve second language speakers (L2S) (e.g. Brouwer, 2003; Brouwer et al., 2004; Kurhila, 2006), as well as an array of interactionist second language acquisition (SLA) studies on a repair-oriented process referred to as negotiation of meaning (Long, 1996; Pica, 1994). However, the research on repair use in L2 oral assessments is rather scarce. Although language testers have positively interpreted test-takers' skills to offer and request clarification (Ducasse & Brown, 2009; Gan, 2010; May, 2011) and to suggest a word when the peer-interlocutor is engaged in a word search (Ducasse & Brown, 2009), research on repair in L2 oral assessments has thus far not been systematic.

In addition, since the Proficiency Guidelines of the American Council on the Teaching of Foreign Languages (ACTFL) were first and foremost created for the assessment of an individual's language abilities and not operationalized with the co-constructed nature of interaction in mind (Huth, in press), it is probably not surprising that they do not include any descriptors for repair. However, the Common European Framework of Reference for Languages (CEFR) describes repair practices such as asking for clarification and self-initiating self-repair, even at low proficiency levels (A1 and A2) (Council of Europe, 2018), but the number of repair scales is limited, and the descriptors are rather vague and do not differentiate well between proficiency levels.

The reason for this gap in repair research in L2 oral tests may be due to the fact that assessing test-takers' use of repair practices is not unproblematic. Thus far, test-takers' orientation to intersubjectivity or mutual understanding, which interactants maintain and restore by means of repair, is not the main goal of (high-stakes) assessments (Seedhouse & Nakatsuhara, 2018). Moreover, repair initiations have mostly been considered disfluencies in L2 testing and therefore rated negatively (de Jong, 2018; Seedhouse & Nakatsuhara, 2018).

Repair is an important component of the construct of IC, but how can repair best be operationalized in an oral assessment? The present study attempts to examine this question. It explores the repair practices that beginning learners of Chinese as a foreign language (CFL) use in a classroom-based oral test interaction with an L1S. In the context of the present study, repair was operationalized in terms of the ability to: (a) other-direct word searches when encountering lexical trouble; (b) other-initiate repair on the interlocutor's turn in the face of non-understanding; and (c) self-repair one's turn in response to a clarification request or other display of non-understanding. Note that (b) and (c) together constitute the practice of other-initiated, self-completed repair, with (b) focusing on the ability to initiate the repair and (c) on the ability to complete it.

Employing CA, we identified the repair practices that the learners enact when interacting with an L1S in the oral assessment. In the next step, we examined whether the actual repair practices produced align with the teacher's conceptualization of repair as reflected in the learning outcomes for the course (including other-directed word searches, other-initiations of repair and self-repaired responses), the students' own reflections on her/his repair use and the scores that the teacher assigned for the use of repair. The extent to which the intended and actual repair practices, student reflections and repair scores align will have implications for the operationalization of repair in the context of this teaching and test setting.

2 Literature Review

2.1 Assessing IC

Paired and group speaking test tasks are considered formats that are suitable to elicit candidates' interactional abilities and, thus, to generate the evidence needed to make inferences about IC (Fulcher, 2003; Fulcher & Davidson, 2007). In comparison to interview-formatted speaking tests such as the ACTFL OPI, paired and group speaking tests usually consist of discussion and/or roleplay tasks that include one or more peer-interlocutors; in some settings, an L1S may also serve as conversation partner. Galaczi and Taylor (2018) emphasize that the construct underlying paired and group speaking tests is broader than interview-formatted tests and aligns more closely with the conceptualization of IC.

Despite the fact that the notion of co-constructed paired and group discourse is not unproblematic for L2 testing as it raises issues of validity, generalizability and rating (Bachman, 2007; Chalhoub-Deville, 2003; Galaczi & Taylor, 2018), language testers have operationalized the construct of IC in paired and group test tasks for standardized tests such as the University of Cambridge ESOL examinations (Galaczi, 2008) and small-scale speaking tests in language programs at schools and universities for placement, exit and achievement testing (Brooks, 2009; Ducasse & Brown, 2009; Gan, 2010).

At the same time, language testers have conducted verbal protocols with raters (Ducasse & Brown, 2009; May, 2011; see also Sandlund & Sundqvist, 2019) and examined the candidate test discourse by means of discourse analysis and CA (Brooks, 2009; Galaczi, 2008) to identify and describe the construct of L2 IC in paired and group test tasks with the goal of obtaining a deeper understanding of what the nature of spoken interactional ability in speaking tests entails. The findings from this body of research have implications for the operationalization of IC, including the development of tasks and the creation of scoring rubrics.

2.2 CA-informed IC assessment

Since the first decade of the 21st century, IC in L2 speaking tests has been increasingly conceptualized from a CA perspective. CA's major tenet is that ordinary talk is systematically organized and socially ordered (Psathas, 1995). For Kasper (2006: 83), CA's object of inquiry is a set of 'sociolinguistic competencies' that interactants use to participate in social interaction. According to her, CA-informed IC can be understood as the set of linguistic and other embodied resources that conversationalists employ in interaction:

(1) to understand and produce social actions in their sequential contexts;
(2) to take turns at talk in an organized fashion;

(3) to format actions and turns, and construct an epistemic and affective stance;
(4) to repair problems in speaking, hearing and understanding;
(5) to co-construct social and discursive identities through sequence organization, actions-in-interaction and semiotic resources; and
(6) to recognize and produce boundaries between activities, including transitions from states of contact to absence of contact and transitions between activities during continued contact. (Kasper, 2006: 86)

This list shows that repair is considered to be an essential component of IC.

CA research methodology is now commonly used for the fine-grained micro-level analysis of specific interactional resources in L2 paired and group test interactions such as topic development (Gan, 2010; Gan *et al.*, 2009), turn-taking practices (Greer & Potter, 2008), contingent responses (Lam, 2018), the formulation of requests (Youn, 2015) and the management of proposal sequences (Youn, 2020). This body of research has contributed immensely to building a more in-depth understanding of the construct of IC in paired and group speaking tests (Galaczi & Taylor, 2018). However, to our knowledge, the use of repair practices in paired and group oral tests has thus far not been studied from a CA perspective. An exploration of these practices is thus the goal of the present study.

2.3 CA literature on repair

Within the CA literature, repair is considered one of the interactional mechanisms that govern talk-in-interaction together with turn-taking, sequence organization and preference organization. Specifically, repair is the mechanism that allows participants to deal with problems in speaking, hearing or understanding (Schegloff *et al.*, 1977). Repair can be either forward-oriented or backward-oriented, depending on the position of the trouble source with respect to the turn-so-far. Forward-oriented repair deals with problems in speaking and occurs when the current speaker is having trouble producing the next relevant item in her/his turn-at-talk; in other words, when the current speaker is having trouble with the continuation of her/his turn, s/he engages in a word search. On the other hand, in backward-oriented repair the trouble source lies in prior talk. Backward-oriented repair can be initiated either by the co-participant or by the speaker of the trouble source.

The seminal studies (Schegloff, 1992, 1997, 2000; Schegloff *et al.*, 1977) on repair practices have been based on interactions in English. Later studies on Chinese (Chui, 1996; Tao, 1995; Wu, 2006; Zhang, 1998; Zhang & Chan, 2013) have shown that repair practices in Chinese are essentially similar to repair practices in English. In what follows we thus provide two examples of repair practices in Chinese. Specifically, we focus on the types of repair that were the instructional targets in the second semester course that is the object of our study: other-directed word searches and other-initiated, self-completed repair addressing understanding problems.

Word searches typically emerge as self-directed practices, with the current speaker withdrawing her/his gaze from the co-participants and verbally indicating that s/he has trouble with the continuation of the turn through various perturbations such as pauses, sound-stretches and hesitation tokens (Goodwin & Goodwin, 1986; Hayashi, 2003; Lerner, 1996). If the current speaker does not manage to produce the outcome of the search, then s/he might ask her/his co-participants for help. An example of other-directed searches in Chinese is provided below (Zhang, 1998: 176).

Excerpt 7.1 Word search in L1 Chinese

```
01  MEI:    ( ) ai   ni  bu  laoshi shuo
                DISC you not always say
             ( ) well you always said

02           yao  gei  wo dianr
             want give me a-bit
             you'd give me some

03           nage shenme, hai   mei gei  wo
             that what       still not give me
             of the what, you haven't given me yet.

04  WU:      sheme a?
             what   Q
             what?

05  MEI:     nage shenme, nage jiao shenme laizhe?
             that what       that call what    PART
             what's that, what's it called?

06  WU:      xiaohuawu ( )
             nitre
             nitre stuff ( )

07  ZHOU:    qinghuawu
             hydride

08  WU:      qinghuawu
             hydride

09  MEI:     a, qinghuawu
             ah, hydride
```

Excerpt 7.1 begins as Mei refers to a promise made by Wu who was supposed to give Mei some hydride but has not done so yet (Lines 1–3). Note how, in Mei's turn, she does not name the item but refers to it with an indeterminate expression: *dianr nage shenme* ('some of the what').

Note here the word *nage* (literally, 'that'), the use of which in the environment of word searches was one of the learning outcomes established by the teacher in the present study (see Table 7.1 in Section 3.1). The slightly rising intonation on *shenme* suggests that Mei is soliciting confirmation of recognition of the item she is mentioning; in other words, she is displaying uncertainty with the continuation of her turn and, although producing a next relevant item, formulates it in a vague way and offers it for confirmation. Wu initiates repair on Mei's turn in Line 4 with an open-class initiator (see below). This action prompts Mei to make the search explicit and other-directed. That is, Mei asks for the name of the substance she is referring to (*nage jiao shenme lai?* 'what's it called?', Line 5). An approximate response is provided by Wu in Line 6 (*xiaohuawu* 'nitre stuff'), while the precise term for the item is delivered by Zhou in Line 7 (*qinghuawu* 'hydride'). This outcome of the other-directed search is then acknowledged through repetitions by both Wu (Line 8) and Mei (Line 9).

Other-initiation of repair occurs when a co-participant initiates repair on the just prior turn, for example by asking for clarification or by requesting a confirmation of her/his candidate understanding. There are various techniques to initiate repair in the next turn; these techniques differ in the degree of specificity with which they locate the trouble source. Open-class repair initiators (such as *shenme a?* 'what?'; see Drew, 1997) generically indicate trouble with the prior turn; typically, a repair initiation done through an open-class repair initiator is understood to address a problem in hearing and is responded to with a repetition of the trouble source turn. Other techniques, instead, allow the co-participant to identify where the trouble source actually is; such techniques include *wh-* interrogatives (e.g. *who?*), partial repetitions with *wh-* interrogatives (e.g. *you saw who?*) and candidate understandings that are offered for confirmation. An example of other-initiation is provided below (Zhang, 1998: 109).

In Excerpt 7.2, the four participants are talking about primary school education. In Line 1, Cong mentions that it is popular to go to preschool classes. The expression *xueqian ban* ('preschool class') is repeated simultaneously by Tian (Line 3) and Cheng (Line 4), while Zhang initiates repair (in overlap) by producing a *wh-* interrogative turn with which he asks the meaning of the expression (Line 5). Note how this repair initiation is very precise in identifying the trouble source (the expression *xueqian ban*) and the nature of the problem (i.e. the meaning of such expression). An extended explanation is then provided by Cheng (Lines 7–9 and 11–13). In this example, the repair is other-initiated and other-completed, in that Zhang initiates repair on Cong's turn and the repair is completed by Cheng. Had Cong (the speaker of the trouble source turn) responded to the repair-initiation, this would have been an example of an other-initiated and self-completed repair.

Excerpt 7.2 Other-initiated repair in L1 Chinese

```
01  CONG:    xianzai yiban     dou shi xueqian    ban    a
             now     commonly all is  preschool  class  PART
             now it's quite popular to go to a preschool class

02           (.)

03  TIAN:    [xueqian    ban
              preschool  class
              preschool class

04  CHENG?   [xueqian    ban
              preschool  class
              preschool class

05  ZHANG:   [xueqian    ban    shi shenme yisi     a?
              preschool  class  is  what   meaning PART
              what does preschool class mean?

06  TIAN:    jiu haoxiang [jiu shi:
             just like     just is
             it's like that:

07  CHENG:              [jiu shi shuo (.)
                         just is  say
                         that's to say (.)

08           ta ba      shangxue      ba    sui
             ta part. attend-school eight year-old
             he goes to school at eight

09           qi-  qi    sui      ban,
             seven- seven year-old half
             seven- seven and half,

10           ba     sui      cai  yao  ba
             eight year-old then need PART
             or eight

11  ZHANG:   °uhm°
             °mm°

12  CHENG:   ba     sui      shangxue,
             eight year-old attend-school,
             go to school at eight,

13           jiu  shangxue      zhiqian,
             just attend-school before
             before going to school,

14           ni  feidei   shang  xueqian   ban   qu xuexi
             you have-to attend preschool class go learn
             you got to go to preschool class to learn

15           jiu  shi shuo gei  ni  peixun yixia
             just is  say give you train  a-bit
             that's to say to give you some training

16  ZHANG:   °uhm°
             °mm°
```

2.4 Repair practices in the L2

Studies on the repair practices used by CFL learners in classroom settings have investigated self-initiated self-repair, that is, CFL students' self-editing practices as they correct their tones, word-order and grammar (Simpson *et al.*, 2013; Tang, 2014; Tao, 2016). As for other-initiated repairs, authors like Rylander (2009) and Tang (2014) have focused on teachers' repair initiations on their students' talk, but not on student-initiated repair sequences.

Since research on repair in L2 Chinese in classroom settings is rather scant, we turn to findings from other languages and, in doing so, we focus on repair sequences accomplished by L2Ss as they freely interact outside the classroom. Prior research on L2 repair practices suggests that L2Ss often engage in word searches (Brouwer, 2003; Eskildsen, 2018; Kurhila, 2006; Theodórsdóttir, 2018) in their interactions with L1Ss outside the classroom. In addition, Hosoda (2000) found that L2 Japanese speakers use verbal and non-verbal cues to solicit L1Ss' help with word searches. Another common practice consists of vocabulary checks (Hosoda, 2006), with L2Ss tentatively producing a lexical item and then offering it to their interlocutor for confirmation. Furthermore, Lilja (2014) illustrated that L2 learners of Finnish used repetition of a part of the trouble source to deal with unknown words/phrases uttered by L1Ss in everyday interaction.

Overall, these studies show that, once the repair sequence is completed (be it forward- or backward-oriented), L2Ss frequently use the newly learned item as they continue the conversation (Brouwer, 2003; Eskildsen, 2018; Lilja, 2014). However, it should also be pointed out that, in one study by Filipi and Barraja-Rohan (2015), it was observed that intermediate students of English failed to orient to non-understanding or misunderstanding issues and did not initiate repair. This finding talks to the importance of encouraging students to initiate repair when they do not understand or when they are being misunderstood (see also Wong & Waring, 2010).

Regarding the development of repair practices over time, longitudinal research on non-instructed L2 IC suggests that, when encountering a problem with the continuation of their turn, less proficient L2Ss simply stop talking (Farina *et al.*, 2012). Over time, though, L2Ss engage in other-directed word searches and ask for help with increasingly diversified resources. It seems, for example, that more proficient L2Ss develop more subtle ways to other-direct word searches (e.g. from metalinguistic questions such as 'how do you say?' to the use of prosodic resources) and that, instead of resorting to their L1, they attempt to paraphrase the meaning of the target lexical item.

As for other-initiation of repair (Brouwer & Wagner, 2004; Hellermann, 2011; Wong, 2000), less proficient L2Ss typically initiate repair in a delayed fashion, thereby showing that they are not immediately able to detect problems in prior talk; furthermore, repair tends to be initiated with open-class repair initiators and tends to target trouble sources in final position. On the other hand, more advanced L2Ss are able to identify with more precision the specific location of the trouble source, thereby increasing the use of more specific repair initiators. With time, L2Ss also seem to become able to identify trouble sources that occur deep inside the prior turn.

As mentioned before, these studies focused on learners/speakers who did not receive IC instruction. In other words, prior research has demonstrated that L2 IC development is observed to occur naturally. This, however, does not exclude a role for L2 IC instruction. Indeed, an increasing number of CA scholars are advocating the importance of CA-informed IC instruction (Betz & Huth, 2014; Carroll, 2010; Wong & Waring, 2010; see also the papers in Salaberry & Kunitz, 2019), while there starts to be evidence pointing to the effectiveness of this type of instruction (see Barraja-Rohan, 2011; Huth, 2006; Huth & Taleghani Nikazm, 2006; Kunitz & Yeh, 2019). It is for these reasons that we decided to follow Barraja-Rohan and Pritchard's (1997) example in the design of instructional materials focusing on other-repair practices to resolve hearing and non-understanding problems and to embrace Wong and Waring's (2010) more general call concerning the importance of teaching self- and other-repair in the L2 classroom.

3 Pedagogical Intervention

3.1 Repair in the L2 IC curriculum: Rationale

Since repair is one of the fundamental mechanisms regulating human interaction (Schegloff *et al.*, 1977), we find it imperative to teach repair starting at the beginning of college-level L2 instruction. Our rationale for IC instruction targeting repair is grounded on: (a) the demonstrated need for explicit IC instruction described earlier (see, in particular, Barraja-Rohan & Pritchard, 1997; Wong & Waring, 2010); and (b) our own observation of students' difficulties during free conversations with L1Ss outside classrooms.

In order to develop empirically based observations concerning the repair practices of students enrolled in our CFL program, we video-taped and examined free conversations between L1Ss and CFL beginning students. During these interactions, the students faced three main challenges in speaking and understanding: (1) they did not know how to say certain words in Chinese; (2) they did not understand what their partners had just said; and (3) their partners did not understand what they had said. More specifically, we noticed that, when facing non-understanding, most students simply refrained from further talk (see Farina *et al.*, 2012; Filipi & Barraja-Rohan, 2015).

Table 7.1 Learning objectives

Continue a conversation when troubles in conversation arise

1. Able to politely ask my partner to repeat questions/statements.
2. Able to politely ask my partner to slow down.
3. Able to ask my partner to explain the meaning of certain words.
4. Able to ask my partner how to say something in Chinese.
5. Able to use 那个 nage 'that' to give myself time search for words.
6. Able to use the new words learned from my partner and continue the conversation.
7. Able to clarify/paraphrase my statement/question when my partner does not understand.
8. Able to refrain from speaking English.

After conducting these observations, we realized that the CEFR (Council of Europe, 2001) does not provide descriptors of repair practices at the A1 level.[1] That is, beginning students are not expected to be able to accomplish repair actions. However, we think it is important that beginning students learn how to use basic repair techniques in order to interact with others. We therefore decided to incorporate the teaching of repair in the first-year Chinese curriculum which aimed to develop students' IC (see also Kunitz & Yeh, 2019; Yeh, 2018a, 2018b).

Our instruction targets three types of repair practices: (1) other-directed word searches (i.e. the ability to ask for help when encountering lexical trouble); (2) other-initiated repair (i.e. the ability to ask for clarification or otherwise display non-understanding of the prior turn); and (3) self-completed repair in response to other-initiation of repair (i.e. the ability to respond to a display of non-understanding such as a clarification request). These repair practices are reflected in a list of learning objectives for repair (Table 7.1), which was given to students at the beginning of the first-year Chinese courses. For both instruction and assessments, repair was operationalized with respect to these learning objectives. Specifically, Objectives 1–3 in Table 7.1 refer to the ability to other-initiate repair in the face of non-understanding; Objectives 4–5 concern word searches, while Objective 7 targets the ability to respond to an other-initiation of repair. Finally, Objective 6 refers to the ability to recycle new words that emerge in the interaction and Objective 8 encourages students to interact exclusively in L2 Chinese, without resorting to the L1 when interactional trouble occurs. These two objectives (6 and 8) do not refer to specific repair practices but reflect the teacher's conceptualization of what it means to handle interactional trouble.

3.2 Instruction and assessment

We used two types of naturally occurring conversations as teaching materials: examples of naturally occurring interactions between L1Ss

Table 7.2 Instructional steps

Step 1 Analysis of the repair practices between L1Ss
Step 2 Analysis of the repair practices between L1Ss and L2Ss
Step 3 Guided written production
Step 4 Guided and free oral production

and examples taken from our corpus of recorded conversations between CFL beginning students (enrolled in the program in previous years) and L1Ss. The instructional steps are illustrated in Table 7.2 (for a more detailed description of the pedagogical cycle, see Kunitz & Yeh, 2019; Yeh, 2018a, 2018b).

Phase 1 aimed to introduce students to an action-based view of language that is typical of CA. Phase 2 was designed to draw students' attention to L2Ss' actions when facing non-understanding, misunderstanding and speaking problems. In Phase 3, the students engaged in written production exercises (e.g. completing multiple turns of interaction by filling in appropriate repair devices). Then, in Phase 4, the students engaged in roleplays with peers and L1 tutors with the goal of students using the interactional practices introduced in the classroom, including repair.

To evaluate the students' learning outcomes, both written and speaking tasks were assigned. The written tasks comprised, for example, short analyses of excerpts of naturally occurring conversations and the writing of dialogues based on given prompts. These written quizzes were designed to assess the students' awareness of the interactional practices discussed in class.

The students were also required to demonstrate their ability to employ the targeted interactional practices and, for this reason, they had to engage in a mid-semester conversation with a peer (formative assessment) and in an end-of-semester conversation with an L1S (summative assessment). Both conversations were video-recorded and later constituted the basis for the students' analysis of and reflection on their own performance.

These conversations were graded with respect to the set of IC teaching objectives and learning outcomes for the course. Scores for repair use were awarded based on a 5-point scale (see Table 7.3) in terms of quality and quantity of repair practices used. For example, 5 points were awarded when various actions were successfully used to continue the conversation

Table 7.3 Scoring rubric for repair

	5–4 points	3–2 points	1–0 point
Manage troubles 20%	Use various actions to continue the conversation when troubles occur.	Use some actions to continue the conversation when troubles occur	Rarely manage to continue the conversation when troubles occur.

when trouble occurred, and 4 points were assigned when various actions were used but did not successfully resolve the trouble encountered by the student. The 3–2 point range differentiates between the successful and unsuccessful use of some repair practices, respectively, while 1 and 0 points were assigned when the student rarely managed trouble. The use of repair made up 20% of the grade for each conversation. Each conversation comprised 6% of the final grade for the course.

4 Participants

The participants in this study were 28 college students enrolled in second-semester CFL courses at a private university in the United States. The participants were non-heritage students who had not studied Chinese before enrolling in college. The students met for three hours a week in class with the teacher who developed the repair instruction for this study.

For the purposes of this study, we first selected the students (18 out of 28) who specifically discussed their repair performance in their evidence-based reflections conducted after their end-of-semester conversation with an L1S. These students displayed awareness of the use of repair in interaction and, specifically, of the importance of achieving/maintaining mutual understanding in interaction with L1Ss. Among these students, we then selected the four highest scoring students (overall speaking score: 5.76/6%; repair score: 4.5/5) and the four lowest scoring students (overall speaking score: 4.4–4.8/6%; repair score: 3.5–4/5) in the speaking test.

Overall, the students with a higher repair score were found to make a consistent use of a greater variety of repair practices than the lower scoring students. In their reflections, the higher scoring students pointed out how they tried to anticipate the meaning of unknown words, but also asked their L1S interlocutor for help when needed. On the other hand, the lower scoring students reported not orienting to their partner for help, even though they had difficulty conversing with her/him.

5 Method

5.1 Assessment task

For their end-of-semester conversation, the students were asked to find an L1S on or off campus and to talk with her/him for about 10 minutes; they were instructed to learn more about the conversation partner and her/his life on campus. All students video-recorded their conversation with the L1S.

The students then watched and reflected on their conversations. To be precise, the students were asked to find and transcribe at least one excerpt of their interaction with the L1S that showed that the student was able to continue the conversation when trouble arose and at least one excerpt where that was not the case. The students were also instructed to share what motivated their excerpt selection and discuss what went wrong and what could have been done differently.

5.2 Procedure for data analysis

Words-only transcripts of all the L1S-L2S interactions were produced; more elaborate transcriptions of focal sequences were transcribed using CA conventions (Jefferson, 2004) and then analyzed to identify the repair practices produced by the students.

We then compared the students' actual use of repair with: (a) the teacher's operationalization of repair as reflected in the learning objectives (see Table 7.1) and in the oral assessment; (b) the repair scores awarded by the teacher; and (c) the students' reflections on their repair use. The goal of the analysis is to investigate the extent to which the intended and actual repair practices, student reflections and repair scores align.

6 Analysis

The analysis presented here focuses on two students, Joe and Jack, and on their end-of-semester conversation with an L1S, after the last unit of IC instruction was implemented in the classroom. Joe received a high score for his speaking skills (5.76/6%) and a fairly high score for repair (4.5/5). Jack, on the other hand, received lower scores (4.8/6% for speaking and 4 for repair). We randomly selected these two students from the respective high- and low-scoring student groups. In what follows we illustrate the repair practices enacted by Joe and Jack and report part of their reflections.

6.1 Joe's repair practices

In his conversation with Liu, the L1S, Joe engaged in word searches and in other-initiations of repair. When it came to word searches, in some cases Joe managed to produce the outcome of the search in Chinese. In other cases he produced the outcome in English. In the latter situation, after the delivery of the English word, he either issued a translation request or managed to produce the Chinese word himself. Whenever he issued a translation request, he recycled the Chinese word in his next turn. We illustrate an example of some of Joe's word search practices in Excerpt 7.3 below.

The excerpt picks up the talk as Liu, the L1S, asks Joe which courses he is taking in the current semester (Line 1). After responding that he is taking five courses (Lines 3–4), Joe goes on to specify which courses he is taking. The heavy perturbations in the delivery of his turn (sound elongations, hesitation tokens, cut-off words and pauses) indicate that Joe is engaging in word searches for each of the courses he mentions: biology

(Line 9), English (Line 12) and Chinese (Line 13). Joe further encounters trouble as he is attempting to say that he is taking other core courses. At this point, in fact, instead of producing the Chinese word *zhuanye*, he uses the English word *major* (Line 15) as an attribute for Chinese *ke* ('class'). Liu receipts Joe's turn with the continuer *mh mh.* (Line 17), thereby not orienting to Joe's turn as problematic. In Line 18, however, Joe produces the Chinese equivalent of *major*, thus orienting to the use of English as problematic. This indeed corresponds to one of the learning outcomes indicated by the teacher (see Table 7.1): the students should refrain from using English. Subsequently (Line 19), by repeating the expression used by Joe (*zhuanye ke* 'core courses'), Liu confirms its accuracy and the sequence soon comes to a close.

Excerpt 7.3 Word search (Joe)

```
01 LIU:   na (0.3) ni:: (.) zhe  xueqi   xiu  shenme.
          so       you      this semester take what
          so (0.3) what do you:: take this semester.

02        (1.3)

03 JOE:   oh. wo wo zhe:: ge xueqi::: (0.6)
          oh  I  I  this  CL semester
          oh. I I this::::: semester (0.6)

04        you:::: (.) uh wu  men ke.
          have           five CL  class
          have::: (.) uh five courses.

05        (0.3)

06 LIU:   mh mh,

07        (0.4)

08 JOE:   wo:: sh- uh = uhm:: (0.4) tch- (0.4) yo::u:: (0.6)
          I                                    have
          I:: b- uh = uhm:: (0.4) tch- ha::ve:: (0.6)

09        sheng,  (0.7)  wu::¿
          bio            logy
          bio, (0.7) logy¿

10        (0.5)

11 LIU:   °°shengwu.°° =
          biology.
          °°biology.°°

12 JOE:   = he:::::: u::::hm: (0.3) yingwen, (0.6)
          and English
          a::::::nd u::::hm: (0.3) English, (0.6)
```

```
13            u:h zhongwen,
                 Chinese
              u:h Chinese,

14            (0.6)

15 JOE:   he:::: (1.1) biede de::: (0.5) major (0.3) ke.
          and            other DE                      class
          a::::nd (1.1) other (0.5) major (0.3) courses.

16            (0.3)

17 LIU:   mh mh. =

18 JOE:   = zhuanye ke.
            major    class
          core courses.

19 LIU:   zhuan[ye ke. ] =
          major    class
          core courses. =

20 JOE:        [(dui.) ] =
               (right)
               (yeah.)

21 LIU:   = [o::h ] okay. =

22 JOE:   [yeah.]

23 JOE:   = mh mh.
```

When it comes to other-initiated repair in the face of non-understanding, Joe uses a variety of different techniques, such as: open-class repair initiators; clarification requests; partial repetitions of the trouble source; and full repetitions of the trouble source followed by a candidate understanding. Excerpt 7.4 presents an example of the latter practice.

Excerpt 7.4 Other-initiation of repair (Joe)

```
01 JOE:   u::::hm: (.) mtch- (0.5)

02            ni::: zhu  zai zhongguo ma¿
              you   live at  China     Q
              u::::hm: (.) mtch- (0.5) do you live in China?

03            (1.2)

04 LIU:   u:::hm wo: shi zai Taiwan (0.7) °uh° zhangda de.
              I   be  at  Taiwan              grow-up DE
          u:::hm it was in Taiwan that I (0.7) °uh° grew up.
```

```
05          ranhou  wo  qi     sui   de  shihou bandao (.)
            then    I   seven  years DE  time   move-to
            then when I was seven I moved to (.)

06          jiazhou.
            California
            California.

07          +(0.7)

08          +((Joe stares ahead))

09  JOE:    jia + zhou:,

10              +((shifts gaze to Liu))

11          (0.3)

12  LIU:    °°mh [mh,°°

13  JOE:         [shi. (0.3) California ma.
                  be.                   Q
            is it (0.3) California.

14          (0.3)

15  LIU:    dui.
            correct
            yes.

16          jiazhou shi Cali[fornia.]
            jiazhou be
            jiazhou is California.

17  JOE:                    [wo ye ] zhu zai (0.2)
                             I also  live at
                             I also live in (0.2)

18          u::hm jiazhou,
                  California
            u::hm California,
```

Here we join the conversation as Joe asks Liu whether he lives in
China (Line 1). Liu responds by saying that he grew up in Taiwan and
then moved to California when he was seven (Lines 4–6). Joe does not
engage with Liu's prior turn, as shown by the 0.7 second that follows it
and by the embodied action of staring ahead. Joe then initiates repair by
repeating the Chinese word *Jiazhou*, with slightly upward intonation
('California', Line 9) as he shifts his eye-gaze to Liu (Line 10). With this
action, Joe is also asking for confirmation of his correct hearing of the
word. Such confirmation is provided by Liu with *mh mh,* (Line 12). Joe

then provides a candidate understanding of the meaning of the Chinese word by asking whether it means California (Line 13); Liu confirms (Lines 15–16) and Joe aptly recycles the new word in his next turn by adding that he also lives in California (Lines 17–18).

Overall, the analysis of Joe's interaction with Liu reveals that his repair practices are diversified. He uses a variety of different repair initiation techniques: in addition to repetitions of the trouble source followed by a candidate understanding, as we have seen in Excerpt 7.4, he also uses open-class repair initiators and clarification requests. He produces word searches as well. Sometimes the outcome of his word search is in Chinese, but if he produces the outcome in English, he issues a translation request and he tends to recycle the Chinese word in the following turn. As we have shown in Excerpt 7.3, he also manages to produce the Chinese word himself after he first delivered the English word. All in all, it is striking that he orients to the norm of avoiding the use of English. At the same time, however, his written reflection shows his persuasion that the knowledge of a shared language might be useful in order to solve potential understanding problems. In any case, he also reports the effort of trying to make educated guesses concerning the meaning of unknown words, in order not to interrupt the conversation. Sometimes, however, he asks what he calls 'casual questions' to confirm the meaning of some words.

6.2 Jack's repair practices

Jack's repair behavior seems to be essentially limited to word searches. In fact, in his conversation with an L1S, he initiates repair on his co-participant's talk only once and he does so with an open-class repair initiator whose use had been discouraged by the teacher. In what follows we report two examples of word search practices (Excerpts 7.5 and 7.6) that differ from Joe's in that Jack makes more use of English and of translation requests. Prior to Excerpt 7.5, Jack had asked Ling about her parents' profession. At the beginning of Excerpt 7.5, Ling reciprocates the question (Line 1) and Jack launches an extended response: his dad is a doctor (Line 3), while his mother is currently unemployed (Line 6). Jack then engages in a word search with several perturbations (Line 7); he eventually continues his turn in English with *she used to* (Line 8), but abandons the turn. It is Ling, in Lines 9–10, who translates and completes Jack's turn in Chinese. In Line 11, Jack accepts the formulation provided by Ling (*yeah*), repeats the Chinese word *zhiqian* ('before') and then confirms his receipt of the word with *okay*. He then attempts to say that his mother used to be a nutritionist (Line 13); the word for his mother's profession is provided in English and neither Jack nor Ling orient to the translation as problematic. The sequence closes with Ling's positive assessment of the profession of Jack's mom.

Excerpt 7.5 Word search 1 (Jack)

```
01 LING:  ni ne?
          you Q
          and you?
```

and you?

```
02        (0.2)
```

```
03 JACK:  u:h wo-de:: baba shi yisheng,
          my       dad  be   doctor
          u:h my:: dad is a doctor,
```

u:h my:: dad is a doctor,

```
04        (0.3)
```

```
05 JACK:  + ((Ling nods))
```

```
06        +u:h wo-de mama meiyou    gongzuo,
             my   mom  not-have job
          my mom does not have a job,
```

my mom does __not__ have a job,

```
07        .hh u:::h (0.2) keshi::: (0.4) #u:::hm:# (1.9)
                          but
          .hh u:::h (0.2) bu:::t (0.4) #u:::hm:# (1.9)
```

.hh u:::h (0.2) __bu:::t__ (0.4) #u:::hm:# (1.9)

```
08        she used to: (0.4) u:::h
```

she used to: (0.4) u:::h

```
09 LING:  °mh.° ta  zhiqian you
               she before   have
          °mh.° before she had
```

°mh.° before she had

```
10        [guo   gongzuo, ta  zhiqian ( )]
           EXPER job       she before
          a job, before she ( )
```

a job, before she ( )

```
11 JACK:  [yeah. ta: (.) zhiqian. okay. ]
                 she      before
          yeah. she: (.) before. okay.
```

yeah. she: (.) before. okay.

```
12        (0.2)
```

```
13 JACK:  gongzuo. .hh u::hm nutritionist.
          job.
          job. .hh u::hm nutritionist.
```

job. .hh u::hm nutritionist.

```
14        (0.7)
```

```
15 LING:  [o:h. ] ting-qi-lai hen  ku.
           oh     sound       very cool
          o:h. it sounds very cool.
```

o:h. it sounds very cool.

```
16 JACK:  [(u:h)]
```

Excerpt 7.6 provides an example of the most common practice that we have observed in Jack's word searches: translation requests. In lines not reported here, Jack has been listing the courses that he is planning to take the following semester. Excerpt 7.6 picks up the talk as Jack is engaging in a word search targeting the Chinese word for 'math'. After a number of perturbations (Line 2), he issues a translation request: >*zenme shuo*< *ma::thȥ* ('how do you say mathȥ'). His partner, however, does not provide an immediate reply (see the 0.4-second silence in Line 4), and Jack attempts to produce the first syllable of the word (Line 5).

Excerpt 7.6 Word search 2 (Jack)

```
01   JACK:   wo ye    xi::a:- (.)  wo ye   xiang
             I  also  wa-          I  also want
             I also w::a:- (.) I also want

02           u:::hm: (0.5) mtch- (0.4) #u:::::::::h# (0.6)

03           >zenme shuo< ma::thȥ
              how    say
             >how do you say< ma::thȥ

04              (0.4)

05   JACK:   sh[::-]
             ma::-

06   LING:   [shu]:::xue.
              ma:::th.

07   JACK:   /tsu/- shuxue.
             /ma/- math.

08              (0.2)

09   LING:   shuxue. [m::h.]
             math. m::h.

10   JACK:           [u::h ]

11              (0.5)

12   JACK:   shuxue:::: (0.3) #u:::::h# (0.3) e:::r yi: yi:,
             math                            two one one
             math::: (0.3) #u:::::h# (0.3) two::: one: one:,

13              (0.3)
```

As soon as Ling produces the word (*shu:::xue* 'math', Line 6), Jack abandons the floor and then successfully repeats the word in the following turn after encountering a pronunciation problem (Line 7). Ling confirms Jack's pronunciation (Line 9) and Jack recycles the word in the next turn as he mentions that one of the courses he would like to take is Math 211 (Line 12).

Overall, Jack uses English more often than Joe; he seems to find it less problematic than Joe to resort to English. In other words, he does not always orient to the relevance of finding an equivalent Chinese word for the English words that he happens to use. However, it is also true that he does often recycle new words in his talk. All these observations relate to Jack's own reflections: he acknowledges an excessive use of English and the need for frequent translation requests. At the same time, he points out his ability to 'make it out of the trouble spot and continue the conversation', but recognizes that he needs to practice 'the phrases for asking what words mean and how to say words in Chinese'.

7 Discussion

7.1 Summary of findings

After an instruction phase that was implemented to teach students how to repair, the students participated in an end-of-semester oral assessment with an L1S. With regard to the learning objectives for repair (see Table 7.1), which are the intended repair practices to be produced in the oral assessment, we found that both Joe and Jack, the two students we are focusing on in this chapter, are able to initiate repair in the face of nonunderstanding and request translations into Chinese. However, the two students do not deploy the following practices: politely asking the partner to slow down; asking the partner to explain the meaning of certain words; using 那个 *nage* 'that' to gain time for a word search; or responding to a repair initiation evidencing lack of understanding on the part of the interlocutor (see below for further discussion).

In addition, while we observed that both Joe and Jack, the higher and the lower scoring student alike, are able to ask for a translation from English into Chinese and incorporate the Chinese word in the following turn, we found that the two students differ in the variety of repair practices used. Joe, who scored higher on repair than Jack, deploys different techniques for repair initiation (open-class repair initiators, clarification requests, partial and full repetitions of the trouble source, candidate understandings). In some cases, Joe produces the outcome of his word search on his own or, after first producing the English word, delivers the Chinese equivalent himself. Jack, however, produces only translation requests and provides one instance of other-initiation of repair through an open-class initiator.

The analysis also revealed that both students try to stay in Chinese for most of their conversation with the L1S and resort to English only when encountering trouble, but while Jack, due to his numerous translation requests, uses English frequently without always orienting to it as problematic (see Excerpt 7.5), Joe is more inclined to enforce the L2-only policy established by the teacher (see Learning Outcome 8 in Table 7.1).

Overall, we can state that of the list of targeted repair practices (see Table 7.1), Joe and Jack actually only produce the following in interaction with the L1S: initiating repair in the face of non-understanding, requesting translations from English to Chinese and recycling the newly learned Chinese word in the next turn. Thus, pedagogically intended and actual repair only partially align.

In addition, Joe, who, as we mentioned above, uses a wider variety of repair techniques than Jack, also received the higher score on repair (4.5/5 versus 4/5 for Jack). However, it needs to be pointed out that Joe and Jack's repair scores are very similar; their scores merely differ by 0.5 points. Therefore, the inferences that we draw from Jack's ability to use repair based on his score, namely that his abilities are lower than Joe's, are hardly justified because the students' scores are almost the same. Changes will have to be made to the rating scale, and the teachers will have to be trained better so as to be able to assign ratings that discriminate more accurately between high and low performers like Joe and Jack. Finally, with respect to the students' reflections, we found that they mainly discuss what the students do to resolve trouble.

7.2 Discussion of findings

We found that some of the repair practices that the students were made aware of during the pedagogical intervention were not used by either student in the interaction with the L1S. For example, the students neither ask the partner to slow down nor do they ask for vocabulary explanations. If we speculate on the reasons why these practices are lacking, we can say that asking someone to speak more slowly or asking for explanations might be rather obtrusive practices which might significantly slow down the progressivity of the ongoing activity. As for the use of hesitation tokens during word searches, it seems that these students only use hesitation tokens such as *uh* and *uhm* that belong to both the L1 and the L2 repertoire; the use of the L2 token *nage* might be too advanced at this stage, especially during a task that aims to engage students in more or less spontaneous speech. Finally, regarding the practice of clarifying/paraphrasing one's own statement/question in case the partner did not understand, it is simply not produced because the L1Ss do not initiate repair on the students' talk. In other words, during the oral assessment the opportunity to use this practice did not open up to the students. Hence, the question arises whether the operationalization of repair should be revised for the present teaching and test setting; it may be more practical to operationalize repair in terms of only two repair practices: repair initiations and other-directed word searches.

Furthermore, as mentioned earlier, both Joe and Jack deploy open-class repair initiators, but whereas Joe uses other repair-initiating techniques as well, Jack initiates repair on his co-participant's talk only once and does so with an open-class repair initiator. In locating the trouble source, nonspecific open-class repair initiators do not indicate what the repairable actually is but rather refer to the entire turn as problematic, whereas repetitions and candidate understandings locate the trouble source more specifically (Schegloff *et al.*, 1977). Being able to locate trouble specifically like Joe may be an indication of a further developed interactional repertoire (Brouwer & Wagner, 2004; Hall, 2018), which should be awarded a higher score on the repair criterion. In fact, Joe received a higher repair score than Jack, whose repair initiations are less varied. However, as we mentioned above, the difference in their repair scores is rather small. Therefore, the scoring rubric for this oral assessment, which currently differentiates the use of repair practices based on quantity and whether or not the trouble could be resolved successfully (see scoring rubric, Table 7.3), could be refined such that it explicitly incorporates this notion of varied repair techniques as a higher level of ability to resolve trouble.

Moreover, teachers may find it difficult to assess students' conversations in which no or hardly any repair is initiated, even though the teacher has the impression that the student does not hear or understand, as is the case with Jack in our dataset. The easiest way out of this dilemma would probably be to subtract points. Yet the problem with that perspective is that we cannot always tell for sure whether a student understands or why a student does not initiate repair. Several scenarios may be at play: the student does not understand but does not know how to initiate repair, s/he does not understand but tries to move the conversation along or s/he actually understands the interlocutor's talk.

Similarly, teachers, such as the teacher in the present study, may find open-class repair initiators ineffective and discourage their students from using this repair-initiating technique because it does not point the interlocutor directly to the trouble source (cf. Wong & Waring, 2010). However, open-class repair initiators have a specific function: they are used to indicate that trouble with the entire turn occurred. It will be impossible for the teacher to determine if a student uses an open-class repair initiator because s/he did not understand the entire turn or because s/he encountered trouble with just one word but did not know any other techniques to indicate trouble except for open-class repair initiators.

One option to remedy this problem of the lack of repair initiations or the sole use of open-class initiators would be to develop oral assessments that elicit these repair practices from the student with the help of the interlocutor. Walters (2013), for example, embedded oral prompts in L1S-L2S discussion tasks. In this test format, the L1S prompts the test-taker to produce certain practices (e.g. a response to an assessment or a compliment). The embedded prompts make the oral test reliable, and yet the discussion task itself facilitates spontaneous talk.

Yet, it may be more practical to assess students in writing rather than in speaking (cf. Huth & Betz, 2019) if the purpose of a test is to assess students' knowledge of certain repair practices. Written tasks can be controlled better as they test one phenomenon at a time. For example, students could be presented with a transcribed repair sequence in the L2 where the repair initiation was taken out. Based on the trouble source in the previous turn and the response to the repair initiation in the following turn, students may be asked to provide an appropriate repair initiator.

Finally, the teacher could also ask her students to reflect on their use of repair in interaction with the L1S (as was done in the present study). These evidence-based student reflections can shed light on the students' perceptions of what they did when they encountered trouble. The insights gained from the student reflections could be incorporated in the rating process.

8 Conclusion

We want to stress that the CA-informed instruction on repair practices that was undertaken prior to the oral assessment was effective. Repair practices are teachable, and even beginning L2 learners can learn how to use repair in interactions with others. However, we also came to realize that students may not necessarily initiate repair or use repair practices in an oral assessment task that was designed to elicit spontaneous talk with an L1S. That may be due to a number of reasons: mutual understanding is not at stake in the conversation; potential misunderstandings can be preempted by the interlocutor; or the student did not grasp from the pedagogical intervention how to properly use repair.

If we as teachers are solely interested in the number of repair practices produced and whether or not trouble is successfully resolved in an oral assessment, we disregard the fact that interaction is co-constructed and that the interlocutor's behavior in the conversation also influences a student's use of repair. Hence, by awarding a low score for little and/or unsuccessful repair use, we may penalize students who are otherwise perfectly able to understand and make themselves understood. It may therefore be beneficial to consider including written tasks or oral prompts, both of which can be designed to elicit a student's knowledge of repair. However, if the objective is to assess a student's repair use in a natural conversation, we may want to discuss the possibility of incorporating repair in an IC sub-construct of 'mutual understanding' and award with a higher score the students who are able to achieve intersubjectivity (e.g. by contingent responses) and, if trouble arises, to maintain or restore intersubjectivity.

Appendix 7.1

DE	modifier marker
DISC	discourse particles
EXPER	experiential marker
PART	utterance final particles
Q	question markers
+ (plus sign)	used to mark the beginning of embodied actions and their co-occurrence with talk

Note

(1) In the 2018 companion volume of the CEFR, descriptors were added to the A1 level of the *asking for clarification* scale.

References

ACTFL (2012) *ACTFL Proficiency Guidelines 2012*. Fairfax, VA: American Council on the Teaching of Foreign Languages. See https://www.actfl.org/publications/guidelines-and-manuals/actfl-proficiency-guidelines-2012.

Bachman, L.F. (2007) What is the construct? The dialectic of abilities and contexts in defining constructs in language assessment. In J. Fox, M. Wesche, D. Bayliss, L. Cheng, C.E. Turner and C. Doe (eds) *Language Testing Reconsidered* (pp. 41–71). Ottawa: University of Ottawa Press.

Barraja-Rohan, A.M. (2011) Using conversation analysis in the second language classroom to teach interactional competence. *Language Teaching Research* 15, 479–507.

Barraja-Rohan, A. and Pritchard, C.R. (1997) *Beyond Talk: A Course in Communication and Conversation for Intermediate Adult Learners of English. Student's Book*. Melbourne: Western Melbourne Institute of Tafe.

Betz, E. and Huth, T. (2014) Beyond grammar: Teaching interaction in the German language classroom. *Die Unterrichtspraxis/Teaching German* 47, 140–163.

Brooks, L. (2009) Interacting in pairs in a test of oral proficiency: Co-constructing a better performance. *Language Testing* 26 (3), 342–366.

Brouwer, C. (2003) Word searches in NNS–NS interaction: Opportunities for language learning? *The Modern Language Journal* 87, 534–545.

Brouwer, C. and Wagner, J. (2004) Developmental issues in second language conversation. *Journal of Applied Linguistics* 1, 29–47.

Brouwer, C., Rasmussen, G. and Wagner, J. (2004) Embedded corrections in second language talk. In R. Gardner and J. Wagner (eds) *Second Language Conversations* (pp. 75–92). London: Continuum.

Carroll, D. (2010) Conversation analysis and language teaching: A call to action. In T. Greer (ed.) *Observing Talk: Analytic Studies of Second Language Interaction* (pp. 7–22). JALT Pragmatics SIG.

Chalhoub-Deville, M. (2003) Second language interaction: Current perspectives and future trends. *Language Testing* 20 (4), 369–383.

Chui, K. (1996) Organization of repair in Chinese conversation. *Text* 16 (3), 343–372.

Council of Europe (2001) *Common European Framework of Reference for Languages: Learning, Teaching, Assessment*. Cambridge: Cambridge University Press.

Council of Europe (2018) *Common European Framework of Reference for Languages: Learning, Teaching, Assessment. Companion Volume with New Descriptors*. See https://rm.coe.int/cefr-companion-volume-with-new-descriptors-2018/1680787989.

de Jong, N. (2018) Fluency in second language testing: Insights from different disciplines. *Language Assessment Quarterly* 15 (3), 237–254.

Drew, P. (1997) 'Open' class repair initiators in response to sequential sources of troubles in conversation. *Journal of Pragmatics* 28 (1), 69–101.

Ducasse, A.M. and Brown, A. (2009) Assessing paired orals: Raters' orientation to interaction. *Language Testing* 26 (3), 423–443.

Eskildsen, S.W. (2018) 'We're learning a lot of new words': Encountering new L2 vocabulary outside of class. *The Modern Language Journal* 102 (Suppl. 2018), 46–63.

Farina, C., Pochon-Berger, E. and Pekarek Doehler, S. (2012) Le developpement de la competence d'interaction: Une etude sur le travail lexical. *TRANEL (Travaux Neuchatelois de linguistique)* 57, 101–119.

Filipi, A. and Barraja-Rohan, A. (2015) An interaction-focused pedagogy based on conversation analysis for developing L2 pragmatic competence. In S. Gesuato, F. Bianchi and W. Cheng (eds) *Teaching, Learning and Investigating Pragmatics: Principles, Methods and Practices* (pp. 231–252). Newcastle: Cambridge Scholars.

Fulcher, G. (2003) *Testing Second Language Speaking.* London: Pearson Longman.

Fulcher, G. and Davidson, F. (2007) *Language Testing and Assessment: An Advanced Resource Book.* London: Routledge.

Galaczi, E. (2008) Peer–peer interaction in a speaking test: The case of the First Certificate in English examination. *Language Assessment Quarterly* 5 (2), 89–119.

Galaczi, E. and Taylor, L. (2018) Interactional competence: Conceptualization, operationalization, and outstanding questions. *Language Assessment Quarterly* 15 (3), 219–236.

Gan, Z. (2010) Interaction in group oral assessment: A case study of higher- and lower-scoring students. *Language Testing* 27 (4), 585–602.

Gan, Z., Davison, C. and Hamp-Lyons, L. (2009) Topic negotiation in peer group oral assessment situations: A conversation analytic approach. *Applied Linguistics* 30 (3), 315–324.

Goodwin, C. and Goodwin, M.H. (1986) Gesture and co-participation in the activity of searching for a word. *Semiotica* 62, 51–75.

Greer, T. and Potter, H. (2008) Turn-taking practices in multi-party EFL oral proficiency tests. *Journal of Applied Linguistics* 5 (3), 297–320.

Hall, J.K. (2018) From L2 interactional competence to L2 interactional repertoires: Reconceptualising the objects of L2 learning. *Classroom Discourse* 9 (1), 25–39.

Hayashi, M. (2003) Language and the body as resources for collaborative action: A study of word searches in Japanese conversation. *Research on Language and Social Interaction* 36, 109–141.

He, A.W. and Young, R. (1998) Language proficiency interviews: A discourse approach. In R. Young and A.W. He (eds) *Talking and Testing: Discourse Approaches to the Assessment of Oral Proficiency* (pp. 1–24). Amsterdam: John Benjamins.

Hellermann, J. (2011) Members' methods, members' competencies: Looking for evidence of language learning in longitudinal investigations of other-initiated repair. In J.K. Hall, J. Hellermann and S. Pekarek Doehler (eds) *L2 Interactional Competence and Development* (pp. 147–172). Bristol: Multilingual Matters.

Hosoda, Y. (2000) Other-repair in Japanese conversations between nonnative and native speakers. *Issues in Applied Linguistics* 11 (1), 39–63.

Hosoda, Y. (2006) Repair and relevance of differential language expertise in second language conversations. *Applied Linguistics* 27, 25–50.

Huth, T. (2006) Negotiating structure and culture: L2 learners' realization of L2 compliment-response sequences in talk-in-interaction. *Journal of Pragmatics* 38, 2025–2050.

Huth, T. (2020) Testing interactional competence: Patterned yet dynamic aspects of L2 interaction. *Papers in Language Testing and Assessment* 9 (1), 1–24.

Huth, T. (in press) Conceptualizing interactional learning targets for the second language curriculum. In S. Kunitz, N. Markee and O. Sert (eds) *Classroom-based Conversation Analytic Research: Theoretical and Applied Perspectives on Pedagogy*. London: Springer.

Huth, T. and Betz, E. (2019) Testing interactional competence in second language classrooms: Goals, formats and caveats. In R. Salaberry and S. Kunitz (eds) *Teaching and Testing L2 Interactional Competence: Bridging Theory and Practice*. New York: Routledge.

Huth, T. and Taleghani-Nikazm, C. (2006) How can insights from conversation analysis be directly applied to teaching L2 pragmatics? *Language Teaching Research* 10, 53–79.

Jefferson, G. (2004) Glossary of transcript symbols with an introduction. In G.H. Lerner (ed.) *Conversation Analysis: Studies from the First Generation* (pp. 13–31). Amsterdam: John Benjamins.

Kasper, G. (2006) Beyond repair: Conversation analysis as an approach to SLA. *AILA Review* 19, 83–99.

Kramsch, C. (1986) From language proficiency to interactional competence. *The Modern Language Journal* 70 (4), 366–372.

Kunitz, S. and Yeh, M. (2019) Instructed L2 interactional competence in the first year. In R. Salaberry and S. Kunitz (eds) *Teaching and Testing L2 Interactional Competence: Bridging Theory and Practice*. New York: Routledge.

Kurhila, S. (2006) *Second Language Interaction*. Amsterdam and Philadelphia, PA: John Benjamins.

Lam, D. (2018) What counts as 'responding'? Contingency on previous speaker contribution as a feature of interactional competence. *Language Testing* 35 (3), 377–401.

Lerner, G. (1996) On the 'semi-permeable' character of grammatical units in conversation: Conditional entry into the turn space of another speaker. In E. Ochs, E.A. Schegloff and S.A. Thompson (eds) *Interaction and Grammar* (pp. 238–276). Cambridge: Cambridge University Press.

Lilja, N. (2014) Partial repetitions as other-initiations of repair in second language talk: Re-establishing understanding and doing learning. *Journal of Pragmatics* 71, 98–116.

Long, M. (1996) The role of the linguistic environment in second language acquisition. In W.C. Ritchie and T.K. Bhatia (eds) *Handbook of Second Language Acquisition* (pp. 413–468). New York: Academic Press.

May, L.A. (2011) Interactional competence in a paired speaking test: Features salient to raters. *Language Assessment Quarterly* 8 (2), 127–145.

McNamara, T.F. (1997) 'Interaction' in second language performance assessment: Whose performance? *Applied Linguistics* 18 (4), 446–466.

Pica, T. (1994) Research on negotiation: What does it reveal about second-language learning conditions, processes, and outcomes? *Language Learning* 44 (3), 493–527.

Psathas, G. (1995) *Conversation Analysis: The Study of Talk-in-Interaction*. Thousand Oaks, CA: Sage.

Roever, C. and Kasper, G. (2018) Speaking in turns and sequences: Interactional competence as a target construct in testing speaking. *Language Testing* 35 (3), 331–355.

Rylander, J. (2009) Repair work in a Chinese as a foreign language classroom. In H.T. Nguyen and G. Kasper (eds) *Talk-in-Interaction: Multilingual Perspectives* (pp. 245–280). Honolulu: National Foreign Language Resource Center-University of Hawaii.

Salaberry, M. and Kunitz, S. (eds) (2019) *Teaching and Testing L2 Interactional Competence: Bridging Theory and Practice*. New York: Routledge.

Sandlund, E. and Sundqvist, P. (2019) Doing versus assessing interaction competence. In R. Salaberry and S. Kunitz (eds) *Teaching and Testing L2 Interactional Competence: Bridging Theory and Practice*. New York: Routledge.

Schegloff, E. (1992) Repair after next turn: The last structurally provided defense of intersubjectivity in conversation. *American Journal of Sociology* 97 (5), 1295–1345.

Schegloff, E. (1997) Third turn repair. In G. Guy, C. Feagin, D. Schiffrin and J. Baugh (eds) *Towards a Social Science of Language. Papers in Honor of William Labov: Social Interaction and Discourse Structures, Vol. 2* (pp. 31–40). Amsterdam: John Benjamins.

Schegloff, E. (2000) When 'others' initiate repair. *Applied Linguistics* 21 (2), 205–243.

Schegloff, E.A., Jefferson, G. and Sacks, H. (1977) The preference for self-correction in the organization of repair in conversation. *Language* 53 (2), 361–382.

Seedhouse, P. and Nakatsuhara, F. (2018) *The Discourse of the IELTS Speaking Test: Interactional Design and Practice*. Cambridge: Cambridge University Press.

Simpson, R., Eisenchelas, S. and Haugh, M. (2013) The function of self-initiated self-repair in the second language Chinese classroom. *International Journal of Applied Linguistics* 23 (2), 144–165.

Tang, X.F. (2014) Self-repair practice in a Chinese as a second language classroom. *Taiwan Journal of Chinese as a Second Language* 9, 101–133.

Tao, L. (1995) Repair in natural Beijing Mandarin Chinese. In D. Branner (ed.) *The Yuen Ren Society Treasury of Chinese Dialect Data, Vol. 2* (pp. 55–77). Yuen Ren Society.

Tao, L. (2016) Metalinguistic awareness and self-repair in Chinese language learning. In H. Tao (ed.) *Integrating Chinese Linguistic Research and Language Teaching and Learning* (pp. 97–120). Amsterdam: John Benjamins.

Theodórsdóttir, G. (2018) L2 teaching in the wild: A closer look at correction and explanation practices in everyday L2 interaction. *The Modern Language Journal* 102 (Suppl. 2018), 30–45.

Walters, F.S. (2013) Interfaces between a discourse completion test and a conversation analysis-informed test of L2 pragmatic competence. In S.J. Ross and G. Kasper (eds) *Assessing Second Language Pragmatics* (pp. 172–195). London: Palgrave Macmillan.

Wong, J. (2000) Delayed next turn repair initiation in native/non-native speaker English conversation. *Applied Linguistics* 21 (1), 244–267.

Wong, J. and Waring, H.Z. (2010) *Conversation Analysis and Second Language Pedagogy: A Guide for ESL/EFL Teachers*. New York: Routledge.

Wu, R. (2006) Initiating repair and beyond: The use of two repeat-formatted practices in Mandarin conversation. *Discourse Processes* 41 (1), 67–109.

Yeh, M. (2018a) Active listenership: Developing beginners' interactional competence. *Chinese as a Second Language Research* 7 (1), 47–77.

Yeh, M. (2018b) Teaching beginners topic development: Using naturally occurring conversation. *Taiwan Journal of Chinese as a Second Language* 17 (2), 89–120.

Youn, S. (2015) Validity argument for assessing L2 pragmatics in interaction using mixed methods. *Language Testing* 32 (2), 199–225.

Youn, S. (2020) Managing proposal sequences in role-play assessment: Validity evidence of interactional competence across levels. *Language Testing* 37 (1), 76–106.

Young, R.F. (2008) *Language and Interaction: An Advanced Resource Book*. London: Routledge.

Young, R.F. (2011) Interactional competence in learning, teaching, and testing. In E. Hinkel (ed.) *Handbook of Research in Second Language Teaching and Learning, Vol. II* (pp. 426–443). London: Routledge.

Zhang, W. (1998) Repair in Chinese conversation. PhD thesis, University of Hong Kong.

Zhang, W. and Chan, A. (2013) Self-repair in Mandarin and Cantonese: Delaying the next item due in casual conversation and news interview. In P. Yuling and D.Z. Kádár (eds) *Chinese Discourse and Interaction: Theory and Practice* (pp. 35–57). Sheffield: Equinox.

8 Observing and Assessing Interactional Competence in Dynamic Strategic Interaction Scenarios

Rémi A. van Compernolle

1 Introduction

This chapter examines the use of dynamic strategic interaction scenarios (DSISs; van Compernolle, 2013, 2014a, 2014b, 2018) for observing and assessing second language (L2) interactional competence (IC). Drawing on Di Pietro's (1987) approach to language learning through scenario performances and Vygotskian sociocultural theory (Vygotsky, 1978, 1986; for L2, Lantolf & Poehner, 2014; Lantolf & Thorne, 2006), particularly the concepts of zone of proximal development and dynamic assessment, DSISs involve three stages: a rehearsal (planning) stage; a performance (spoken interaction in L2) during which support is provided; and a debriefing (feedback). The goal of DSISs is to observe current independent abilities but also to provoke abilities that are still in the process of maturing. Consequently, DSISs result in the dual assessment of past or completed development (i.e. what the person can already do) and of a learner's trajectory for future development, as evidenced by what becomes possible with assistance.

DSISs involve footing shifts between scenario performances in which a teacher and the student are playing scenario-defined roles and pedagogical interaction in which the interactants break character to negotiate linguistic or interaction assistance (van Compernolle, 2013). It therefore becomes possible to assess the learner's linguistic and interactional resources that are required for the scenario proper as well as some of the real-world interactional competencies the learner may be required to demonstrate outside of a pedagogical/assessment context (e.g. with L1 users of the language), such as performing word searches, repair sequences, and so on. Previous work on DSISs has focused on the sociolinguistic and pragmatic competencies specifically targeted by these tasks; the current chapter expands the purview of assessment to include the interactional competencies that become relevant as the learner and assessor interact and negotiate the boundaries between scenario performance and pedagogical support.

2 Background

2.1 Assessing speaking as a co-constructed achievement

Assessments of L2 learners' speaking abilities have traditionally made two broad assumptions. The first is that speaking ability resides in the individual. The second is that speaking is an abstract, generalizable skill. Consequently, the goal of assessing speaking is (i) to create a context in which the individual can demonstrate his or her ability so that (ii) the individual's speech sample can be evaluated in terms of some set of criteria that transcend the specific context of the assessment.

The Oral Proficiency Interview (OPI) used by the American Council on the Teaching of Foreign Languages (ACTFL) is one such assessment tool. The OPI aims to rate a candidate's speaking ability based on general descriptors that are hierarchically organized into five levels (as well as several sub-levels): Distinguished, Superior, Advanced, Intermediate and Novice (see ACTFL, 2012). The proficiency levels are defined with reference to the topics the speaker can speak about (e.g. familiar versus abstract topics), control over grammar and lexis, length of discourse (e.g. short utterances versus oral paragraphs), and so on. References to an interlocutor are generally focused on the degree to which the candidate's accent or linguistic errors might lead to miscommunication. For instance, in describing the Advanced level of oral proficiency, the ACTFL guidelines state: 'Such errors, if they do occur, do not distract the native interlocutor or interfere with communication' (ACTFL, 2012: 5). Numerous critiques of the ACTFL OPI, and other similar interview-style assessments, have been published over the last 30 years or so and should be familiar to the reader (e.g. Bachmann, 1990; Johnson, 2000, 2001; Johnson & Tyler, 1998; Kitajima, 2009; Lantolf & Frawley, 1985; Lazaraton, 1996; McNamara, 1997; Salaberry, 2000; Shohamy, 1988; van Compernolle, 2011; van Lier, 1989), so they will not be repeated here. It suffices to say that concerns have been raised about the adequacy of the interview context for assessing speaking ability as a single, abstract construct as well as the lack of attention paid to the interactive nature of the interview, which is by definition a co-constructed activity.

An alternative view of assessing speaking assumes that abilities are situated in their context of occurrence and are co-produced between interlocutors (van Compernolle, 2015, 2018). This perspective relocates speaking abilities in the interaction between people. Although each individual certainly draws on their interactional repertoire (Hall, 2018) of the various semiotic resources appropriated from past experiences using language, the specific speaking abilities one observes during an assessment – or any other interaction – depend on the resources made relevant to the interaction across speaker turns. This is a kind of *interactional competence* that, as Mehan (1982: 65) described it, 'is the competence necessary for effective interaction. ... [and] it is the competence that is available in the interaction between people'. In the L2 field, calls to focus on IC in teaching and testing have come out as a reaction to proficiency models (e.g. ACTFL, 2012) based on an individualistic operationalization of communicative competence (for overviews, see Kramsch, 1986; Hall *et al.*, 2011).

The central argument is that 'IC is not the knowledge or the possession of an individual person but is co-constructed by all participants in a discursive practice, and IC varies with the practice and with the participants' (Young, 2011: 428). Because IC is co-constructed and variable across discursive practices and participants, any assessment of speaking must take into account the features that define the practice in question (e.g. appropriate topics, turn-taking norms, language register) as well as the ways in which the assessor and learner jointly accomplish the interaction together. For instance, ACTFL's OPI can be seen as a variety of interaction in its own right (Seedhouse, 2013) which follows an expected, institutionally determined interactive script (i.e. learners are required to provide second-turn responses to teacher/assessor first-turn questions) that is more aligned with an interview (Johnson, 2001) or the classroom practice of initiation-response-feedback (van Compernolle, 2011) than an everyday conversation. Consequently, we are compelled to specify the kind of IC demonstrated in such contexts – responding to questions and expanding topics while controlling an appropriate discourse register (e.g. academic spoken language) – rather than assuming generalizability to any and all contexts of speaking as well as the role of the assessor's interaction style in co-producing the quality of the interaction.

To be sure, some speaking assessments break away from the interview speech event by engaging learners in roleplay, which aims to evaluate the learner's ability to negotiate a specific kind of real-world task. Indeed, the ACTFL OPI can include a 'situation with complication', which can be used to assess a learner's strategic competence in interaction (Ross & O'Donnell, 2013). However, it is still the case that learners are evaluated on the basis of their individual contributions to the interaction with little – if any – regard for the ways in which the assessor's turns-at-talk shape the interaction and, consequently, the learner's performance. This chapter is concerned with this specific aspect of speaking assessments involving roleplay, with particular focus on a task referred to as dynamic strategic interaction scenarios (DSISs; van Compernolle, 2018). As described below, DSISs are carried out not only with the assumption that interaction is co-constructed but, to take it even further, that co-construction wherein the assessor intentionally assists the learner is fundamental to assessing a learner's current and emerging abilities.

2.2 Dynamic strategic interaction scenarios

DSISs are adaptations of Di Pietro's (1987) strategic interaction approach to teaching language through performing dramatic scenarios. Scenarios are based on a shared context, and the drama is grounded in a kind of conflict between each interactant's role. For example, a scenario may involve two friends deciding where to go for lunch, and each has a different preference for cuisine and/or price. The goal of the scenario then is to negotiate the conflict. Learners may try to convince the other participant, offer a compromise or even end the scenario without any agreement.

DSISs were originally proposed as a component of van Compernolle's (2014a, 2014b, 2016, 2018) concept-based pragmatics instruction research as an approach to assessing and supporting the continued growth of L2 pragmatic abilities in spoken interaction. They were designed to be carried out between a learner and a teacher. As such, DSISs combine teaching and assessment as a unified activity, drawing on insights from research on dynamic assessment (DA) (Poehner, 2008). The basic argument, grounded in Vygotsky's (1978) concept of the zone of proximal development (ZPD), is that we gain greater insight into the full range of learners' abilities if our assessments capture what becomes possible with assistance than if we only consider what learners are able to do alone. In other words, by integrating pedagogy into the assessment procedure, we may be able to provoke – and therefore assess – emerging abilities that may not be captured in unassisted contexts. Thus, as noted earlier, DSISs – like all forms of DA – not only acknowledge the potential role of an assessor in influencing a learner's performance, but indeed embrace the role of the assessor as a mediator who supports the learner in performing beyond his/her independent abilities.

DSISs involve three basic phases (van Compernolle, 2018). The first is a planning stage. Here, the learner and assessor, or mediator, discuss the context of the interaction and what kind of language would be appropriate or useful for carrying out the learner's agenda. Importantly, the learner is not aware of what is on the mediator's agenda, although they know there will be some kind of conflict. The second phase is the performance. During the performance, the mediator may offer assistance when the learner encounters difficulty. In principle, this assistance should be tailored to the needs of, and negotiated with, the learner in the moment. This means that assistance should only be as explicit as is necessary for the learner to regain control over the performance (see Aljaafreh & Lantolf, 1994). Incidentally, while there is an explicit goal on the part for the assessor to negotiate appropriate forms of support in DSIS tasks from the outset, the effectiveness of the tasks for assessment purposes depends on the assessor's own IC (van Compernolle, 2013). In the third phase, the mediator and learner self-evaluate the performance. Here, the mediator may offer additional instruction or feedback on difficulties the learner experienced during the performance. In addition, the learner may ask questions or request further assistance. This may include additional practice with language forms or interactional strategies, explicit metalinguistic instruction or even re-performing parts of the scenario that were especially problematic.

2.3 A CA-for-SCT perspective on assessing IC

As noted, this study is grounded in Vygotskian sociocultural theory (SCT). Indeed, Di Pietro's (1987) original strategic interaction approach drew on Vygotsky's (1978) concepts of mediation and internationalization, with specific reference to three types of psychological regulation: object-regulation, other-regulation and self-regulation. In L2 development, Di Pietro argued that the language under study mediated learner ability (i.e. object-regulation) because it affords but also constrains the learner's potential course of action in interaction. Other-regulation refers to the various roles played by the teacher and possibly other students who may be able to assist the learner in gaining control over the language. Lastly, self-regulation depends on the extent to which the individual learner has gained control over the language (i.e. the process of internalization). In the DSIS model (van Compernolle, 2013, 2014a, 2014b, 2018), other- and self-regulation are foregrounded in the form of explicit feedback from others (i.e. the teacher and other students), which is intended to foster greater individual control over the language in order to assess not simply a learner's or a group's current ability to self-regulate but more importantly their responsiveness to mediation from others (cf. the ZPD concept).

While SCT provides the psychological foundation for DSIS task design and implementation, the approach also draws on conversation analysis (CA) in two ways. The first is at a conceptual level. SCT and CA share a focus on human action in its sociocultural context, namely with respect to the idea that human action is co-constructed, or co-regulated (van Compernolle, 2015), through the turn-taking system and action sequencing (Schegloff, 2007). Indeed, such a view underpins IC scholarship in general, including within SCT where it is conceptualized as mediated action (van Compernolle, 2015). This is to say that IC depends not only on an individual's repertoire but, more importantly, on what becomes available and relevant in specific contexts of human action.

The second way in which CA informs DSIS is at an analytic level. As I have argued elsewhere (van Compernolle, 2015, 2016), while SCT provides a robust psychological theory of human functioning and development, especially with regard to the relationship between social interaction and internalization, it lacks a solid analytic apparatus for documenting the processes through which mediational means (e.g. language, interactional resources) may first become available on the interpersonal plane (i.e. between people) and subsequently appropriated to mediate one's own functioning on the intrapersonal plane (i.e. within the person). This is unfortunate since this movement from the interpersonal to the intrapersonal – or what Vygotsky (1978) referred to as the genetic law of development – underpins the entire theory. CA is useful in this regard because of its detailed focus on the microinteractional features of turn-taking, action sequencing, and speech timing and delivery. Thus, a CA-for-SCT approach (van Compernolle, 2016) appropriates the methodological apparatus of CA for analyzing interactional data in order to offer a more systematic, rigorous and trustworthy account of the potential movement from interpersonal to intrapersonal functioning than would otherwise be possible.

3 Methods

3.1 Data and participant

This chapter focuses on one scenario performed by an intermediate US university-level learner of French. She was recruited to participate in a pilot study of DSISs to be used for assessing French students' IC in a range of social-interactive situations. The learner had taken three years of French classes in high school, but it had been about 18 months since she last studied French in a formal context. She was placed into her current course (Intermediate French II) by examination. As the researcher, I performed the DSISs with the student in a university office. The interactions were audio- and video-recorded for subsequent analysis. Although CA informs the present study, the data have not all been transcribed in an extremely detailed fashion. Rather, only the main interactive features that are relevant to understanding the sequence organization of talk, as well as some of the speech delivery and nonverbal behaviors that assist in disambiguating parts of the interaction, have been included.

3.2 DSIS procedure

The scenario under analysis in this chapter was titled 'Saturday plans'. It involved two friends trying to decide what to do on a Saturday. The student received a piece of paper that described the general context and her goal for the interaction. The student's goal was to try to convince her friend to go to the zoo, while my role was to propose going to see a movie. Note that while I knew what the student's goal was, she was unaware of my preference for seeing a movie, which was intended to be the conflict we would have to negotiate in the scenario.

As noted earlier, DSISs involve three phases. In the first, the student and I reviewed her role and discussed useful strategies and appropriate language for accomplishing her goal. We then performed the scenario. The student was told in advance that I would be able to offer help during the performance if she needed it. The assistance was intended to be graduated and contingent (Aljaafreh & Lantolf, 1994), meaning that it would (1) be only as explicit as deemed necessary *in situ* by the mediator in order to help the student resolve the problem, and (2) be provided only when deemed necessary. These two principles aim to avoid over-assisting the learner, on the one hand, and to push the learner to struggle to some extent to solve problems independently before intervening, on the other. The third phase centered on a debriefing in which we discussed and evaluated the performance and engaged in additional language practice if sought by the participant or mediator.

3.3 Assessment focus

Since DSISs are relatively open ended, it is not possible to determine specific linguistic features or interactional practices to assess in an a priori fashion. Rather, a more general framework is used for assessing a learner's IC, drawing on operationalizations of the construct in the literature (e.g. Hall, 1993; Rine, 2009; Young, 2011). In the present study, the assessment's focus was on turn-taking management (i.e. how to project and respond to actions as well as to repair problems in interaction).

4 Analysis

The analysis is presented in four sections that are representative of the dimensions of IC observed in the data. Section 4.1 will underscore the co-constructed nature of DSIS assessment tasks with respect to turn-taking (i.e. sequence organization and appropriate next actions). I then turn my attention to the way in which turn-taking management is central to dealing with repairing troubles in interaction and what such instances reveal about L2 learners' IC in the context of an assessment. In the excerpts that follow, the student and mediator are identified as S and M, respectively.

4.1 DSIS tasks as co-constructed events

The first examples illustrate the co-constructed nature of DSIS tasks and highlight the ways in which IC is on display at all times. In particular, they help to demonstrate how a subset of the semiotic resources in one's interactional repertoire (Hall, 2018) are made relevant from moment to moment, which has implications for the assessment of IC. Excerpt 8.1 displays the opening of a scenario in which the student and mediator are meeting for lunch. The two interlocutors are playing the roles of pen pals who are meeting in person for the first time.

Excerpt 8.1

```
1    M:    AH (.) bon↑jour.
           Ah        hello
2    S:    bonjour.
           hello
3    M:    ça va?
           things going well
4          (.)
5    S:    eh ↑oui. (.) c'est b↑ien.
           uh  yes             it's good
6          (.)
7          comment ça va.
           how       are things for you
8    M:    bah bien. bien. merci.
           yeah good good       thanks
9          (0.2)
10         alors ce restaurant a l'air bon,
           so     this restaurant looks good
```

The mediator opens the scenario with a first-pair part greeting (Line 1), which makes a second greeting (Line 2) the relevant next action. Note here that in addition to the student providing the right kind of turn in Line 2, she also reciprocates the mediator's greeting with the same salutation, *bonjour* 'hello'. This is an important observation because it shows alignment in the second turn with the mediator's initial choice: alternative salutations, such as the more informal *salut* 'hey', would not necessarily match the register initiated by the mediator in this scenario. The greeting sequence continues with the how-are-you expression *ça va?* (Line 3), a relevant response and follow up from the student (Lines 5–7), and finally the sequence-closing response and thanks from the mediator (Line 8), who in turn transitions to a new topic focused on the restaurant they have met in front of. Just as in the case of the opening *bonjour* greeting, here the mediator shapes the how-are-you sequence by using *ça va* (Line 3), which is picked up and reused by the student in her follow up (Line 7). Thus, while action categories are projected from turn to turn (e.g. salutation, how-are-you), so too are the specific semiotic resources that can be seen as appropriate for use (e.g. *bonjour, ça va?*). It is in this sense that we need to understand speaking, or rather talk-in-interaction, as a co-constructed phenomenon in which next actions, and the specific semiotic resources needed to accomplish them, are made relevant by prior turns-at-talk.

Excerpt 8.2 shows the next part of the restaurant scenario and a less routinized co-construction of action sequencing and use of relevant semiotic resources. Here, we see the mediator and student begin to negotiate one of the conflicts in the scenario. Their characters are pen pals who have never met in person until now. The student's character has been lying about being rich and a member of the DuPont family for several years, and the mediator's character is going to her for $15,000 to help pay for his mother's medical expenses. The restaurant they have met at is quite expensive.

Excerpt 8.2

```
14    M:    euh oui.
            uh yes
15          ça a l'air euh: un peu cher,
            this looks  a bit expensive
16          mais euh:: mais euh t'es de: des DuPont. hein?
            but uh      but uh      you're a   DuPont right?
17          donc euh ça [va.
            so   uh  that's fine
18    S:                [non. euh:
                         no   uh
19          je pense que:: uh (.) nous devrions (.)
            I think that   uh    we    should
20          partager le (.) l'addition.=
            split   the     the check
21    M:    AH↓ (.) >partager l'addition pour ce restaurant?<
            oh       split   the check   for this restaurant
22    S:    uh oui.
            um yes
23    M:    ah d'accord.
            oh okay
24          (.)
25          parce que moi je pensais que tu payais.
            because  I thought that you were paying
26          (0.2)
27    S:    uh non.
            uh no
28          (.)
29          c- (.) c'est-
            i-     It's
30          (.)
31          je'n suis pas: (.) très riche.
            I'm not         very rich
```

In Lines 15–17, the mediator provides an assessment of the restaurant (i.e. it looks expensive), but dismisses his observation because the student is from the DuPont family. The student reads this turn as suggesting that she should pay for the meal. This is evident in her response, which begins with a *non* 'no' (Line 18) that overlaps the end of the mediator's turn, thus explicitly rejecting the idea that she pay, and continues with the alternative suggestion that the two split the bill (Lines 19–20). The student's response is particularly important for evaluating her IC because: (1) it demonstrates that she has relevant and appropriate L2 semiotic resources for rejecting an implicit request and suggesting an alternative; and (2) it shows that she is capable of reading her interlocutor's intent in the prior turn, which is comprised of three separate utterances (i.e. noting the price of the restaurant in Line 15, acknowledging the student's family's last name in Line 16 and then concluding in Line 17 that it, presumably the price, is fine).

The student's rejection in turn shapes the remainder of the sequence. The mediator initially responds to the suggestion that they split the check with some surprise, as heard in the tone and delivery of Line 21 (i.e. emphatic delivery of AH, speeded up delivery of *partager l'addition pour ce restaurant* 'split the check for this restaurant' with final rising intonation). Upon the student's confirmation (Line 22), the mediator explicitly reveals his prior assumption that the student would pay (Line 25), which leads to the student's admission that she is not in fact rich (Line 31). Note that this sequence closure – admitting to not being rich – is assessable as part of the student's IC: her claimed identity as a member of the rich DuPont family, previously mentioned by the mediator, becomes relevant to providing an account for why she will not pay for the meal. By admitting she is not rich, she is able to excuse her refusal to pay, which in the turn following Excerpt 8.2 leads the mediator and student to leave the restaurant in search of cheaper fare elsewhere.

The two examples presented above have focused on the co-constructed nature of DSIS tasks in general. In what follows, I emphasize the role of IC in dealing with troubles in turn-taking management.

4.2 Use of English and identity work

The following examples of turn-taking management center on the use of L1 English as a resource for dealing with troubles in interaction. The data shown here are a single continuous episode. However, they have been divided into two excerpts for ease of reading and analysis.

Excerpt 8.3 displays the opening of the scenario performance. S launches a greeting sequence in Line 1, which is reciprocated by M in Line 2. S in turn begins the scenario proper by asking M if he wants to go to the zoo (Line 3). Note that S used the formal/deferent second-person form *vous* here, which M oriented to as problematic in Lines 4–5. What is important here is that M switches to English, S's L1, to engage in a peda- gogical turn-at-talk, questioning her use of *vous* 'if we're friends'. In this way, he indexes their identities as teacher and student, which makes a cor- rection of S's utterance relevant. S responds with the English change-of- state token, 'ah okay' (Line 6), and both participants laugh (Line 7), and she in turn rephrases her question using the more appropriate informal/ socially close *tu* form (Line 8). The point here is that M's use of English to focus on the form of S's utterance is read by S as a shift in footing to teacher-student interaction (as opposed to scenario performance) without any additional negotiation, which is an important part of one's IC.

Excerpt 8.3

```
1     S:    bonjour.

            hello

2     M:    bonjour.

            hello

3     S:    uh voudrez-vous aller au z[oo?

            Uh do you/would you like to go to the zoo

4     M:                              [you wanna say vous

5           if we're friends?

6     S:    ah okay.

7           ((both laugh))

8           veux-tu aller au zoo aujourd'hui?

            Do you want to go to the zoo today
```

A similar example is shown in Excerpt 8.4. M responds to S's suggestion that they go to the zoo by proposing instead to go to the movies (Lines 9–10). S rejects the counter-suggestion (Line 11) and follows up with a reason to go to the zoo: it is *fun* (Line 12). However, she apparently does not know the French word for *fun*: she hesitates with a pause before uttering *fun* in English, which is read by M as a request for assistance. He provides the French equivalent in Line 13, which is repeated by S (Line 14) and then used by her (Line 15) as the scenario continues. In other words, here, S's use of English initiates a mediation sequence (van Compernolle, 2013, 2015), put- ting the scenario on hold so they can deal with a linguistic problem and consequently indexing M and S's identities as teacher and student.

Excerpt 8.4

```
9    M:    bah le zoo euh ça je sais pas.

           Well the zoo uh I don't know about that

10         je voulais plutôt voir un film.

           I kind of wanted to go see a movie

11   S:    ah non je ne veux pas voir les films aujourd'hui

           Ah no I don't want to see a movie today

12         je pense que le zoo (.2) est très uh (3.5) fun.

           I think that the zoo is very

13   M:    amusant?

           fun

14   S:    amusant.

           fun

15         est plus amusant que voir un film.

           Is more fun than seeing a movie
```

The two previous examples illustrate two important aspects of IC. The first is S's ability to recognize and initiate shifts in footing from scenario performance to teaching-learning activity (i.e. an explicit focus on language). Second, S demonstrates an ability to recognize and deploy relevant interactional resources for participating in such footing shifts – in these cases, the use of L1 English. From an assessment perspective, this information is useful inasmuch as we have evidence that S is able to take up as well as seek out assistance from a more competent person through the use of English, which is relevant to a wide range of contexts within but also beyond formal pedagogical settings (e.g. in conversation with multilinguals who speak English and French).

4.3 Repair initiation

The following excerpts illustrate S's competence in initiating conversational repair. Different from correction (Hall, 2007) and seeking assistance (van Compernolle, 2015), repair is a mechanism for dealing with troubles in the progressivity of talk (Schegloff *et al.*, 1977). Troubles may include mishearing, misunderstanding, lack of knowledge about a current topic of conversation, linguistic ambiguity, and so on.

In Excerpt 8.5, M – in an attempt to dissuade S from going to the zoo – observes that it may rain (Line 1). S responds with the open-class repair initiator (Drew, 1997) *comment?* 'what?', which signals that something in M's prior utterance is problematic but without specifying the exact source of trouble. Consequently, M repeats the main idea expressed in the utterance, *il va peut-être pleuvoir aujourd'hui* 'it might rain today' (Line 3), which involves two modifications to his utterance from Line 1. First, he omits the turn-initial *d'accord mais* 'okay but' in order to 'disencumber the trouble-source turn from elements now superfluous' (Schegloff, 2004: 99). Second, he makes his utterance an assertion rather than the negated interrogative (i.e. *it might rain* versus *is it not supposed to rain*), which similarly simplifies the utterance only to the main idea worth repeating. The repair is successful as evidenced by S's response in Line 4 (*je ne pense pas* 'I don't think so') and subsequent continuation of the scenario performance.

Excerpt 8.5

```
1    M:    d'accord mais il va pas pleuvoir peut-être aujourd'hui?

           Okay     but is it not supposed to rain today

2    S:    comment?

           what

3    M:    il va peut-être pleuvoir aujourd'hui.

           It might rain today

4    S:    je ne pense pas.

           I don't think so
```

The second example of repair initiation (Excerpt 8.6) also involves the open-class initiator *comment* 'what' (Line 2) with rising interrogative intonation and raised eyebrows. What is different here is that M and S must negotiate the scope of the trouble in order to accomplish the repair together. M's initial repetition of the problematic utterance *on peut faire les deux alors* 'we can do both then' (Line 3) does not repair the problem. This is evident from the way S moves her head back and shrugs her shoulders during the pause in Line 4, which can be interpreted as a nonverbal repair initiator. Consequently, another attempt at repair from M is necessary in order to maintain progressivity in interaction: M begins to enumerate the two activities, going to the zoo (Line 5) and going to the movies (Line 7). Note that S's *oui* 'yes' utterances in Lines 6 and 8 are read by M as confirming her comprehension, and therefore successful repair: in Line 9, he closes the sequence and the two co-participants move on with the scenario.

Excerpt 8.6

```
1    M:    on peut faire les deux alors.

           We can do both then

2    S:    comment? ((raises eyebrows)

           What's that

3    M:    on peut faire les deux alors.

           We can do both then

4          ((2.0) ((S moves head back and shrugs shoulders; gazes at M))))

5          le zoo cet après midi, et

           The zoo in the afternoon and

6    S:    oui. oui.

           Yes yes

7    M:    et le cinéma plus tard?

           And the movies later

8    S:    oui.

           yes

9    M:    d'accord. peut-être.

           Okay maybe
```

The two instances of repair initiated by S demonstrate the co-constructed nature of IC. Although S initiated both repair sequences, the repair itself was managed by both S and M: drawing on S's displays of understanding (or lack thereof), M modified his speech to repair the problem and closed the sequence only when S was able to continue.

4.4 Rejecting assistance

The final example of IC demonstrated in the DSIS is shown in Excerpt 8.7. Here, M is responding to S's previous suggestion that they go to the zoo today and go to a movie the following weekend. The problem according to M is that the movie he wants to see is showing this week but not the next (Lines 1–3). This pushes S to modify her suggestion and propose they do both the zoo and a movie today (see Excerpt 8.6, above, for the resolution to the problem – that they can do both). However, in initiating her response, S struggles to formulate her utterance (Line 4). Note the long pauses after the turn-initial *um puis* 'um then' and after the subject pronoun *nous* 'we'. M reads this second pause, as well as the co-occurring gaze shift, as signaling trouble with the verb: he offers a candidate verb form *pouvons* 'can' with rising intonation (Line 5), signaling that it is a suggestion but not a corrective or directive move. In turn, S self-corrects with a different verb: *nous allons au zoo* 'we'll go to the zoo' (Line 7), thus rejecting M's offer of assistance. The reader will note S's scrunched yes and head shake, which can be taken as evidence that she registered and rejected the suggestion.

Excerpt 8.7

```
1     M:    on va voir parce que je pense que Marry Poppins passe
            We'll see because I think that Mary Poppins is showing

2           cette semaine mais la- la semaine prochaine, le film
            This week but next week the movie

3           ne passe plus.
            Is no longer showing

4     S:    um puis {(7.5) puis nous (3.0) ((looking up and to left))}
            Um then       then we

5     M:    pouvons?
            can

6     S:    ((scrunches eyes and shakes head once))

7           nous allons au zoo aujourd'hui pour le (1.2) pour l'après-midi,
            We go to the zoo today        for    for the afternoon

8           et voir le film ce um (.4) soir.
            And see the movie this um evening

9     M:    ah ce soir?
            Oh this evening

10    S:    à ce soir.
            At this evening
```

The preceding example is important in terms of observing and assessing IC because it shows that S is capable of asserting her own meaning rather than simply uptaking a possible correction from a more expert speaker of French. To be sure, S still has progress to make, as evidenced in the same excerpt. Note that in Line 9, M utters a confirmation of S's suggestion that they go to the movies this evening: *ah ce soir?* 'oh this evening'. S hears this as a correction and takes it up by repeating *à ce soir* 'at this evening', which is ungrammatical (i.e. she replaces the change-of-state particle *ah* from M's utterance with the locative preposition *à*), possibly because of the *um* that preceded her own utterance in Line 8: *et voir le film ce um soir* 'and see the movie this um evening'.

5 Conclusion

This chapter has considered some of the dimensions of IC that may be observed and, in turn, made the object of assessment in the context of

DSISs. The analysis focused on the co-constructed nature of interaction and subsequently on instances in which troubles in performance arose that had to be resolved in order for the scenario to continue. These moments are authentic instances of a learner's IC inasmuch as they are not simply performances for a task (e.g. performing appropriate speech acts). In other words, these examples provide a glimpse into the learner's real-life ability to negotiate and manage the turn-taking system.

Because the examples shown in the analysis were not specifically prompted, it is not possible to assess a learner's IC based on an a priori coding scheme or rubric. Instead, as an assessment procedure, it is likely more beneficial to document a learner's repertoire of interactive practices that become relevant. In this sense, an assessment of IC would involve constructing an inventory of the various semiotic resources used to accomplish specific context-bound actions. For instance, such an inventory for S in this study would include picking up and reusing register-specific language in her second-turn greetings, using English to solicit vocabulary assistance, initiating other-repair through an open-class initiator and rejecting unnecessary assistance. To be sure, the inventory is short because only one scenario was analyzed for this chapter. The reader is reminded, however, that S performed six different scenarios in this assessment procedure, which yielded a greater number of examples and a larger set of interactive practices that can be used to assess her IC.

Documenting a learner's repertoire of interactive practices in this way has the potential to be a useful approach to assessing his or her IC at a single moment in time. However, the approach may prove especially useful for tracking IC development longitudinally. Indeed, research conducted in more naturalistic settings (Pekarek Doehler & Pochon-Berger, 2018) has adopted a similar approach to documenting the development of L2 IC as the expansion of context-sensitive interactional repertoires. The point of assessing IC over time through DSISs would, therefore, be to trace the growth of a learner's repertoire (e.g. resources for managing turn-taking and repair) and his or her ability to deploy resources in a context-sensitive way over time. Naturally, assessing IC in this way may also provide educators with information relevant to classroom pedagogy, including developing remedial lessons to teach learners additional resources that are either absent or inappropriately used in DSISs as well as modifying curricula at the program level (e.g. developing materials, revising course objectives). Although it is not necessarily feasible for teachers to conduct and analyze one-on-one DSIS tasks, especially if they have large class sizes, there are interesting models for adapting the procedure for classroom contexts (van Compernolle, 2018; van Compernolle & Ballesteros Soria, 2020). Such work involves students performing scenarios in small groups and using a post-performance debriefing stage (Di Pietro, 1987) as a context for providing feedback on the performance and mediating future development for the group as well as for other students, drawing additional insights from approaches to conducting group/class-room dynamic assessment (e.g. Poehner, 2009). Future work in this important domain would do well to focus on strategies for documenting learner repertoires in a formal fashion that can be used to make within-learner and across-learner comparisons across time, and that can be used effectively for making pedagogical decisions.

References

ACTFL (2012) *ACTFL Proficiency Guidelines 2012*. Fairfax, VA: American Council on the Teaching of Foreign Languages. See https://www.actfl.org/publications/guide-lines-and-manuals/actfl-proficiency-guidelines-2012.

Aljaafreh, A. and Lantolf, J.P. (1994) Negative feedback as regulation and second language learning in the zone of proximal development. *The Modern Language Journal* 78, 465–483.

Bachman, L.F. (1990) *Fundamental Considerations in Language Testing*. Oxford: Oxford University Press.

Drew, P. (1997) 'Open' class repair initiators in response to sequential sources of troubles in conversation. *Journal of Pragmatics* 28, 69–101.

Di Pietro, R.J. (1987) *Strategic Interaction: Learning Languages Through Scenarios*. Cambridge: Cambridge University Press.

Hall, J.K. (1993) The role of oral practices in the accomplishment of our everyday lives: The sociocultural dimension of interaction with implications for the learning of another language. *Applied Linguistics* 14, 145–167.

Hall, J.K. (2007) Redressing the roles of correction and repair in research on second and foreign language learning. *Modern Language Journal* 91, 511–526.

Hall, J.K. (2018) From L2 interactional competence to L2 interactional repertoires: Reconceptualising the objects of L2 learning. *Classroom Discourse* 9 (1), 25–39.

Hall, J.K., Hellermann, J. and Pekarek Doehler, S. (eds) (2011) *L2 Interactional Competence and Development*. Bristol: Multilingual Matters.

Johnson, M. (2000) Interaction in oral proficiency interview: Problems of validity. *Pragmatics* 10, 215–231.

Johnson, M. (2001) *The Art of Nonconversation: A Reexamination of the Validity of the Oral Proficiency Interview*. New Haven, CT: Yale University Press.

Johnson, M. and Tyler, A. (1998) Re-analyzing the OPI: How much does it look like natural conversation? In R. Young and A.W. He (eds) *Talking and Testing: Discourse Approaches to the Assessment of Oral Proficiency* (pp. 27–51). Amsterdam: John Benjamins.

Kitajima, R. (2009) Negotiation of meaning as a tool for evaluating conversational skills in the OPI. *Linguistics and Education* 20, 145–171.

Kramsch, C. (1986) From language proficiency to interactional competence. *Modern Language Journal* 70, 366–372.

Lantolf, J.P. and Frawley, W. (1985) Oral proficiency testing: A critical analysis. *The Modern Language Journal* 69, 337–345.

Lantolf, J.P. and Poehner, M.E. (2014) *Sociocultural Theory and the Pedagogical Imperative in L2 Education*. New York: Routledge/Taylor & Francis.

Lantolf, J.P. and Thorne, S.L. (2006) *Sociocultural Theory and the Genesis of Second Language Development*. Oxford: Oxford University Press.

Lazaraton, A. (1996) Interlocutor support in oral proficiency interviews: The case of CASE. *Language Testing* 13 (2), 151–172.

McNamara, T. (1997) 'Interaction' in second language performance assessment: Whose performance? *Applied Linguistics* 18, 446–466.

Mehan, H. (1982) The structure of classroom events and their consequences for student performance. In P. Gilmore and A.A. Glatthorn (eds) *Children In and Out of School: Ethnography and Education* (pp. 59–87). Washington, DC: Center for Applied Linguistics.

Pekarek Doehler, S. and Pochon-Berger, E. (2018) L2 interactional competence as increased ability for context-sensitive conduct: A longitudinal study of story-openings. *Applied Linguistics* 39 (4), 555–578.

Poehner, M.E. (2008) *Dynamic Assessment: A Vygotskian Approach to Understanding and Promoting Second Language Development.* Berlin: Springer.

Poehner, M.E. (2009) Group dynamic assessment: Mediation for the L2 classroom. *TESOL Quarterly* 43 (3), 471–491.

Rine, E.F. (2009) Development in dialogic teaching skills: A micro-analytic case study of a pre-service ITA. Unpublished dissertation, Pennsylvania State University.

Ross, S.J. and O'Connell, S.P. (2013) The situation with complication as a site for strategic competence. In S.J. Ross and G. Kasper (eds) *Assessing Second Language Pragmatics* (pp. 311–326). New York: Palgrave Macmillan.

Sacks, H., Schegloff, E. and Jefferson, G. (1974) A simplest systematic for the organization of turn-taking for conversation. *Language* 50, 696–735.

Salaberry, R. (2000) Revising the revised format of the ACTFL Oral Proficiency Interview. *Language Testing* 17, 289–310.

Schegloff, E.A. (2004) On dispensability. *Research on Language and Social Interaction* 37, 95–149.

Schegloff, E.A. (2007) *Sequence Organization in Interaction: A Primer in Conversation Analysis, Volume 1.* Cambridge: Cambridge University Press.

Schegloff, E., Jefferson, G. and Sacks, H. (1977) The preference for self-correction in the organization of repair in conversation. *Language* 53, 361–382.

Seedhouse, P. (2013) Oral proficiency interviews as varieties of interaction. In S.J. Ross and G. Kasper (eds) *Assessing Second Language Pragmatics* (pp. 199–219). New York: Palgrave Macmillan.

Shohamy, E. (1988) A proposed framework for testing the oral proficiency of second/foreign language learners. *Studies in Second Language Acquisition* 10, 165–180.

van Compernolle, R.A. (2011) Responding to questions and L2 learner interactional competence during language proficiency interviews: A microanalytic study with pedagogical implications. In J.K. Hall, J. Hellermann and S. Pekarek Doehler (eds) *L2 Interactional Competence and Development* (pp. 117–144). Bristol: Multilingual Matters.

van Compernolle, R.A. (2013) Interactional competence and the dynamic assessment of L2 pragmatic abilities. In S. Ross and G. Kasper (eds) *Assessing Second Language Pragmatics* (pp. 327–353). Basingstoke: Palgrave/Macmillan.

van Compernolle, R.A. (2014a) *Sociocultural Theory and L2 Instructional Pragmatics.* Bristol: Multilingual Matters.

van Compernolle, R.A. (2014b) Profiling second language sociolinguistic development through dynamically administered strategic interaction scenarios. *Language and Communication* 37, 86–99.

van Compernolle, R.A. (2015) *Interaction and Second Language Development: A Vygotskian Perspective.* Amsterdam and Philadelphia, PA: John Benjamins.

van Compernolle, R.A. (2016) CA-for-SCT: Dialectics and the analysis of cognition on the ground. *Language and Sociocultural Theory* 3 (2), 173–193.

van Compernolle, R.A. (2018) Focus on meaning and form: A Vygotskian perspective on task and pragmatic development in dynamic strategic interaction scenarios. In M. Ahmadian and M.P.G. Mayo (eds) *Recent Trends in Task-based Language Learning and Teaching* (pp. 79–97). Berlin: Mouton De Gruyter.

van Compernolle, R.A. and Ballesteros-Soria, N. (2020) Developing interactional repertoires in the classroom through dynamic strategic interaction scenarios. *Vigo International Journal of Applied Linguistics* 17, 141–169.

van Lier, L. (1989) Reeling, writhing, drawling, stretching, and fainting in coils: Oral proficiency interviews as conversation. *TESOL Quarterly* 23, 489–508.

Vygotsky, L.S. (1978) *Mind in Society: The Development of Higher Psychological Processes*. Cambridge, MA: Harvard University Press.

Vygotsky, L.S. (1986) *Thought and Language*. Cambridge, MA: MIT Press.

Young, R.F. (2011) Interactional competence in language learning, teaching, and testing. In E. Hinkel (ed.) *Handbook of Research in Second Language Teaching and Learning, Vol. 2* (pp. 426–443). London and New York: Routledge.

9 Using Social Deduction Board Games to Assess and Strengthen Interactional Competence in ESL Learners

Shane Dunkle

1 Introduction

Roleplay activities have been a staple tool for eliciting contextualized, pragmatically realistic utterances in the second language classroom (Brown & Lee, 2015; García, 2018; Houck & Tatsuki, 2011; Hughes & Beatrice, 2017; Lin, 2009; Scrivener, 2005). This is because roleplay activities usually allow for large amounts of student language production that can be used by an instructor to assess knowledge of grammatical forms, meanings and pragmatic use, as well as being an overall popular activity for communicative language teaching classes (Brown & Abeywickrama, 2010). The assessment context of these student productions, in best case scenarios, will feature aspects of speaking/conversation that mirror real-world production. Carless's (2007) learner-oriented model of assessment (LOA) is one possible assessment context for roleplay activities, since LOA aims to 'mirror real-world applications of the subject matter'. In the language classroom, roleplay activities are the assessment tool that comes closest to simulating the kind of real-world utterances a student would produce after classroom instruction.

One pedagogical goal of a roleplay activity is to have students transfer the same utterances and situational knowledge to similar real-world contexts. Götz (2013) considers 'fluent' English to contain productive (speech rate, unfilled pauses), perceptive (accuracy, intonation, pragmatic features, register, sentence structure) and nonverbal (gestures, facial expressions, body language) features – all of which should be present in student utterances during a roleplay activity if it is to reflect real-world usage of the target language. The assessment feedback for student production may take the form of a scored rubric or written/oral feedback that outlines how 'fluent' the student's production was along with areas the student should focus on when practicing.

While roleplays are a commonly used assessment tool/task for student production, they do have inherent limitations. While roleplays provide simulated contexts for learners to produce target pragmatic features at a relativity high frequency (Culpeper *et al.*, 2010), modifications to the context and/or roles may be needed in order to allow students to produce more contextually appropriate utterances (Brandl, 2008; Neff & Rucynski, 2013). In addition, roleplays may not elicit the full range of problematic interferences that would arise if students produced the same utterances outside of the roleplay activity in real-world situations, as students 'simply seem to do different things' once they leave the classroom (Eskildsen & Majlesi, 2018). One specific style of roleplay, closed,[1] is often used as a production tool to assess a student's understanding and usage of learned language by an instructor. However, closed roleplays often have students studying the exact context, roles and positionality of interlocutors before any utterances are produced in order to successfully produce the target linguistic and non-linguistic/pragmatic forms necessary for 'successful' production in the roleplay scenario. Thus, students are allowed access to materials and pre-structured utterances that can be utilized during production (Crowther-Alwyn, 1999; Scrivener, 2005). This scaffolding and preparation, while necessary for learner production in a classroom context, becomes problematic when students are expected to produce the same utterances in real-life contexts without such scaffolding. In these closed roleplays, students are not exposed to or allowed to experience and navigate through the unpredictable and uncontrolled aspects of real-world conversational contexts, and are instead practicing 'speaking' rather than 'talking' (Rover & Dai, this volume) – not to mention the other non-linguistic aspects inherit in all roleplay activities that cover a wide spectrum from perceived learned needs to instructor training and uptake of such topics in a language classroom (Young & Sachdev, 2011).

Even harder than providing appropriate contexts in which learners can produce utterances is that of assessing how well a learner has internalized the understanding and/or control of pragmatic areas that extend beyond the more easily demonstrable areas of utterances such as tense, aspect and pronunciation. Implementing assessment tasks that focus on these areas of learner output places an overemphasis on the linguistic utterances themselves and does not include 'communicative stress' so that students at higher levels have the 'opportunity of practicing speaking in more stressful situations' (Brown & Yule, 1991). Another roleplay style, open roleplays, are one way of adding this stress back into student utterances, as there is no extensive scaffolding and students can produce whatever utterances they feel match the current interactions with interlocutors since open roleplays do not feature a predefined outcome for a given scenario.

Students are also free to use any linguistic and non-linguistic tools that they feel comfortable employing to reach any kind of conclusion for the roleplay scenario. Even though open roleplays may better simulate real-world contexts, students may still feel they are 'on stage' and it becomes hard for an instructor to separate things like performance anxiety from linguistic knowledge when observing and assessing students.

While both styles of roleplay activities (and other styles) have advantages and disadvantages for student production and assessment/feedback in the language classroom context, the use of social deduction games is another activity that can be used that will allow for more learner agency and creativity while still introducing the spontaneity and stress of real-life contexts and reducing the 'on stage' feeling that students may feel when participating in a roleplay activity. This was first anecdotally observed by myself when playing social deduction board games with students outside of the classroom in a board game group and noticing that student utterances seemed more realistic in terms of the skills that we practiced in class than they were during the formative assessment roleplay tools I used during the production time after instruction in class. I saw that, indeed, students seemed to be doing different things outside of class. It was then that I decided to bring these social deduction games into the classroom and to integrate them into my speaking curriculum. Therefore, the research in this chapter on using social deduction board games in the language classroom is firmly contextualized in my own experience as an applied linguistics classroom-based English language instructor seeking a new and novel way to engage students and to produce more learner agency and creative utterances both inside and outside of the classroom context. In this way, the primary motivation of the research was situated in the context of giving formative assessment to students (action research), rather than furthering any specific topic or idea in the field in general. It can also be firmly situated in the idea of 'instructional pragmatics', where I wanted to focus on the pedagogical component of interlanguage pragmatics (Bardovi-Harlig, 2020; Ishihaha, 2010) and how to better incorporate this into a higher-level language classroom for students who already have a firm grasp and command/use of English.

By using social deduction board games as a formative assessment[2] tool for the production of certain pragmatic skill sets, the assessment of these student utterances/performances will be more reliable as the speech acts will be in the realm of what an English-dominant speaker might also produce given the same contextual parameters. Also, using these social deduction board games, in lieu of or at least in conjunction with a roleplay activity, will 'allow inferences as to [students'] ability to engage in social interactions and are therefore more likely to support real-world uses that include the ability to deploy language in interactive situations for social purposes', as outlined by Roever and Kasper (2018). If social deduction games reflect some aspects of roleplays, specifically open roleplays as defined by Culpeper *et al.* (2010) and Kasper and Rose (2002), in that the speaker and listener assume roles and coordinate their contributions through turn-taking and the outcomes of the games/roleplays are not pre-determined in a situational scenario, they can then be used as a formative assessment tool for student production when their one-on-one or group interactions are audio- and video-recorded by an instructor so that student performances may be viewed again to find student production done overtly or subtly.

One aspect of assessing speaking that should be addressed at this point is that the assessment of both linguistic and non-linguistic skills together in a specific context can be an attribute of interactional competence (IC) as outlined by Roever and Kasper and 'cannot be separated from performance' (2018). For the context of this chapter though, IC is treated as more of a 'global' skill that includes both IC and interlanguage pragmatic performative features. This means that some key features of IC, such as 'negotiating communicative norms and conventions on the fly' (Jenks, 2013) were not discretely assessed in the research project presented here. One aspect of IC that is included within the scope of this chapter is the display of pragmatic competence – although it is treated as local, discrete skill. While students do assume roles in social deduction board games as they would in a role play activity, these roles, such as werewolves or a freedom fighter in a dystopian future, are not situated in reality and do not reflect the contexts of traditional conversation. These roles have generally been specifically created for the context of the game in order to facilitate winning and losing and to bring the game to a close, so these roles only have strategic in-game functions and do not have any prescribed contextualized pragmatic attributes. The outcomes, however, are real in that there will be a tangible winner(s) and loser(s) of the game. Roleplay activities in the pedagogical sense, on the other hand, are usually designed to simulate a specific linguistic or non-linguistic aspect (or more) of conversation inherit in the roleplay scenario, which is usually the target structure that the instructor wants a learner to demonstrate in order to assess their understanding and usage of the skill. Social deduction board games can achieve the same outcomes, but in a very different production context. The differences between these two contexts can be better seen by defining what a social deduction game is, the roles that participants take and how winning a social deduction game is accomplished.

2 Social Deduction Board Games

Social deduction board games, also known as social deduction games (SDGs), are a style of board game where players are given roles and asked to complete a specific individual/team/group objective(s). The roles that players are given feature specific actions that will allow the winning objectives to be accomplished when used strategically by the players during the game; however, some roles are secret and feature actions that allow an individual or team to win by completing objectives that are in conflict with those of the rest of the players. A lot of these games feature objectives where players must find and expose the players engaged in trying to complete these secret objectives.

SDGs differ from traditional board games in that the primary game mechanism that players are engaging with is produced by the players themselves, rather than by any specific game mechanism designed into the game. For example, in the popular board game 'Monopoly', the main game mechanism is dice rolling. 'Monopoly' also features interaction through trading, and these trades are usually based on mutual positive outcomes for both traders. Additionally, there is no hidden information, so trades are based on known variables such as player positions on the game board and how many rounds might be left in the game. In SDGs, there is usually an element of hidden information as each player's winning goals/actions are not known to the other players. In this way, when players interact, they cannot rely only on the information that the game presents or generates randomly through such mechanisms as dice rolls, but they must also analyze the players themselves to determine their hidden motivations. This is known as 'metagaming', or when players make a play or decision that has been influenced by external knowledge rather than based on fundamental strategy alone (Carter *et al.*, 2012).

The main game mechanic of SDGs then becomes the ability of the player to use linguistic forms and pragmatic skills like negotiation, bluffing and turn-taking to achieve their objectives in the game and win. The popular social deduction game 'Werewolf' features two or more players in a group playing the role of a werewolf that 'eats' and eliminates players in a night phase, whereas the rest of the players in the group are villagers trying to find the werewolves during a day phase. There is usually a moderator who facilitates game aspects such as setting the length of the phases (night phase usually only being a couple of minutes long and the day phase being as long or as short as the moderator deems necessary) and who does not actively participate in the playing of the game. As a side note, this role provides the class instructor with an excellent opportunity to observe and record student utterances as they play, while also allowing the game to fit into any length of class time. The day phase of the game has all players trying to find the werewolves through questions, accusations and deductions. There is no turn order as to who can speak and there are no limitations on what can be said in the game. The challenge is for the werewolf player(s) to be able to successfully deflect accusations made against them if a villager player starts to suspect that they are a werewolf and, conversely, for the villager players to successfully detect who might be bluffing. If there are ever more werewolves than villagers, they win (see Appendix 9.2 for complete rule set). SDGs like 'Werewolf' are challenging not because of the rule set or gaming mechanism, but rather because of the challenge they present to players' pre-existing knowledge and employment of social norms and speaking skills. They are challenging to play for English-dominant speakers precisely because they challenge pragmatic skills and shared cultural expectations (i.e. breaking Grice's cooperative maxim) that speakers may or may not usually actively employ when speaking, based on the interlocutors and context.

3 Using SDGs as a Formative Measure of Pragmatics

Because of the unique features that are present in SDGs, learners can produce target pragmatic skills, but in a context that promotes learner agency and creativity and focuses more on the skill itself, rather than on the specific context. Using board games for the purpose of language learning is not a new or novel strategy and is commonly used to promote speaking skills (Gaudart, 1999; Tilton, 2019; Vlachopoulos & Makri, 2017; Whitton, 2011). However, employing SDGs in the second language classroom as a formative assessment tool can facilitate a context for utterances that better reflect a learner's skill and production level of a learned pragmatic area, which then encourages transfer to other contexts.

For assessment purposes, SDGs fulfill the requirements for useful assessments: practicality, reliability, various forms of validity, and beneficial consequences (Green, 2014). SDGs are practical because how-to-play resources and free versions can be found online (see boardgamegeek.com; also see Appendices 9.1 and 9.2) and commercially produced games can be found in most local gaming stores. They can be considered reliable since the underlying rules and game systems do not change from game to game. When played again with the same group of learners, the strategies for winning the game will remain the same, but new opportunities for learners to produce and improve on the same pragmatic utterances and speech acts will be present. This contrasts with open roleplays where the outcomes can be widely different depending on how a student approaches the given scenario and closed roleplays where a student may only have one path to an outcome without the creativity necessary to produce novel utterances. Finally, SDGs have beneficial consequences due to the gamification aspect of the SDGs. Learners become focused on rules and strategy, so speech acts and linguistic forms become integrated into the overall strategy of trying to win the game. In other words, learners put less emphasis on actively producing target structures through utterances and so learners' actual production levels can be observed by an instructor, something that this chapter shows is true in two out of three instructional contexts. By using SDGs to elicit learned pragmatic speech acts, the learner experiences a similar contextual stress load in that they must be able to integrate specific utterances and speech acts that align with their current strategy for winning the game. Learners who are able to successfully accomplish this task are given positive feedback in that they have a greater opportunity to win the game. Those learners who win the game gain the knowledge that they were able to manipulate and incorporate the pragmatic skill sets to the extent that they won the game, receiving positive reinforcement about their ability to use the skill(s). As an added bonus, other participants in the SDG will be more likely to emulate a winning strategy to try and win future games.

In roleplays (open or closed), feedback is usually given by the instructor after they have assessed the degree to which a student has 'successfully' navigated the scenario presented by the roleplay. In SDGs, that 'success' is intertwined with the winning of the game. Instructors can still give discrete feedback later after reviewing student performances, from notes taken during the game or after watching a recording of the game and analyzing student utterances for the presence of target skills, either linguistic, non-linguistic or pragmatic.

In this study, the most problematic aspect of assessing pragmatic skills is identifying what can be considered to be a display of a pragmatic utterance in a speech act (i.e. defining the intended assessment construct). This is summed up by Culpeper and Haugh (2014) in such areas as production format, participation status, participation framework and production roles, which are all part of participant footing. For example, an instructor must distinguish between a pragmatic utterance of bluffing in relation to a statement of truth and whether a student was either consciously or actively producing such an utterance. There are also many factors that must be controlled for in order to correctly assess if a learner has effectively demonstrated the ability to bluff. In closed or open roleplays, unless certain aspects of the roleplay such as position and intention of a speaker are spelled out for the speaker and kept hidden from other participants, they would be unknown to the student speaker and those they interact with during the roleplay. In this way, roleplays introduce a wide spectrum of variables that are rarely known in advance in naturally occurring interactions.

Other contextual factors that may not be represented in role plays are the stakes of the participants. In a roleplay where one participant is buying a car, since there is no tangible real-life outcome, this may affect the utterances and attitudes of the participants. In SDGs, while the contexts within the game, i.e. finding werewolves or being a member of the mafia, are not realistic, the context of winning a game is – that is, the tangible outcome of either playing 'Monopoly' or any SDG is that a player will win the game, and that is the tangible real-life outcome. The context does not need to be controlled for, as it is unrealistic to begin with, and thus lowers the affective filter of student production. Some aspects like intonation, verbal and non-verbal signals and grammatical accuracy can be assessed in both SDGs and roleplays; however, capturing naturally occurring utterances for a skill like bluffing can be problematic in SDGs in that unless the instructor understands the intent behind an utterance, they might miss the attempt by a student to mislead in a given context – something that can be somewhat controlled for if the instructor knows which roles each student is playing before they begin the game. Roleplays allow an instructor to know all the roles and information of the production context and thus can better assess when a learner has attempted to produce a specific utterance and the degree to which they were successful, as in an achievement test. SDGs, on the other hand, provide a tangible outcome in that if a learner successfully produces utterances that fulfil the pragmatic requirements of a speech act, then the learner will gain an advantage in the SDG over the other participants and possibly win the game. In this way, SDGs provide tangible results that motivate participants to actively use such skills that may not be present in a roleplay, although it can be noted that sufficient scaffolding by the instructor in regard to the game rules and playing strategy/outcomes is a large variable in this equation. From a pedagogical assessment angle, though, this fits nicely with communicative language assessment that is learning oriented as the SDG 'correspond[s] in demonstrable ways to language in non-test situations' (Bachman & Palmer, 1996). In other words, even if there is a successful negotiation sequence in the car purchase roleplay, the purchasing students do not actually receive a car and this fact would probably influence utterances and be different from those used when buying a car in a real-life situation. In the SDG context, if a successful negotiation sequence is performed, the student might win the game, which is a real-life outcome.

4 Game Design

I had been using SDGs in my advanced level English spoken communications class as a last-day social bonding activity and outside of class in a separate board game group that was open to any domestic or international student wanting to participate. It was during these sessions in the last-day social bonding activity and board game group that I saw anecdotal evidence emerging that students were producing more novel and interesting utterances, similar to those of native speakers, for the skills they had practiced during the class than they were producing during the roleplays that were being used as production tools to assess certain pragmatic competencies taught in class. After one quarter (a full eight-week academic term at the institution where the study was conducted), I incorporated SDGs into the class curriculum as practice activities to gather more anecdotal evidence as to their pedagogical effectiveness as assessment tasks. During this period, I still used roleplays as the primary formative assessment tool, but students were also given feedback on their utterances produced during gameplay. I collected more anecdotal evidence over the next two quarters that SDGs were a useful production task/tool to assess a student's comprehension and production of certain pragmatic skills studied in class. Then, keeping the SDG rules intact, I designed formative assessment tasks that were administered three times over the duration of the course. The study was run during the fourth consecutive quarter of using SDGs in the spoken communications class, after IRB approval.

4.1 Participants

In order to investigate whether it was possible to use SDGs in lieu of roleplay activities, or at least in conjunction with them, as a formative assessment tool, two treatments groups – a roleplay group and SDG group – were created with the international student participants that were enrolled in an English communication class at my higher education institution. All students were given a pre-study online survey at the start of the course. The participants ($n = 16$, see Table 9.1) included six female and ten male students who were all enrolled as full-time graduate, doctoral or postdoctoral students at an accredited Midwestern private R1 university. They were rated as Intermediate Mid to Advanced High (on the ACTFL scale) by myself, a trained but not certified ACTFL rater. Participating students also filled out a pre- and post-survey to better understand their English study (see Table 9.2) and pragmatic study backgrounds, and to indicate if they had ever participated in a roleplay and/or SDG and if they found the roleplay or SDG beneficial to their overall English-speaking strategies. Two of the participants indicated that they had studied linguistics before participating in the study. The majority of participants (72%) had played board games (card, dice or board strategy) in both their native languages and in English. Four participants indicated that they had played

Table 9.1 Participant native languages

Chinese	7
Japanese	3
Portuguese	2
Spanish	2
Arabic	1
Korean	1

Table 9.2 Participant years of English study

0–5 years	1
5–10 years	5
10–15 years	8
15–20 years	1
20–25 years	1
Over 25 years	0

social deduction games in their native language and two indicated that they had played SDGs in English on their pre-surveys.

4.2 Task design

The research covered three pragmatic skill areas: negotiation, turn-taking (specifically next speaker selection) and bluffing. In order to find tokens of usage of the target skills by a speaker, what constituted production of these skills was clearly defined in advance so that it could be made clear to a student what they were expected to produce when they practiced using these forms in the production and assessment sections of each class. The following section will outline how each skill was defined and then assessed/encoded in the student production videos.

4.3 Negotiation

Negotiation sequences were grouped by negotiation actions as defined by Mulholland (1991), and were also based on the grouping of speech acts for negotiation (such as accept, refuse, reject, approve, disapprove, agree, disagree, correct and retract) as established by Weisser (2018). Students were given a 30-minute lesson outlining aspects of negotiation as used by native speakers, both to achieve a common positive outcome during an exchange of goods or information through positive face work with the purpose of reaching an equitable positive face saving outcome, and to maintain a clear communication channel (politeness) with an interlocutor (Brown & Levinson, 1987; Cutting, 2015; Mulholland, 1991; Strauss & Feiz, 2014) – usually through clarification sequences (Deen, 1997). The SDG group played the game 'Coup', and the roleplay group participated in a car buying scenario where one person was a car salesperson and the others were a husband and wife. The baseline SDG native speaker video also featured the game 'Coup', and was used to assess in the student SDG utterances whether the SDG context allowed students to produce utterances in the same quantity and quality as the native speakers. This was then compared to the roleplay group to see if this number was higher or lower.

For the native speaker video, an example of a negotiation token/ sequence is the following:

Example 9.1 Native speaker – negotiation

```
(1)   Sp 1:  [foreign ai:d]
(2)          being ↑two ↓coi::ns now if anyone i::::s a ↑duke (.) would
(3)          anyone ↑choose [↑to blo:ck?] NEGOTIATE - OFFER
(4)   Sp 2:  [↑I'm gonna ] block,
(5)          ((moves index finger in arc)) NEGOTIATE - ACCEPT
(6)   Sp 1:  ↑she sa::ys that she's [a ↑duke]
```

```
(7)    Sp 3:  [that yo]u're a ↓du:ke
(8)    Sp 2:  [↑mm::::]
(9)    Sp 1:  [are you] calling ↑her ↑↑ou::t?  ASK - CLOSED QUESTION
(10)   Sp 3:  ↑you're a ↑du:ke  ACCUSE
(11)   Sp 1:  or are <you: letting go::> your foreign aid
(12)   Sp 2:  [>you know what< I won't ] block you again
              NEGOTIATE - OFFER
(13)          [((pointing hand at Speaker 3))]
(14)   Sp 4:  huh
(15)   Sp 3:  ↑after ↑↑this? ((gaze to Speaker 2))
(16)   Sp 2:  ↑yea:h I did ↑i:t (0.4) I'm do:ne (0.4) [so]
(17)   Sp 3:  [ok]ay that's like somewhat of an alliance
(18)   Sp 2:  [↑yea:h, ↑yeah] (0.4) [it's ] (?) ↑yeah]  NEGOTIATE - ACCEPT
(19)          [((nods head))]
(20)   Sp 3:  [o↑kay]  NEGOTIATE - ACCEPT
```

In this exchange, Speaker 2 challenges Speaker 3 on his action of taking 'foreign aid' during their turn. This action may be blocked by the Duke character in the game. Speaker 2 claims to be the Duke and asserts that they can block Speaker 2 from completing the 'foreign aid' action and denying the action they wanted to take. Speaker 3 then has the option of challenging Speaker 2 on their claim that they are the Duke character. Before Speaker 3 decides to initiate a challenge, Speaker 2 first initiates a negotiation sequence and states that if Speaker 3 does not challenge them on their claim to be the Duke character, that they will not block them on future turns. It is unclear if Speaker 2 means that they will not block future 'foreign aid' actions or not block all of Speaker 3's actions. This may or may not be an intentional deception strategy to not completely define the contexts in which Speaker 2 will block any or all of Speaker 3's claims or actions.

4.4 Bluffing

Contexts in which the speaker has claimed to be a role that they were not or denied being a role that they were in possession of and playing as when accused were used as tokens of bluffing. Carson's (2010) second and third definition of lying where 'S makes a false statement X to S1' and 'S states X in a context in which S thereby warrants the truth of X to S1' were the basis of encoding tokens of bluffing made by English-dominant and learner speakers in both roleplay and SDG contexts (Carson, 2010: 30). The students played an SDG called 'The Resistance', and the roleplay group participated in a scenario where each person was a member of a computer company debating if they should recall a specific computer software due to problems possibly caused by one of the members in the group. Only instances where the primary researcher knew that the speaker was bluffing about the character they held (or their position on a topic in the roleplay), or the speaker was challenged (in an SDG) and showed that they were bluffing were considered for coding in the research. There were many instances of speakers claiming to be or not to be a specific character in an SDG that went unchallenged, but due to the nature of the SDG, it was unknown if the speaker was bluffing or telling the truth. In the roleplay, some students would not offer certain details of what they knew about the scenario context/other participant roles and level of involvement in the problem according to their character's position in the scenario. In the native speaker video for bluffing in which the same SDG was used, 'The Resistance', there were many instances of a participant being challenged as to what character they were actually playing:

Example 9.2 Native speaker – bluffing

```
(1) Sp 1:  You're a spy ((points to Speaker 2)) Challenge
(2) Sp 2:  No, seriously I didn't think it through
(3) Sp 1:  You're a spy (0.3) you're a spy
(4) Sp 2:  No,((points to Speaker 1)) I am not a spy Bluff
(5) Sp 1:  You are two are the spies
(6) Sp 2:  No n:o
```

4.5 Turn-taking: Next speaker selection

The speech act of a current speaker selecting next speaker was chosen as the target skill for students, as Wong and Waring (2010) consider it a clear aspect of turn-taking that can be taught in the language classroom. The SDG group played a game called 'Insider', which combines the premise of 20 questions with a secret spy role; if the group successfully guesses the chosen word, then they must find the spy to win the game. The spy helps the group guess the word chosen as they, along with the person who chose the word, know the answer and try to provide questions that will lead the group to a correct guess. The roleplay group participated in a scenario where they were all members of a movie production company and collectively had to decide if they were going to produce a movie with a large budget and risky production schedule for worldwide distribution.

Three main ways of next speaker selection are (a) eye contact, (b) gesture and (c) using names (LoCastro, 2012). When coding eye contact, the eye contact turn-giving sequence would sometimes also have an accompanying gesture pointing at the intended next speaker. For coding purposes, the first action undertaken by the speaker (head turn to establish gaze or pointing with one finger or open palm) was used as the primary initiator of selecting the next speaker. Sometimes gestures occurred before the eye contact, such as when the speaker was looking at their game role or roleplay instruction sheet and then giving a turn by pointing first, speaking while looking at their item and then looking up, while most of the time a speaker would establish gaze and then point. Due to the rapid-fire question and answer context of the first part of the SDG, 'Insider', one speaker (A) was able to select the next speaker (C) multiple times by quickly asking follow-up questions, until a speaker not involved in the adjacency pair (B) self-selected and started a new turn sequence, usually selecting the same speaker (C) as before. These rapid-fire turn sequences were only treated as one token when A was selecting C, and then a new token was recorded when B selected C. Sometimes A would select B and B would select A for the next turn and these were all treated as unique instances for coding purposes. Examples of each are as follows:

Example 9.3 Native speaker eye contact example

```
(1)    Sp 1:    ↑Is it ((gaze to speaker 2)) ↑↑a::n action?
(2)    Sp 2:    n:::o
(3)    Sp 3:    ((gaze to Speaker 2)) Isn't that ↑the same
                thing as a
(4)             ↑↑a function?
(5)    Sp 1:    ((gaze to speaker 1)) I:: don't know.
```

Example 9.4 Native speaker gesture example

```
(1)    Sp 1:    Is it dairy?((gestures towards speaker 2))
(2)    Sp 2:    n:o
```

Example 9.5 Native speaker name example

```
(1)    Sp 1:    Eliza::beth,
(2)    Sp 2:    ↑psshhhh::
(3)    Sp 1:    you were just really good [an:] an:,
(4)             no  offense  (.)  it  just  happens  with  <uh>
                mishearing an:
(5)             answer (.)
(6)    Sp 2:    ahh, (0.1) I think it was you dude
```

5 Methodology

During the first half of a class, all students received the same lecture on specific linguistic utterances and pragmatic skills that would be used to strengthen their overall English-speaking skills, which in turn would hopefully improve their IC. The students then practiced these skills either in an SDG group or a roleplay group in the second half of the same class. Both groups were video- and audio-recorded as they participated in the production activities. The utterances and skills were criterion referenced from the middle 10 minutes of native speaker videos on YouTube for the SDG treatment group. Since the research study focused only on the SDG treatment context, the criterion reference for the roleplay group was based on existing materials such as *Pragmatics: Teaching Natural Conversation*

(Houck & Tatsuki, 2011). The overall formative assessment was also designed as a predictive validity assessment for future student success in using the target utterances and pragmatic skills (Brown & Abeywickrama, 2010). Before implementation of the assessment, the participants were randomly placed into either the roleplay treatment group or the SDG treatment group. Both groups were video-recorded and the middle 10 minutes of the student productions of both groups were transcribed according to Jeffersonian CA conventions. The transcriptions were encoded for tokens of production of the target utterances and pragmatic skills. Students were then given written feedback as to their performance in the roleplay or SDG as compared to the criterion-referenced target utterances and skills. This process was repeated twice more in two other classes following the same procedure. After the class ended, the total number of tokens from each pragmatic skill area and SDG were tallied and put into the context of the research question to see if the SDG treatment group were producing utterances and skill tokens at a rate equal to or greater than the native speaker SDG video tokens. Since the research question does not challenge the authenticity of pragmatic skills and linguistic utterances produced while engaging in roleplay activities/tasks, the criterion-referenced product validity was based on the course curriculum/materials for the specific pragmatic skills in the roleplay groups, rather than seeking videos of native speakers performing in similar roleplay contexts. At the conclusion of the academic quarter, all students were given an exit survey.

5.1 Materials

The instruction materials for the lecture section of the class were adapted from *Teaching and Learning Pragmatics* by Ishihara and Cohen (2014), along with *Pragmatics: Teaching Natural Conversation* (Houck & Tatsuki, 2011) and *Pragmatics: Teaching Speech Acts* (Tatsuki & Houck, 2010). The three SDG games used in the SDG treatment group were: (1) 'Coup', published by Indie Board and Cards, 2012; (2) 'Insider', published by Oink Games, 2016; and (3) 'The Resistance', published by Indie Board and Cards, 2009. The roleplays were adapted from 'Business Roles 2' by

Table 9.3 Instruction skill and material breakdown

Skill	Social deduction game used	Roleplay used
Negotiation	'The Resistance' (Indie board and cards)	Car purchase (Instructor created based on existing materials)
Bluffing	'Coup' (Indie board and cards)	Computer software recall (Business roleplays 2)
Turn-taking	'Insider' (Oink Games)	Producing a movie (Business roleplays 2)

Cambridge University Press and a car purchase roleplay created by myself based on existing materials found online (Johnson, 2003; see also Appendix 9.2).

The pre- and post-surveys were given through the online survey tool Qualtrics. The pre-survey had 33 multiple choice, slider and fill-in-the-blank questions. The post-survey had 16 multiple choice, slider and fill-in-the-blank questions. Two video cameras on tripods were used to capture the video of participant verbal and non-verbal production and two iPads for each group were placed at equidistant ends of where the participants were sitting to capture the linguistic production of participants.

5.2 Procedures

The study was conducted over the course of three academic classes during one (eight-week) quarter, each class covering one specific pragmatic skill: negotiation, bluffing and turn-taking. Students were notified when they enrolled in the class that they would be part of this study, but that both the roleplay and SDGs were already part of the current class curriculum. Students who did not want to participate were given the option of not being video-recorded and their data not being included in the study, but were informed that they would still be assessed and receive feedback on their utterances produced during the SDG activity. This spoken communications class is a non-credit bearing pass/fail English support class where students self-select for enrollment based on a desire to improve their speaking skills. All students signed a consent to research waiver before enrolling in the class and all enrolling students volunteered to participate in the study, i.e. no enrolling student declined to participate in the research study.

Each class was 80 minutes long and was broken up into three distinct sections: (A) 30 minutes of explicit pragmatic instruction; (B) 10 minutes of instruction on how to play the SDG or the context and roles of the roleplay; and (C) 40 minutes of practice where half of the class played an SDG and half of the class participated in a roleplay, both of which were uninterrupted by the instructor. Both groups were video-recorded and audio-recorded during performance.

In cases where there were an odd number of students, preference was given to the SDG group to receive more students. All students received the same 30 minutes of explicit pragmatic instruction (Kasper & Rose, 2002; Norris & Ortega, 2000) as a whole class, consisting of studying a specific speech act, understanding the grammatical and linguistic forms and viewing examples in media of English-dominant speakers using similar speech acts. The pragmatic instruction also included discussion of how the speech acts are the same or different in a student's home culture in order to give multiple points of reference so that the students would be exposed to a variety of both cultural and linguistic usages. This also provided an opportunity for them to understand what they would be assessed on in the production practice activity (Ishihara & Cohen, 2014).

After the 30 minutes of instruction, each student received an index card labeled 'role play' or 'social deduction board game'. They were then separated into two rooms. Students in the SDG room were given an explanation of the rules of the game that they would play (see Appendix 9.2). Students in the roleplay classroom were allowed time to review the scenario, role and goal worksheets that had been given to them before they moved into their room. Students were video-recorded during the 40-minute production session either performing a roleplay or playing an SDG. Over the course of the class each student participated in at least two roleplay activities or played two SDGs.

After all the classes were complete, the middle 10 minutes of each recorded session were transcribed into CA Jeffersonian format and then analyzed for the number of tokens of production of the target pragmatic skill in speech acts for that lesson. The rationale behind choosing the middle 10 minutes of each video was that students' production would be at its peak as they would understand the practice activity fully after 10 minutes but would not have become tired after 20 minutes of production (Cohen, 2018). Ten minutes of three videos of native speakers playing the same SDG were also transcribed and analyzed for the same pragmatic tokens as were outlined and taught to students. Two of these videos were publicly available on YouTube and featured a full play-through of each game (see Appendix 9.1) and a third video was recorded with the permission/release of participants of a group playing the SDG 'Insider'. The number of native speaker tokens collected from these videos was then compared to the number of tokens collected from the student videos to see if the students were producing pragmatic tokens at a rate close to or equal to the native speakers. The number of student SDG pragmatic tokens was also compared to the roleplay amount to see if the SDG students were producing the target pragmatic structures at an equal or higher rate.

Since roleplay activities are already an established classroom practice, instead of native speaker roleplay videos, classroom scaffolding materials for the skills being taught were the baseline for student production. The native speaker videos used to compare student output to in the SDG context were necessary to establish a baseline since the SDG context is novel and experimental. Roleplays did not have any native speaker videos as a baseline since students were exposed to model utterances during the instructional section of the class.

After class I reviewed video-recorded student output to confirm the written assessment notes I had made during student production. I also made these videos available to students for their own reference. Oral feedback was given in the subsequent class on individuals' and groups' performance, based on their performance in the videos with regard to the quality and quantity of their pragmalinguistic production as compared to the models/examples introduced in the instructional section of the class. Students were also given feedback in written format on an exit form given to them at the end of the quarter, where each pragmatic skill had production comments that followed the predictive validity for the formative assessment task. Finally, the results of the pre- and post-survey questions were analyzed to consider the students' preference for participating in either a roleplay or SDG in order to practice the target pragmatic skill.

6 Analysis

6.1 Negotiation

Negotiation sequences were present in the student negotiation videos, similar to those found in the native speaker video. One example is as follows:

Example 9.6 Student – negotiation

```
(1)    Sp 1:   ↑so::::, (2.2) I'm the ↑duke (.) I'm gonna take ↑three
(2)            (2.0)
(3)    Sp 2:   may↑be (0.6) °oh that's all ri:ght°  NEGOTATION – ATTEMPT
(4)    (2.2)
(5)    Sp 3:   °°anyone have to challenge he:r°° (0.8) ↑three?
                NEGOTIATE – OFFER
(6)    Sp 4:   (lef-) two ↑ca::rds [$you ha[ve two ca::rds$]
(7)            ((gaze to Speaker 2))  NEGOTIATE – OFFER
(8)    Sp 3:   [huh huh [huh huh huh]
(9)    Sp 2:   [huh huh huh] huh huh
(10)   Sp 1:   one ((points with one finger))
(11)   Sp 4:   ↑challenge you  NEGOTIATE – OFFER
(12)   Sp 1:   ↑okay
(13)   Sp 4:   °a::::h°
(14)   Sp 1:   challenge [↑not acep]ted  NEGOTIATE – REJECT
(15)   Sp 2:   [↑huh ↑huh]
(16)   Sp 3:   huh
```

Like the native speaker negation sequence, Speaker 1 is claiming to be the Duke character and wants to perform the action of that character. However, in this negotiation sequence Speaker 4 is trying to have Speaker 2 challenge Speaker 1 instead of challenging Speaker 1 themselves. Speaker 4 knows that if they challenge Speaker 1 and fail, then they will be eliminated. Speaker 2 has two cards remaining, so if they are wrong, then they will still be in the game with one card remaining. Speaker 2, however, does not want to challenge Speaker 1, and only laughs in response to the negotiation offer. It is Speaker 1 that verbalizes the rejection of the offer by stating in a humorous tone of voice, 'challenge not accepted'. There is no further offer or objection by either Speaker 2 or Speaker 4, so the next player takes their turn. It is also interesting to note that Speaker 1 is using humor to soften the rejection in this sequence as a face-saving strategy for Speaker 4. This may show that Speaker 1 is 'making full use of an internal feedback system that allows [them] to keep track of output on a number of different levels' and that might only have been produced in the absence of an instructor and 'in the company of peers' (Morrison & Low, 1983).

6.2 Bluffing

Students producing bluffing sequences that were similar to native speaker bluffing sequences were also found and coded. These tokens are most apparent whenever a speaker was accused of being on the traitor team:

Example 9.7 Student – bluffing

```
(1)  Sp 1:  You're a spy ((gestures towards Speaker 2))
(2)         ((gaze to Speaker 3))
(3)         He's spy::  Challenge
(4)  Sp 2:  N::o because I choose [th::] the first one  Bluff
(5)  Sp 3:  ((gaze to Speaker 1)) You don't know
```

In both the native speaker and SDG student groups, the actual traitors were directly accused of working against the group by voting against the team's objectives and in both videos those accused would deny that they were the traitor and try to either reflect the accusations onto another player or give an extended explanation for their actions. In the native speaker SDG, the accuser and the accused would use a pointing gesture at each other and would maintain direct eye contact. In the student video, the accuser was a Japanese male and when he made the accusation, he looked at another speaker (not the accused) when making the accusation. The student was given feedback after the session about how he should have maintained eye contact when he was making the accusation so that the listener (the student he was directly accusing) understood that it was them that was being accused of being the spy. On a side note, in this example Speaker 3 was a spy and knew that Speaker 1 was also a spy, hence the challenge to the accusation.

The roleplay group did not accuse each other of creating the problem or point out the information that they knew about who had created the problem that necessitated the recall, therefore assigning blame and/or work. Rather, the focus of the group's interaction was on solving the problem and figuring out the technical details of how to go about recalling and fixing the software problem presented in the scenario. This could be due to the explanation of the scenario's parameters and outcome that could have made it clearer that most of the work should be assigned to the individuals who created the problem.

6.3 Turn-taking

Student videos that were encoded for turn-taking production, specifically giving a turn, also produced tokens of production that were consistent with the native speaker videos using the same pragmatic strategies:

Example 9.8 Student eye contact example

```
(1)  Sp 1:  Is it ↑a ↑↑building? ((gaze to speaker 2))
(2)  Sp 2:  no
```

Example 9.9 Student gesture example

```
(1)  Sp 1:  Is it ↑a ↑↑tool? ((points at speaker 2))
(2)  Sp 2:   I:m ↑sorry?
(3)  Sp 1:  Is it ↑a ↑↑tool? ((points at speaker 2)) ↑you ↑↑say?
```

Example 9.10 Student name example

```
(1)  Sp 1:  A:kira,
(2)  Sp 2:  Akira
(3)  Sp 1:  Okay (0.1) So, fi::ve minutes
(4)  Sp 3:  W::ell
(5)  Sp 1:  come clean ((gestures towards Speaker 3))
(6)  Sp 3:  huh huh huh
(7)  Sp 1:  huh huh huh
```

7 Results

By using social deduction board games in lieu of a roleplay activity as a formative assessment task, I hypothesized that students learning these skills in an ESL classroom context would produce better linguistic and non-linguistic displays of three IC/pragmatic skill areas: negotiation, bluffing and turn-taking. The negotiation context produced an equal number of tokens for both the SDG and the roleplay. However, there was some variation in the negotiation sequences in terms of how the specific negotiation turns occurred, as some speakers used direct questions as a negotiation offer and others presented the offer as indirect statements. While the SDG did not have students producing more negotiation sequences, it did not have them producing sequences at a lower rate than the roleplay.

Table 9.4 Negotiation sequence production

Negotiation video	Time	Number of people	Number of negotiation sequences
Native speaker SDG 'Coup'	10 min	4	7
Student SDG 'Coup'	10 min	4	6
Student roleplay 'Car purchase'	9.5 min	3	6

Table 9.5 Bluffing sequence production

Bluffing video	Time	Number of people	Number of negotiation sequences
Native speaker SDG 'The Resistance'	10 min	5	8
Student SDG 'The Resistance'	10 min	5	4
Student roleplay 'Computer software recall'	10 min	4	0

Bluffing showed the greatest production of the target pragmatic skill. While students participating in the SDG produced half as many sequences of bluffing as the native speakers, they did produce sequences that were almost identical to those of the native speakers. In both groups, Player A would accuse Player B of working against the group as a traitor, and Player B, who was in fact a traitor, would strongly deny this and assert that Player A was wrong while maintaining eye contact and projecting confidence through tone and stress in their utterances. In the student roleplay group, there were no instances of a negotiation sequence. This could be due to the chosen scenario not allowing students more opportunities for bluffing to take place, although the participant roles were somewhat at odds with one another as to who would be responsible for leading the effort to recall and fix software based on who the group agreed was responsible for the problem. It could also be that the more 'realistic' context of the roleplay pushed students to focus more on other pragmatic skills, such as preservation of face or power structures, over the target pragmatic structures of bluffing.

Finally, turn-taking showed the most dramatic context in which the SDG allowed students to produce far more opportunities to engage in selecting the next speaker, as was outlined in the lecture section of the turn-taking class. This is due in part to the rapid-fire question and answer section of the SDG. Students who participated in the roleplay tended to have much longer turns and use longer utterances, since the context of the roleplay simulated a business meeting where students would have to explain their rationale in detail for the decisions they were making in the context of the simulation – an outcome aspect of the roleplay design that could be further revised in future iterations to better match the outcome of the SDG. The SDG context provided more opportunities for a speaker to select the next speaker by name, since turns were relatively short and the constrained time limit for each round in the SDG meant that speakers were overlapping. If a specific speaker wanted another specific speaker to reply to their questions or utterance, they would select that speaker by name to verbally signal that they were giving a turn to that speaker directly. Lastly, both the SDG and roleplay group produced more tokens of giving turns through gestures than the native speaker SDG group. It is also worth noting that all of the native speaker SDG participants were friends, so they were familiar with each other's names and were thus able

Table 9.6 Turn taking by selecting next speaker production

Turn-taking video	Time	Number of people	Number of turn-taking sequences		
			Eye contact	Name	Gesture
Native speaker SDG 'Insider'	10 min	4	73	3	1
Student SDG 'Insider'	10 min	4	26	2	3
Student roleplay 'Producing a movie'	10 min	4	7	0	3

to use them more as turn-giving strategies than the students since the student participants only met each other during class time.

The results of exit surveys given to participants ($n = 16$) revealed that that students liked the SDG activities (94%) and that they also enjoyed doing the roleplay activities (64%). Participants also felt that the SDGs were equally as helpful in producing the target structures (76%) as the roleplay activities (76%). Moreover, participants reported that they enjoyed participating in the SDGs (76%) far more than in the roleplay activities (23%). However, when asked which activity was better, 52% reported that the roleplay was better for practicing English, compared to 42% who preferred SDGs. In other words, even though participants found the SDG activity equally valuable for producing target structures and far more enjoyable than the roleplay activity, the roleplay activity was seen as having more face validity as a formative assessment task for producing utterances for these skills. In a limited follow-up interview, some participants were asked to explain why they felt the roleplay activity was better for in-class practice. Some participants reported that the roleplays seemed 'more academic' as compared to just 'playing a game' in the SDG activity. This discrepancy could be attributed to the fact that SDGs are still not widely used in the academic setting. Since few students encounter them in this context, they do not have the face validity that roleplay activities have due to the widespread use of roleplays in language classrooms. However, it could be argued that if the board game/SDG task is seen as more enjoyable for students and less 'academic', this may help reduce the affective filter and allow for more dynamic and creative production of pragmatic utterances.

8 Conclusion

The SDGs provided an equal, if not better, context for target pragmatic forms of turn-taking and bluffing. For negotiation, it was at least equal to that of the roleplay group. Moreover, the SDG groups tended to produce shorter, phrase-level utterances that more closely resembled the 'natural' and 'fluent' speech that native speakers use in casual spoken conversation. The roleplay groups tended to view their turns more as monologues than as dialogues with other members in the group. This may be an effect of the roleplays selected rather than a feature of the interaction of the participants. This study was very limited in scope and participants, so further research is needed to see if the results would hold up over multiple games and target structures. The limited number of participants does not equivocally show that the SDG activity/context allows for the learning of target structures over time, as the assessment of the target structures was limited to the SDG/roleplay activity and a more formative assessment methodology would need to be implemented to see if the benefits of participating in the SDG activity would be as beneficial as participating in a roleplay over the course of an entire program or even over multiple classes. Another limitation of the current study was that the instructional/production time for both the roleplay and board game activities were limited. Since the aim of this study was to compare SDGs and roleplays in an academic classroom context, and the length of the study's class was 80 minutes, the target structure instruction was limited to 30 minutes and both activities were limited to 40 minutes of production time. Some participants commented in the exit questionnaire that the production time seemed limited. Thus, one major takeaway from the current study is that the SDG activity should be allowed sufficient time allocation for a more authentic experience and to allow multiple opportunities for student production of target utterances. One other limitation that must be acknowledged is that of cost. Roleplay activities usually cost nothing or at the maximum the cost of making copies of materials for students. SDGs and board games must be purchased before they can be used in the classroom, which introduces problematic cost and availability issues as funds will have to be allocated to acquire SDGs which will hinder their use in the classroom context.

The most limiting aspect of this study is that the target utterances/ skills/contexts for using SDGs in the classroom as an assessment tool are restricted in scope as to what target utterances and pragmatic skills can actually be assessed using these types of games. The three target skills in this study – bluffing, negotiation and turn-taking (specifically giving turns) – are three skills that are present in the SDGs I selected to practice these skills. Other important pragmatic skill areas such as politeness strategies or apologizing, while being able to be somewhat integrated into a board game activity, would take effort and would not be directly elicited by SDGs depending on the context of the SDG (i.e. werewolves, mafia family, etc.). It would also take time to seek out and research the social deduction board games that would elicit such utterances as there is no specific resource that aligns games to specific pragmatic skills that would be useful for an instructor.

What cannot be overlooked is that in each of the SDG contexts, students were performing a task that required them to produce each of the target pragmalinguistic forms in what could be described as learner agency that allowed for creative production of utterances. Each SDG group had a winner that emerged at the end of the game that did not occur only because of a specific logical strategy based on odds or luck as might be seen in other types of board game like 'Monopoly'. The car purchase roleplay featured in this study ended in a car not being bought, because the couple wanted to just leave and go to another car dealership. While this may be authentic for some car purchasing experiences, it requires an extensive scenario with multiple roles that must be heavily controlled for, and after the roleplay is finished, there is no actual outcome where the participants will have actually purchased a car if they succeed in their negotiation efforts. Knowing that, if an instructor were to assess and give feedback on the utterances that a student produced, the expectation would be that if they incorporated that feedback into their linguistic toolbox, they would achieve success when going to purchase a car in real life. The roleplay scenario did not extend into other more intense verbal areas of purchasing a car such as financing and leasing that might occur throughout the scenario in real life.

In an SDG, the forms that pragmatic utterances take can be the focus of the lesson/activity and if the student uses them appropriately, they have the more dynamic goal of winning the game. Also, since SDGs can be replayed over and over and the context stays the same, this allows for practice through repetition and might increase the chance that students will have better retention of the pragmalinguistic forms so that they can adapt those forms to any context or situation they encounter rather than only in the one context presented in a roleplay scenario. Since roleplay activities are an established and well-researched activity for student production, it is not the position of this research that SDGs should replace roleplay activities, but rather that SDGs allow for similar, or possibly more, opportunities based on the SDG and the target pragmatic skill, in order to produce more learner agency and create 'fluent' and 'natural' utterances. Thus, my position is that SDGs can and should be used more in the academic language classroom context to further expand and enhance the toolset used to elicit speech for assessment and feedback with the overall goal of supporting and helping language learners.

Appendix 9.1

- 'Coup' – play through video link: https://www.youtube.com/watch?v=k2YUYPDq7gQ
- 'The Resistance' – play through video link: https://www.youtube.com/watch?v=g_QRczGzXqw

Appendix 9.2

- Rules for 'Coup': https://upload.snakesandlattes.com/rules/c/CoupTheResistance.pdf
- Rules for 'The Resistance': https://en.wikipedia.org/wiki/The_Resistance_(game)

- Rules for 'Insider': https://oinkgames.com/en/games/analog/insider/
- Rules for 'Werewolf': https://www.instructables.com/Play-Werewolf/
- Outline used for Car Purchase roleplay: https://calper.la.psu.edu/publications/publication-items/project-work-esl/Lets_Make_a_Deal.pdf

Acknowledgments

The author would like to thank Julie Matsubara, University of Chicago, for feedback on the implementation of the research methodologies, and Ahmet Dursun, University of Chicago; Rue Burch, Kobe University; and M. Rafael Salaberry, Rice University, for their feedback on the writing of this chapter.

Notes

(1) Closed roleplay activities feature a specific outcome to a scenario and may have pre-defined utterances, interactions, etc., that must be enacted by a student for the roleplay to be considered successful – similar to cued dialogues.
(2) Formative assessment in that students will be given discrete ongoing feedback, either written or orally, by an instructor as to the student's strengths and weaknesses in some aspect of the target skill.

References

Bachman, L. and Palmer, A. (1996) *Language Testing in Practice.* New York: Oxford University Press.

Bardovi-Harlig, K. (2020) Pedagogical linguistics: A view from L2 pragmatics. *Pedagogical Linguistics* 1 (1), 44–65.

Brandl, K. (2008) *Communicative Language Teaching in Action: Putting Principles to Work.* Upper Saddle River, NJ: Pearson Education.

Brown, G. and Yule, G. (1991) *Teaching the Spoken Language: An Approach Based on the Analysis of Conversational English.* New York: Cambridge University Press.

Brown, H.D. and Abeywickrama, P. (2010) *Language Assessment: Principles and Classroom Practices.* White Plains, NY: Pearson Education.

Brown, H.D. and Lee, H. (2015) *Teaching by Principles: An Interactive Approach to Language Pedagogy* (4th edn). White Plains, NY: Pearson Education.

Brown, P. and Levinson, S.C. (1987) *Politeness: Some Universals in Language Usage.* Cambridge: Cambridge University Press.

Carless, D. (2007) Learning-oriented assessment: Conceptual bases and practical implications. *Innovations in Education and Teaching International* 44 (1), 57–66.

Carson, T.L. (2010) *Lying and Deception: Theory and Practice.* New York: Oxford University Press.

Carter, M., Gibbs, M. and Harrop, M. (2012) Metagames, paragames and orthogames: A new vocabulary. *Proceedings of the International Conference on the Foundations of Digital Games* (pp. 11–17). New York: Association for Computing Machinery.

Cohen, A.D. (2018) *Learning Pragmatics from Native and Nonnative Language Teachers.* Bristol: Multilingual Matters.

Crowther-Alwyn, J. (1999) *Business Roles 2: 12 More Simulations for Business English.* Cambridge: Cambridge University Press.

Culpeper, J. and Haugh, M. (2014) *Pragmatics and the English Language*. New York: Palgrave Macmillan.

Culpeper, J., Mackey, A. and Taguchi, N. (2010) *Second Language Pragmatics: From Theory to Research*. New York: Routledge.

Cutting, J. (2015) *Pragmatics: A Resource Book for Students*. New York: Routledge.

Deen, J. (1997) *Dealing with Problems in Intercultural Communication: A Study of Negotiation of Meaning in Native-Nonnative Speaker Interaction*. Tilburg: Tilburg University Press.

Eskildsen, S.W. and Majlesi, A.R. (2018) Learnables and teachables in second language talk: Advancing a social reconceptualization of central SLA tenets. Introduction to the special issue. *The Modern Language Journal* 102, 3–10.

García, N.M. (2018) Using dialogues, role plays, songs, and poetry in teaching speaking. In *The TESOL Encyclopedia of English Language Teaching*. Wiley Online Library. doi:10.1002/9781118784235.eelt0259

Gaudart, H. (1999) Games as teaching tools for teaching English to speakers of other languages. *Simulation & Gaming* 30 (3), 283–291.

Götz, S. (2013) *Fluency in Native and Nonnative English Speech*. Philadelphia, PA: John Benjamins.

Green, A. (2014) *Exploring Language Assessment and Testing*. New York: Routledge.

Houck, N.R. and Tatsuki, D.H. (2011) *Pragmatics: Teaching Natural Conversation*. Mattoon, IL: United Graphics.

Hughes, R. and Beatrice, R.S. (2017) *Teaching and Researching Speaking*. New York: Routledge.

Ishihara, N. (2010) Instructional pragmatics: Bridging teaching, research, and teacher education. *Language and Linguistic Compass* 4, 938–953.

Ishihara, N. and Cohen, A.D. (2014) *Teaching and Learning Pragmatics: Where Language and Culture Meet*. New York: Routledge.

Jenks, C. (2013) Interactional Competence versus Pragmatic Competence: Implications for Language Teaching. Academic presentation at Temple University, Osaka, Japan, September. See https://jalt.org/events/osaka-chapter/13-09-07.

Johnson, K.E. (2003) *Let's Make a Deal: A Sample Project for Advanced ESL Learners*. CALPER Pedagogical Materials: Project Work, No. 1. University Park, PA: Pennsylvania State University, Center for Advanced Language Proficiency Education and Research.

Kasper, G. and Rose, K.R. (2002) *Pragmatic Development in a Second Language*. Malden, MA: Blackwell.

Lin, Y. (2009) Investigating role-play implementation: A multiple case study on Chinese EFL teachers using role-play in their secondary classrooms. PhD thesis, University of Windsor. See https://scholar.uwindsor.ca/etd/425.

LoCastro, V. (2012) *Pragmatics for Language Educators: A Sociolinguistic Perspective*. New York: Routledge.

Morrison, D.M. and Low, G. (1983) Monitoring and the second language learner. In J.C. Richards and R.W. Schmidt (eds) *Language and Communication* (pp. 228–250). New York: Longman.

Mulholland, J. (1991) *The Language of Negotiation: A Handbook of Practical Strategies for Improving Communication*. New York: Routledge.

Neff, P. and Rucynski, J. Jr. (2013) Tasks for integrating language and culture teaching. *English Teaching Forum* 51 (2), 12–23.

Norris, J. and Ortega, L. (2000) Effectiveness of L2 instruction: A research and quantitative meta-analysis. *Language Learning* 50, 417–528.

Roever, C. and Kasper, G. (2018) Speaking in turns and sequences: Interactional competence as a target construct in testing speaking. *Language Testing* 35 (3), 331–355.

Scrivener, J. (2005) *Learning Teaching*. Oxford: Macmillan Education.

Strauss, S. and Feiz, P. (2014) *Discourse Analysis: Putting our Worlds into Words*. New York: Routledge.

Tatsuki, D.H. and Houck, N.R. (2010) *Pragmatics: Teaching Speech Acts*. Mattoon, IL: United Graphics.

Tilton, S. (2019) Winning through deception: A pedagogical case study on using social deception games to teach small group communication theory. *Sage Open*. See https://journals.sagepub.com/home/sgo.

Vlachopoulos, D. and Makri, A. (2017) The effects of games and simulations on higher education: A systematic literature review. *International Journal of Educational Technology in Higher Education*, 10 July. doi:10.1186/s41239-017-0062-1

Weisser, M. (2018) *How to Do Corpus Pragmatics on Pragmatically Annotated Data*. Amsterdam: John Benjamins.

Whitton, N. (2011) Game engagement theory and adult learning. *Simulation & Gaming* 42 (5), 596–609.

Wong, J. and Waring, H.Z. (2010) *Conversation Analysis and Second Language Pedagogy: A Guide for ESL/EFL Teachers*. New York: Routledge.

Young, T.J. and Sachdev, I. (2011) Intercultural communicative competence: Exploring English language teachers' beliefs and practices. *Language Awareness* 20 (2), 81–98.

10 Assessing Interactional Competence in Secondary Schools: Issues of Turn-taking

Dagmar Barth-Weingarten and Britta Freitag-Hild

1 Introduction

Since the interactional turn in pragmatics, it has also become widely acknowledged in second language acquisition (SLA) research that mastery of a foreign language does not only comprise language skills but also the ability to participate successfully in interaction (cf., for example, Kasper & Youn, 2018: 592). In the meantime, such skills – described with various models and labels (cf., for example, Pekarek Doehler, 2019) – are also a crucial component of assessing speaking in second/foreign languages. Consequently, assessment models started incorporating *inter*action into their testing and grading procedures (e.g. Galaczi, 2014; Ikeda, 2017; Youn, 2015; for problems involved, cf. Plough *et al.*, 2018; Roever, 2018; see also Roever & Dai, this volume; Youn & Chen, this volume). And especially when the assessment target is natural talk-in-interaction, the concept of interactional competence (IC) – i.e. 'members' practices ... for organizing social interaction' (Pekarek Doehler, 2018: 5) – seems to be particularly useful (cf., for example, Roever & Kasper, 2018; Taguchi & Roever, 2017; Wong & Waring, 2010). At the same time, research on the interactional dynamics of talk-in-interaction – such as conversation analysis (CA; cf., for example, Sidnell & Stivers, 2013) and interactional linguistics (IL; cf., for example, Couper-Kuhlen & Selting, 2018) – turned to second/foreign language interaction and has already shown a wide array of features and aspects to be relevant in this regard. They include not only specific practices of turn-taking organization, repair, action accomplishment and sequence organization, but also their interplay (for a survey, see, for example, Pekarek Doehler, 2019). As a result, assessing IC may be hard to manage (cf. Roever & Kasper, 2018; Waring, 2018: 60–62), and even more so when assessment resources are scarce, such as in the ordinary secondary school FL classroom, where both assessment staff and assessment time are limited.

This chapter suggests a way to handle the complexity of assessing IC systematically with an eye to managing scarce assessment resources. Our approach adopts the idea of describing IC in terms of the generic organizational contingencies participants need to deal with in interaction in general, such as turn-taking, action formation, overall structural organization and dealing with trouble (cf. Schegloff, 2007: xiv; Wong & Waring, 2010). In addition, we propose that IC may be systematically assessed by focusing on these aspects one by one, with assessment resources determining assessment granularity. Our chapter demonstrates this approach with the example of turn-taking in paired peer speaking tasks (roleplays; cf. Kasper & Youn, 2018) in a German secondary school EFL classroom (see also Barth-Weingarten & Freitag-Hild, in preparation).

In the following sections, we will first briefly survey current knowledge on assessing IC (Section 2) and then topicalize the challenges it poses to analysts and teachers in the ordinary (German) secondary school EFL classroom, in particular (Section 3). Section 4 will sketch our proposal for solving these challenges with the example of the assessment of EFL learners' turn-taking (TT) behavior. This includes a proposal of key points regarding sequence organization for assessing TT in roleplays, which may help ordinary FL teachers include IC into their testing procedures in school while using their assessment resources efficiently.

This chapter will hopefully contribute to classroom interaction research as well as the improvement of formal assessment methods, even though it cannot claim to offer an approach tested formally for its impact and outcomes. At the same time, however, and perhaps even more so, it is geared towards the ordinary FL teacher in that we hope to inspire further attempts to help future FL teachers develop the skills necessary to assess IC in the ordinary FL school classroom. Beyond this, we would like to contribute to making formal assessment frameworks like the Common European Framework of Reference for Languages (CEFR; Council of Europe, 2012) better applicable to the FL classroom. This chapter thus not only attempts to respond to questions concerning the incorporation of research findings on the dynamics and situated nature of language use (re *inter*action) into interactionally less constrained test situations (e.g. conversation and argument versus interview), but also to questions concerning the practical challenges of assessing interaction with less manpower. The approach presented here is currently being (further) developed and tested in a collaboration of researchers specialized in CA/IL and TEFL in the framework of EFL teacher training at the University of Potsdam, Germany.

2 Assessing IC

As Huth (2018) points out, formal SLA assessment like the CEFR not only requires controlled and replicable testing contexts, but also seems to mainly still aim at individual learners' linguistic output assumed to be produced independently of local contingencies and assessed relative to fixed scales. These assumptions are in stark contrast to the dialogic, interactional, multimodal, temporal/online and locally (viz. sequentially) and globally (viz. situationally) situated nature of talk-in-interaction (cf., for instance, Deppermann, 2011; Ford, 2004). Especially when the assessment/teaching target is natural talk-in-interaction (e.g. Taguchi & Roever, 2017; Wong & Waring, 2010), accomplishing action successfully in a foreign language, particularly in the spoken mode, is an inherently *interac*tional accomplishment (cf. Kramsch, 1986; Young, 2008; also the work by Hall). It therefore requires IC, viz.

> members' methods (Garfinkel, 1967) for managing social interaction, i.e., systematic procedures (of turn-taking, repairing, opening or closing a conversation, etc.) by which members of a social group organize their conduct in a mutually understandable and accountable way … that … is not simply transferred from the L1 to the L2, but … recalibrated, adapted in the course of L2 development. (Pekarek Doehler & Pochon-Berger, 2015: 235; see also Kasper, 2006; Markee, 2008; Pekarek Doehler, 2018, for example)

As such, IC is a crucial component of assessing speaking in an FL context. And since IC is constituted by 'situation-based, context-bound, and "publicly" observable practices', it is 'observable … not only for co-participants, but also for the researcher' (Pekarek Doehler, 2018: 5), and the rater/grader. In studying IC, however, not only a range of subskills, but also a wide array of features and aspects needs to be taken into account. These include verbal and prosodic as well as kinetic resources and practices, such as gaze, gesture and bodily movement (cf. Kasper, 2006; Pekarek Doehler, 2018: 20; also Plough, this volume). Moreover, these resources are to be described at one, or several, specific points in time, for determining a single learner's current level of competence and tracing his/her development (cf. Pekarek Doehler, 2018; Pekarek Doehler *et al.*, 2018, for example). Accumulated single-case analyses across foreign language learners (FLLs), in turn, allow us to compare learners' skills in a target group, for instance (cf., for example, Al-Gahtani & Roever, 2013).

More recently, assessment models have incorporated interactional dynamics. For one, they have expanded their test methods to interactionally less constrained test situations (e.g. conversation and argument versus interview) (Galaczi, 2014: 554) and tasks. Since the interactional turn in pragmatics, language training and assessment in particular favor roleplays (Crookall & Saunders, 1989: 15–16; see also Stokoe, 2014: 257) as they help us 'overcome … the problem of "construct underrepresentation"' (Kasper & Youn, 2018: 591). Roleplays allow us – at least better than other speaking tasks – to elicit interactional behavior, while at the same time controlling it (note the issue of the co-participant's/co-test taker's influence, though; cf. Roever, 2018).

Second, assessment models have also expanded their objects of assessment to inherently interactional skills, such as TT management. For these, Galaczi (2014), for instance, found advanced learners using more back-channels, plus confirmation of understanding, fewer inter-turn gaps and intra-turn pauses, more starts with latching/overlap and more turn prefaces than B1/2 learners. However, while these findings strike us as intuitively plausible, some questions remain as to the adequate description of the complexity of the data. Assessing inter-turn gaps and intra-turn pauses appropriately would, for instance, require the inclusion of inaudible, kinetic behavior, which can equally well serve TT (Mondada, 2016; Plough, this volume). Moreover, prosody can project continuation at points of lexico-syntactic completion (see, for instance, Ford & Thompson, 1996). In addition, existing studies use relatively complex categories, which may be hard to replicate; compare, for instance, Galaczi's (2014: 566–567) category of 'listener support moves', which seems to be relevant for both TT management (continuers) and action accomplishment/stance taking (confirmation of understanding) (cf. Ikeda, 2017; Youn, 2015). Hence, the complexity of the object of study seems to challenge formal language testing (cf. Roever & Kasper, 2018; Waring, 2018: 60–61; also Roever & Dai, this volume).

How can such issues be managed better in formal language testing? And how can they be managed when time and staff resources for assessment are scarce, as in the ordinary secondary school FL classroom? In the following section, we will present an approach to assessing IC systematically and under ordinary EFL classroom conditions, which we developed for EFL teacher training in Germany.

3 Handling the Challenges of Assessing IC in the EFL Classroom

3.1 A general challenge: Handling the complexity of IC

As shown in quite a number of studies (cf. Section 2), IC is a complex assessment construct. In order to deal with this complexity, it seems to be useful to (1) start with qualitative studies (cf. Kasper & Youn, 2018; Roever & Kasper, 2018) and (2) break down IC into its components, which are potentially more manageable than the *gestalt* notion itself. For the latter, Pekarek Doehler (2019: 43) suggested using the 'generic orders of interaction', viz. 'the various organizations of practice that deal with the various organizational contingencies of talk-in-interaction' (Schegloff, 2007: xiv). 'Contingencies' here basically refer to problems participants need to solve for smooth interaction. According to Schegloff (2007: xiv), they include:

- The TT problem. Who can start speaking when and how? How can turns be held and/or yielded?
- The action formation problem. How can participants design their contributions such that they accomplish actions that fit their position in

the turn, the sequence and the overall interactional situation, and thus are recognizable to their interlocutors?

- The sequence-organizational problem. How can speaker contributions be lined up and grouped coherently?
- The repair problem. How can trouble in speaking, hearing and/or understanding be repaired such that the interaction can continue smoothly?
- The overall structural-organization problem. How can participants structure an entire exchange?[1]

While this list has been compiled from studies of L1 interaction (see, for instance, Couper-Kuhlen & Selting, 2018; Sidnell & Stivers, 2013), work on FL classroom interaction has shown that: (1) these problem types are also relevant for L2 interaction; and (2) L2 IC actually seems to develop in the direction of native speakers' interactional behavior (see, for instance, Hellermann, 2009; Kasper & Youn, 2018; Pekarek Doehler, 2019; Pekarek Doehler & Pochon-Berger, 2015; Roever, 2018; Wong & Waring, 2010).

At the same time, it is not always easy to classify specific linguistic patterns with regard to the contingency type to which they belong. The German token *ähm*, for instance, can serve to hold the turn (TT) while at the same time projecting self-initiated self-repair (Couper-Kuhlen & Selting, 2018: 89, 117). We nevertheless support the idea that adopting the generic orders of interaction as basic categories for assessing IC turns its description into a more systematic and thus more feasible and replicable undertaking.[2]

3.2 A specific challenge: Handling scarce assessment resources

While the challenge discussed in Section 3.1 is relevant for all professional purposes of investigating IC, assessing IC in the ordinary secondary school classroom has to cope with additional challenges and demands. First, the assessment of speaking skills and IC usually needs to fulfill specific pedagogical purposes. Depending on whether the assessment is diagnostic, formative or summative, it will be used by the teacher either to plan and direct further teaching and learning processes, or to provide feedback during the learning process or to finally evaluate the students' learning processes against a predefined learning target, such as the CEFR (Diehr & Frisch, 2008: 23–26; Hallet, 2011: 178–185).

Second, formal language testing is often done by trained testers who, at least for English, are also frequently native speakers of the target language. The ordinary secondary school EFL classroom, in contrast, at least in Germany, often neither has the luxury of one-on-one testers nor do the teachers have extensive training in assessing IC.

Third, this challenge not only embraces the assessment side of it but, to date, also the assessment object. Spoken language and, in particular, talk-in-interaction as a genre, still receive inadequate attention in both course books and teacher training (Helmke *et al.*, 2007: 40; also Pekarek Doehler, 2019: 43).

Fourth, talk-in-interaction is also challenging to the ordinary FL teacher due to their lack of training in assessing the unique nature of the construct. Thus, teachers need an appreciation for cut-offs, repetition and collaborative completions (see Wong & Waring, 2010: 218–220, for instance), as well as multimodality, which necessitates knowledge in the realm of prosody and kinetic behavior.

Fifth, the non-permanency of spoken interaction often requires, at the very least, recording and repeated listening/viewing, if not also transcription, of the language material to be assessed.

For these reasons, teacher trainees not only need to be trained in the basic concepts of IC and their systematic observation, but also in recording ethics and the transcription of spoken language material. Furthermore, the scarcity of testers in the secondary school classroom will remain a challenge unless we accept even more basic solutions, such as administering paired peer speaking tasks like roleplays (e.g. Kasper & Youn, 2018).

Overall, however, the greatest challenge for FL teachers in the ordinary school classroom is predicated on time constraints (cf. Youn, 2015: 218). At least in German secondary schools, this challenge arises from:

- much less time reserved for assessing than teaching the foreign language;
- a large group of 'test-takers', up to 30 FLLs per group;
- the need
  - ○ to ensure an objective and comprehensive evaluation based on clear assessment criteria,
  - ○ to provide useful feedback to the FLL to help them improve their speaking skills, and
  - ○ to use the test or assessment results for monitoring one's own teaching and support for further learning processes.

Therefore, the solution to this problem is to work selectively regarding:

- The number of tests taken. While the implementation of oral exams in the FL classroom is generally seen positively due to the 'washback effect' the exams have on teaching speaking skills (Matz *et al.*, 2018: 2), the manageability and feasibility of several oral exams or tests throughout the school year remains limited. What may be helpful here is the idea of using the recordings of selected FLLs' tests as a basis, not for summative assessment, but for awareness-raising activities. Here, all students can participate in meta-discussions on the IC exhibited by the selected test-takers (see, for instance, Wong & Waring, 2010: 46–47).
- The parts of the recording analyzed in detail. Analyzing/diagnosing IC comprehensively throughout the entire exchange will, again, most likely unduly strain the FL teachers' time resources. We therefore

propose focusing the analysis on key points for each IC subskill (see Section 4.2.2 for key points for TT, for instance) and merely scan the rest of the exchange for relevant diversions – with the granularity necessitated by fairness considerations, of course.

While the ultimate test task and granularity of assessment is determined by the test purpose and the assessment resources available, the principles of systematicity and selectivity, as suggested above, are promising solutions to the challenges of assessing IC, at least in the ordinary FL classroom. In the following section, we will illustrate our approach to testing IC with the example of TT in FLL roleplays recorded in the EFL classroom of a German secondary school.

4 The Example of Turn-taking

4.1 TT as an object of study in SLA

While TT is considered a fundamental phenomenon in CA (cf. Sacks *et al.*'s seminal 1974 paper), to date, classroom interaction studies offer only relatively few findings on FLLs' TT skills. According to the longitudinal studies by Pallotti (2001) and Cekaite (2007; see also Young & Miller, 2004), learners' TT behavior seems to develop from 'not taking turns', through 'inappropriate turn-taking by producing long pauses and/or using competitive strategies', to 'using fewer pauses, more precision-timing and even latching and overlap' (see, for example, Galaczi, 2014; Pekarek Doehler, 2019: 29). According to Pekarek Doehler and Pochon-Berger (2015: 241), learners' skills may also be influenced by the language proficiency needed to recognize possible completion points (Wong & Waring, 2010: 14–24; see also the notion of 'transition-relevance place' (TRP) in Sacks *et al.*, 1974). We can use these findings as anchor points for our observations, yet there is still much need for research in this regard – a situation that, at least for now, also forces us to develop our own criteria.

4.2 Operationalizing the concept of TT

CA/IL examine talk-in-interaction from an emic perspective, viz. the question of what the participants orient to as relevant, as an error or as appropriate, etc. However, assessing IC, even if CA-driven, needs to 'eticize' the analysis in order to achieve reliability, validity and generalizability (see Wagner *et al.*, 2018: 25–28, for instance; also Burch, personal communication). Moreover, 'de-emic-ization' (as one reviewer put it) is a constant danger in studying FLLs' talk-in-interaction, as non-native speaker paired peer interaction may be more difficult to reconcile with the idea of using participant orientation as a methodological tool: for one, co-participants tend to 'favor the progressivity of interaction' (Pekarek Doehler, 2019: 21; see also Firth, 1996; Schegloff, 1979). In addition, we as analysts (and competent users of the L2) may feel tempted to question the basic assumption of 'order at all points' (see, for example, Hutchby & Wooffitt, 1998: 17–23) in the material at hand. One way to – at least partly – solve the latter problem is to focus on the observable practices employed by the FLLs (Waring, 2018: 58), viz. their methodic solutions to the generic problems in talk-in-interaction. These may be specific to a certain learner at a certain point in that learner's L2 development, or they may be typical of learners with a particular L1. In any case, though, they are recurrent and therefore recognizable (Pekarek Doehler, 2019: 18).

In diagnosing our FLLs' TT skills, we will start from the categories and models established in studying native speaker talk for three reasons: (1) their relevance was established by numerous CA studies (see Sidnell & Stivers, 2013); (2) we assume that especially with TT we are dealing with a basic IC, viz. 'interactional abilities … developed since infancy' which L2 speakers need to 'recalibrate … in the course of L2 development' (Pekarek Doehler, 2018: 6; see also Hellermann, 2018: 40; Kecskes *et al.*, 2018); and (3) we can also see them at work in the data (see Section 4.3).

4.2.1 Practices relevant for assessing TT with FLLs

In the CEFR, TT is understood as a basic precondition of interaction (Council of Europe, 2012: 57, 84; for other assessment tests, see Council of Europe, 2012: 194–195), and 'turntaking and turngiving [sic]' are framed as collaborative strategies (Council of Europe, 2012: 73, 119, 124). As with other competencies in the CEFR, benchmarks are provided as 'illustrative descriptors' (Council of Europe, 2012: 25). For C2, for instance, learners

> [c]an interact with ease and skill, picking up and using non-verbal and intonational cues apparently effortlessly. Can interweave his/her contribution into the joint discourse with fully natural turntaking [sic], referencing, allusion making, etc. (Council of Europe, 2012: 28)

For C1, learners

> [c]an select a suitable phrase from a readily available range of discourse functions [sic] to preface his/her remarks appropriately in order to get the floor, or to gain time and keep the floor whilst thinking. (Council of Europe, 2012: 86)

It is to be noted, though, that the descriptors unfortunately only resulted from a study of Swiss FL teachers using sample scales provided to them for discussing and comparing FLLs' proficiency and are, thus, essentially based on intuition, meta-statements and questionnaires (Council of Europe, 2012: 217–225), viz., at best, 'second-hand knowledge' on how interaction works. Moreover, the descriptors strike us as relatively vague (cf. Galaczi, 2014: 555). While it may be necessary to include as wide a range of FLLs' spoken language use as possible, it often poses a challenge to a straightforward and systematic description of IC, at least from a CA/IL point of view. Moreover, selected resources are mentioned on a par with interactional contingencies and actions (compare, for instance, 'non-verbal and intonational cues' for C2 and prefacing phrases for C1 versus 'turn-taking, referencing' for C2 and 'keep the floor' for C1 versus 'allusion making' for C2 and 'gain time' for C1). In addition, the description also frequently lacks straightforwardly operationalizable descriptions (see 'fully natural' for C2 and 'readily available' for C1). The description of B2 strikes us as more applicable in these regards:

> Can intervene appropriately in discussion, exploiting appropriate language to do so. Can initiate, maintain and end discourse appropriately with effective turntaking [sic]. Can initiate discourse, take his/her turn when appropriate and end conversation when he/she needs to, though he/she may not always do this elegantly. Can use stock phrases (e.g. 'That's a difficult question to answer') to gain time and keep the turn whilst formulating what to say. (Council of Europe, 2012: 86)

This specifies the distinction, and relationship, between resources (for instance, 'stock phrases') and interactional outcomes (for instance, to 'keep the turn') more clearly and refers to conditions for appropriateness (for instance, 'when appropriate'). However, here too the descriptors refer to different interactional (sub)skills for the various learner levels (compare the illustrative descriptors for C2, C1 and B2), which in essence also suggests that – as one reviewer pointed out – this assumes that learners at different levels cannot, or do not, relevantly orient or use these resources (but see, for example, Burch & Kasper, 2016). (For the CEFR Companion (Council of Europe 2018), see Barth-Weingarten & Freitag-Hild, in preparation.)

For these reasons, in our project we aimed to develop a rubric more feasible for EFL teachers. We started off from the CA concept of TT and its terminology, not only because it has been successfully employed in studying talk, but also because employing special-purpose terminology has the advantage of being usable efficiently without losing precision. To be able to use the terminology, graders, just like their learners, then also need a basic understanding of TT organization. This includes knowledge on:

- The concept of 'turn', as a fully fledged speaker contribution (versus continuer, for instance; see, for example, Barth-Weingarten, 2016: 181–186; Schegloff, 1982) and opportunity to act (Schegloff, 2007: 3–5), as well as:
- The CA model of TT, which basically embraces three main subskills:
  (1) turn-holding, i.e. keeping the floor for a full turn-constructional unit (TCU) or a multi-unit turn, until a possible transition-relevance place (TRP);
  (2) turn-yielding, i.e. giving up the floor (and often allocating it to another participant);
  (3) turn-taking, i.e. taking the floor when appropriate.
- The working of the TT system with its components of turn-allocation and turn-construction.
- The relevance of timing, with 'precision timing' (see, for example, Galaczi, 2014; Wong & Waring, 2010: 49) not only referring to no-gap

turn starts at TRPs, but also being dependent on a range of 'situational' factors, such as sequential position (initiative turns versus responsive turns), action (see the notion of 'preference' in Pomerantz & Heritage, 2013, for instance) and stance-taking (see, for example, Couper-Kuhlen, 1993). All of these may lead to various kinds of gap and overlap (Jefferson, 1983, 1986), and even competition for the floor (French & Local, 1983). What the participants must do for this in any case is monitor their co-participants' turn for completion.

- Language-specific resources relevant for the three subskills mentioned above, including phenomena such as lexico-syntax, prosody-phonetics and paraverbal as well as kinetic means.

For further details on these issues, see also Sacks *et al.* (1974), Clayman (2013), Hayashi (2013), Schegloff (2007: 3–5) and Wong and Waring (2010: Ch. 2), for instance.

This background enables us to diagnose TT with FLLs with precision and thereby provides the basis for identifying learner-specific practices as well as benchmarks for a rubric of TT skills with regard to the teaching target. The relevant part of our rubric is shown in Figure 10.1.

Pts.	Interactional skills Turn-taking
9-10	The FLL holds/yields/takes turns successfully **throughout the role play**, i.e. transitions are well-timed and designed appropriately re: context), multi-unit turns are efficiently secured, both done with a **broad** (and target-variety-like) **variety** of means.
7-8	... **mostly** successfully... ... **a variety** of (target-variety-like) means.
5-6	... **partially** successfully... ... **several** means(, but few target-variety-like).
3-4	... **rarely** successfully... ... **some** means(, but mostly not target-variety-like).
1-2	... **hardly able, or unable, to** hold/yield/take turns, viz. transitions exhibit significant gaps and/or are inappropriately designed re: context), and/or multi-unit turns are secured with much trouble. The student tries to use some means that are (not target-variety-like) and mostly kinetic, though.

Figure 10.1 Rubric for assessing TT (for rubric columns for further IC skills, see Barth-Weingarten & Freitag-Hild in prep., for instance)

The criteria are based on CA findings on TT and they may also include target-variety likeness of the resources employed, when this is part of the teaching goals – hence the bracketing. The specific degree of competence is captured by degree adverbs. Note that the adverb 'convincingly' maintains room for local contingencies which may even lead to trouble in L1 interaction. Each competence level is then associated with two specific grades, one lower and one higher, which proved to be more practicable than just five competence levels when it came to the actual grading (see Section 4.3.3). In general, though, lower grading is associated with lower TT competence. Overall, this generalized and unified way of capturing TT competence helps us keep the main assessment aspects consistent across the learner levels and therefore allows us to rank our FLLs with regard to similar criteria more fairly. At the same time, the diagnostic granularity is not fixed in advance and can be determined anew for each assessment situation on the basis of both the teaching target and the unit goals as well as the test type and the assessment resources.

4.2.2 Selecting key points for observing TT with FLLs

As mentioned in Section 3.2, secondary school EFL teachers in Germany have to cope with scarce assessment resources. To handle the challenge of lack of time, we moreover propose focusing the diagnosis on relevant sequence-organizational **key points**. For our current purposes – assessing TT – we see these at the following sequence-organizational positions:

- Beginning of the character introduction[3] → taking the turn
- Character introduction → mainly turn-holding
- End of character introduction → turn-yielding
- Beginning of the interactive part[4] → all subskills

To ensure a comprehensive assessment, we moreover propose to, at least, scan the other parts of the roleplay for additional points relevant to assessing TT skills ('bird's-eye view'). In some of the roleplays, for instance, the learners entered into a more heated debate. There, overlaps and interruptions are the sequence-organizationally preferred option (see, for example, Kotthoff, 1993).

4.3 Assessing EFL learners' TT skills – a pilot study

4.3.1 Data and methods

As material, we selected representative roleplays from a larger collection of semi-open face-to-face roleplays (Kasper & Youn, 2018: 591–592; also Huth, 2010), recorded by one author during her service at a secondary school in an 8th grade class (German EFL learners aged 13–14 years in their third year of learning English in the secondary school). The learners are expected to have acquired an A2 language proficiency at this stage, although some had started learning English earlier or more extensively and consequently surpassed this level. The roleplays were designed to elicit natural interactional behavior. Yet, their consequentiality (Schegloff, 1991; see also 'authenticity' in Kasper & Youn, 2018: 613) is potentially limited, as they were based on the students acting in the role of the fictitious inhabitants of a fictitious town, which the students had created as part of a simulation project (see Freitag-Hild, 2014).

Moreover, against this background and in addition to the actual roleplay, the FLLs had also been asked to start by introducing their character. This complemented the roleplays with a different genre: character introductions. The roleplays resemble everyday conversation in the FLLs' status as addressed ratified participants (Goffman, 1981; also Dynel, 2011), although the conversational event as such was elicited by, and mainly for, the teacher (TEA) (addressed audience). In the character introductions, in contrast, the TEA is the ratified addressed participant (see, for instance, Nat's gaze behavior in the sample transcript in Section 4.3.2, Line 0:06a). TEA's rights to the floor are somewhat restricted, though, due to the rather monologic nature of the genre. Others present in the room constitute the addressed audience; this includes the FLL's roleplay partner who at times, however, becomes an addressed ratified participant, such as when they are topicalized as a relative (see Joe's gaze behavior, for instance, in Line 0:31a). Moreover, roleplay partners also have the right to initiate repair (see Line 0:36). Despite these differences, we consider material from both genres for our current purposes because the character introduction – as its length is not fixed – also requires the current speaker to hold, and yield, the turn at particular points (see Section 4.2). In addition, the character introduction is a less complex interactional situation, which therefore also constitutes a good starting point for novice IC assessors (see Sections 3.2 and 4.2.2).

Apart from what the FLLs had prepared on their specific character, the students were provided with role cards for the actual roleplay informing them about the specific interactional situation they would find themselves in. As the specific unit aimed to develop argumentative skills, the learners were asked to pursue conflicting projects in a parent-child argument, such as texting versus doing one's homework, listening to loud music versus reducing the volume, etc. (cf. van Compernolle, this volume). This required the learners to use the following resources: their language skills, their IC with regard to TT, action accomplishment and repair, as well as their knowledge of family life[5] and the contributions of their co-participant. (For our experiences with the consequences of the latter issue, see Section 4.3.) The unexpectedness necessary to avoid construct underrepresentation (Roever, 2018) was introduced by the fact that no FLL knew the specific role card of their co-participant.[6] The students were asked first to introduce their character and then to start with the interactive part of the roleplay. The teacher did not specifically allocate the initiating turns for either of the speaking tasks.

In our systematically selective analysis of the FLLs' TT skills, we will employ the methodology of IL, viz. scrutinizing the material in a CA-inspired way for the role language patterns play in the organization of interaction (see, for example, Couper-Kuhlen & Selting, 2018).

4.3.2 Two EFL learners' TT practices

We now illustrate our approach, and its value with regard to assessment, by presenting the analysis of the TT skills of two of our FLLs – Joe and Natalie (Nat) – in what we consider a representative example of our roleplays. As is general practice in CA, these will be two detailed qualitative single-case analyses, which afterwards, however, allow us to compare specific details of the TT behavior of two members of the same learner group. Such single-case analyses can then, in a next research step, lead to a better understanding of the distribution and nature of IC in a larger learner group.

Our roleplay requires Joe (the son) to obtain leave of absence from, and Nat (the mother) to make her son join, a family gathering. The relevant role cards are shown in Figure 10.2.

On this basis, the following ensues. For transcription conventions, please see the Appendix 10.1.

Father/mother	Son/daughter
It is Friday afternoon and you are just about to phone a restaurant and book a table for tomorrow night because your brother has arranged to visit you for the weekend. When your son/daughter comes home from school, she asks you for permission to go to a friend's party Saturday night.	It is Friday afternoon and you come home from school. A friend from school has invited you to a party Saturday night. You would very much like to go to the party, but your uncle is coming to stay for the weekend. Just as you return from school, your mother/father is about to call a restaurant in order to book a table for Saturday night.

Figure 10.2 Role card for Excerpt 'Oh mum'

Excerpt 10.1 'Oh mum' RP011, sec. 0:00–1:52 (expanded basic transcript; focus on TT)

Tea: teacher; Nat: mother; Joe: son

? intonation ending between mid and high
▌Nat looking at Joe

0:00	Tea:	okay-
		|_____
		|
0:00a		((Nat looks at Tea))
		__ |_____
		|
0:01		off you [GO.]
0:02	Nat:	[uh:m: -]
0:03		i:'m natalie DEAN? (.)
0:04		i:'m: firty free¹ years OLD? (.)
0:06		äh my job is (.) ähm i'm a NURSE? (.)
		|_____|
		|
0:06a		((glances at Tea))
0:09	Joe:	[((moves lips))] [((smiles))]
0:10	Nat:	[i've got] [free² CHILdren- (.)]
		|
0:10a		((with slight smile))
0:11		a:nd (.) a HUSband?
		|_____|
		|
		((Joe waves and smiles to (audience)))
0:12		and i'm from GERmany?
		|_____
		|
0:12a		((looks at Tea))
		____|
		|
0:14		(--)
0:14:30	Joe:	h[h°]
0:15	Nat:	[Y]ES; thAt's it.
		|
		((slightly smiling))
		|
0:16	Joe:	°hh m_HM,
		|__|
		|
0:16a		((nods once))
0:16:50	Nat:	[((laughing, nods extensively))]
0:17	Joe:	[((click)) _i'm ((l)aughs))=°h i'm joe DEAN-=
		|
0:17a		((Joe briefly glances at Nat))
0:19		=i'm fifteen YEARS o:ld, (.)
0:21		(ähm/and) my hobbie:s a:re °h footba foot to play FOOTba:ll,

_____

¹ thirty-three
² three

```
0:25                   as a (.) QUARterback,=
0:27                   =a:nd (-) °h go to SCHOO:L,
0:30                   meet my FRIENDS, (.)
0:31                   ((click)) ä:hm yes my mom is NAtalie dean-
                                                          |
0:31a                            ((briefly looks at Nat, then away again))
0:33                   my father is (.)  MOE dean,
                       (-)
0:35                   (MORma[nny),        ]
0:36      Nat:              [ (MORman)]  ((la[ughs with fingers covering mouth))]
0:37      Joe:                          [          <<smiling>   °h]h> a:nd
                       YEAH;=i('m) come from: (-) yu es AY.
                                         |_____
                                         |
0:37a                       ((looks at Nat))
                        __ |
                          |
0:41      Nat:         YES;
                       <<laughing> hm,>
                                   |____
                                   |
0:41a                       ((looks at Tea, slightly smiling))
                        _____ |
                             |
0:43                   oKAY;
0:43:30               ähm (-) my bro|ther\
0:44                   ähm can we START?
                            |_____
                                   |
0:44a                 ((Nat looks at Tea))
                            | |_____
                            |         |
0:44b                       |   ((Joe looks at Nat, scratching his mouth and chin))
                        _|_____       |
                            |  |       |
0:45      Tea:         m_H[M?]  |
                           |_____|
                        _|_
                          |
0:45:80   Nat:         [oK]AY.=
0:46                   =°h my brother called me ähm to VIsit us tomorrow;
0:49      Joe:         °h ↑Oh !MOM!;=
                            |
0:49a                      ((quick glances at Nat))
                            |
0:50                   =ähm (°h) i want to go to a !PAR!ty (.) yesterd äh
                       tomorrow-
0:54                   (-)
                       |__
                          |
0:54a                 ((Joe looks at Nat))
                       _____ |
                             |
0:54:50   Nat:         ähm NO.
```

((44 sec omitted))

1:38	Joe:	but i the party is me very important.
1:38a		((Joe looks at Nat))
		|————————|————————|
1:40	Nat:	but he will see you ähm ALso.
1:43	Joe:	(-) °h yEs but
1:44	Nat:	((l[aughs))]
1:44:50	Joe:	[((laughs))]
1:45	Nat:	no exCUse.
1:46	Joe:	!^MO:M.!
		((quick glance at Nat))
1:46:50	Nat:	[<<laughing>h°>]
1:47	Joe:	[it's ver]y imPORtant for m[e::;]
1:48	Nat:	[^No:.]
1:49	Joe:	i u\
1:50		<<laughing sigh>h°>
1:50a		((hits his leg with fist, smiling))
1:52	Nat:	there will äh be aNOther party;
		((Joe quickly glances at Nat))

For reasons that will become clear in the comparison of the two FLLs, we will start our discussion with Joe. The line numbers in the following analysis reflect the line numbers in the transcript and as such refer to seconds in the recording.

Judged against the rubric, Joe's TT behavior is successful and appropriate regarding timing and situation throughout the roleplay with only a few exceptions. He uses efficient practices from all linguistic dimensions, most of which are even native-like. In his character introduction, he holds his turn by a range of prosodic resources: level or mid-rising final intonation (e.g. Lines 0:17 and 0:19); vowel lengthening (e.g. *a:re* in Line 0:21); and latching (viz. the prosodically phonetically tight connection between TCUs, as in *QUARterback,= =a:nd* in Lines 0:25–0:27; compare 'rush-through' in Wong & Waring, 2010: 32–33, for instance). He projects continuation by clicks (e.g. Line 0:31) and in-breaths (e.g. Line 0:37) as well as lexico-syntactic means (e.g. *a:nd* in Line 0:27). Also, *ähm* (e.g. Line 0:31) can be seen to serve this purpose, with native-like frequency, although pronunciation-wise Joe uses the German variant of this filler word. As regards kinetic cues, Joe does not gaze at his co-participant while talking (see, for example, Lines 0:36–0:37). At the end of his introductory turn, Joe yields his turn successfully, appropriately and native-like: he uses low-falling intonation and gazes at his co-participant (Line 0:37).

Also, for TT, Joe can be observed to successfully employ various means. At the beginning of his character introduction (Lines 0:16–0:17), for example, he starts on time with a precision-timed in-breath accompanied by a head nod and followed by a response particle and a click that is tightly connected to his first content word. This strong projection secures him the floor to such an extent that he can even interweave a laugh particle responding to Nat's laugh before he restarts and continues his turn (Line 0:17). Joe's close monitoring of his co-participant for the relevance of TT is also visible (e.g. Line 0:44b).

In the rest of the roleplay, we can also find some less native-like uses of TT organization cues. In Line 0:50, Joe uses level intonation at a point where he waits for Nat to take the turn. Nat, in turn, seems to orient to the holding effect of this final intonation contour and does not come in. Therefore, a pause ensues, in the course of which Joe uses the opportunity to repair his TT cues prosodically and kinetically: he prolongs his pause and now starts looking at his co-participant (Line 0:54a), thereby signaling turn-yielding more explicitly (Deppermann, 2013; Rossano, 2013, for instance). This little sequence, in fact, also shows that while peer testers' opportunities to (re)act are dependent on each other (Roever & Kasper, 2018), non-target behavior does not necessarily lead to non-assessability of IC, provided that the latter is understood as a complex skill repairable on-line (see Burch, 2014).

Joe's gaze behavior actually seems to be in need of further development in general: at other TRPs, too, he looks down at his role card instead of using his gaze to cue turn-yielding (and allocate the turn) (e.g. Line 1:38). Moreover, he – at least temporarily – has to retreat to kinetic resources when Nat keeps claiming the floor persistently (Lines 1:49–1:50). However, overall, such more learner-like TT behavior is rare on his side.

Nat's TT behavior, in comparison, is also successful and appropriate regarding the timing and situation. However, while she uses efficient TT practices, these are fewer in number and type and some of them are still L1-like. In her character introduction, for instance, she manages to hold her turn. Apart from some level intonation (e.g. Line 0:10), though, she often uses a practice to end her intra-turn TCUs which – with its ladle-like final intonation contour (dipping low and rising higher than normal on the final syllable) being followed by a pause (e.g. Lines 0:03, 0:04, etc.) – strikes us as less L2-like. It may work nevertheless because, for one, Nat's gazing behavior does not indicate readiness to yield the turn – she does not look at Joe for most of the character introduction (and when she does (Line 0:10), she, interestingly, uses a more L2-like holding final intonation contour). Nat thus would be able to use other resources successfully at the earlier points, too. Second – and here is where an additional need for further research comes into play – this practice can also be observed with other German FL learners, and it may work in the situation at hand because of it being a 'members' method' (Garfinkel, 1967), viz. part of the set of shared 'systematic procedures … by which members of a social group organize their conduct in a mutually understandable and account-able way' (Pekarek Doehler & Pochon-Berger, 2015: 235); that is, Joe – being a (German) FLL (of English) himself – knows and therefore understands it. However, Nat also projects continuation by the conjunction *and* (Line 0:11) and the German filler word *äh(m)* (e.g. Line 0:06), with the latter being slightly more frequent on her part than with Joe (see, for example, Lines 0:43:30, 0:44, 0:46, 0:54:50, 1:40, 1:52). In effect then, it seems to be a combination of resources that helps Nat to hold her turn.

Nat also has some difficulties in turn-yielding at the end of her character introduction: perhaps due to an on-line change of plan, she needs to repair her turn-holding pattern at the end of Line 0:12 into a turn-yielding one. For this, she uses a German (re)confirmation particle followed by an explicitly turn-yielding phrase ending in L2-like low-falling intonation (*YES; thAt's it.*, Line 0:15). At this point, she also efficiently uses her gaze to select the next speaker: from a clarification check with TEA (Line 0:12:00a), she moves her gaze to her co-participant (Line 0:15, cf. 0:46) and keeps closely monitoring him for most of his multi-unit character introduction (Lines 0:16–0:37). In this way, then, she arguably also recognizes Joe's turn-yielding cues and responds with a precision-timed confirmation (*YES*, in Line 0:41).

Nat then – after another visual clarification check with TEA (Line 0:41:00a) – initiates and projects moving into the interactive part of their exchange with a sequence-structuring particle (oKAY, Line 0:43) (Beach, 1993) and the German filler *ähm* (Line 0:43:30) (see also the in-breath and her bodily reorientation to Joe at the re-start in Line 0:46). Later, Nat's turn-holding practices also include latching (Lines 0:45:80–0:46), and the low-falling intonation used at that point shows that she at least has that resource at her disposal (Line 0:45:80).

In the more heated part of their exchange, Nat eventually manages to take advantage of Joe's less active TT behavior with laughing (Line 1:45) and an early, recognitional onset (Line 1:48) (Jefferson, 1983). This arguably leads to Joe retreating to kinetic means of expression (Line 1:50a) and thus frees the way for Nat to make another content point in the clear (Line 1:52).

4.3.3 Identifying and differentiating competence levels of TT

Based on our observations, we can now start comparing the competence levels of our FLLs with regard to their TT skills.[7] Nat, for instance, uses fewer linguistic practices of turn-holding than Joe in number and type, while some of her practices are also more L1-like (compare her high mid-rising intonational turn-holding practice and the frequency of *äh(m)*). At the same time, she seems to be better able than Joe to manage more exceptional TT situations (the heated debate), while both FLLs are able to employ alternative resources (Pekarek Doehler, 2019: 40) (compare, for instance, Nat's gazing behavior in the character introduction and Joe's turn-yielding repair in 0:54a).

Applying our rubric (see Section 4.2.1) then, we would see them at the second-best competence level, with Joe at 9 points and Nat at 7 points. It needs to be kept in mind, though, that the actual grading is highly dependent on the overall teaching target as well as the learning outcome of the relevant teaching unit.[8] If native-ness is a teaching target, for instance, Joe did somewhat better. Also, if diversification of 'methods for getting the same interactional business accomplished' (Pekarek Doehler, 2019: 18) is a basic feature of L2 interactional development – as has been observed by longitudinal studies (see also Pekarek Doehler & Pochon-Berger, 2015: 262–263) – we would assume that Joe has indeed already developed a higher competence level in TT than Nat.

5 Summary and Some Conclusions for Research and Teacher Training

In this chapter, we presented our approach to assessing IC systematically under the conditions of scarce assessment resources. We advocated the systematic analysis of IC by focusing on subtypes of IC determined by the generic orders of talk-in-interaction but conceded that their overall number and the detail of their study is to be determined by the assessment resources available for the assessment situation at hand. When the latter are scarce, as is the case in the German secondary school EFL classroom, we suggested proceeding selectively, but systematically, with regard to the number of IC skills analyzed (focus on TT, action accomplishment or repair) as well as the comprehensiveness of the analysis (focus on sequence-organizational key points for analysis and a bird's-eye view on the rest of the exchange). For illustration, we analyzed the TT skills of two exemplary, intermediary FLLs of English in a semi-open roleplay starting with character introductions recorded in a German secondary school classroom. We hope to have shown that, with sufficient attention to interactional detail, already such a pilot study can result in valuable insights with regard to (relevant aspects of) the IC of FLLs.

While our results seem to confirm overall learner characteristics known from longitudinal studies of TT (compare the issue of diversification in Section 4.3.3, for instance), in particular the IL part of our study shows that there is more to the development of TT skills than the three stages longitudinal studies had described so far (see Section 4.1). In particular, we can see finer distinctions in addition to these stages when looking at the set of linguistic resources and practices employed by the FLLs of one learner group. These finer distinctions seem to be particularly relevant when it comes to (assessing) intermediate and more advanced learners. Therefore, while further research is undoubtedly needed, these findings demonstrate that adopting the generic orders of talk as basic assessment categories is able to turn the description of IC into a more systematic undertaking, which may also help improve the replicability of the assessment, even if the emic CA/IL approach needs to be eticized.

Moreover, our observations suggest that there exist L1-specific learner IC practices that may contribute to smooth interaction with learner peers. Whether they are problematic for interaction with L2 native speakers is an empirical question, the answer to which will also have repercussions on the value of language learning 'in the wild' (see, for instance, Pekarek Doehler, 2019). Further research is definitely needed here.

In addition, our pilot study provides evidence for the assumption that 'different levels of IC are observable and measurable' (Roever & Kasper, 2018: 348; also Roever, 2018), and that we can use situations for testing this, which are interactionally less constrained but do not have to be prototypically interactive (see the role of the character introductions in the assessment procedure). Moreover, our pilot study suggests that such insights can already be obtained under scarce assessment resource conditions, when the analysis is restricted to only two FLLs, for instance. Undoubtedly, though, analysis of a larger collection of roleplays done by a range of FLLs will provide us with more insight and an opportunity to study TT across learners of the same proficiency level. This will help us develop a better idea of how FLLs are faring with regard to certain IC benchmarks and, in turn, allow us to improve our benchmark scales.

Our analysis also led to some conclusions about the possible influence of co-test takers on an FLL's IC. While peer testers' opportunities to (re-) act are undoubtedly dependent on each other (see Roever & Kasper, 2018), non-target behavior does not necessarily lead to non-assessability of IC or unfair grading, provided the test situation allows for, and is understood as, an interactional situation co-constructed by the peer test-takers. Moreover, IC must be understood, and analyzed, as a complex skill, which is repairable on-line. The design and analysis of such complexity is what we would like to see CA/IL-inspired work provide for with its close attention to interactional details when assessing IC in FLLs talk-in-interaction.

Finally, we would like to point out again that, no doubt, acquiring the necessary skills for assessing IC in their FLLs' talk will be a challenge for FL teachers. They will need to develop an appreciation for the target of the study and their teaching – (everyday) interaction – as such (see Section 3.2), as well as the necessary expert knowledge on the specific aspect of IC (see Section 4.2.1). Moreover, teachers will need to hone their assessment skills in order to assess their learners' IC reliably on the basis of clear assessment criteria – skills for which sufficient practice and training should be provided as part of pre-service as well as in-service teacher training. What is more, especially in a school context, assessment serves pedagogical purposes in that teachers should use it to reflect on their own teaching methods and contents and how they need to be developed further in the interest of their students' language learning progress (for more detail on pedagogical implications, see Freitag-Hild & Barth-Weingarten, 2020). All of this, no doubt, requires time, both in teacher training and teaching practice, even if the ways to save resources we have suggested above are used. But helping our students to tackle the challenges of real talk-in-interaction will doubtlessly be all the more appreciated by them, the more they come into contact with language 'in the wild'.

Appendix 10.1: Transcription Conventions

(cf. Couper-Kuhlen & Barth-Weingarten, 2011; for kinetic transcription, Selting *et al.*, 1998)

Minimal transcript

Sequential structure

[ ]	overlap and simultaneous talk
[ ]	

In- and outbreaths

°h/h°	in-/outbreaths of approx. 0.2–0.5 second duration
°hh/hh°	in-/outbreaths of approx. 0.5–0.8 second duration

Pauses

(.)	micro pause, estimated, up to 0.2 second duration approx.
(-)	short estimated pause of approx. 0.2–0.5 second duration
(--)	intermediary estimated pause of approx. 0.5–0.8 sec. duration

Other segmental conventions

and_uh	cliticizations within units
uh, uhm, etc.	hesitation markers, so-called 'filled pauses'

Laughter and crying

haha, hehe, hihi	syllabic laughter
((laughs)), ((cries))	description of laughter and crying
<<laughing> >	laughter particles accompanying speech with indication of scope

Continuers

hm, yes, no, yeah	monosyllabic tokens
hm_hm, ye_es,	bi-syllabic tokens

Other conventions

((coughs)), <<coughing> >	non-verbal vocal actions and events with scope
(may i)	assumed wording
((…))	omission in transcript

Basic transcript

Sequential structure

=	fast, immediate continuation with a new turn or segment (latching)

Other segmental conventions

:	lengthening, by about 0.2–0.5 second
::	lengthening, by about 0.5–0.8 second

Accentuation

SYLlable	focus accent
!SYL!lable	extra strong accent

Final pitch movements of intonation phrases

?	rising to high
ˀ	intonation ending between mid and high
,	rising to mid
—	level
;	falling to mid
.	falling to low

Fine transcript

Accentuation

SYLlable	focus accent
sYllable	secondary accent
!SYL!lable	extra strong accent
↑	smaller pitch upstep
^SO	rising-falling focus accent

Kinetic cues

▓	Nat looking at Joe

Acknowledgments

We are grateful to Rue Burch and Taiane Malabarba as well as two anonymous reviewers for comments on an earlier version. Needless to say, all remaining errors are our own.

Notes

(1) The domains of these problems also suggest that language proficiency cannot be clearly separated from IC (see Galaczi, 2014: 572; Pekarek Doehler, 2019: 40). However, for our current purposes – the study of FLLs' TT – they seem to be less important than for action accomplishment, for instance.

(2) As mentioned towards the end of Section 1, more formal studies supporting this goal are still needed.

(3) For the phases of the roleplay, see Section 4.3.1.

(4) In our material this usually still included the first post-expansion adjacency pair after the base adjacency pair.

(5) In any future project we recommend creating roles as close to the students' social experience as possible to tackle the issue of (in)authenticity (Kasper & Youn, 2018: 592–593; also Roever, 2018). Moreover, the more control over the test situation needs to be exerted, the more detailed instructions are needed. However, this seems to us less relevant for TT.

(6) Some of the role cards used will need to be improved, though, in further work, with regard to how much they already tell the FLL about the project of their co-participant. This is more relevant for assessing action accomplishment and, possibly, repair, though.

(7) Barth-Weingarten and Freitag-Hild (in preparation) discuss a similar procedure for the assessment of action accomplishment in sequential context.

(8) Back then, our FLLs in fact had not profited from a unit on TT.

References

Al-Gahtani, S. and Roever, C. (2013) 'Hi doctor, give me handouts': Low-proficiency learners and requests. *ELT Journal* 67, 413–424.

Barth-Weingarten, D. (2016) *Intonation Units Revisited: Cesuras in Talk-in-interaction.* Amsterdam: John Benjamins.

Barth-Weingarten, D. and Freitag-Hild, B. (in preparation) Assessing interactional competence in secondary schools: Issues of action accomplishment. To appear in 2022 in *Applied Pragmatics*, in the special issue 'Assessing Interactional Competence: Between Observation and Grading' (ed. D. Barth-Weingarten, E. Betz and T. Malabarba).

Beach, W.A. (1993) Transitional regularities for 'casual' 'Okay' usages. *Journal of Pragmatics* 19, 325–352.

Burch, A.R. (2014) Pursuing information: A conversation analytic [sic] perspective on communication strategies. *Language Learning* 64 (3), 651–684.

Burch, A.R. and Kasper, G. (2016): 'Like Godzilla': Enactments and formulations in telling a disaster story in Japanese. In M.T. Prior and G. Kasper (eds) *Emotion in Multilingual Interaction* (pp. 57–85). Amsterdam: John Benjamins.

Cekaite, A. (2007) A child's development of interactional competence in a Swedish L2 classroom. *The Modern Language Journal* 91 (1), 45–62.

Clayman, S.E. (2013) Turn-constructional units and the transition-relevance place. In J. Sidnell and T. Stivers (eds) *The Handbook of Conversation Analysis* (pp. 150–166). Oxford: Wiley-Blackwell.

Council of Europe (2012) *Common European Framework of Reference for Languages: Learning, Teaching, Assessment.* Cambridge: Cambridge University Press.

Council of Europe (2018) Common European Framework of Reference for Languages: Learning, Teaching, Assessment. Companion volume with new descriptors. https://rm.coe.int/cefr-companion-volume-with-new-descriptors-2018/1680787989. (access May 05, 2021).

Couper-Kuhlen, E. (1993) *English Speech Rhythm: Form and Function in Everyday Verbal Interaction*. Amsterdam: John Benjamins.

Couper-Kuhlen, E. and Barth-Weingarten, D. (2011) A system for transcribing talk-in-interaction: GAT 2. English translation and adaptation of Selting, Margret *et al.* (2009): Gesprächsanalytisches Transkriptionssystem 2. *Gesprächsforschung – Online-Zeitschrift zur verbalen Interaktion* 12 (1), 1–51.

Couper-Kuhlen, E. and Selting, M. (2018) *Interactional Linguistics: Studying Language in Social Interaction*. Cambridge: Cambridge University Press.

Crookall, D. and Saunders, D. (eds) (1989) *Communication and Simulation*. Clevedon: Multilingual Matters.

Deppermann, A. (2011) Konstruktionsgrammatik und Interaktionale Linguistik: Affinitäten, Komplementaritäten und Diskrepanzen. In A. Lasch and A. Ziem (eds) *Konstruktionsgrammatik III* (pp. 205–238). Tübingen: Stauffenburg.

Deppermann, A. (2013) Turn-design at turn-beginnings: Multimodal resources to deal with tasks of turn-construction in German. *Journal of Pragmatics* 46, 91–121.

Diehr, B. and Frisch, S. (2008) *Mark their Words. Sprechleistungen im Englischunterricht der Grundschule fördern und beurteilen*. Braunschweig: Westermann.

Dynel, M. (2011) Revisiting Goffman's postulates on participant statuses in verbal interaction. *Language and Linguistics Compass* 5 (7), 454–465. doi:10.1111/j.1749-818x.2011.00286.x

Firth, A. (1996) The discursive accomplishment of normality. On 'lingua franca' English and conversation analysis. *Journal of Pragmatics* 26, 237–259.

Ford, C.E. (2004) Contingency and units in interaction. *Discourse Studies* 6, 27–52.

Ford, C.E. and Thompson, S.A. (1996) Interactional units in conversation: Syntactic, intonational, and pragmatic resources for the management of turns. In E. Ochs, E.A. Schegloff and S.A. Thompson (eds) *Interaction and Grammar* (pp. 134–184). Cambridge: Cambridge University Press.

Freitag-Hild, B. (2014) Lernaufgaben im genre-basierten Englischunterricht: Kompetenzen zum monologischen und dialogischen Sprechen entwickeln. In C. Fäcke, M. Rost-Roth and E. Thaler (eds) *Sprachenausbildung – Sprachen bilden aus – Bildung aus Sprachen. Dokumentation zum 25. Kongress für Fremdsprachendidaktik der Deutschen Gesellschaft für Fremdsprachenforschung (DGFF) 2013* (pp. 77–89). Baltmannsweiler: Schneider Verlag Hohengehren.

Freitag-Hild, B. and Barth-Weingarten, D. (2020) Pragmatische Kompetenzen im Englischunterricht beurteilen: Ein interdisziplinäres Seminar zur Entwicklung von Diagnosefähigkeiten für interaktionale Fähigkeiten in der ersten Phase der Lehrerbildung [Assessing pragmatic skills in the English classroom: An interdisciplinary course on developing diagnostic skills for interactional competencies in university teacher training]. In H. Limberg and K. Glaser (eds) *Pragmatische Kompetenzen im Fremdsprachenunterricht [Pragmatic Competencies in the Foreign Language Classroom]* (pp. 381–408). Frankfurt am Main: Peter Lang.

French, P. and Local, J. (1983) Turn-competitive incomings. *Journal of Pragmatics* 7, 17–38.

Galaczi, E.D. (2014) Interactional competence across proficiency levels: How do learners manage interaction in paired speaking tests? *Applied Linguistics* 35 (5), 553–574.

Garfinkel, H. (1967) *Studies in Ethnomethodology*. Cambridge: Polity Press.

Goffman, E. (1981) *Forms of Talk*. Philadelphia, PA: University of Pennsylvania Press.

Hallet, W. (2011) *Lernen fördern: Englisch. Kompetenzorientierter Unterricht in der Sekundarstufe I*. Seelze: Kallmeyer in Verbindung mit Klett.

Hayashi, M. (2013) Turn allocation and turn sharing. In J. Sidnell and T. Stivers (eds) *The Handbook of Conversation Analysis* (pp. 167–190). Oxford: Wiley-Blackwell.

Hellermann, J. (2009) Looking for evidence of language learning in practices for repair: A case study of self-initiated self-repair by an adult learner of English. *Scandinavian Journal of Educational Research* 53 (2), 113–132.

Hellermann, J. (2018) Languaging as competencing: Considering language learning as enactment. *Classroom Discourse* 9 (1), 40–56.

Helmke, A., Helmke, T., Kleinbub, I., Nordheider, I., Schrader, F.-W. and Wagner, W. (2007) Die DESI-Videostudie. *Der fremdsprachliche Unterricht – Englisch* 41 (90), 37–44.

Hutchby, I. and Wooffitt, R. (1998) *Conversation Analysis: Principles, Practices and Applications.* Cambridge: Polity Press.

Huth, T. (2010) Can talk be inconsequential? Social and interactional aspects of elicited second-language interaction. *The Modern Language Journal* 94, 537–553.

Huth, T. (2018) On graded scales: Interaction, proficiency, and assessment frameworks. Abstract of the presentation at the CLIC conference 'Assessing Speaking on Context – New Trends', Rice, 4–5 May.

Ikeda, N. (2017) Measuring L2 oral pragmatic abilities for use in social contexts: Development and validation of an assessment instrument for L2 pragmatics performance in university settings. Unpublished PhD dissertation, University of Melbourne.

Jefferson, G. (1983) Notes on some orderliness of overlap onset. In V. D'Urso and P. Leonardi (eds) *Discourse Analysis and Natural Rhetorics* (pp. 11–38). Padua: Cleup Editors.

Jefferson, G. (1986) Notes on 'latency' in overlap onset. *Human Studies* 9, 153–183.

Kasper, G. (2006) Beyond repair: Conversation analysis as an approach to SLA. *The Modern Language Journal* 88, 551–567.

Kasper, G. and Youn, S.J. (2018) Transforming instruction to activity: Roleplay in language assessment. *Applied Linguistics Review* 9 (4), 589–616. doi:10.1515/applirev-2017-0020

Kecskes, I., Sanders, R.E. and Pomerantz, A. (2018) The basic interactional competence of language learners. *Journal of Pragmatics* 124, 88–105.

Kotthoff, H. (1993) Disagreement and concession in disputes: On the context sensitivity of preference structures. *Language in Society* 22 (2), 193–216.

Kramsch, C. (1986) From language proficiency to interactional competence. *The Modern Language Journal* 70, 366–372.

Markee, N. (2008) Toward a learning behavior tracking methodology for CA-for-SLA. *Applied Linguistics* 29 (3), 404–427.

Matz, F., Rogge, M. and Rumlich, D. (2018) What makes a good speaker of English? Sprechkompetenz mit mündlichen Prüfungen erfassen. *Der fremdsprachliche Unterricht Englisch* 153, 2–7.

Mondada, L. (2016) Challenges of multimodality: Language and the body in social interaction. *Journal of Sociolinguistics* 20 (3), 336–366.

Pallotti, G. (2001) External appropriations as a strategy for participating in intercultural multi-party conversations. In A. Di Luzio, S. Günthner and F. Orletti (eds) *Culture in Communication. Analyses of Intercultural Situations* (pp. 295–334). Amsterdam: John Benjamins.

Pekarek Doehler, S. (2018) Elaborations on L2 interactional competence: The development of L2 grammar-for-interaction. *Classroom Discourse* 9 (1), 3–24.

Pekarek Doehler, S. (2019) On the nature and the development of L2 interactional competence: State of the art and implications for praxis. In M.R. Salaberry and S. Kunitz (eds) *Teaching and Testing L2 Interactional Competence: Bridging Theory and Practice* (pp. 25–59). New York: Routledge.

Pekarek Doehler, S. and Pochon-Berger, E. (2015) The development of L2 interactional competence: Evidence from turn-taking organization, sequence organization, repair organization and preference organization. In T. Cadierno and S. Eskildsen (eds) *Usage-based Perspectives on Second Language Learning* (pp. 233–268). Berlin: de Gruyter.

Pekarek Doehler, S., Wagner, J. and González-Martinez, E. (2018) (eds) *Longitudinal Studies on the Organization of Social Interaction.* London: Palgrave Macmillan.

Plough, I., Banerjee, J. and Iwashita, N. (2018) Interactional competence: Genie out of the bottle. *Language Testing* 35, 427–445.

Pomerantz, A. and Heritage, J. (2013) Preference. In J. Sidnell and T. Stivers (eds) *The Handbook of Conversation Analysis* (pp. 210–228). Oxford: Wiley-Blackwell.

Roever, C. (2018) Assessing interactional competence: Features, scoring, and practicality. Presentation at the CLIC conference, 'Assessing Speaking on Context: New Trends', Rice, 4–5 May.

Roever, C. and Kasper, G. (2018) Interactional competence as a target construct in testing speaking. *Language Testing* 35 (3), 331–355.

Rossano, F. (2013) Gaze in conversation. In J. Sidnell and T. Stivers (eds) *The Handbook of Conversation Analysis* (pp. 308–329). Oxford: Wiley-Blackwell.

Sacks, H., Schegloff, E.A. and Jefferson, G. (1974) A simplest systematics for the organization of turn-taking for conversation. *Language* 50, 696–735.

Schegloff, E.A. (1979) The relevance of repair to syntax-for-conversation. In T. Givón (ed.) *Discourse and Syntax* (pp. 261–286). New York: Academic Press.

Schegloff, E.A. (1982) Discourse as an interactional achievement: Some uses of 'uh huh' and other things that come between sentences. In D. Tannen (ed.) *Analyzing Discourse: Text and Talk* (pp. 71–93). Washington, DC: Georgetown University Press.

Schegloff, E.A. (1991) Reflections on talk and social structure. In D. Boden and D.H. Zimmerman (eds) *Talk and Social Structure: Studies in Ethnomethodology and Conversation Analysis* (pp. 44–70). Berkeley, CA: Polity Press.

Schegloff, E.A. (2007) *Sequence Organization in Interaction. A Primer in Conversation Analysis, Vol. 1.* Cambridge: Cambridge University Press.

Selting, M., Auer, P., Barden, B., *et al.* (1998) Gesprächsanalytisches Transkriptionssystem (GAT). *Linguistische Berichte* 173, 91–122.

Sidnell, J. and Stivers, T. (eds) (2013) *The Handbook of Conversation Analysis.* Oxford: Wiley-Blackwell.

Stokoe, E. (2014) The conversation analytic role-play method (CARM): A method for training communication skills as an alternative to simulated role-play. *Research on Language and Social Interaction* 47, 255–265.

Taguchi, N. and Roever, C. (2017) *Second Language Pragmatics.* Oxford: Oxford University Press.

Wagner, J., Pekarek Doehler, S. and González-Martinez, E. (2018) Longitudinal research on the organization of social interaction: Current developments and methodological challenges. In S. Pekarek Doehler, J. Wagner and E. González-Martinez (eds) *Longitudinal Studies on the Organization of Social Interaction* (pp. 3–35). London: Palgrave Macmillan.

Waring, H.Z. (2018) Teaching L2 interactional competence: Problems and possibilities. *Classroom Discourse* 9 (1), 57–67.

Wong, J. and Waring, H.Z. (2010) *Conversation Analysis and Second Language Pedagogy.* New York: Routledge.

Youn, S.J. (2015) Validity argument for assessing L2 pragmatics in interaction using mixed methods. *Language Testing* 32 (2), 199–225.

Young, R.F. (2008) *Language and Interaction: An Advanced Resource Book.* London and New York: Routledge.

Young, R.F. and Miller, E.R. (2004) Learning as changing participation: Discourse roles in ESL writing conferences. *The Modern Language Journal* 88 (4), 519–535.

Part 4

Using New Technologies to Assess Speaking

11 Design and Implementation of a Classroom-based Virtual Reality Assessment

Jayoung Song and Wei-Li Hsu

1 Introduction

Computer technology has increasingly been used in all aspects of language testing, including test design and development, test administration, scoring and analysis. While assessing oral language proficiency via computer or other forms of multimedia technology has become a popular trend in the field of language testing, it has some limitations, including eliciting different language functions and skills compared to face-to-face (F2F) tests. Although it would be ideal to administer F2F speaking tests to all language learners, using F2F tests has been limited by the difficulty of getting test-takers and examiners in the same physical location and the coordination of arranging a large number of assessments. New technologies such as virtual reality (VR) might help decrease some of these challenges, making it more feasible to administer testing at a convenient time and place while eliciting relatively natural data by providing sufficient social and situational information through the immersive nature of VR technology.

The current study proposes a classroom-based VR oral assessment, which could be used for placement or formative tests. The chapter first discusses design-related issues that were taken into consideration when creating the VR oral assessment. Then, it presents a small-scale pilot study, including students' performances and perceptions of the VR test that we developed.

2 Literature Review

2.1 Second/foreign language assessment using computer-mediated technology

Given that it takes a vast amount of money and time to facilitate one-on-one F2F interviews or roleplays, language practitioners have become interested in alternative forms of speaking assessments that incorporate technology, including computerized oral proficiency instruments (COPI) or semi-direct oral proficiency instruments (SOPI). Although previous studies found that COPI or SOPI could be comparable to F2F in terms of test-takers' performance (Clark & Hooshmand, 1992; Kenyon & Malabonga, 2001), these computer-based tests of speaking generally elicit monologic speech and so do not provide direct evidence of communicative competence.

With the increasingly widespread use of video-mediated communication tools such as Skype or virtual environments, videoconferencing technology has been used to assess L2 oral ability (Davis *et al.*, 2017; Ockey *et al.*, 2017). These tools have the potential to combine the convenience and consistency related to computer-based assessments with the ability to elicit samples of interactive language. Studies have investigated the possibility of using technology to deliver International English Language Testing System (IELTS) (Nakatsuhara *et al.*, 2017), classroom-based oral interviews via videoconferencing (Kim & Craig, 2012), or group discussions in a virtual environment (Ockey *et al.*, 2017). Kim and Craig (2012) reported the comparability of videoconferencing and F2F interviews in terms of comfort and accessibility as well as test-takers' speaking scores. Similarly, in the study of Ockey and colleagues (2017), the results showed the feasibility of virtual environments in terms of eliciting evidence of interactive aspects of oral performance. Test-takers also reported a feeling of engagement and social presence in the virtual environments where test-takers were represented as avatars to participate in group discussions.

Some questions remain regarding the reliability and usefulness of video-mediated communication for assessment purposes (Davis *et al.*, 2017). One is whether video communication technology is stable enough to support interaction between speakers. In Ockey *et al.*'s (2017) study, one-third of the students reported problems hearing the other test-takers in the virtual environment oral assessment. The study reported that these technological glitches lasted for a few seconds, after which the connection returned to normal. Recent research also suggested that video-mediated technology might not be stable for assessment purposes. For example, Davis *et al.* (2017) reported problems in all of the 25 sessions that they conducted in China, in which 22 sessions dropped the video and five sessions dropped the call. Disruption in the audio or video can obviously lead to communication interference, thus making it hard for raters to make accurate judgments on test-takers' actual L2 oral ability. That is, long pauses or silence might be due to technical glitches rather than the test-takers' inability to carry out the conversation.

The other concern is associated with the visual input for supporting speech production. Previous studies have found that the visual input provided by single-camera video or two-dimensional video is inadequate to support the full range of features found in communication (Groen *et al.*,

2012). Limited visual input could impact test-takers in a variety of ways. For instance, communication could be hampered by an inability to see other test-takers' body language in the case of virtual environments where participants are represented as avatars (Davis *et al.*, 2017). More recent technology such as virtual reality could complement the shortcomings of current computer-based assessments while at the same time eliciting nuanced language with the visual depth that three-dimensional videos could provide.

2.2 Possibilities of virtual reality for assessing L2 oral ability

Several characteristics of VR render it well suited to the development of L2 speaking assessment. First, its immersive environment provides test-takers with a wide array of contextualization cues that are necessary for choosing appropriate speech acts and styles. In contrast, in traditional discourse completion tasks (DCT), SOPI or COPI, which may be written or oral, each task requires the test-taker to either write or orally produce what they would say in the situation described in a prompt. As such, they must figure out what speech acts are appropriate based on the prompt's stated contextual factors, which will include the relative power of the interlocutors, the degree of social distance between them and the degree of imposition implied by their interaction (Brown & Levinson, 1987). Nevertheless, it seems reasonable to expect that such written descriptions of conversational contexts will not display a fully rounded picture of them, and thus may be unable to best elicit the test-taker's speech acts production. Moreover, some researchers have expressed a concern that advanced learners are at an advantage over less-advanced learners due to their superior ability to read and comprehend prompts (Moon & Ahn, 2005). VR technology, on the other hand, has the potential to address these issues by providing an environment with overall levels of realism sufficient to support situated experiences (Hanson & Shelton, 2008). For instance, in an oral assessment designed to measure a person's ability to make a complaint, the subject could watch a 360-degree video set in a restaurant where the wrong menu item is served. Test-takers watching the video might feel that they are in the restaurant and be able to take advantage of the portrayed contextualization cues such as the various foods that people at nearby tables order, how they order it, the behavior of the servers, and so forth. The visual depth that VR videos provide in situations like this could elicit more nuanced speech acts compared to those that traditional DCTs or computer-mediated assessments could offer.

Second, VR can create a sense of perceived presence (a sense of presence defined as 'being there' in a virtual environment; Slater, 2003), which results in evoking desired reactions to the situation (Poeschl & Doering, 2014). That is, perceived presence in the VR is expected to help create an atmosphere in which test-takers might feel that they are engaged in a conversation with their interlocutor(s), as opposed to regular video-recorded or audio-recorded interaction.

A final advantage of VR testing is its practicality, which is likely to be enhanced further through advances in computer technologies that make it more accessible to a broader population at a lower cost. The primary monetary investment in VR-based language testing would be in its initial filming, editing and implementation. Once it has been built, it can be used an unlimited number of times without arranging for either human interlocutors or test centers. Affordable VR equipment and technology, including 360-degree cameras and phone-enabled headsets, enable educators to create their own VR learning and assessment materials.

2.3 Theoretical framework of VR-mediated L2 oral assessment

Responding to the call of communicative language pedagogy (Canale & Swain, 1980), language testers propose that tests should reflect language use in target contexts (Bachman, 1990; Bachman & Palmer, 1996). In line with this, speaking as the most basic way of communication should consider oral exchanges in specific contexts. Therefore, this section discusses VR-mediated L2 oral assessment within a pragmatics theory (Leech, 1983) and the speech act theory (Brown & Levinson, 1987; Fraser, 1990). Although we are aware that oral exchanges between two persons are co-constructed, the feature of co-construction between two human beings via VR was not readily available when the study was conducted in 2018. Accordingly, in the study, we define oral ability that is assessed as the ability to orally produce discourse to respond to discrete items presented visually and aurally (adapted from Fulcher, 2003; Luoma, 2004).

Pragmatics is chosen to represent some constructs of oral ability because pragmatics emphasizes language use in a social context and the effect of the language use on other interlocutors (Crystal, 1997; Levinson, 1983; Mey, 2001). Leech (1983) categorized pragmatics into two sub-areas: pragmalinguistics and sociopragmatics. Pragmalinguistics focuses on how well speakers utilize linguistic tools, such as phonological and grammatical skills, to produce speech (Roever, 2013). On the other hand, sociopragmatics is concerned with knowledge of social norms in a given context, and the knowledge is situation dependent (Roever, 2013; Thomas, 1983; Youn, 2015).

Speech act theory (Brown & Levinson, 1987) is selected for its ability to systematically familiarize language learners with linguistic forms that are regarded as culturally appropriate when communicating with the target community (Cohen, 2008; Ishihara & Cohen, 2010). Levinson (2017) summarizes four approaches to categorizing speech acts. One of the four approaches is to identify the functions of communicative utterances; some common functions are thanking, complimenting, requesting, refusing, apologizing and complaining. Competent L2 speakers can interpret and respond with the intended meaning of linguistic forms within a given situation. For example, when being invited to a dinner party, test-takers are required to appropriately perform the target speech acts, which could be thanking or apologizing. Based on speech act theory, Hudson *et al.* (1995) develop multiple measurements, and a measure is open-ended DCT. The DCT tasks aim at three speech acts: request, refusal and apology. Various situations are developed, representing different degrees of three parameters: relative power, degree of imposition and social distance.

The current study adopts VR-mediated oral assessment for increasing learners' access to common speech acts in the target languages. Therefore, L2 oral ability is evaluated through common speech acts in social situations. The elicited responses will be cataloged into pragmalinguistic and sociopragmatic areas, which will be discussed further in the next section.

3 The Current Study

The current study attempts to investigate the use of VR for a classroom-based L2 speaking assessment. Due to the study's exploratory nature, the study was limited to the humble goal of collecting initial evidence of the feasibility and usability of VR technology to assess L2 speaking ability. Specifically, the study addressed three questions:

(1) Does the VR test elicit comparable scores to the F2F test?
(2) What language functions does the VR test elicit compared to the F2F test?
(3) What are the Korean as a foreign language students' perceptions of the VR test compared to the F2F test?

3.1 Design of the VR oral assessment: Students at a campus café

The development and design of the VR oral assessment followed the five stages recommended by Jianda (2007) and Birjandi and Rezaei (2010). First, the researchers identified and classified situations that would be most relevant to the test-takers. Based on an analysis of their textbooks, classroom materials and target-language conversations, it was concluded that the speech acts that most commonly arose for first-year Korean classes were greetings, invitations, acceptances or refusals, and apologies. This analysis led to an on-campus café for the VR video filming and an invitation to a movie or dinner for the conversational prompt. Second, the researchers took account of how contextual variables, including relative power, degree of imposition and social distance, would be reflected in the test. It was concluded that an interlocutor of roughly the same age as the participants, coupled with the conversational context that starts with a casual greeting in a campus café, would give test-takers sufficient evidence about social distance and relative power to enable them to choose a contextually appropriate speech style. Thus, a native speaker of Korean, of approximately the same age as the participating test-takers, portrayed the interlocutor in the recorded VR video. Third, the researchers piloted the proposed scenarios with two participants in order to validate the scenarios used to elicit test-takers' speech act production and gauge the time required for immersion in the VR environment to serve effectively as a prompt. Lastly, based on analysis of the pilot study data, the time requirements for each prompt were adjusted, after which it was piloted again with a non-overlapping group of two learners, upon whom it was found to have good construct validity, i.e. that 'the test scores reflect the area(s) of language ability we want to measure', and authenticity, 'the degree of correspondence of the characteristics of a given language test task to the features of a target language use task' (Bachman & Palmer, 1996: 21, 23).

3.2 VR equipment

Due to their relatively low cost, user-friendliness and high-quality output, *Samsung Gear 360* and *Insta 360* cameras were used for all filming. Both proved easy to carry and use but had different strengths. *Samsung Gear 360* recordings can be managed and viewed on Samsung phones, making it easy to check recorded files on the spot without exporting them to a computer first. *Insta 360*, on the other hand, has an internal stabilizer that enables the shooting of cleaner, less shaky videos with less effort. From among the various commercially available types of VR goggles that the participating test-takers might have used, the researchers selected HTC VIVE as being a cost-effective means of providing a truly immersive learning experience.

3.3 Task design

Two common tasks aimed at eliciting ratable oral performance are DCTs and roleplays, each of which has its pros and cons. An advantage of a DCT is practicality, insofar as it enables the elicitation of many ratable responses in a short time. One shortcoming of DCT items, identified by Hudson and his colleagues (1995), is that the responses they elicit tend to be shorter than those observed in ethnographic studies. Roleplays, in turn, can simulate plausible situations in which target-language use occurs while allowing testers to control contextual variables within a predefined framework (Kasper & Youn, 2018).

To overcome DCTs' shortcoming of eliciting shorter responses while maintaining their communicative nature, the researchers designed two roleplay-like DCT tasks, based on the study of Hudson and colleagues (1995). Each of the 'roleplays' is divided into multiple oral DCT items. We first selected two common social situations for the two roleplays, which represented certain degrees of power, imposition and social distance.

These two tasks are: to accept a friend's invitation to (1) a movie or (2) dinner, resembling a more equal relationship with lower imposition and shorter social distance, different from the teacher-student relationship common in F2F roleplays. The target speech acts of the two tasks are greetings (receptive and productive), invitations (receptive), suggestions (productive) and closing (receptive and productive). Based on roleplay responses with corresponding purposes, each VR oral-task video was divided into the following five phases: greetings (by both the VR inter-locutor and the learner); small-talk about typical weekend activities (again by both parties); an invitation to a movie on Friday (by the VR interlocu-tor); the suggestion of a different time and meeting location (by the learner); and closing (by both parties). The greeting and closing phases each contain one DCT item, while the small-talk phase comprises three, and the invitation and suggestion phases comprise two each.

To elicit more elaborate responses, contextual information regarding the schedule conflict is provided in the task's prompt, written in English, while other information relevant to subsequent DCT items is elicited by previous items. Each DCT item allows the learner 30 seconds to respond (a time the researchers determined to be sufficient via roleplay). To increase the authenticity of any resulting gaps, learners are able to see and hear the VR interlocutor's verbal and nonverbal behavior indicating active listenership (i.e. engaging with prior speakers' talk through receipts, assessments, etc.; Brouwer & Wagner, 2007). Although each task contains multiple oral DCT items, it was recorded continuously.

3.4 Rubric development and scoring

In order to assess both pragmalinguistic and sociopragmatic variables, a rubric was developed based on Ockey's (2009) and Youn's (2015) studies. The rubric consisted of four categories: delivery, language use, sensitivity to situation and engaging with interaction, with the first two correspond-ing to pragmalinguistic areas and the last two to sociopragmatic areas. Delivery was assessed in terms of appropriate speaking speed, pauses and comprehensible pronunciation. A range of linguistic resources and prag-matic strategies (i.e. pragmalinguistics; Leech, 1983) is crucial in conveying meanings appropriately, which is what the language use category was intended to measure. In addition to appropriate language use, one's social perceptions and sensitivity towards situations (i.e. sociopragmatics; Leech, 1983; Thomas, 1983) also constitute pragmatic competence. For example, when declining an invitation, acknowledging decline as a dispreferred action shows one's sociopragmatic competence. Dispreferred or negative actions invoke interactionally appropriate pauses between turns and hesi-tation such as 'well' or 'uh', often followed by account for decline (such as schedule conflicts), rather than a direct 'no' to the situation without any explanation. Therefore, the sensitivity to situation category measured one's consistent evidence of awareness of and sensitivity to situation. Lastly, engaging with interaction measured the degree of test-takers' engagement during the task. Features such as acknowledgment tokens and nonverbal features (e.g. gestures or embodied displays) were assessed. Based on this, an analytic rubric was developed, and it provided ratings on a 3-point scale for each of the four subscales.

4 Main Pilot Study

4.1 Participants

The participants were 24 university students enrolled in the second semester of first year Korean at a private university in the United States. The first researcher, who was also the course instructor, utilized the VR technology throughout the semester in line with the main objective of the class. Half of the students had experienced VR outside the Korean classroom for entertainment purposes, and the others had no such out-of-class experience.

4.2 Data collection

The 24 students were randomly assigned to two groups based on their scores in the previous oral exam. The two groups did not differ in terms of their Korean speaking ability ($t = 0.15$). The first group took the VR test first followed by the F2F test. The other group took the F2F test first followed by the VR test. The topic of the test tasks was counterbalanced: the first group took Topic 1 (invitation to a movie) first while the other group took Topic 2 (invitation to a dinner) first. The research design is shown in Table 11.1.

For the VR test, the researchers administered individual VR tests to all 24 students during class time. At the beginning of each session, a proctor set up a computer connected to the HTC VIVE goggles. The proctor then introduced herself to the students and briefly explained the VR assessment's setting, tasks and steps. Then, a brief written prompt was presented to the students and the assessment started one minute later. An example prompt was: 'Your friend will invite you to go shopping with her to buy a present. Please respond to your friend's invitation based on the following schedule. You are available on Saturday night, but unavailable on Friday night.' After the students had read the prompt, the proctor helped them wear the VR goggles, after which the task started immediately (Figure 11.1a).

Table 11.1 Research design

	First test	Second test
Group 1 ($n = 12$)	VR (Task 1)	F2F (Task 2)
Group 2 ($n = 12$)	F2F (Task 1)	VR (Task 2)

Figure 11.1 (a) VR and (b) F2F tests

Each test-taker's performance was video-recorded in a way that also captured the VR video they were watching.

The F2F test format was the same as that of the VR test, with the difference being the location where the actual conversation took place. Students were invited to the researcher's office and were provided with the same written prompt. The researcher acted as the interlocutor of a conversation similar to the one in the VR test (Figure 11.1b).

After all test-takers had finished the VR and F2F assessments, they were given an online perception questionnaire that was developed by the present researchers based on prior work by Ockey *et al.*, (2017). It consisted of 11 items, of which 10 were answered via the same 6-point Likert scale, with 6 = 'strongly agree', 5 = 'agree', 4 = 'slightly agree', 3 = 'slightly disagree', 2 = 'disagree' and 1 = 'strongly disagree'. These 10 items were followed by an open-ended question about the advantages and challenges of the VR test. The questionnaire items were divided into four dimensions based on previous studies: efficacy (how well they think they did in the test); anxiety (how nervous they were in the test); easiness (how easy it was to take the test); interaction category (how easy it was to manage interaction); and enjoyment (how much they enjoyed taking the test). After completing the survey, four test-takers selected at random were invited to an individual interview to provide detailed feedback on their VR assessment experiences. Individual interviews were audio-recorded and then transcribed.

4.3 Data analysis

To address the first research question, about whether the VR assessment elicited comparable scores to F2F assessment, all the recorded VR and F2F assessments were scored by two raters. The two raters had graduate degrees in Korean language education and experience in rating similar oral tests. The researcher provided training to the raters with three purposes: (a) familiarizing the raters with the assessment tasks, testing modes and rating criteria descriptions; (b) establishing a shared understanding of differentiating test-takers' oral communication abilities according to the rating criteria descriptions; and (c) practicing scoring and discussing cases. After training, the raters graded independently. The interrater reliability was 0.90, which shows high reliability. Students' scores on the VR and F2F test were analyzed using MANOVA.

In order to answer the second question, which is whether the VR test appropriately elicits the language functions targeted for the test tasks, all 24 recordings were analyzed using a language-function checklist for evaluating a synchronized computer-assisted speaking test (Nakatsuhara *et al.*, 2017, which is modified from O'Sullivan *et al.*, 2002 and Brooks, 2003). The checklist includes 25 language functions under three major functional categories (i.e. informational, interactional and managing interaction). The first researcher and a trained assistant familiar with the checklist coded the elicited language functions independently and completed the checklist. They discussed the checklist and came to an agreement on the scoring. Following the approach of Nakatsuhara *et al.* (2017), the coding was conducted to determine whether each function was elicited in each part of the test, rather than how many instances of each function were observed. The number of people who used each language function in both testing modes was compared using McNemar's chi-square tests.

To answer the last question, i.e. students' perceptions towards the VR testing mode compared to the F2F mode, the perception questionnaire was analyzed using MANOVA. Test-takers' open-ended comments and interviews were also coded and thematically analyzed.

5 Results and Discussion

5.1 Research question 1

Descriptive statistics indicated slightly lower scores under the VR testing condition. However, repeated-measure MANOVA showed no main effect for mode (F (1,46) = 2.3, p = 0.13, partial η^2 = 0.02), indicating that the mean differences between VR and F2F tests were not statistically different. Table 11.2 shows descriptive statistics of students' scores in the VR and F2F assessment.

Table 11.2 Descriptive statistics of students' scores

Rating category	Mode	Mean	SD
Delivery	VR	2.22	0.66
	F2F	2.22	0.72
Language use	VR	1.93	0.56
	F2F	2.14	0.71
Sensitivity to situation	VR	2.18	0.76
	F2F	2.47	0.71
Engaging with conversation	VR	2.10	0.69
	F2F	2.35	0.56

Note: The possible score range was from 1 to 3.

Overall, the results of students' oral scores showed that the VR assessment generated similar scores compared to the F2F assessment, suggesting the VR as a potential tool for classroom-based assessment. This result is consistent with previous research, which examined comparability between F2F tests and videoconferencing tests (Craig & Kim, 2010, 2012; Nakatsuhara *et al.*, 2017). It is interesting that in the available literature, and in this study, a consistent trend was observed for the computer-mediated speaking test mean scores to be slightly lower, although that difference was not statistically significant. It might be possible that the VR testing mode was more challenging than the F2F mode, due to the lack of affordances embedded in the VR mode such as co-construction of meaning and backchanneling from the interlocutor. This might have affected students' performance in terms of engaging with conversation.

What is encouraging is that test-takers were able to complete the VR assessment without encountering major technology issues. There were two instances out of 24 sessions in which the VR videos were not set up appropriately and test-takers did not see anything through their goggles. The test-takers reported this after putting on the goggles and the issue was resolved quickly. It needs to be highlighted here that the results of both the statistical analyses are only indicative, given the exploratory nature of this study with a small sample size.

5.2 Research question 2

Of the 25 language functions examined for a computer-assisted speaking test (Nakatsuhara *et al.*, 2017; see Appendix 11.1 for a complete list of the language functions), the majority of functions were elicited in the VR assessment, including advanced language functions such as *interactional* and *managing interaction*. There were, however, two language functions that test-takers used significantly less in the VR, as shown in Table 11.3. These were *asking for information* and *negotiation of meaning*.

Only one-fourth of the students showed *asking for information*. It seemed that since the VR assessment was pre-recorded, and students figured this out while engaging with the conversation, they instantly knew that the interlocutor would not respond to their questions and thus did not ask questions.

Table 11.3 Result of McNemar's chi-square tests

Function	Test mode	Count	Mean	SD	X^2 (df = 1)	Sig.
Asking for information	VR	4	0.16	0.40	4.0	0.04
	F2F	12	0.50	0.55		
Negotiation of meaning	VR	4	0.16	0.32	7.1	0.02
	F2F	19	0.79	0.34		

Another language function that was least elicited by the VR assessment was *negotiation of meaning*. Negotiation of meaning is achieved by checking one's own understanding, checking others' understanding, asking for clarification, etc. However, as the test-takers understood that the VR interlocutor would not answer their questions, students used this strategy significantly less than others in the language function category. Although the current VR test tasks elicited most of the language functions, they showed major weaknesses in eliciting language samples indicative of joint meaning construction due to the pre-recorded nature of the current assessment.

The results indicated the contextual validity of the VR test. Although the VR assessment successfully elicited most language functions, the recorded nature of the assessment might have facilitated the test-takers' use of some of the language functions less, especially *asking for information* and *negotiating meaning*. Given that these language functions are critical in jointly constructed conversation, the current VR assessment shows a limitation observed in oral DCT.

5.3 Research question 3

There were 12 items in the questionnaire, two or three items in each of the five categories. Internal consistency was measured for each category and all showed high internal consistency (i.e. efficacy $\alpha = 0.87$, anxiety $\alpha = 0.83$, easiness $\alpha = 0.80$, interaction management $\alpha = 0.80$, enjoyment $\alpha = 0.87$). Table 11.4 shows descriptive statistics of students' perceptions in the VR and F2F assessment.

Descriptive statistics indicated lower scores under the VR testing condition. MANOVA showed main effect for mode ($F (1,46) = 5.38, p = 0.025$, partial $\eta^2 = 0.105$), indicating that the students felt differently across the two modes. Using a Bonferroni correction that established the significance level at .01 to correct an inflated Type 1 error, we calculated t-test. Post hoc analysis showed a significant difference between the two modes in easiness of test-taking and interaction management.

The three categories that did not show significant difference were efficacy, anxiety and enjoyment. This result indicated that the students felt that they showed true ability in the VR mode, experiencing comfort and enjoyment. This is reflected in their responses to the open-ended questionnaire and interview.

The participants' key terms in describing the VR test were *enjoyment*, *engagement* and *a relaxed atmosphere*. The majority of the students commented that the environment was interesting and enjoyable, which was consistent with previous research on implementations of innovative technology for oral ability assessment (Ockey *et al.*, 2017). It seemed that the immersive aspect of VR technology contributed to feelings of engagement and social presence. As one student (ID 7) put it, 'The VR equipment was immersive. It felt a lot less awkward than I expected'. Another (ID 2) speci-fied that social presence was elicited by the immersive nature of the VR technology, commenting, 'The machine made it feel like I was actually talking to the person. It was like speaking to a Korean friend and having to think on my feet'. This finding is consistent with those of Rupp and col-leagues (2019) and Snelling (2016), who both reported that the immersive environments contributed to learners' engagement and social presence.

Some students reported that they felt they did well on the test because the VR had provided a more standardized setting than they were accus-tomed to. One of this group said, 'I think it is nice that VR is standardized and prefer this over pairing up for oral exams because not everyone in the class is at the same level or has conversational chemistry'.

However, there were some challenges with the VR test. The challenges included difficult-to-manage interactions and conversational unnatural-ness. In particular, the questionnaire data for *interaction* indicated that more than half of the test-takers had a hard time managing their time during the task. They either felt that there was too much silence or that their speech was interrupted by the next turn, leading to feelings that they could not say what they wanted. Although the system included a timer based on the pilot study's results to indicate how much time was left for each DCT item, many students still felt that it was too long or too short. This could have been due to a widespread but incorrect assumption, which also emerged from the open-ended question responses. The assumption was that they would be penalized for not fully utilizing the time indicated on the timer. If the students had known that their scores were not affected by how much time they spent talking, as long as their speech acts were appropriate, their views of the experience would undoubtedly have been different. As ID 1 explained, 'I found the virtual reality exam rather dif-ficult to work with because the set time was restricting'. Many also found it difficult to engage in conversation with the pre-recorded VR videos. As ID 2 noted, 'I prefer face-to-face because it's more dynamic and the speak-ers can interact in response to current situations'. ID 3 said, 'The VR was a bit harder since you can't tell what the person is going to ask and how/when you should respond'.

In sum, the test-takers generally showed positive attitudes towards the VR assessment in terms of providing a relaxing and enjoyable atmosphere. On the whole, however, the results indicated that the students generally preferred F2F testing, which is congruent with previous studies that com-pared F2F with other computer-mediated testing modes (Kenyon & Malabonga, 2001; Qian, 2009). This could be attributed to the students' lack of experience with the new testing mode. All participants indicated that they had taken interview-type proficiency tests in the past; however, none of the students had previously taken a test in VR. As such, it is pos-sible that they favored the F2F mode because it allowed them to more easily predict what the test would entail and thus maximize their performance. That is, the novelty of the VR environment seems to have led test-takers to question its reliability. Another reason could be found in the aforementioned limitation of the current VR test, i.e. not allowing for co-construction that students usually do in interaction.

5 Conclusion

The preliminary analysis shows some strengths of the VR test, especially regarding delivery. The other three categories showed slightly lower means in the VR test although the difference was not statistically significant. Consistent with the results from the study examining the language functions, including speech acts, of a computer-mediated speaking assessment (Nakatsuhara *et al.*, 2017), our VR assessment was able to elicit most of the examined functions, indicating its potential for scaffolding speech acts via VR videos. Regarding the affective factors of VR assessment, the analysis also suggests that the potential of VR assessment for more and easier access for practicing and self-assessing oral ability outside of class.

We note that the current study presents only an initial assessment of the VR testing. A major limitation is that the study did not analyze actual language data elicited by the two modes. Without looking at the language data, it would be difficult to conclude that the VR test could yield comparable performances to the F2F test. The other limitation is that the test was administered to students at only one proficiency level. Students who are at advanced level might show different results in terms of speaking performance and perceptions. Future studies should examine students with varying levels of language proficiency.

Table 11.4 Students' perceptions towards the VR and F2F test

Category	Mode	Mean	SD	$t(df = 46)$	Sig.
Efficacy	VR	3.13	1.02	−3.28	0.02
	F2F	4.00	0.78		
Anxiety	VR	4.45	1.25	−3.98	0.69
	F2F	4.60	1.29		
Easiness	VR	3.40	1.06	−5.01*	0.00
	F2F	4.70	0.70		
Interaction	VR	3.70	0.90	−5.43*	0.00
	F2F	4.97	0.72		
Enjoyment	VR	4.35	1.07	−1.79	0.08
	F2F	4.83	0.76		

Note: The possible score range was from 1 to 6. *$p < .05$ (Bonferroni adjustments).

This study provides practical guidelines for future VR assessments. Given that adapting oneself to a VR environment is likely to consume more cognitive resources than F2F communication, it is seen as desirable for future VR assessment to visually present task prompts in the VR videos and make them easier to be retrieved, which may reduce students' cognitive load. Additionally, to overcome the awkward silence between each DCT item, each DCT item could be divided into shorter clips, after which the multiple clips comprising a given task could be compiled and ordered into a 'playlist'. This would enable learners to skip to the next DCT item as soon as they finish their responses. Advanced technology could bring the possibility of an AI avatar that can actually respond to the test-takers in real time.

At its current stage of development, it is recommended that this type of VR test is used for placement or formative evaluation. The VR test could supplement F2F roleplays, especially when quicker and easier assessment of students' speaking ability is needed, such as placement test or formative test for remote teaching or large language classes. The VR test also provides a less stressful environment for students than the F2F test; it could be used as a formative test in which students could practice repeatedly to familiarize themselves with speech acts in common social situations.

While technology is advancing and language classes are being delivered online due to the current pandemic, more synchronized interaction using VR technologies is becoming available, such as Microsoft Teams and Hololens, Moot with Zoom, and Spatial. However, purchasing the apps and equipment is still expensive, and building a virtual context in these apps requires more technical skills than our study, which may be a major challenge for many language instructors and programs. Additionally, although synchronized computer-mediated communication is ideal, it also requires a stable internet connection, especially in the circumstances of high-stakes tests. The present VR test allows students to download the videos in advance and record their responses without worrying about delayed responses while taking the test. Furthermore, compared with synchronized VR apps, the equipment required to take our VR assessment is becoming cheaper. The VR videos can be played on a smartphone with affordable VR goggles. In another advantage of our VR assessment over synchronized apps, a computer-mediated oral assessment offers relatively easy means to provide corrective feedback, such as pointing out which DCT item in the task could use which linguistic form, along with the grading rubric. For these reasons, we hope that the current VR test could provide some insights for feasible and useful VR assessment for current and future classroom-based evaluations.

Appendix 11.1: Language Function Analysis

Category	Description
Informational	Providing personal information
	Expressing opinions
	Elaborating on or modifying an opinion
	Justifying an opinion
	Comparing
	Speculating
	Describing a sequence of events, things, people
	Summarizing
	Suggesting
Interactional	Agreeing
	Disagreeing
	Modifying or commenting on the other speaker's utterance
	Asking for opinions
	Persuading
	Asking for information
	Self-initiated repair
	Checking own understanding
	Indicating understanding of point made by the other speaker
	Establishing common ground/purpose
	Asking for clarification
	Responding to requests for clarification
Managing conversation	Initiating any interaction
	Changing the topic
	Sharing the responsibility for developing the interaction
	Coming to a decision

References

Bachman, L.F. (1990) *Fundamental Considerations in Language Testing.* Oxford: Oxford University Press.

Bachman, L.F. and Palmer, A.S. (1996) *Language Testing in Practice: Designing and Developing Useful Language Tests, Vol. 1.* Oxford: Oxford University Press.

Birjandi, P. and Rezaei, S. (2010) Developing a multiple-choice discourse completion test of interlanguage pragmatics for Iranian EFL learners. *ILI Language Teaching Journal (Special Issue: Proceedings of the First Conference on ELT in the Islamic World)* 6 (1–2), 43–58.

Brooks, L. (2003) Converting an observation checklist for use with the IELTS Speaking Test. *Cambridge ESOL Research Notes* 11, 20–21.

Brouwer, C.E. and Wagner, J. (2007) Developmental issues in second language conversation. *Journal of Applied Linguistics and Professional Practice* 1 (1), 29–47.

Brown, P. and Levinson, S.D. (1987) *Politeness: Some Universals in Language Usage.* Cambridge: Cambridge University Press.

Canale, M. and Swain, M. (1980) Theoretical bases of communicative approaches to second language teaching and testing. *Applied Linguistics* 1, 1–47.

Clark, J.L. and Hooshmand, D. (1992) 'Screen-to-screen' testing: An exploratory study of oral proficiency interviewing using video teleconferencing. *System* 20 (3), 293–304.

Cohen, A.D. (2008) Teaching and assessing L2 pragmatics: What can we expect from learners? *Language Teaching* 41 (2), 213–235.

Craig, D.A. and Kim, J. (2010) Anxiety and performance in video-conferenced and face-to-face oral interviews. *Multimedia-Assisted Language Learning* 13, 9–32.

Craig, D.A. and Kim, J. (2012) Performance and anxiety in video-conferencing. In F. Zhang (ed.) *Computer-enhanced and Mobile-assisted Language Learning: Emerging Issues and Trends* (pp. 137–157). Hershey, PA: IGI Global.

Crystal, D. (1997) *A Dictionary of Linguistics and Phonetics.* Oxford: Basil Blackwell.

Davis, L., Timpe-Laughlin, V., Gu, L. and Ockey, G.J. (2017) Face-to-face speaking assessment in the digital age: Interactive speaking tasks online. In J.M. Davis, J.M. Norris, M.E. Malone, T.H. McKay and Y.A. Son (eds) *Useful Assessment and Evaluation in Language Education* (pp. 115–130). Washington, DC: Georgetown University Press.

Fraser, B. (1990) Perspectives on politeness. *Journal of Pragmatics* 14, 219–236.

Fulcher, G. (2003) *Testing Second Language Speaking.* London: Longman/Pearson Education.

Groen, M., Ursu, M., Michalakopoulos, S., Falelakis, M. and Gasparis, E. (2012) Improving video-mediated communication with orchestration. *Computers in Human Behavior* 28 (5), 1575–1579.

Hanson, K. and Shelton, B.E. (2008) Design and development of virtual reality: Analysis of challenges faced by educators. *Journal of Educational Technology & Society* 11 (1), 118–131.

Hudson, T., Detmer, E. and Brown, J.D. (1995) *Developing Prototypic Measures of Cross-cultural Pragmatics.* Technical Report No. 7. Honolulu, HI: University of Hawaii, Second Language Teaching and Curriculum Center.

Ishihara, N. and Cohen, A.D. (2010) *Teaching and Learning Pragmatics: Where Language and Culture Meet.* Harlow: Pearson Longman.

Jianda, L. (2007) Developing a pragmatics test for Chinese EFL learners. *Language Testing* 24 (3), 391–415.

Kasper, G. and Youn, S.J. (2018) Transforming instruction to activity: Roleplay in language assessment. *Applied Linguistics Review* 9 (4), 589–616.

Kenyon, D.M. and Malabonga, V. (2001) Comparing examinee attitudes toward computer-assisted and other oral proficiency assessments. *Language Learning & Technology* 5 (2), 60–83.

Kim, J. and Craig, D.A. (2012) Validation of a videoconferenced speaking test. *Computer Assisted Language Learning* 25 (3), 257–275.

Leech, G. (1983) *Principles of Pragmatics.* London: Longman.

Levinson, S.C. (1983) *Pragmatics.* Cambridge: Cambridge University Press.

Levinson, S.C. (2017) Speech acts. In Y. Huang (ed.) *The Oxford Handbook of Pragmatics* (pp. 199–216). Oxford: Oxford University Press.

Luoma, S. (2004) *Assessing Speaking.* Cambridge: Cambridge University Press.

Mey, J.L. (2001) *Pragmatics: An Introduction* (2nd edn). Oxford: Blackwell.

Moon, Y.I. and Ahn, H.J. (2005) Effects of DCT types in eliciting interlanguage pragmatics data from low-level learners. *English Teaching* 60 (4), 277–297.

Nakatsuhara, F., Inoue, C., Berry, V. and Galaczi, E. (2017) Exploring the use of video-conferencing technology in the assessment of spoken language: A mixed-methods study. *Language Assessment Quarterly* 14 (1), 1–18.

Ockey, G. (2009) Developments and challenges in the use of computer-based testing for assessing second language abilities. *The Modern Language Journal* 93 (Suppl. 1), 836–847

Ockey, G.J., Gu, L. and Keehner, M. (2017) Web-based virtual environments for facilitating assessment of L2 oral communication ability. *Language Assessment Quarterly* 14 (4), 346–359.

O'Sullivan, B., Weir, C.J. and Saville, N. (2002) Using observation checklists to validate speaking-test tasks. *Language Testing* 19 (1), 33–56.

Poeschl, S. and Doering, N. (2014) Effects of simulation fidelity on user experience in virtual fear of public speaking training – an experimental study. *Annual Review of Cyber Therapy and Telemedicine* 12, 66–70.

Qian, D.D. (2009) Comparing direct and semi-direct modes for speaking assessment: Affective effects on test takers. *Language Assessment Quarterly* 6 (2), 113–125.

Roever, C. (2013) Assessing pragmatics. In A.J. Kunnan (ed.) *The Companion to Language Assessment* (pp. 125–139). Oxford: John Wiley & Sons.

Rupp, M.A., Odette, K.L., Kozachuk, J., Michaelis, J.R., Smither, J.A. and McConnell, D.S. (2019) Investigating learning outcomes and subjective experiences in 360-degree videos. *Computers & Education* 128, 256–268.

Slater, M. (2003) A note on presence terminology. *Presence Connect* 3 (3), 1–5.

Snelling, J. (2016) *Virtual Reality in K-12 Education: How Helpful Is It?* See https://eon-reality.com/virtual-reality-k-12-education-helpful/.

Thomas, J. (1983) Cross-cultural pragmatic failure. *Applied Linguistics* 4, 91–112.

Youn, S.J. (2015) Validity argument for assessing L2 pragmatics in interaction using mixed methods. *Language Testing* 32 (2), 199–225.

12 Operationalising Interactional Competence in Computer-mediated Speaking Tests

Noriko Iwashita, Lyn May and Paul J. Moore

1 Introduction

An increasing number of studies investigating various aspects of interactional competence (IC) in both assessment and classroom contexts has led to a reconsideration of the construct of speaking proficiency in language assessment research (Plough, 2018). In particular, evidence from studies of speaking tests employing a face-to-face format supports the claim that IC is an essential component in the co-construction of dialogue (e.g. Plough *et al.*, 2018).

The incorporation of IC into the L2 speaking construct coincides with the increasing use of computer-mediated tests (CMTs; e.g. TOEFL iBT, Pearson PTE) which include speaking components. These tests reflect both advances in technology and the reality of communication in an age where spoken interactions through automated systems have become increasingly common. This phenomenon has been further accelerated during the global pandemic. Although some aspects of IC are elicited through the speaking tasks in these tests (e.g. responding), test-taker performances tend to be scored mainly in terms of fluency, accuracy and content, reflecting an arguably narrowly defined construct of speaking proficiency in the psycholinguistic tradition. The challenge of incorporating IC into task design is attributed to a lack of interactivity due to the current unidirectional nature of CMTs (Galaczi & Taylor, 2018; Plough *et al.*, 2018).

In this chapter we review the emergence of IC in L2 assessment in both rating scales of existing tests (face-to-face and CMT) and empirical studies, and explore two current approaches to CMT in terms of affordances for incorporating IC: (1) existing tests (e.g. Pearson) where candidates produce monologues in response to predetermined questions; and (2) the offering of existing face-to-face interviewer-led tests via videoconferencing (e.g. IELTS). We then report on three recent developments, including the use of virtual environments and speech technologies, and discuss their potential for eliciting and assessing aspects of IC. While attempts to incorporate IC in CMTs are promising (e.g. Davis *et al.*, 2018; Nakatsuhara *et al.*, 2017a, 2017b; Ockey *et al.*, 2017), issues of technological reliability and test-takers' accessibility to and familiarity with the devices have posed a challenge for wide implementation of face-to-face speaking assessment in a virtual environment. Furthermore, research has shown that technology provides a different context from a face-to-face environment, which has opened up a new avenue for assessing IC. The chapter presents a discussion on the assessment of IC, focusing on task design and implications for the L2 speaking construct. In particular, we will identify affordances and constraints for operationalising IC in CMTs. Despite the clear limitations of incorporating the assessment of IC in CMTs at present, with continuing technological advances and the ongoing efforts of language testing researchers we anticipate that it will become possible to elicit and assess IC in CMTs in the near future.

2 The Emergence of Interactional Competence as a Construct in L2 Assessment

The notion of IC originally evolved from linguistic anthropology to broaden the concept of communicative competence (Hymes, 1974). In the context of second language, Hymes' notion of communicative competence was articulated by Canale and Swain (1980), and then further elaborated incrementally to suit classroom contexts (e.g. Celce-Murcia, 2008; Celce-Murcia *et al.*, 1995) and assessment (Bachman, 1990). Kramsch (1986), who first introduced the term 'interactional competence' to the field of applied linguistics, was critical of the notion of proficiency used in foreign language education in the United States. She argued that current models lacked attention to communication skills and did not acknowledge the inherently co-constructed nature of interaction in which conversational participants' behaviours are contingent on their interlocutors; that is, whether people are able to interact effectively or not is subject to the effects of context and interlocutors (Ross, 2018; Young, 2011). It is now generally agreed that IC comprises knowledge about the language and context of communication and the ability to deploy this knowledge for communication (Hall & Pekarek Doehler, 2011; Young, 2008). IC is thus considered as both 'the competence necessary for effective interaction' and 'the competence that is available in the interaction between participants' (Mehan, 2013: 130).

Building on earlier work, Roever and Kasper (2018) further contribute to the conceptualisation of IC, referring to generic properties of interaction such as turn-taking to perform actions, opening and closing interaction, and conversational repair, and suggest how participants adapt various devices of conversation according to specific interactional contexts that involve interlocutors. Whether participants are able to employ appropriate turn-taking and to open/close interaction depends on their interlocutors' interactional behaviours, thus reflecting the inherently co-constructed nature of interaction.

The contingency of IC on the interactional behaviours of co-participants has also been articulated by Young (2011), who presents strong and weak views of IC. While the weak view of IC considers an individual's interactional ability to be contingent on the interactional behaviour of the co-participants, referred to as the co-constructed nature of IC, a more radical and stronger view disregards individual contributions to the interaction. As interest grows, the notion of IC has been revisited. Hall (2018) recently pointed out that, in conceptualising the notion of IC, drawing from work in two different fields (i.e. linguistic anthropology and conversation analysis) had resulted in some confusion about the fundamental notion of IC, and then called for competence to be replaced by repertoire, as the term 'interactional repertoire' moves away from the more static, linear and traditional concept of 'competence'.

The growing interest in IC has been reflected in the field of L2 assessment, leading to IC receiving increased attention as paired and group tasks were implemented widely in both classroom and assessment contexts. Traditionally, test tasks were developed focusing on individual ability guided by psychometrics, but with the increasing use of pair- and group-based tasks an interactional view of assessment has been employed in task design, drawing upon non-cognitive perspectives. The shift from an individualistic view of assessment to a view incorporating co-construction is conceptualised in terms of moving from a psycholinguistic (psychological) to a sociolinguistic view of assessment that recognises its fundamentally social nature (Roever & Kasper, 2018). This movement has been termed the 'social turn' in second language assessment (McNamara, 1997).

As noted by Roever and Kasper (2018), perspectives on the speaking construct impact on task design, administration, scoring and inferences made about test-takers' ability from the score. Assessment tasks based on sociolinguistic perspectives elicit purposeful interactive language use to provide evidence about test-takers' ability to tailor their talk to their interlocutor and context for communication. It is important to note, however, that this type of assessment is not free from limitations. For instance, standardisation is often difficult and interlocutors' interactional behaviour contributes to test-takers' interactional behaviour; therefore it is difficult to identify each participant's individual contribution to the interaction (Brown & Hill, 1998). In light of the fundamentally co-constructed nature of interaction, some scholars recommend that a shared score be awarded for interactional aspects of performance (May, 2009), but shared scores may result in unfairness (Nakatsuhara, 2013). There is also the necessity in high-stakes tests to have an individual score for a candidate, which limits the extent to which IC can be operationalised in rating scales.

In contrast, in psycholinguistic assessment, the language elicited is not usually embedded in interaction, as social interaction is not considered a part of the assessment criteria. Within this perspective, the speaking construct is described in terms of efficiency of processing and automaticity (van Moere, 2012). Van Moere (2012) points out that the language assessment literature pays little attention to the notion of automaticity (referred to as 'near effortless processing of language', van Moere, 2012: 326) as a characteristic of a competent L2 speaker, and argues that in order to assess well-defined psycholinguistic constructs, tasks should require evidence of a test-taker's capacity to handle language (morphology, syntax and lexis) that would be processed in real-life domains. From this perspective, interactional strategies (such as turn-taking, organising ideas) are considered as social skills, and if these were incorporated into speaking assessment, the test conditions would become less standardised and thus measurement would be less reliable. Furthermore, incorporation of these strategies may result in considering other factors such as personality (referred to as a 'construct irrelevant trait', van Moere, 2012). Similarly, scholars such as Kormos (2006) and Dörnyei and Kormos (1998), drawing on the speech processing production model (de Bot, 1992; Levelt, 1989), argue that communicative success largely depends on an individual speaker's ability to employ linguistic resources. In the next section, we explore how the conceptual development of IC in language assessment discussed above is employed in the rating scales of existing large-scale speaking assessments.

2.1 Interactional competence in the rating scales of face-to-face speaking tests

The criteria used in many major tests of speaking are based on what Roever and Kasper (2018) call a primarily psycholinguistic-individualist perspective on language competence, as shown in the description referring to IC in the four major tests summarised in Appendix 12.2. In addition to a focus on complexity, accuracy, fluency and pronunciation, some tests attempt to incorporate IC, by explicitly (and, in some cases, implicitly) assessing interactive aspects of task fulfilment, turn-taking (including initiation and elaboration of turns), repair and topic negotiation (Cambridge English: First, Cambridge English, 2011; Examination for the Certificate of Competency in English, Michigan Assessment, 2020; Trinity College London, 2015). In contrast, despite the introduction of the interlocutor frame, or script (see O'Sullivan & Lu, 2006), the IELTS Speaking Test retains a level of contingency between interactants. Although this link to IC is not made explicit in the descriptors, it appears to be implicated in the criterion 'develops topics fully and appropriately' (Seedhouse, 2019: 248). Seedhouse *et al.* (2014), for example, argue that the question-answer format of Sections 1 and 3 involves a level of 'discoursal involvement' that is not explicitly addressed in the criteria. They make the following recommendation:

> that consideration be given to the explicit inclusion in the ratings process of the quality of candidate discoursal participation or interactional competence. In particular, we recommend including in the band descriptors 'the ability to answer questions'. (Seedhouse *et al.*, 2014: 24)

Furthermore, Seedhouse and Morales (2017) propose the introduction of a candidate question into the IELTS Speaking Test, in order to provide the opportunity for more naturalistic, two-way interaction.

Recent rating studies conducted to simulate interaction in the classroom (Ikeda, 2017; Youn, 2015) attempted to incorporate the assessment of IC-related criteria employing roleplay tasks. Rating criteria from two of these tasks reveal a strong focus on topic negotiation, turn organisation, appropriateness of linguistic expressions, repair and interactional engagement (see Appendix 12.3). The descriptors in these two related tests provide clear evidence of the sociolinguistic-interactional perspective that Roever and Kasper (2018) claim is necessary for the evaluation of IC. Both rubrics are task specific, and the level of detail in Ikeda's (2017) rubric suggests that this level of incorporation of IC is not scalable to the level required for the larger tests outlined above. These can be contrasted with Seedhouse *et al.*'s (2014) minimal recommendation for the IELTS Speaking Test (outlined above). Although limited, the recent initiatives in large tests and small in-house tests have shown the potential for incorporating features of IC in speaking tests.

2.2 Empirical studies on IC in face-to-face speaking assessment

There has been continuing research interest in exploring IC in speaking assessment. Many IC researchers have employed conversational analysis (e.g. Galaczi, 2014; Nakatsuhara, 2013; Schegloff, 2007) to identify features of IC. Galaczi and Taylor (2018), for example, categorised IC features into topic management, turn management, nonverbal behaviour, breakdown repair and interactive listening. Earlier studies mainly identified features of IC observed in classroom assessment, focusing on identifying various interactional features observed in paired or group interaction assessment (e.g. Galaczi, 2008; Gan, 2010; Gan *et al.*, 2008; He & Dai, 2006; Luk, 2010; Nakatsuhara, 2011). These studies primarily aimed to validate pair/group oral assessment and/or to investigate how interlocutor variables (e.g. proficiency, personality traits, interaction patterns) may have some impact on the features of observed IC. These studies employed conversational analysis methods drawing on non-cognitive, more sociolinguistic or sociocultural perspectives, and reported features of IC observed in fine-grained analyses.

More recent studies have compared IC features observed in different levels of performance so that some features could be explicitly incorporated into existing rating scales (e.g. Galaczi, 2014; Lim, 2018; Roever & Kasper, 2018). The findings of these studies have shown differences of the features under study across levels. However, it may be challenging to incorporate the features observed (i.e. Galaczi – topic development, turn-taking and listener support; Lam – listener responses; Roever & Kasper – preliminaries) into existing rating scales because the observance of these features could be task-dependent. It could be quite possible that these features are task dependent. Furthermore, there is an issue of generalisability of CA-based studies (e.g. Skogmyr Marian & Balaman, 2018), which is more an issue for large-scale assessments than for small-scale/classroom assessments. In classroom assessment, a small number of features of IC in the curriculum can be selected and tested without considering implications for a wider context.

Features of IC have also been investigated in rater studies. Several studies have examined interactional features of performance ratings by analysing verbal protocols collected during rater assessment of paired speaking test performances. Interpreting the findings, both May (2009) and Ducasse and Brown (2009) pointed out that the interaction aspect of performance in general was not always fully described in the rating scales used in the studies, and suggest a scale that reflects the complexities of IC in a paired speaking test in order to assess test-takers' IC. Such a scale would incorporate interactive listening and the use of body language as part of the IC construct.

Focusing on pragmatic competence in interaction, Ikeda (2017) and Youn (2015) conducted validation studies in the context of a university EAP setting. Based on discourse analysis of speaking performance on roleplays, rating scales were developed focusing on the features of pragmatic competence and used for assessment (see Appendix 12.3 for a summary of the scales). The results of both studies revealed that rating scales discriminate features of performance on tasks designed for the studies across the levels.

A small number of studies have explored a range of interactional strategies (e.g. negotiation of meaning, responding to clarification requests) test-takers employed during test performance based on psycholinguistic and cognitive underpinnings (e.g. Ramazani et al., 2018; van Batenburg et al., 2018). Van Batenburg et al. (2018) investigated interactional abilities (i.e. use of self-supporting and other-supporting strategies) assessed in the performance of six dialogic tasks with scripted speech by pre-vocational learners in the Netherlands. The performance was assessed using both holistic categories (focusing on linguistic accuracy and interactional ability) and analytic categories (in terms of compensation, meaning negotiation and correcting misinterpretation). High levels of agreement among the three raters in the study were interpreted by the researchers as providing justification for the assessment of interactional ability by examining individual test-takers' use of strategies. Van Batenburg *et al.* (2018) thus concluded that IC can be regarded as an individual trait and an integral part of speech production.

In summary, in response to the growing recognition of IC as an integral part of speaking assessment, features of IC have been incorporated into tasks and rating scales of speaking assessment regardless of theoretical orientations. A rich volume of studies in both assessment and classroom contexts have provided further insights into the construct of IC as an integral part of speaking proficiency but, as noted by Galaczi and Taylor (2018), the findings have posed a number of challenges. Although various features of IC have been researched in both classroom and assessment studies and the notion of IC is broadly defined, many features of IC are not adequately defined or researched (Galaczi & Taylor, 2018). This issue is especially important for classroom-based assessments. That is, some questions remain regarding which features of IC should be included in assessment scales, and on what basis (construct definition of IC). Similarly, as mentioned above, considering the contingent nature of features of IC observed in test and classroom discourse, it is not clear how these features might be discriminated, nor how their assessment can be scalable. Although the number of studies investigating IC features across the levels is increasing and the findings of the studies provide further insights into IC features observed in assessment contexts, the implications of these studies, given the broad nature of the construct of IC, are not yet clear. Researchers from a psycholinguistic-individualistic perspective have attempted to incorporate individuals' contribution to interaction as a measurable construct (van Batenburg *et al.*, 2018). Others (e.g. van Moere, 2012) have also pointed out limitations regarding the face validity of purely psycholinguistic assessment.

3 Technology, IC and L2 Teaching and Learning

The challenges posed in the empirical research discussed above point to additional complexities in incorporating IC into computer-mediated assessment. Galaczi and Taylor (2018) note the unidirectional and predetermined nature of performances elicited through technology-mediated prompts. These concerns are also raised by Plough *et al.* (2018: 439), who conclude that 'computer-based tests currently lack interactivity, which means that certain aspects of the IC construct cannot be operationalised'. The ways in which working with new technologies may change how language skills are taught and assessed is an issue addressed in detail by Chapelle and Voss (2016). Language learning and teaching now incorporate technologies to the extent that Winke and Isbell (2017: 314) point to the 'oncoming normalization ... of tech-infused language assessment'.

This reflects the reality of many language learners who are now accustomed to communicating and learning with and through personal, social and institutional technologies. It is interesting that this rationale for the use of technology in language assessment echoes the call for a focus on IC in language assessment from Kramsch (1986), who argued for the need for speaking assessment to reflect the communicative orientation and widespread use of paired and group speaking tasks in L2 learning contexts. It is therefore timely that we now consider the ways in which IC could be operationalised in computer-mediated language assessment to reflect the reality of language learning and use in our increasingly tech-infused lives.

3.1 Technology and the computer-mediated assessment of L2 speaking: Affordances and constraints

The capacity of current technologies has led to the narrowing of the construct of speaking operationalised in standardised, high-stakes computer-mediated L2 speaking tests, with concern about construct under-representation due to the inability to elicit features of IC (Galaczi, 2010; see also Schmidgall & Powers, 2017). The impact on tasks is also noted by Lim (2018), in that there has been a resurgence of dictation and read-aloud tasks that many imagined had been relegated to the past. At this point, technology is still not mature in terms of capacity for meaningfully including and eliciting IC in speaking assessment tasks.[1] Lim (2018: 216) suggests that rather than focusing on constraints, 'it is perhaps more fruitful to consider how new and emerging technologies can be used or developed in ways that are fit for purpose', which may lead to broadening the L2 speaking construct. This is particularly salient when considering the changing nature of communication, with a prediction that by 2020 'the average person will have more conversations a day with bots [chatbots] than they do with their spouse' (Pemberton, cited in Deloitte, 2018). While this prediction may not be fully realised, currently the first point of phone communication with banks, telcos and most large companies will typically be through an interaction with an automated speaking system, capable of generating instructions and questions, and recognising and following up on our responses in a limited way. The realisation that so much of our communication is not face-to-face could be said to support the use of CMTs of L2 speaking, in order to capture the reality of communicating with both human beings and automated systems.

3.2 Computer-mediated assessment of L2 speaking: Current approaches

In line with the previous assessment of the potential role of technology to reconceptualise the construct of IC, we report on two current approaches to the computer-mediated testing of speaking, in terms of affordances for incorporating IC: (1) existing tests (e.g. Pearson, Aptis) where candidates produce monologues in response to pre-recorded questions or tasks; and (2) the offering of existing face-to-face interviewer-led speaking tests (e.g. IELTS) via videoconferencing.

First, existing standardised computer-based speaking tests, which are essentially monologic and unidirectional, reflect a psycholinguistic orientation to the L2 speaking construct. Bernstein *et al*. (2010: 358) explain the principles underlying Versant: 'These automated tests share many aspects of task design and scoring technology, and all purport to measure the construct *facility* in the spoken language. Facility can be defined as the ability to understand the spoken language on everyday topics and to speak appropriately in response at a native-like conversational pace in an intelligible form of the language'. The criteria for TOEFL iBT (ETS, 2014), Pearson Education (2018) and Aptis (British Council, 2019a) are designed to focus on the (lexical and grammatical) complexity, accuracy and fluency of candidates' speech, as well as pronunciation and task fulfilment (see summary of the scales in Appendix 12.1). This perspective is often made explicit by the test developers, as exemplified in the following statement from the creators of Aptis: 'As Aptis is an online test with a semi-direct format in which test-takers respond to pre-recorded prompts, some aspects of the speaking and writing construct were not being tested, such as interaction' (Fairburn & Dunlea, 2017: 14). However, the creators also state that 'the theoretical framework for Aptis has, from the start, made flexibility and adaptation an explicit part of the test system' (Fairburn & Dunlea, 2017: 5), which holds promise for future developments. This flexibility is apparent in the recently developed *Aptis for Teens* (British Council, 2019b), designed for 13–17 year olds, where a new speaking task in which candidates present from a poster has been introduced in order to reflect typical classroom speaking tasks for this age group. Although the poster presentation task is monologic in form, a target audience is given, with candidates instructed to *make your presentation as interesting and informative for your classmates as possible*. From these examples of existing standardised speaking tests, it is clear that technology impacts on both the tasks that can be developed and the construct that is operationalised, with implications for the potential to assess IC, which is not currently included.

The second context for computer-mediated testing is the offering of existing face-to-face speaking tests such as IELTS through a video-mediated platform, such as Skype. In a study that compared the two modes, Nakatsuhara *et al*. (2017a) found that the scores were basically identical. However, there were differences found in terms of the comparability of the candidate language that was elicited in the two modes of the test. In the video-mediated mode, more candidates asked examiners for clarification in Parts 1 and 3 of the test. Although the increased incidence of clarification requests was initially thought to reflect issues with the sound quality, this was improved in later phases of the study and clarification requests remained as a notable feature. Nakatsuhara *et al.* (2017b) interpreted this finding as evidence of tapping into a change of construct elicited through the videoconferencing mode, incorporating both interactive listening and conversation repair skills, including ways to indicate and solve break-downs in communication. The researchers also found that candidates used the language functions comparing and suggesting more in the face-to-face version of the test.

The impact of the two modes was not limited to candidates: differences were also found in examiners' use of verbal and nonverbal tokens, such as back-channelling and nodding, with one examiner reporting that he used these more in the face-to-face version to signal comprehension and encourage candidates, while others reported nodding more in the video mode to achieve the same purpose. Body language and gestures were also issues for examiners, as in the videoconferencing mode it was more difficult for them to use natural gestures and they experienced challenges in reading test-takers' gestures as well (Nakatsuhara *et al.*, 2017a). Turn-taking was also found to be challenging in the videoconferencing mode, with examiners reporting difficulties in signalling turn initiation and determining when a candidate's turn had been completed. Another interesting aspect of IC was the possibility that limited eye contact in the video mode impacted negatively on rapport. While it is important to note that IC is presently not explicitly operationalised in the IELTS rating scale (see Appendix 12.2), the aspects of difference between face-to-face and video modes that emerged in this study point to the integral role it plays, and the context-dependent nature of IC.

3.3 Computer-mediated assessment of L2 speaking: Recent developments

We now turn to three recent developments and discuss their potential for eliciting and assessing aspects of IC: (1) the creation of new paired and group speaking tests using videoconferencing technologies (Davis *et al.*, 2018); (2) the use of virtual environments to simulate contextualised group discussions (Ockey *et al.*, 2017); and (3) the use of speech technologies to enable multi-turn interactions, with questions and follow-up responses to a candidate generated through the use of automated speech recognition and interactive spoken dialogue systems (Litman *et al.*, 2018).

First, the design and potential of new group speaking tests for delivery through videoconferencing has been explored by Davis *et al.* (2018), who report on a study where a video-mediated communication tool (Skype) was used to facilitate speaking assessment in small groups. As video-mediated technology enables both speaking and visual input to occur together, it has the potential to tap into interactional resources, along with the convenience of candidates and examiners not having to be in the same location. The study investigated the feasibility of delivering interactive speaking assessment tasks using current videoconferencing technology, and the participants' perceptions of video-mediated speaking tests delivered online. Researchers developed prototype speaking tasks that incorporated a moderator and two or three participants, including both monologic and dialogic responses. Aspects of IC incorporated in the scoring rubric are turn-taking, collaboration, engagement and appropriateness.

The study found that technological reliability and test-taker familiarity with access to technology were challenges, echoing concerns from Nakatsuhara *et al.* (2017b). They also conceded that the full range of visual input available to participants in face-to-face interaction was not accessible through video. The current practice of using a single-camera video for each participant results in diminished visual input which limits the communication of body language and gestures. However, they concluded that as speaking, including conversations and job interviews, now often takes place through video-mediated platforms, this should be reflected in the ways in which we assess speaking.

Davis *et al.*'s (2018) study highlights the potential for new kinds of collaborative tasks involving small groups in the computer-mediated assessment of speaking, while acknowledging the need for more reliable technology if videoconferencing is used in high-stakes testing contexts. It also points to the need to align the type of interaction that is increasingly part of our everyday lives with the way that speaking is assessed, in order to enhance authenticity and tap into key aspects of IC, which is in marked contrast to the approach taken by many existing CMTs.

We now turn to another approach to CMT, which is the use of web-based virtual environments (VEs) to facilitate interactive speaking assessment. Ockey *et al.* (2017: 347) note that 'with the advent of three-dimensional (3D) graphics, motion-speech synchronisation, and video communication platforms, it is now possible to pursue this potential'. These technological affordances enabled the researchers to develop tasks designed to tap into interaction among multiple users and use the immersive virtual environment as the context in which communication took place. Their exploratory study involved the use of avatars, through which test-takers interacted to participate in an academic discussion in a virtual library setting. They aimed for the avatars to be able to nonverbally signal social presence, but this proved impractical for a full representation of body language. This limitation highlighted the importance of nonverbal communication in interaction.

While acknowledging the limitations, the researchers felt that there was great potential for the use of this technology in assessing interactive speaking, as VEs were able to provide a rich virtual context for group speaking tests. Although it is unlikely that the use of VEs would be feasible in large-scale speaking tests, they could be used in small-scale tests for specific purposes, such as assessing speaking in the context of an

English for Business course where the VE could be a boardroom and candidates negotiate a deal or each provide and respond to a marketing pitch, or in the context of an Aviation English course where the VEs could be the cockpit of a plane and the control tower. This exploratory study demonstrates a way for group discussions, which pose challenges logistically in face-to-face speaking tests, to be conducted in a virtual environment that helps to contextualise the interaction. While the use of avatars may pose a threat to both authenticity and construct validity, in that aspects of non-verbal communication cannot be meaningfully assessed, the use of VEs for contextualised synchronous communication in Ockey *et al.*'s (2017) study demonstrates the affordances of technology to elicit aspects of IC including turn-taking, responding and building on the contributions of other participants, rather than restricting candidates to monologues as many existing CMTs currently do.

Finally, another intriguing development involves the potential of automatic speech recognition (ASR) and interactive spoken dialogue systems (SDS) for the assessment of L2 speaking. The progress that has been made in ASR and SDS is described as 'significant' by Litman *et al.* (2018). There is, however, an important caveat: only if speaking ability is defined in psycholinguistic terms can features relevant to the construct be measured by present-day systems.

Despite this limitation, Litman *et al.* (2018) identified the opportunity for SDS to elicit a targeted range of interactive spoken language from a candidate. They use the example from an IELTS speaking test, where the examiner asks, '*Do you work or are you a student?*', to which the candidate replies, '*I'm a student in university*'. The examiner then follows up with, '*And what subject are you studying?*'. A sample finite state dialogue manager could also generate the questions for this IELTS speaking test interaction, following up on key words in the response to the initial question 'Do you work or are you a student?' through providing the next question as either 'What kind of work do you do?' or 'What subject do you study?'. If the response is not intelligible, this would trigger the request 'I'm sorry, but I didn't understand. Can you repeat that?'.

The potential value of these systems, as they continue to be developed and refined, would primarily be to the developers of semi-direct speaking tests (such as Pearson Test of English Academic and Aptis) which currently involve monologic tasks. Incorporating these systems could enable candidate responses over a series of several short turns to be elicited, thus enabling the assessment of certain aspects of IC, including interactive listening and providing contingent responses. They could also generate generic requests for clarification and elaboration of responses from a candidate. However, Roever and Kasper (2018: 350) caution that although 'monologic tasks set up as speaking to an audience (imaginary or real) do require recipient design of talk, which is an element of IC, ... they severely underrepresent the IC construct'. The limitations of the short, heavily constrained responses that would result from the use of SDS in its current form would thus need to be acknowledged by test developers and reflected in the interpretations that could be made regarding IC on the basis of performance on these tasks.

Overall, the more promising developments for the elicitation and assessment of IC seem to lie in the design of interactive speaking tasks using videoconferencing technologies and web-based virtual environments. These enable multiple candidates to interact in real time without having to be in the same location and, in the case of videoconferencing technology, reflect the context in which a great deal of academic and professional communication is being carried out in current times. VE technologies enable an immersive experience that could be particularly effective for ESP assessment where the provision of a specific visual context (e.g. a cockpit and control tower or a doctor's surgery) would add to authenticity.

4 Conclusion

This chapter has explored the role of IC in tests of second language speaking, at a time when developers of large-scale standardised tests are increasingly interested in the affordances offered by emerging technologies, while recognising the fact that much modern communication is technologically mediated. We began by reviewing the genesis of current perspectives on the notion – and, more recently, construct definition – of IC, highlighting the tension between so-called psycholinguistic-individualist and sociolinguistic-interactional perspectives on language competence (Roever & Kasper, 2018). Limitations of current psycholinguistic approaches to language testing were then discussed, with a particular focus on what has been identified as a primary focus on salient features of language production, at the expense of a focus on IC as an essential component of face-to-face interaction. Similarly, challenges in incorporating IC in language tests were identified, including issues related to discriminability and scalability. This discussion was supported by an examination of approaches to IC taken in various large-scale and classroom approaches to testing, as exemplified in rating descriptors.

We then examined two current approaches to computer-mediated testing in terms of task design and the extent to which IC is incorporated as an essential component of the L2 speaking construct. We began with an examination of current large-scale computer-based tests that explicitly draw on current technologies, and a strong psycholinguistic framework, in the testing of monologic speech. While this approach is acknowledged as deliberately underrepresenting the L2 speaking construct, it acts as a baseline for examining the present-day affordances of computer-mediated testing. Slightly further down the continuum towards future-oriented innovation is research comparing face-to-face and video-mediated delivery of the IELTS Speaking Test. Such research continues to provide insights into relevant linguistic (e.g. differences in the use of clarification checks) and non-linguistic (e.g. nonverbal and perceptual/experiential) influences of the technologies used.

In the final section, we introduced three recent developments and discussed their potential for eliciting and assessing aspects of IC. The more innovative, small-scale studies into online testing, involving interaction with humans and/or chatbots, explore both the limits and potential future affordances of such technologies. The influence and effectiveness of the more aspirational claims is dependent on the extent to which the hype of emerging technologies is sustained by future realities. While Litman *et al.* (2018) note that there is some way to go before the technology is able to provide a fuller treatment of IC, it is clear that there has been some movement towards this future capability and, as argued by researchers over the past 15 years (e.g. Chapelle & Douglas, 2006: 108), 'communicative language ability needs to be conceived in view of the joint role that language and technology play in the process of communication'. The review of research presented in this chapter shows that, despite present-day limitations, there is evidence of a strong motivation among researchers to pursue the possibilities afforded by current and emerging technologies in language testing.

Appendix 12.1: Criteria Used in Major Semi-direct Speaking Tests (CMT)

Name of test	TOEFL Speaking Rubrics (ETS, 2014)	Pearson Scoring Criteria (Pearson, 2018)	Aptis (British Council, 2019a)
Rating categories	• Delivery • Language use • Topic development	• Content • Oral fluency • Pronunciation	Task fulfilment/topic relevance, grammatical range and accuracy, vocabulary range and accuracy, pronunciation, fluency and cohesion
Example descriptors (highest rating)	Delivery: (4) Generally well-paced flow (fluid expression). Speech is clear. It may include minor lapses, or minor difficulties with pronunciation or intonation patterns which do not affect overall intelligibility	Oral fluency: (5) Native-like	(5) Uses a range of complex grammar constructions accurately. • Uses a range of vocabulary to discuss the topics required by the task • Pronunciation is clearly intelligible • Backtracking and reformulations do not fully interrupt the flow of speech • A range of cohesive devices is used to clearly indicate the links between ideas

Appendix 12.2: Criteria Used in Major Direct Speaking Tests

Name of test	IELTS Speaking Band Descriptors – Public Version (IELTS n.d.)	Trinity ISE II Speaking & Listening Scale (Trinity College London, 2015)	Examination for the Certificate of Competency in English (ECCE) (Michigan Assessment, 2020)	Cambridge English: First (Cambridge English, 2011)
Rating categories	Fluency and coherence	Communicative effectiveness	Overall communicative assessment	Interactive communication
Example descriptors of one criterion (highest rating)	Fluency & coherence: (9) • Speaks fluently with only rare repetition or self-correction • Any hesitation is content-related rather than to find words or grammar • Speaks coherently with fully appropriate cohesive features • Develops topics fully and appropriately	Fulfils the task very well: (4) • Initiates and responds appropriately, both actively and receptively • Maintains and contributes to the interaction by elaborating his/her utterances spontaneously • Says or signals in basic ways that he/she did not follow and these signals are always effective	• Conveys information and ideas, and asserts a viewpoint very comprehensibly • Expresses ideas readily, including details and complexities • Sustains talk quite independently without interlocutor support • Understands interlocutor speech without grammatical or lexical simplification at normal pace • Highly interactive participant: often spontaneously elaborates on new topics and can contribute substantially to topic development; self-initiates topic commentary and easily initiates exchanges	Interactive communication: (5) • Initiates and responds appropriately, linking contributions to those of other speakers • Maintains and develops the interaction and negotiates towards an outcome

Appendix 12.3: Rating Categories of Two IC Studies that Also Targeted Pragmatic Competence

Name of task	Rating criteria for roleplay with a professor (Youn, 2015)	Rating rubrics – roleplay dialogue tasks (Ikeda, 2017)
Rating category and example descriptors (highest rating: Youn: 3; Ikeda: 4)	*Content delivery* • Clear, concise, fluent (especially speech act delivery) • Smooth topic initiations with appropriate transitional markers and clear intonations (i.e. smooth turn initiation) *Language use* • Pragmatically appropriate linguistic expressions (bi-clausal, conditional: I was wondering if, I don't think I can; modal verbs, would, could, might) • Good control of grammar and vocabulary that doesn't obscure meaning *Sensitivity to situation* • Consistent evidence of awareness and sensitivity to situations exists in contents or tone *Engaging with interaction* • A next turn shows understandings of a previous turn throughout the interaction (i.e. shared understanding) • Evidence of engaging with conversation exists (e.g. clarification questions, backchannel, acknowledgement tokens) *Turn organisation* • Complete adjacency pairs (e.g. question and answer, granting a request and thanking) • Interactionally fluid without awkward pauses or abrupt overlap	*Social actions to achieve the communicative goal* The test-taker's performance shows understanding of the given or ongoing situation with clear, necessary and appropriate actions and information to prevent the problem and promote success in the situation *Facility with the language* Clear and fluent throughout the speech/conversation and sound variation (e.g. intonation, stress) and speed control is explicitly seen. Repairs/restatement, insertions may be used to elaborate and/or to stress or to mitigate the content, but these actions are well managed and fluency is not seriously flawed *Language use to deliver the intended meanings* The test-taker's performance shows explicit control of linguistic resources with few unclear parts to deliver the intended meanings throughout the speech *Language use for mitigation* Lexical choices and/or combinations well mitigate imposition with devices including bi clausal, conditional: I wonder if/whether and/or modal verbs such as 'would' 'could' 'might' in statement form *Engagement in interaction* A next turn clearly shows understanding of a previous turn response to the interlocutor (feedback to the interlocutor, clarification backchannel, acknowledgement tokens, questions) [and is] well-tailored for the ongoing context throughout the interaction *Turn organization* Smooth, natural turn-taking throughout the conversation

Note

(1) There are, however, promising developments, including speech recognition technology and web-based virtual environments, which are discussed later in this chapter.

References

Bachman, L.F. (1990) *Fundamental Considerations in Language Testing*. Oxford: Oxford University Press.

Bernstein, J., Van Moere, A. and Chen, J. (2010) Validating automated speaking tests. *Language Testing* 27 (3), 355–377.

British Council (2019a) *Aptis Candidate Guide*. See https://www.britishcouncil.org/sites/default/files/aptis_candidate_guide-web.pdf.

British Council (2019b) *Aptis for Teens Candidate Guide*. See https://www.britishcouncil.org/sites/default/files/aptis_for_teens_candidate_guide_0.pdf.

Brown, A. and Hill, K. (1998) Interviewer style and candidate performance in the IELTS oral interview. In L. Taylor and P. Falvey (eds) *IELTS Collected Papers: Research in Speaking and Writing Assessment* (pp. 37–61). Cambridge: Cambridge University Press.

Cambridge English (2011) *Assessing Speaking Performance – Level B2*. See https://www.cambridgeenglish.org/images/168619-assessing-speaking-performance-at-level-b2.pdf.

Canale, M. and Swain, M. (1980) Theoretical bases of communicative approaches to second language teaching and testing. *Applied Linguistics* 1 (1), 1–47.

Celce-Murcia, M. (2008) Rethinking the role of communicative competence in language teaching. In E. Alcón Soler and M.P. Safont Jordà (eds) *Intercultural Language Use and Language Learning* (pp. 41–45). New York: Springer.

Celce-Murcia, M., Dörnyei, Z. and Thurrell, S. (1995) Communicative competence: A pedagogically motivated model with content specifications. *Issues in Applied Linguistics* 6 (2), 5–35.

Chapelle, C.A. and Douglas, D. (2006) *Assessing Language Through Computer Technology*. Cambridge: Cambridge University Press.

Chapelle, C. and Voss, E. (2016) 20 years of technology and language assessment in Language Learning & Technology. *Language Learning & Technology* 20 (2), 116–128.

Davis, L., Timpe-Laughlin, V., Gu, L. and Ockey, G. (2018) Face-to-face speaking assessment in the digital age: Interactive speaking tasks online. In J.M. Davis, J. Norris, M. Malone, T. McKay and Y.A. Son (eds) *Useful Assessment and Evaluation in Language Education* (pp. 115–130).Washington, DC: Georgetown University Press.

de Bot, K. (1992) A bilingual production model: Levelt's Speaking Model adapted. *Applied Linguistics* 13, 1–25.

Deloitte (2018) Chatbots point of view. *Deloitte Digital*, March.

Dörnyei, Z. and Kormos, J. (1998) Problem-solving mechanisms in L2 communication. *Studies in Second Language Acquisition* 20 (3), 349–385.

Ducasse, A.M. and Brown, A. (2009) Assessing paired orals: Raters' orientation to interaction. *Language Testing* 26 (3), 423–443.

ETS (2014) *TOEFL Speaking Rubrics*. Princeton: Educational Testing Service. See www.ets.org/s/toefl/pdf/toefl_speaking_rubrics.pdf.

Fairburn, J. and Dunlea, J. (2017) *Speaking and Writing Scales Revision*. Aptis Technical Report TR/2017/001. London: British Council.

Galaczi, E.D. (2008) Peer–peer interaction in a speaking test: The case of the First Certificate in English examination. *Language Assessment Quarterly* 5 (2), 89–119, DOI: 10.1080/15434300801934702

Galaczi, E.D. (2010) Face-to-face and computer-based assessment of speaking: Challenges and opportunities. In L. Araujo (ed.) *Computer-Based Assessment of Foreign Language Speaking Skills.* JRC Scientific and Educational Reports. Luxembourg: Publications Office of the European Union.

Galaczi, E.D. (2014) Interactional competence across proficiency levels: How do learners manage interaction in paired speaking tests? *Applied Linguistics* 35 (5), 553–574.

Galaczi, E.D. and Taylor, L. (2018) Interactional competence: Conceptualisations, operationalisations, and outstanding questions. *Language Assessment Quarterly* 15 (3), 219–236.

Gan, Z. (2010) Interaction in group oral assessment: A case study of higher- and lower-scoring students. *Language Testing* 27 (4), 585–602.

Gan, Z., Davison, C. and Hamp-Lyons, L. (2008) Topic negotiation in peer group oral assessment situations: A conversation analytic approach. *Applied Linguistics* 30 (3), 315–334.

Hall, J.K. (2018) From L2 interactional competence to L2 interactional repertoires: Reconceptualising the objects of L2 learning. *Classroom Discourse* 9 (1), 25–39. doi:10.1080/19463014.2018.1433050

Hall, J.K. and Pekarak Doehler, S. (2011) L2 interactional competence and development. In J.K. Hall, J. Hellermann and S. Pekarak Doehler (eds) *L2 Interactional Competence and Development* (pp. 1–15). Bristol: Multilingual Matters.

He, L. and Dai, Y. (2006) A corpus-based investigation into the validity of the CET-SET group discussion. *Language Testing* 23 (3), 370–401.

Hymes, D.H. (1974) Ways of speaking. In R. Bauman and J. Sherzer (eds) *Explorations in the Ethnography of Speaking* (pp. 433–452). Cambridge: Cambridge University Press.

IELTS (n.d.) *Speaking: Band Descriptors (Public Version).* See www.ielts.org/-/media/pdfs/speaking-band-descriptors.ashx?la=en.

Ikeda, N. (2017) Measuring L2 oral pragmatic abilities for use in social contexts: Development and validation of an assessment instrument for L2 pragmatics performance in university settings. Unpublished PhD dissertation, University of Melbourne.

Kormos, J. (2006) *Speech Production and Second Language Acquisition.* Mahwah, NJ: Lawrence Erlbaum.

Kramsch, C. (1986) From language proficiency to interactional competence. *The Modern Language Journal* 70 (4), 366–372. doi:10.1111/modl.1986.70.issue-4

Levelt, W.J.M. (1989) *Speaking: From Intention to Articulation.* Cambridge, MA: MIT Press.

Lim, G.S. (2018) Conceptualising and operationalising second language speaking assessment: Updating the construct for a new century. *Language Assessment Quarterly* 15 (3), 215–218.

Litman, D., Strik, H. and Lim, G. (2018) Speech technologies and the assessment of second language speaking: Approaches, challenges and opportunities. *Language Assessment Quarterly* 13 (3), 294–309.

Luk, J. (2010) Talking to score: Impression management in L2 oral assessment and the co-construction of a test discourse genre, *Language Assessment Quarterly* 7 (1), 25–53. https://doi.org/10.1080/15434300903473997

May, L. (2009) Co-constructed interaction in a paired speaking test: The rater's perspective. *Language Testing* 26 (3), 397–422.

McNamara, T.F. (1997) 'Interaction' in second language performance assessment: Whose performance? *Applied Linguistics* 18 (4), 446–466.

Mehan, H. (2013) *Learning Lessons: Social Organization in the Classroom.* Cambridge, MA: Harvard University Press. doi:10.4159/harvard.9780674420106

Michigan Assessment (2020) *ECCE Speaking Rating Scale.* See https://michiganassessment.org/wp-content/uploads/2014/11/ECCE-Rating-Scale-Speaking-20140220.pdf.

Nakatsuhara, F. (2011) Effects of test-taker characteristics and the number of participants in group oral tests. *Language Testing* 28 (4), 483–508.

Nakatsuhara, F. (2013) *The Co-construction of Conversation in Group Oral Tests.* Frankfurt am Main: Peter Lang.

Nakatsuhara, F., Inoue, C., Berry, V. and Galaczi, E. (2017a) Exploring the use of video-conferencing technology in the assessment of spoken language: A mixed-methods study. *Language Assessment Quarterly* 14 (1), 1–18.

Nakatsuhara, F., Inoue, C., Berry, V. and Galaczi, E. (2017b) Exploring performance across two delivery modes for the IELTS Speaking Test: Face-to-face and video-conferencing delivery (Phase 2). *IELTS Research Reports Online* 2017/3.

Ockey, G.J., Gu, L. and Keehner, M. (2017) Web-based virtual environments for facilitating assessment of L2 oral communication ability. *Language Assessment Quarterly* 14 (4), 346–359.

O'Sullivan, B. and Lu, Y. (2006) The impact on candidate language of examiner deviation from a set interlocutor frame in the IELTS Speaking Test. *IELTS Research Reports Online* 2006/4. See https://www.ielts.org/-/media/research-reports/ielts_rr_volume06_report4.ashx.

Pearson Education (2018) *PTE Academic Score Guide (Version 9).* See https://pearsonpte.com/wp-content/uploads/2017/08/Score-Guide.pdf.

Plough, I. (2018) Revisiting the speaking construct: The question of interactional competence. *Language Testing* 35 (3), 325–329. DOI: 10.1177/0265532218772322

Plough, I., Banerjee, J. and Iwashita, N. (2018) Interactional competence: Genie out of the bottle. *Language Testing* 35 (3) 427–455.

Ramazani, M., Behnam, B. and Ahangari, S. (2018) Psychometric characteristics of a rating scale for assessing interactional competence in paired-speaking tasks at micro-level. *Journal of English Language Pedagogy and Practice* 11 (23), 180–206.

Roever, C. and Kasper, G. (2018) Speaking in turns and sequences: Interactional competence as a target construct in testing speaking. *Language Testing* 35 (3), 331–355.

Ross, S.J. (2018) Listener response as a facet of interactional competence. *Language Testing* 35 (1), 357–375.

Schegloff, E.A. (2007) *Sequence Organization in Interaction: A Primer in Conversation Analysis.* Cambridge University Press. https://doi.org/10.1017/CBO9780511791208

Schmidgall, J.E. and Powers, D.E. (2017) Technology and high-stakes language testing. In C. Chapelle and S Sauro (eds) *The Handbook of Technology and Second Language Teaching and Learning* (pp. 317–331). Hoboken, NJ: John Wiley & Sons.

Seedhouse, P. (2019) The dual personality of 'topic' in the IELTS Speaking Test. *ELT Journal* 73 (3), 247–256. doi:10.1093/elt/ccz009

Seedhouse, P. and Morales, S. (2017) Candidates questioning examiners in the IELTS Speaking Test: An intervention study. *IELTS Research Reports Online Series* 2017/5. See https://www.ielts.org/-/media/research-reports/ielts_online_rr_2017-5.ashx.

Seedhouse, P., Harris, A., Naeb, R. and Üstünel, E. (2014) The relationship between speaking features and band descriptors: A mixed methods study. *IELTS Research Reports Online* 2014/2. See https://www.ielts.org/-/media/research-reports/ielts_online_rr_2014-2.ashx.

Skogmyr Marian, K. and Balaman, U. (2018) Second language interactional competence and its development: An overview of conversation analytic research on interactional change over time. *Language and Linguistics Compass* 12 (8), 1–16. doi:10.1111/lnc3.12285

Trinity College London (2015) *Integrated Skills in English (ISE): Specifications – Speaking & Listening.* See https://www.trinitycollege.com/site/?id=3634.

van Batenburg, E., Oostdam, R., van Gelderen, A. and de Jong, N. (2018) Measuring L2 speakers' interactional ability using interactive speech tasks. *Language Testing* 35 (1), 75–100.

Van Moere, A. (2012) A psycholinguistic approach to oral language assessment. *Language Testing* 29 (3), 325–344. doi:10.1177/0265532211424478

Winke, P.M. and Isbell, D.R. (2017) Computer-assisted language assessment. In S. Thorne and S. May (eds) *Language, Education and Technology: Encyclopedia of Language and Education* (3rd edn). Cham: Springer.

Youn, S.J. (2015) Validity argument for assessing L2 pragmatics in interaction using mixed methods. *Language Testing* 32 (2) 199–225. doi:10.1177/0265532214557113

Young, R. (2008) Language learning and discursive practice. *Language Learning* 58, 135–181.

Young, R. (2011) Interactional competence in language learning, teaching and testing. In E. Hinkel (ed.) *Handbook of Research in Second Language Teaching and Learning, Vol. 2* (pp. 426–443). London and New York: Routledge.

13 Assessing Speaking in the Post-COVID-19 Era: A Look Towards the Future

M. Rafael Salaberry and Alfred Rue Burch

1 Introduction

Two years ago, when we launched the project that has become the final version of this volume, we were intent on broadening the scope of thinking and application of assessment practices of the theoretical construct of speaking ability. At the end of our publication journey, and in the wake of the still ongoing COVID-19 health crisis, it has become clear that many longstanding institutional practices and structures need to be evaluated with a critical eye. After all, the theoretical construct of speaking ability is central to our social interactions across contexts and settings of communication. We are mindful that – against the background of the health crisis – our chosen topic stands small compared to the urgency of many other educational, social, political, economic and health challenges. Despite such comparison, however, the potential misalignment of theoretical constructs and institutionalized assessment procedures has important social consequences that may not be apparent to test-takers or even test administrators. Ironically, the consequences of the current health crisis on the nature of our personal interactions have brought to the surface an increased level of awareness about important features of our speaking competence such as multimodality, co-construction of discourse, recipient-design of interactions, etc.

In the introductory chapter to this volume, we outlined some of the advantages of the construct of speaking ability prompted by the expanded sociolinguistic definition of language use, as well as some of the challenges faced by the designers of testing instruments intent on assessing such a broad construct. As described in that chapter, the theoretical framework and research findings from conversation analysis (CA) are best suited to assess the new interactional perspective on language use and language assessment (see Roever & Dai and Plough, this volume). However, CA's methodology and epistemology entail four aspects that have proven to be challenging for the design and administration of second language tests: (1) the co-constructed nature of interaction; (2) the expansion of the concept of speaking to include nonverbal behavior (embodiment); (3) the *emic* perspective on interactional events; and (4) the re-specification of cognitive/ psychological phenomena as interactionally observable, rather than being purely individual and intra-psychological (Kasper, 2009).

In this concluding chapter, we reflect on the empirical data and the theoretical claims advanced in the chapters in this volume to gather some ideas and proposals for the development of assessment instruments focused on the construct of speaking in context. By necessity, our analysis is mindful of the challenges described in the paragraph above. Our objective is to evaluate the viability of both established and new testing instruments that are appropriate to appraise the new sociolinguistic construct of speaking ability and that are, at the same time, feasible from a logistical and financial perspective. We divide this analysis into four distinct areas. We first address the conceptual and logistical challenge of scaling up the implementation of promising (albeit small-scale) projects designed to assess the construct of IC. Then, we review the strategic functional allocation of test types and methodologies to match the requirements of different types of assessment instruments. Third, we evaluate the affordances and constraints of new communication media and settings to incorporate new ways of assessing and redefining the construct of speaking ability. Finally, we acknowledge that the process of assessing language ability rests on the development of a business product that is required to be financially viable, and thus we close the chapter with some thoughts on the development of viable educational-business partnerships.

2 The Long View: Scaling Up Small-scale Projects

Three of the four constitutive dimensions of the construct of IC (as part of a CA approach) described in detail in previous chapters (i.e. co-constructed interaction, embodiment and *emic* perspective) entail a broader and more localized definition of speaking ability than is the case in traditional (mostly cognitive-based) tests of language competence focused primarily on the generalizability of findings of testing. Thus, by definition, there is an unavoidable logistical constraint brought about by this more expansive, interactional concept of speaking. More specifically, it is possible that the requirements of IC-based descriptions of speaking ability are not scalable to the requirements imposed by standardization needs inherent to the types of tests administered on a large scale (cf. Ikeda, 2017; van Moere, 2014). On this point, the chapters in the section on the design and implementation of novel procedures to assess speaking ability (Chapters 7–10) are representative of small-scale studies that may or may not be scalable given the potential logistical demands of doing so. For instance, Barth-Weingarten and Freitag-Hildt analyze the options to assess turn-taking in L2 English in high schools (in Germany) whereas Kley, Kunitz and Yeh survey the viability of options to evaluate repairs in L2 Chinese in college-level courses (in the United States). Even though the aforementioned chapters and the others in that section present strong arguments for the potential replication of the results of their projects on a larger scale, we must concede that the keyword used in this description is 'potential'. Until such projects have achieved scalability, it is necessary to consider that small-scale and large-scale projects are inherently distinct in nature. Consider, for instance, the logistical hurdle of providing training to language testers as it was done in the study of Barth-Weingarten and Freitag-Hildt, or the time and investment it would take to reproduce a similar pedagogical setup as accomplished by Dunkle. Even more daunting would be developing the professional expertise developed by the team of researchers-teachers exemplified by Kley, Kunitz and Yeh and their colleagues at CLIC on how to teach and assess IC, or by van Compernolle on the topic of sociocultural theory. Furthermore, a widespread diffusion of these practices would mean intervening both in pre-service and in-service teacher education.

One advantage of small-scale studies is that they represent a type of experimental laboratory for the dissemination of information on how to implement such small-scale protocols (as explicitly advocated by the authors of those chapters). In this way, these exploratory projects function as the reference point to adapt the successful small-scale ventures to larger scale implementations that can be used with large numbers of test-takers. In this scenario, the challenge is twofold. First, second language testing companies and institutions need to identify concrete benefits afforded by such exploratory projects in order to invest time and resources into implementing similar testing instruments on a larger scale. Conversely, language teachers and local innovative language test designers need to go beyond their own limited time and resources to launch any project (i.e. even a small-scale project constitutes a big endeavor for language teachers). There is a potential synergy between these two groups of stakeholders that may hold the key to the successful implementation of CA-/IC-based testing instruments. Given that the ideas about IC were introduced about two decades ago, it is possible that the convergence of small exploratory projects and their large-scale implementation is just ready to launch now or in the near future. Another way to address the limitations of scaling up localized assessment studies is simply not to do it. That is, if one of the most important goals of language teaching is to encourage students to interact, the small-scale approach of the projects described in the chapters in this volume is most valuable when they are implemented on-site in the actual classroom environment. This perspective brings up the strategic nature of some decisions about language assessment. We next address the functional division of assessment goals according to the strategic deployment of specific affordances and constraints of test instruments.

3 Strategic Functional Division of Labor

Another important dimension of analysis of testing instruments, parallel to the division of small-scale versus large-scale projects, is represented by the categorization of speaking events on a continuum of individual to collaborative representation of the speaking act. Even though, on a programmatic scale, we can visualize and pursue the transition from an individualistic psycholinguistic conceptualization of assessment to a sociolinguistic one (i.e. the fourth constitutive dimension of CA/IC), it may be more appropriate to consider a comprehensive approach that incorporates both of these views. The rationale for this approach is that, from both a theoretical point of view and also from the perspective of test administration, we can match different types of tests with distinct functional uses of language. That is, a test that measures the ability of test-takers to respond to prerecorded prompts can be dissociated from the measurement of, for instance, the ability to interact with co-workers to improve workplace interactional dynamics (i.e. a sub-construct that would require high levels of recipient-design and co-construction of the interaction). In essence, the identification of distinct various functional aspects of the overall construct of speaking lends itself to the strategic 'division of labor', so to speak, whereby distinct aspects of the theoretical construct can be allocated to different types of tests.

In this way, the argument for the use of traditional tests (e.g. ACTFL-OPI) becomes valid to the extent that such tests are used for the purpose of assessing the (sub-)construct they are designed to address (e.g. the ability to use an institutional type of interview) and not any other type of construct that would not be adequately assessed through that test (e.g. the ability to participate in an interactional event defined primarily by co-construction and recipient-design). There is, however, one major logistical hurdle faced by this otherwise rational approach to the allocation of testing instruments. That is, as eminently viable as this strategic approach is, it does require a joint collaborative approach by major test designers to purposefully and explicitly describe to test-takers and institutions the range of uses each specific test may be able to address. Furthermore, it brings into focus the important role played by end-users of tests. Beyond test designers and test administrators, this third constituency has a responsibility to become stakeholders in the process as well. For instance, the latest movement focused on social justice and equal opportunity may prompt end-users to place higher or lower value on testing practices on large- or small-scale tests (e.g. small-scale uses are more valuable to the learners, because they assess language use that is more relevant to day-to-day tasks and responsibilities), thus encouraging them to forego their participation in large-scale assessment practices that they may deem less valuable on the scale of social goals that they consider relevant.

4 Strategic Use of Affordances and Constraints to Assess IC

The previous point on social goals and end users brings up another strategic dimension that is worth considering for the design and development of testing instruments: The analysis of the construct of speaking against the background of the overall context of communication in the era of social media. New technologies have continued to expand the range of features to be considered as part of the definition of the concept of speaking. For instance, the innovation of means for communication via social media, as represented in the interactive bots and avatars that are becoming prevalent in online communication, focuses our attention on the variety of cues that can be associated with interactions that are largely based on speaking modes of communication. Even though online communication is very much a live interactional event (unless it is asynchronous), it has become very prevalent in our daily lives as the result of the health emergency caused by SARS-CoV-2 (e.g. the ever-present app Zoom in many educational settings). More importantly, online communication represents a type of interactional environment that requires a close look at how we define IC (see chapters by Song & Hsu and Iwashita, May & Moore, this volume).

The introduction of new technologies may also be relevant and useful to address some of the challenges brought about by the expanded scope of a theoretical definition of speaking that considers the actual interactional aspects of a wide range of functional spoken communication (see chapters by Plough, Burch & Kasper and Compernolle, this volume). As was the case for previous technologies, the strategic use of specific features of each technology brings up new options to assess specific aspects of the construct being tested. For instance, the advent of telephone answering services justified asking test-takers to leave a message as a natural realistic task (albeit of a monologic nature). Given that these testing protocols reflect features of at least some of the speaking tasks we perform in our daily lives, by definition they accurately reflect some components of the theoretical construct of speaking ability. Furthermore, one could also argue that, indirectly, they assess the type of interactional ability prompted by the given task (attention to expected audience, adaptation to limited but still existent interactional features of the communicative event, etc.). Examples from both old and new technologies (e.g. interactions via telephone or Zoom) confirm that it is both the affordances and the constraints of uses of technology that may be strategically used for the design of future speaking tests. With regard to constraints, for instance, telephone conversations, by definition, do not provide access to visual information available to process the message. Similarly, during Zoom meetings, the limitation of visual cues (compared to our normal face-to-face interactions) affects the timing of turn-taking and requires an adaptation to the medium.

Among the multiple types of interactions prompted by newer technologies, it is increasingly common for our interlocutors not to be another human being, but rather a type of automated system such as a prerecorded voice cued by prompts (typical of many phone interactions), a bot (social media and websites) or other similarly designed automated systems. The rapid integration of these new technologies into our daily lives entails that the concept of IC need not only consider human-to-human interactions, but also the increasingly prevalent type of communication in which recipient design and co-construction of knowledge have been predetermined in advance of the interaction based on data analysis of previous similar interactions or simply based on heuristics associated with expected communicative events. On the other hand, as long as prior contributions, even digital/mechanical, influence the contributions of the 'living' speaker, and the living speaker's contributions shape the options for the digital responses, there is still co-construction, albeit of a different type.

5 Testing as Risk-taking Business

Finally, we need to address the elephant in the room: language testing represents big business and, as such, we must recognize that changes to assessment instruments need to be viable from a financial perspective (both for producers and for users of tests). To what extent is the construct of IC relevant or necessary to address goals and objectives pursued by major companies and institutions in the business of second language assessment? For instance, are the end-users of speaking tests (i.e. the academic institutions administering the assessment of learners) interested in carrying out the assessment of IC? Are the advocates for learners (i.e. parents and public officials such as local boards of education) aware of the range of constructs conjured up by vague descriptors such as 'speaking ability'?

The relevance of the financial aspects of designing, implementing and administering a major test cannot be overlooked. Despite the best intentions of test designers who may be intent on finding as perfect a match as possible between a test instrument and the construct under analysis, the logistical and, ultimately, financial aspects of the endeavor need to be taken into account. In general, the administrators of major tests currently on the market may be reluctant to substantially modify their testing framework and methodology if they do not see a need to do so. Not only have companies made substantial investments in the design and administration of widely used tests, but they have also refined and improved their tests on the basis of their extensive experience in administering them over the years. The well-known examples are the ACTFL-OPI in the United States and the IELTS in Europe/UK.

Despite the need to keep the 'bottom line' in sight when we describe the ideal process of designing and administering speaking tests, it is nevertheless relevant to remind ourselves of the opportunities available to critique both the expansion of the construct and the actual implementation of the test that will faithfully represent such a construct. First, the argument that major tests have refined their chosen instruments on the basis of a massive database and of multiple studies focused on those tests may be true on the face of concrete investments and data collection. On the other hand, if such (streamlined) tests do not track precisely the construct of IC, and if we agree that the sociolinguistic view of IC is valid, there is a viable argument to question the foundation of the language assessment enterprise. For instance, despite the fact that, as Ross (2017: 13) points out, the OPI is 'one of the most developed task-based language assessments methods in use', it is also the case that there are inherent liabilities in the design of these tests, as shown in this volume (Burch & Kasper). Second, as described above, end-users need to play the role of stakeholders in this process. In the eyes of end-users, the concept of a speaking test may be overly simplified (and thus misrepresented), in part due to the sketchy and commonsensical definition provided in the marketing of popular tests. For instance, test-takers may conclude that, because they can pass a test like the TOEFL or the ACTFL-OPI, they have enough language competence to use the language in a wide range of contexts.

6 Conclusion

The strong support of a wide range of academics and researchers for the adoption of a concept like IC for the assessment of speaking is evident, not just from the list of contributors to this volume, but from a quick review of the lists of publications cited in this volume as well. As discussed in this concluding chapter, however, beyond the need to develop more precise and realistic definitions of a wide range of conceptualizations of speaking ability, we also need to be mindful of the logistical constraints that require appropriate strategic decisions on how to deploy distinct types of tests that will match such constraints. Our analysis in the previous paragraphs focused on the opportunities afforded across four distinct areas: (a) the division of goals pertinent to small-scale and large-scale projects; (b) the strategic functional allocation of test types and methodologies to match different types of assessment instruments; (c) the affordances and constraints of new communication media; and (d) the conceptualization of speaking assessment instruments as a business product that needs to be financially viable.

Throughout this final chapter, we have made the assumption that the integration of the theoretical development of the construct of IC with logistical affordances is viable. One possible theoretical rationale for the type of strategic allocation of resources described above is to posit that the construct of IC is composed of two sub-constructs (i.e. a static one and a dynamic one) as has been proposed by Young (2011, 2019) and Hall (2018), inter alia. For instance, Hall (2018: 28) advocates theoretically demarcating these two sub-constructs, assigning the term 'interactional repertoires' to the 'variable, L2-specific semiotic resources comprising the objects of learning' that learners encounter in their interactions with other language users. The other sub-construct defined by Hall (inheriting the general label of IC) is thus restricted to the actual (generalizable) competence represented by the 'basic interaction infrastructure of human sociality'. In essence, Hall makes a distinction between, on the one hand, the 'underlying competence' of learners to participate in social interaction and, on the other hand, the repertoires of L2 resources as the object of learning. Decoupling the notion of generalizable competence from the actual deployment of interactional resources (i.e. the stability of underlying competence versus the variability of the object of learning) provides a pathway to integrate distinct pathways to test design (e.g. small-scale versus large-scale).

The chapters in this volume provide a point of departure to think about the multitude of ways in which such research can be reflected on the design of new types of tests and the implementation of a variety of tests to match specific sub-components of the construct of speaking. The objective of this final chapter has been to evaluate the practicality of using established testing instruments as well as new ones to properly appraise the new sociolinguistic construct of speaking ability. Overall, we hope the main contribution of this volume will spur additional research on both the assessment of the complex construct of speaking in a second language and the means to accomplish such an ambitious goal.

References

Hall, J.K. (2018) From L2 interactional competence to L2 interactional repertoires: Reconceptualising the objects of L2 learning. *Classroom Discourse* 9, 25–39.

Ikeda, N. (2017) Measuring L2 oral pragmatic abilities for use in social contexts: Development and validation of an assessment instrument for L2 pragmatics performance in university settings. Unpublished PhD dissertation, University of Melbourne.

Kasper, G. (2009) Locating cognition in second language interaction and learning: Inside the skull or in public view? *International Review of Applied Linguistics* 47, 11–36.

Ross, S. (2017) *Interviewing for Language Proficiency: Interaction and Interpretation.* Basingstoke: Palgrave Macmillan.

van Moere, A. (2014) Raters and ratings. In A.J. Kunnan (ed.) *The Companion to Language Assessment Volume III: Evaluation, Methodology, and Interdisciplinary Themes* (pp. 1358–1374). Malden, MA: Wiley Blackwell.

Young, R.F. (2011) Interactional competence in language learning, teaching, and testing. In E. Hinkel (ed.) *Handbook of Research in Second Language Teaching and Learning, Vol. 2* (pp. 233–268). New York: Routledge.

Young, R. (2019) Interactional competence and L2 pragmatics. In N. Taguchi (ed.) *The Routledge Handbook of Second Language Acquisition and Pragmatics* (pp. 93–110). New York: Routledge.

Index

Note: References in *italics* are to figures, those in **bold** to tables; 'n' refers to chapter notes.